The Functioning
of Complex
Organizations

The Functioning of Complex Organizations

Edited by

George W. England
University of Oklahoma

Anant R. Negandhi
University of Illinois

Bernhard Wilpert
Science Center Berlin

 Oelgeschlager, Gunn & Hain, Publishers, Inc.
Cambridge, Massachusetts

 Verlag Anton Hain
Königstein/Ts.

International Standard Book Number: 0-89946-067-4 (U.S.A.)
3-445-12098-1 (Germany)

Library of Congress Catalog Card Number: 80-21966

Printed in West Germany

Library of Congress Cataloging in Publication Data
Main entry under title:

Functioning of complex organizations.

Papers presented at a conference held in Berlin, Dec. 17-20, 1978.
Includes index.
1. Organization — Congresses. I. England, George W. II. Negandhi, Anant R. III. Wilpert, Bernhard.
1936-
HD29.F86   302.3'5   80-21966
ISBN 0-89946-067-4

Contents

v

List of Figures

List of Tables

Foreword

The International Institute of Management of the Science Center Berlin in its two main strands of research preoccupation — industrial structure policies and labor market policies — is continuously confronted with the need to better understand the intricate interrelationships between modern industrial and public organizations as well as between them and their socioeconomic and policy contexts. The problems encountered cover the whole gamut from the impact of intraorganizational incentive systems on productivity; through interorganizational networks and their response to deglomeration, sectoral, or labor market policies; all the way to societal and value barriers to social change and technological innovation. While our knowledge may be fairly advanced when it comes to describing and understanding the dynamics on one level (e.g., group characteristics and leader behavior), little is known about cross-level effects (e.g., employer characteristics, organizational structure, and investment behavior of companies). What is called for are conceptual frameworks that strive toward bridging interlevel dynamics.

The International Institute of Management and Comparative Administration Research Institute in 1978 encouraged such an ambitious attempt by supporting the efforts of former staff members of the International Institute of Management, professors England, Negandhi, and Wilpert, to call on colleagues in the field of organization theory to submit papers to a conference on "The Functioning of Complex Organizations" (held in Berlin, December 17-20, 1978). The papers were to relate to four levels of variables presumed to affect organizational functioning — individual, group, organizational, and societal level variables. Some sixty papers were screened, of which the collection in this volume was finally chosen after a thorough review process and various rewriting stages in an effort to make them compatible with the overall purpose. As the editors of the volume themselves conclude, time and the state of art in organization theory may not be ripe as yet to provide fully integrated frameworks that span the relationships from micro- to macrolevels. But it is hoped that the present volume will constitute another significant steppingstone to bring organization theory closer to that urgently needed goal achievement.

Hans-Jürgen Ewers
Acting Director
International Institute of Management
Science Center Berlin

Preface

This volume attempts to provide coherent perspectives on the functioning of complex organizations. Selected organizational scholars have prepared chapters in their respective content areas that (1) identify the major conceptual and theoretical thinking in the area, (2) critically review the research studies undertaken, and (3) provide overall conclusions from the research studies and the promise of the area for the future.

Using this common framework, the functioning of complex organizations (including organizational design, organizational structure, and organizational performance) is viewed as the dependent variable(s) that we are trying to understand and explain. We have purposefully included chapters concentrating on four levels of independent or potential explanatory variables — the individual, the group, the organizational, and the societal. The intent of this selection is to provide for an integration of the impact of these four levels of variables on the functioning of complex organizations. It is important to know how each level of independent variables affects organizational functioning, but it is equally important to consider the impacts in relation to each other. Indeed, it is the interlocking of various parts of subsystems within a given system that provides the main differentiating attributes of a system (England, Negandhi, and Wilpert, 1979).

Chapters 1 through 4 are addressed to research and issues concerning the individual and the functioning of complex organizations. Hendrick reviews research and concepts stemming from the work of Piaget, Harvey, Hunt and Schroder, and Kohlberg that identify developmental patterns of conceptual thinking and moral reasoning. The level of conceptual thinking in terms of abstractness-concreteness of organizational members (particularly leaders) is posited as a powerful explainer of current organizational functioning problems. In Hendrick's words, "concreteness-abstractness, then, appears to be a transcendent human dimension that helps integrate and explain the commonality of present organization structure, norms, and practices." Conceptual thinking determinism may be as powerful in organizations as technological determinism. The promise of the area is seen in the development of interventions that increase the abstractness level of organizational leaders, which would permit organizational functioning to become more in line with that desired by organizational members.

Weitzel, Dawis, and Mason view the competence potential of the individual both as a determinant of efficient organizational functioning and as influenced by the nature of organizational functioning. Competence potential influences organizational functioning largely in terms of decisionmaking and prescribed work role performance. The nature of organizational functioning influences competence potential development through task requirements that more fully realize potentials and through participative mechanisms that induce motivation to realize potentials. The promise of the area is in developing procedures and strategies of prescribing organizational roles in a manner that induces both motivation to perform and development of competence potential. The dynamics of this type of matching of human capacities with organizational requirements is complex and not well understood in either a research sense or an application sense.

Mahoney proposes a new conceptual formulation of job satisfaction that incorporates and integrates various aspects of job satisfaction models, including needs, expectancies, and values. A key feature of this formulation is in the separation of satisfaction-dissatisfaction-producing elements in the work situation into those for which the notion of optimality is relevant (e.g., hours of work, closeness of supervision, and workplace temperature) and those for which optimality is not relevant (e.g., interesting work, skill development, and personal growth). Related to this distinction is the formulation of job satisfaction as having two components — deprivational aspects and aspirational aspects. Overall satisfaction is measured by summing aspirational and deprivational values individually across all potential elements and then combining the two sums. The promise of this model is in its conceptual integration of previous models and research results and the potential it offers for increased understanding of the relationships between satisfaction concepts and work behavior concepts.

Miner reviews the research literature concerning nine major theories of organizational motivation. Each theory is considered in terms of a series of major questions:

What is the real nature of the constructs of the theory?

What methods of measurement are available to measure the constructs of the theory?

What are the limits of the theory's domain?

Does the theory predict performance levels?

Does the theory predict work satisfaction?

Are the motivational processes specified by the theory involved in organizational and vocational choice?

How and to what extent can the motivational processes specified by the theory be externally influenced?

What is the talent supply of the motivational components posited by the theory in the population at large and in relevant subgroups?

The promise of this comparative mapping of theories of organizational motivation is in detecting unexplored areas, conflicting explanations, and potential areas where integration seems possible. In Miner's words, "there is no systematically constructed map to fill in," but "it is clear that when the multidimensional puzzle falls together, it will provide a high level of scientific understanding . . . ."

Four chapters (5 through 8) deal with issues concerning decisionmaking and leadership in organizational functioning. These are focused primarily at the levels of the group and the organization, but contain linkages to the individual level.

Hall develops a model of organizational decisionmaking that combines evolutionary theory of organizing with behavioral theory of the firm. Key elements in the model include the organization's enacted environments, enactment processes, selection and retention processes, and organizational learning and memory. Arguments are made for integrating different levels of analysis — the individual, the group, and the organization — into a model for the organization as an entity with its own "organizational mind." The proposed model is described and illustrated for a limited set of short-run budget-related decisions. The major promise of the model is in showing how the organization acquires purpose, meaning, and orientation and a quasi-official map of causality. Insights into underlying causes of pathologies of decisionmaking and related prescriptions are also provided through the model.

Kmetz reviews leadership studies and organizational structure studies and suggests that a synthesis is needed between the two research areas if we are to make significant progress in understanding organizational functioning. While theoretical linkages between leadership and organization structure have long existed, research into each topic has proceeded largely independently of the other. Kmetz develops an integrated model of leadership and organization structure based on the two sets of literature and the few studies directly linking the two areas. The promise of the model lies in the opportunity to redirect research in the two areas, which allows greater understanding of how they jointly function both as organizational control devices and organizational focusing processes.

Miles reviews and evaluates changes that have taken place in the organizational roles of leaders and of the led during the last three decades in the United States. A narrowing of the "zone of acceptance" and an enlarging "zone of conditional acceptance" of leadership are noted. In viewing the future, Miles argues "that in the United States during the 1960s and early 1970s (and more recently in Western Europe), most managers have played with change in leader and led roles, but have not taken the full implications of their 'experiments' seriously. That is, with few exceptions, efforts to expand subordinate roles to include more involvement in decisionmaking and more self-direction and self-control have not been accompanied by total system redesign." "There is simply nothing in current theory or practice to suggest a major continuing commitment to role restructuring in Western societies. Work organizations, for the near future at least, will probably continue to be the only arena in which most people are expected to stop growing." In terms of longterm predictions, Miles forecasts that "role change will become an economic must rather than an ethical ought and will occur as a matter of course."

Bryson and Kelley review theory and research concerning leadership, politics, and the functioning of complex organizations. They create a framework for relating these three areas and suggest a series of propositions relating leadership, politics, and the functioning of organizational and interorganizational networks. This framework attempts to merge supervisory behavior with more broadly defined "leader" behavior and to relate leader behavior to a broad range of individual, processual, structural, environmental, and effectiveness variables. In short, it attempts to relate leadership to overall organizational and interorganizational network functioning. The value of this approach for integrating micro- and macroviews of leadership, politics, and functioning of organizations is seen in terms of better understanding, explanation, prediction, and prescription in the area. A series of "next steps" required by this approach is outlined.

Chapters 9 and 10 deal with structural and interorganizational issues in organizational functioning. Reimann and Inzerilli review and synthesize research findings concerning technology and organizational structure. Their review indicates that "studies focusing on the unit level of the organization or those defining technology in terms of environmental inputs and outputs (rather than transformation processes) seem to be remarkably consistent in their support of technological determinism." When sufficient comparative controls are exercised, "it becomes apparent that most of the controversy centers around studies focusing on the impact of transformation technology at the level of the organizational system." The authors propose the development of a "consistent theory" for relating technology and structure at the system level as a guide for future research. "This theory should recognize that a given complex organization may operate with a variety of 'core' — or 'first-order' — transformation technologies, in addition to which it will typically utilize one or more 'second order' technologies to support, coordinate, and control its 'first order' activities." This task of theory development is viewed as extremely difficult but necessary for further progress.

Koenig reviews a diverse range of literature in attempting initial steps toward a more complete understanding of interorganizational relations among a network of organizations. Interorganizational relations (IOR) are based on exchange of resources between two or more organizations. Major attributes of this exchange of resources or of these transactions include density, centrality, directionality, and intensity. Interorganizational relations are further defined in terms of their systemic properties, such as being controlled and oriented toward a condition of equilibrium or balance around mutually shared goals of cooperation. Moreover, the system or network is open and subject to influences from its environment. Problems concerning the dynamics of interorganizational relations or network change are discussed in terms of defining and establishing baselines for change detection and for identifying the directionality of change. As Koenig states, "the conceptualization itself of an IOR system remains difficult, let alone delineation of boundaries and dynamics." Conceptual formulations such as that presented seem crucial to further development of the area.

In Chapter 11, which focuses directly on the societal level, Beres and Portwood review, evaluate, and synthesize recent research dealing with sociocultural influences on organizations and organizational functioning. The two most pressing theoretical problems impeding our understanding of sociocultural influences on organizations are identified as (1) lack of an operationalizable definition of culture and (2) lack of clear conceptualization of how culture affects organizations and their functioning. The authors' review of the cultural causal issue in terms of recent studies leads them to propose two hypotheses:

1. The greater the physical constraints on organizational functioning, the less variance there will be across cultures in the organization's mode of functioning.
2. Within a society, culture (a) leads to the emergence of certain types of organization, (b) determines the type of organization that will be most common, and (c) influences the distributional mix of organizational types.

The promise of the area is seen in terms of cultural studies (if broadly and rigorously pursued) providing a catalyst for a new synthesis in organizational theory.

In total, these authors are arguing for conceptual and theoretical development as a necessity for increasing our understanding of organizational functioning. While it is far from novel to hear such pleas and arguments, it is altogether another matter to do something about the situation. Here we find research-directed evaluation and synthesis and suggested areas of needed concentration concerning the impact on organizational functioning of major variables, including conceptual thinking, leadership-led roles, organizational motivation, technology, interorganizational networks, and sociocultural influences. New integrative models have been developed in the areas of competence potential, job satisfaction, organizational decision-making, and organizational leadership. The "need to know" seems sufficient; the "will to find out" can be tested only in the future.

The reader is reminded that the final summary chapter will, based on the picture displayed in the preceding chapters, try to identify those problem fields in need of greater attention in the future. Four main areas are identified. First, the chapter discusses the discrepancy that exists between the claims and realities of a systems approach to organization studies. That discrepancy is seen to highlight the need for a great emphasis on multivariate considerations and a more thorough analysis of cross-level effects (i.e., the study of influence factors transcending systems borders). Second, it points to the need for linking the well-established structural approaches of organization research to dynamics of organizational behavior. Third, it calls for a reevaluation of the dynamics and indeed the frequent functionality of intra- and interorganizational conflicts — a topic widely neglected by traditional approaches. And fourth, it appeals to students of the issues of organizational functioning to consider new types of dependent variables that must be conceptualized and researched as a consequence of emergent changes in the socioeconomic and political environment if complex organizations are to survive and to serve their own and wider interests.

REFERENCE

England, G. W.; A. R. Negandhi; and B. Wilpert, eds. 1979. *Organizational Functioning in a Cross Cultural Perspective.* Kent, Ohio: Kent State University Press.

Acknowledgments

The editors would like to express their gratitude to the International Institute of Management of the Science Center Berlin and the Comparative Administration Research Institute for supporting the development of this volume. Critical reviews and comments were given by a large number of colleagues. Among them, we are especially grateful to Klaus Bartölke, Peter Dachler, Walter Goldberg, Frank Heller, Marion Kostecki, Ewa Masļyk, Derek Pugh, Makato Takamiya (whose sudden death recently shocked and saddened all of us), and M. Van de Vall. We would also like to thank Prasad Vasireddi for his editorial assistance and Ilona Köhler for her unfailing administrative support.

Berlin, February 1980   G.W.E.
                                                                 A.R.N.
                                                                 B.W.

Chapter 1

Competence Potential and Organizational Functioning

William Weitzel,* Rene V. Dawis,** and Nancy Mason**

OVERVIEW

The effective functioning of complex organizations depends on the effective functioning of its individual members. This truism is rarely disputed, but only occasionally is it systematically integrated (Argyris, 1964). To bring together the individual and the organization requires the writer to move between these two levels of abstraction and across several disciplines. The individual level is largely the domain of the psychologist. Too often psychologists give only ceremonial nods to the impact of the environment and its institutions on the behavior of individuals. The level of the organizatic⁻ is treated mainly by sociologists and political scientists. They usually acknowledge the individual and differences related to individuals and then focus their primary attention on environmental variables and

*   University of Oklahoma.
** University of Minnesota.

organizational operations and activities. The consequence of maintaining these separate ways is to reduce our knowledge of how each impacts upon the other. In this chapter we will begin with dependent variables related to the functioning of the organization and link them to the behaving individual, particularly to the variables related to the competence potential of organization members. Our focus will be on both content issues and the measurement of these issues.

The organizational variables to be addressed are organizational structure, the concepts important to design, and organizational performance. These relate respectively to preparation for organizational functioning, methods or approaches related to organizational change and the influence of internal conditions on the organization, and the assessment of the organization's operations and output. Evaluation of each of these aspects of organizational functioning requires the development of criteria. Our focus will be on the general nature of these criteria and how they relate to the individual member level of organizational activity.

The individual variables related to competence potential need to be treated from two perspectives — the level of the observable or the index variable level and the more abstract level often referred to as the level of potential, about which we can only draw inferences. After having indicated the possible relationship between the organizational variables and the individual variables, we will focus on the latter. We want to show the relationship between organizational aim or purpose and organizational task with individual skill and individual ability. We hope to show the natural linkages between these constructs and their behavioral indicants. There are several general models of intellectual competence from which we will draw. We also want to expand the general model of competence potential to include some abilities virtually unmapped in the psychological literature, abilities that are of importance to an individual in an organizational setting. Those individuals who possess what appear to be interpersonal competence or people skills seem to be accorded higher positions in organizations. The abilities underlying these skills are not well known. Without having well-developed measures reflecting these abilities, it is hard to know just what aspects of interpersonal interaction ought to be studied further. Other abilities not being pursued today seem to be those related to the handling of things (person-object interaction). For example, mechanical abilities are often evaluated through abstract verbal descriptions. This appears to require those with mechanical abilities to possess verbal skills in order to demonstrate successfully their mechanical skill potential.

THE ORGANIZATION

Organization Structure

Few characteristics about the organization stand out like its structure. Most organization members can tell an outsider how work is carried out within an organization and who has the authority for particular aspects of the work being carried out by the organization, and often they can tell the general principles by which the organization operates as it pursues its goals and objectives. Each of these things is related to the organization's structure. Following the work of Vollmer (1968), we propose to describe organization structure using three broad categories — policies and practices, functions, and roles. Each of these categories addresses one aspect of the translation of organizational goals and objectives into organizational action. Policies, functions, and roles specify how the organization will operate.

Policies are intended to provide direction to organizational members. They indicate in general ways how organizational behavior should occur. Policies are the guidelines from which organizational members obtain direction when standard procedures are judged inappropriate for a particular activity.

Functions are combinations of related activities carried out in the organization. These related activities may be grouped around a particular product or group of products. For example, the collection of all activities related to the production of welding equipment products might be collected into a welding products division. Or, activities may be grouped around a part of the production process. Those activities related to the maintenance of equipment used to manufacture welding equipment products would be brought together as the maintenance department. In similar fashion, one or more departments might be formed by grouping similar activities in the production of welding equipment such as grouping together machining of parts, grinding and polishing of parts, and plating of parts. To round out this definition of functions, organizations usually identify and locate together those activities connected with purchasing of raw materials and those activities related to selling of the finished products. With increased organizational size, supporting activities are grouped into clusters of similar activities such as those related to personnel and to financial control and accounting.

It would appear that rational conditions for grouping of activities into divisions or departments are conceptual and/or physical similarity of action. But organizational activities simply may be linked together by less elegant and more pragmatic criteria that are more directly related to achieving organizational objectives. For example, conditions such as variation in customer demands or concentration of customers in several locations may be met by grouping the selling function by location and placing it in close physical proximity to the customers even if that is away from the place of manufacture.

Roles are best described as that combination of activities, rights, and expectations that one or more individuals assumes within the organization and that are related to achieving the objectives and goals of the organization. It is this aspect of structure that is closest to the main thrust of this chapter. Connected with the formal and sometimes unstated demands of the organization for the individual role holder are the individual's aspirations for career and desires for need fulfillment from the work setting. What the individual carries into the work setting is influenced by the person's experience in educational situations and other work settings. Also of importance, influencing the expectations of the individual role holder, are the interests, aptitudes, abilities, and skills that the person brings to the work situation. The role-individual match has been described by Dawis, England, and Lofquist (1964). Basically there is an exchange of skill for reward that occurs within the structure of the work role. It is in this exchange that the individual-organizational accommodation (sometimes called the socialization process) occurs. This accommodation occurs on both the individual's part and on the organization's part. An individual may influence the size of the work role he or she has. But also, over time individuals move to places within the organization where they may influence other aspects of structure such as the changing of or the setting of policy and the changing of or the formation of the functional groupings of the organization. In this way, individual role holders; their abilities and skills; and their perceptions, aspirations, and interests all combine to influence the structure of the organization.

Design of the Organization

It is apparent from the previous discussion that a number of factors need be considered to produce the most effective structural arrangement for meeting the objectives of the organization. Those activities related to identifying the important variables to consider, to specifying the procedures for diagnosis of issues and potential problems in the situation, and to the implementation of changes identified as important to carry out may be classified as design activities. The important question for all of these activities is, How are they to be carried out? And most importantly for this discussion, What mechanism or approach to design is likely to influence and be influenced by competence potential?

There are several ways to proceed in the design of organizations. One approach is based upon the work of industrial engineering and the scientific management school of thought (Vollmer, 1968). This approach begins with an analysis of the flow of work and of methods and procedures (and in some cases tools) for handling the flow of work and an assessment of the skill of the persons who are involved in the performance of the tasks. Additionally, there is a need to analyze the information flow, because information functions as the feedback component in organization operations. Flow of work and flow of information may be handled in a rational analysis. Both are the basic building blocks in the analysis and design of organizations from this perspective.

Another approach, the behavioral approach, starts with persons in their work roles, observes them, and involves them in self-role analysis regarding their work situation. This guided introspective analysis by the role occupant, in addition to providing the basic ingredients for organizational design, leads to greater commitment of the role occupants to their jobs and to the organization. It can also improve their knowledge of their roles and can influence favorably persons' job behavior. The operating assumptions are founded upon a belief in the self-actualizing nature of the individual and that given the opportunity, each person will attempt to reach for his or her highest level. Practically, this approach assumes that productivity improvements will follow from personal growth of the role holder. Design and redesign emerge out of discussions with the role holders, and their views of the situation are taken as the best available information. Further, there is assumed to be a greater willingness to act on recommended changes in the design due in part to the role holder's ownership of the change itself. This approach to design requires a greater degree of participation on the part of the individual role holder than does the previously described approach. The previous approach, however, does not preclude participation by the role holders. In fact, most successful rational approaches to design of organizations and adjustment in their flow of work emphasize the utility of involvement of persons in their roles.

It appears that the degree of directiveness or participativeness in attempts to design the organization will be one of the variables that will influence the nature and acceptance of the design. It is necessary, however, to consider the design mechanism in relation to the competence potential of the individual role holder. The more competent the role holder, the more likely it is that the person will be able to contribute usefully to the design of the organization. Further, given the increasing attempts to involve organization members in decisions affecting them (Thorsrud, 1976; Heller, 1976), there is a greater likelihood that role holders will expect to be involved. This involvement is reputed to increase the motivational level of role holders and, by so doing, to influence favorably their desire to utilize their abilities and skills on the job. The design mechanism that achieves the greatest degree of involvement and participation consistent with the development of the most efficient flow of work and information would be consistent with our orientation toward obtaining, and then utilizing to the fullest, the competence potential of organizational role holders.

Organizational Performance

Performance of organizations is judged in a number of ways. For capitalist business organizations, performance might be evaluated in terms of the degree of profitability consistent with long-term organizational survival. The greater the level of profit, the higher the level of performance. A more immediately meaningful assessment of organizational performance is in terms of its utilization of organizational resources. Return and/or output per unit of investment or asset would fit into this framework. Still others prefer to make comparative judgments between organizations recognizing the impact of factors and variables outside of the control or the boundaries of the organization. In some cases industry comparisons are used, such as in retailing, when one buyer's sales of a particular product are compared with sales of other buyers in different companies who are also selling the same product (in some cases within the same market). Or one can make comparisons in terms of the share of the market the organization has, continues to maintain, or is able to take from competitors.

Each of these comparisons focuses upon the resources of the organization — finances, materials, facilities and equipment, and people. Each of these comparisons assumes something about the way the organization is arranged or structured so that these resources may be utilized. In some cases it appears that these comparisons assume that all other things are equal with regard to the methods and procedures of the organization, with respect to the environment within which the organization operates, and concerning the quality of the human and other resources present and available. It is assumed that the organization will have the capacity to arrange itself so there is an opportunity for at least "satisficing" performance, given the available resources and the constraints of environmental demand — namely, social-cultural, political-legal, and market. We may summarize this part of our discussion by saying that organizational performance is a function of its efficient resource utilization, the effectiveness of methods and procedures, and the degree of and cost of environmental predictability.

Our treatment of these organizational issues is in terms of the individual and his or her capacity and competence in the situation. It is the individual who selects the alternative from those available. The more competent the individual, the better the decision (ceteris paribus). This competence of the human resource may be observed in various activities, but it is especially evident with respect to the decisions made by the organization's members regarding managerial, technical, production, and support activities. We usually evaluate the impact of the individual's decisions or the organization in terms of short-term and long-term goal achievement. The greater the goal achievement, the greater the organizational effectiveness. This linkage between individual performance, organizational performance, and judged organizational effectiveness requires some additional elaboration (Steers, 1975). Let us consider it within the framework of organizational effectiveness. Then we can attempt to link the more usual psychological treatment of individual members to the activities of the organization.

Organization Effectiveness

Organization effectiveness can be defined (Gibson, Ivancevich, and Donnelly, 1976: 60) as "the extent to which organizations achieve their missions, goals, and objectives within the constraints of limiting resources." There are two aspects of this definition — first, the construct of goal achievement, and second, the impact of resource constraint. Comparative organizational effectiveness may be evaluated in terms of organizational efficiency, defined as the ratio of outputs to inputs or maximizing results with minimum use of resources. Achieving organizational goals is a necessary condition for effective performance. The efficient use of constrained resources may result in effectiveness but is not a necessary condition for effectiveness. An organization can, therefore, be effective and inefficient. And further, an organization can be efficient and not effective. However, maximization of both effectiveness and efficiency is the usual long-run goal of organizations. Individual competence in decisionmaking contributes to organizational effectiveness through selection of efficient resource utilization alternatives.

One consequence of efficiency is the creation of useful surplus in some form (Katz and Kahn, 1978). The alternative uses of surplus are usually identified and then selected by individual decisionmakers. The surplus could be used to expand capacity, develop technology, or perhaps even lower prices to consumers. Selection from these choices will be by individual decisionmakers as they interrelate the long- and short-term goals of the organization. But the concept of an effective organization must also be considered in relation to the environment within which it operates. The effective organization may no longer remain effective when that environment changes (Burns and Stalker, 1961; Woodward, 1965; Lawrence and Lorsch, 1967). In Weber's (1947) completely programmed bureaucracy, knowledge of all pertinent cause and effect relationships, both inside and outside the organizational boundaries, was complete. The organization was built to operate efficiently, consistent with that knowledge. But rapid changes occurring within those pertinent cause and effect relationships force the organization to prepare to adapt. This is accomplished by key role holders. Again, structure and individual competence interact.

Individual–Organization–Environment Relationship

Burns and Stalker (1961) pointed out that dynamic environments require effective organizations to coordinate activities through flat structure and require greater self-control by personnel. Stable environments permit tall organizational structures and personnel control by rules and procedures. Thompson's (1967) discussion supports the relationship between degree of structure and "task environment" predictability but points out that the variable contributing to this relationship is the time and cost of obtaining needed information by organizational decisionmakers. Length of time and cost required by the organization to respond to the environmental changes are functions of their internal structural design and the cost of altering the production process.

Galbraith (1977) has elaborated the relationship of time, availability, cost, and amount of information required to differences in organizational design. Following Thompson, he argues that the organization needs information about the environment to regulate internal operations. Differences in the amount and timeliness of the information required forces organizations to utilize their resources differentially, partly as a function of availability of necessary information. Available relevant information requires one or more of three kinds of strategies: (1) those that keep the organization on an acceptable time schedule (by sampling incoming information or adding personnel to absorb the information); (2) those that keep the organization within budget (by sampling incoming information or delaying action until the incoming information has been sifted for meaning); and (3) those that enable the organization to utilize the available information regardless of time or budget (e.g., by delaying action until the information has been sifted for meaning through adding personnel). When the information comes from many sources (such as when the organization is geographically dispersed) coordination problems compound the difficulty. Over time, organizations establish the most cost-effective information-monitoring analysis and utilization strategies for those potentially changing elements of the environment critical to survival of the organization.

When previously used sources of information are not producing adequate, relevant information, the previously mentioned three strategies (meeting time schedules, operating within budget, and utilizing available information) are augmented by adding personnel to search for additional information, utilizing forecasting devices, and operating by plan. Usually the needed information is obtained by those with experience — that is, those who know what information is relevant to the needs of the organization. However, even those without such organizational experience but who know how to obtain information are used. For example, research scientists in development laboratories often have little product or organizational knowledge but have great amounts of information potentially relevant for organizational or product change. Thompson (1967) describes how this need for information about the environment is influenced by the level of complexity and technology of the activity of the organization to be changed. Thompson's discussion precipitated that of Galbraith (1977) and Terreberry (1968). A fourfold table (Table 1-1) helps to describe the organizational situation and the kind of information gathering needed by organizations.

In each case, the fundamental integrating organizational unit which assimilates information from these disparate sources is the individual decisionmaker. The nature and level of individual competence required of these "integrating units" can be stated in broad terms for each quadrant.

Table 1-1. Kind of Information Gathering Needed by Organizations

Organization Activity	*External Environment*	
	Stable	*Shifting*
Simple	I	III
Complex	II	IV

Source: Adapted from Thompson (1967).

Quadrant I includes cases where technology is simple and where environment is stable. Here the organization would use standard procedures for gathering periodic information. Little flexibility in procedure would be required since the environment changes so little. Control by rules and procedures and appeal to hierarchy for any changes describe the coordination process. Individual competence required in decisionmaking need only be to classify well, to follow rules, and to apply them.

Quadrant II indicates cases where there is complexity or high level technology involved in the organizational activity being considered. Information gathering about environmental changes would need to be accomplished by persons knowledgeable about the complex or highly technical internal activity that was being influenced by the environment. However, even though the environment is relatively stable, if the activities were the sale of complex, technical products in a number of different markets, the boundary organizational units would need to be specialized both by having knowledge of the different markets and by reflecting the internal technology. Since the external environment is predictable (stable), each of the role holders in the boundary units would be rule appliers and would request approval for changes by appealing up the hierarchy. Individual competence required by role holders in these units would be that they classify well, follow rules and apply them, and have a good grasp of the technology represented by their internal production or service process.

Quadrant III refers to cases where the environment is increasingly less stable but where the technology of the internal production process is reasonably simple and straightforward. In such cases, the organizational boundary unit would be deployed to insure the most complete surveillance possible of the changing environment. Individual competence required in these units would be the need to develop responses to the changes in the environment rather than just apply rules, but their technical competence need not be as great as that required in Quadrant IV.

Quadrant IV describes the situation where there is less stability and greater change in the environment and where the activity to be carried out is complex or requires high technology. The organization needs to be able to respond quickly to changing demands, but more importantly, to anticipate the changes well in advance since much lead time is required to change the complex or high technology of internal activity. To facilitate such responses, the organization might be arranged into self-contained programs directed toward various environmental segments. These programs will have within them their own support system capable of handling the technological demands of the task in a changing environment. The more change there is in the environment, the more difficult it is for the organization to respond quickly and efficiently. The level of individual competence required in these units would need to be more knowledgeable technically than that in Quadrant III and able to do more than simply follow rules and procedures as in Quadrants I and II.

The diagram in Figure 1-1 presents the three levels of analysis referred to along with the topics and concepts used from each level. The arrows indicate the principal flow of influence between the environment, organization, and individual constructs as the organization operates over time. Up to this point, we have focused attention on the organizational side of the individual-organizational nexus. We have discussed the structure, design, and performance of organizations and how these influence and are influenced by the individual organization member. Our discussion has drawn largely from sociological sources, which focus principally on organizational and environmental variables and minimally on individual variables. We wished to present a general but complete description of the dependent variable — organizational functioning — for no discussion of competence potential can be complete if its context is not understood. Still to be discussed fully is the independent variable — competence potential — its assessment, and the specifics by which it affects organizational functioning.

THE INDIVIDUAL

Skill and Task

A useful starting point in the discussion of competence potential and its assessment is the concept of skill. To begin with, skill might be defined with reference to task — that is, a skill can be defined as behavior emitted in the performance of a task. A task, in turn, is a performance requirement of the individual that ordinarily implies some more or less well-defined set of behaviors. For many typical work tasks, the set of behaviors is clearly defined. But in other instances, even the performance requirement (goal, objective) may be poorly defined, and different individuals confronted with the same task may exhibit strikingly different sets of behaviors. This latter circumstance will make it difficult sometimes to define the task in terms of the behaviors required, especially in those instances in which new behaviors can be "invented" by the individual in order

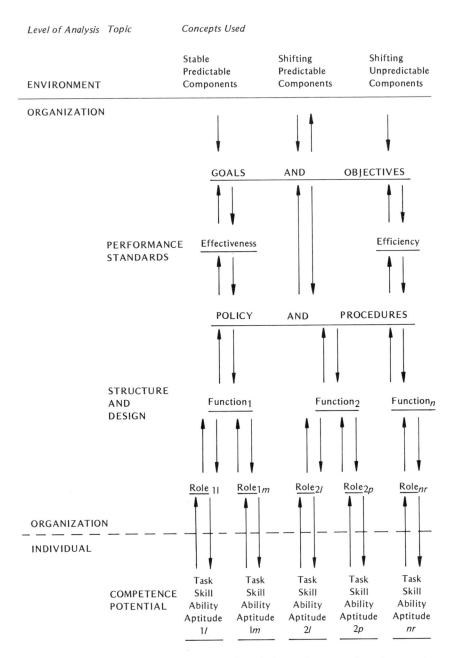

Level of Analysis Topic   *Concepts Used*

ENVIRONMENT	Stable Predictable Components	Shifting Predictable Components	Shifting Unpredictable Components

ORGANIZATION

GOALS   AND   OBJECTIVES

PERFORMANCE   Effectiveness   Efficiency
STANDARDS

POLICY   AND   PROCEDURES

STRUCTURE
AND   Function$_1$ Function$_2$ Function$_n$
DESIGN

Role$_{1l}$ Role$_{1m}$ Role$_{2l}$ Role$_{2p}$ Role$_{nr}$

ORGANIZATION
— — — — — — — — — — — — — — — — —
INDIVIDUAL

COMPETENCE POTENTIAL	Task Skill Ability Aptitude $1l$	Task Skill Ability Aptitude $1m$	Task Skill Ability Aptitude $2l$	Task Skill Ability Aptitude $2p$	Task Skill Ability Aptitude nr

Figure 1-1. Summary of the levels of analysis, topics covered, and concepts used in describing organizational functioning and individual competence potential.

12

to accomplish the task. To complicate matters even further, a task is a behavior demand regardless of source. Thus, there can be self-imposed tasks as well as tasks required by the organization.

Limiting discussion for the moment to well-defined tasks imposed or required by the organization, one may define a skill (more precisely, a work skill) as a behavior sequence with a definable beginning, a definable end, and usually a definable middle. The beginning and end points (and usually what should occur in between, although this latter may vary) are defined by the task. Any skill exhibited by a group of persons will produce individual differences in time of performance (time required to do the task) and quality of performance (in terms of either its form or its product, sometimes easily discerned on a single dimension such as accuracy or level of difficulty, sometimes complex enough to require several qualitative dimensions). Whichever of these dimensions is used — speed or quality — individual differences in the manifested skill behavior can be used to define a dimension of skillfulness or, more simply, a skill dimension (Lofquist and Dawis, 1969).

Since skills are identified by referring to tasks, there are in principle at least as many skills as there are tasks. This situation creates a continuing problem of classification. Several approaches to task classification have been proposed, which Fleishman (1975) categorized into (1) behavioral description, as in the work of McCormick (1976) and Fine (1963); (2) behavior requirements, as in Miller's (1962) approach; (3) ability requirements, the approach employed by Fleishman (1972); and (4) task characteristics, as exemplified in Hackman's (1970) work.

Both McCormick and Fine have been searching for more basic kinds of work behavior than are more generally applicable to the description of jobs (a "job" being defined as a collection of tasks). McCormick identified 189 such basic behaviors ("job elements"), which are incorporated in the Position Analysis Questionnaire (McCormick, Jeanneret, and Mecham, 1972), one of the best developed of current instruments available for the study and description of jobs.

Fine's earlier research on "worker functions" (Fine, 1955), as contrasted with "worker traits," was an effort also to identify basic behavior descriptors of tasks and jobs. His major conclusion was that such worker functions were of three kinds, those dealing with data, with people, and with things. This conclusion has withstood the scrutiny of job analysts of the U.S. Employment Service to the extent that the present nine digit Dictionary of Occupational Titles (DOT) code system incorporates the data-people-things behavior descriptors in the middle three digits of the DOT code.

Ability

For the purposes of the present chapter, Fleishman's ability approach is adopted for two reasons: it coincides with the present authors' conceptual understanding of competence potential, and it allows for the integration of large portions of the literature in both basic and applied psychology. The following discussion elaborates on the present authors' conceptualizations of competence potential in ability terms, based in large part on the ideas of Fleishman, Ferguson (1954, 1956), and Guilford (1967) — authors who have espoused the concept of ability as the essential link with basic psychology, especially the psychology of learning. Buss (1973), elaborating on the ideas of Ferguson and Fleishman, has shown how ability and learning can be conceptually related through the phenomenon of transfer. Guilford (1967) has shown the identity or similarity between abilities he has identified in his research and learning tasks typically used in the psychological experimental laboratories.

We start with the premise that competence potential is best operationalized in terms of skills. That is, a person's competence potential is best described in terms of what skills are present and what skills are possible for the person. Since skills are so numerous, however, it becomes necessary in discussing skills to adopt some data reduction strategy that provides for the regeneration or recapturing of the original skill data. This is, of course, the type of problem for which factor analysis was invented. Using a factor analytic (i.e., linear) model, we can reduce the data on skill variables to scores on some smaller set of latent (nonobserved) factors, which we now identify as abilities. That is, following Lofquist and Dawis (1969), abilities may be defined as reference dimensions by which skills may be described in linear fashion (in terms of a factor pattern). In principle, all skills, old or newly invented, can be described as a weighted linear combination of ability scores. The work of French (1951) exemplifies the search for such reference or ability dimensions.

It should be noted that the concept of ability as used here is more specific than that used by many investigators (cf., for example, Dunnette, 1976). Abilities are factor descriptors of skill variables, identified in the factor analysis of skills. The present state of the art in ability measurement, therefore, represents only a primitive realization of this concept and definition. Likewise, the present state of the art in describing skills in terms of abilities, as best typified by the U.S. Department of Labor's (1970) Occupational Aptitude Patterns, represents only a promising beginning.

Having distinguished between skill and ability, it is now possible to define "aptitude." In the present context, "aptitude" should refer to skill. An aptitude is the potential for a skill. Following Ferguson (1954, 1956), having a particular combination of abilities makes it possible to infer either possession of a particular skill or potentiality (aptitude) for that skill. Potentiality is inferred because the potential skill is presumed to lie within the transfer gradients for the ability combination.

Competence Potential Assessment

Competence potential with reference to a particular job can be defined in terms of a person's aptitude for each skill required for the job. One might consider all of the required skills, or one might limit consideration to only the important or necessary ones. In either case, an overall index of potential might be derived from the differing potentials for the separate skills.

Such a conceptualization of competence potential would require a careful task analysis of each job as a necessary precondition to competence potential assessment. It is not difficult to see why assessment of competence potential has been problematic for those jobs for which the component tasks — or even more critically, the requisite skills — are difficult to specify — for example, management jobs, professional positions. For such jobs, competence potential assessment will continue to be problematic so long as persons filling such jobs can continue to define their tasks to a significant extent and/or to "invent" new skills with which to complete broadly defined tasks.

Even after having determined the important critical skills, however, the assessment of competence potential on each skill can become an impossible task. Here is where we have recourse to abilities as descriptors of skills. Knowledge of a person's ability level on each of a manageable number of abilities should enable the estimation of that person's aptitude for the required skills — hence, assessment of the person's competence potential. This capability, however, is predicated on knowing the ability combinations required for the different skills.

In the present context, therefore, given a set of ability scores for a person, one should be able to estimate that person's actual or potential standing on every skill for which an ability combination definition (such as a regression equation) is available. From this perspective, the critical information is ability scores, and the assessment of competence potential reduces to the assessment of abilities.

There are many difficulties with the proposed approach to competence potential assessment. For one thing, the number of abilities that have been identified and for which there are adequate measures is small and limited in range. For another, the number of skills for which there are validated ability combination descriptions (that is, regression or prediction equations) is not large. Empirical determination of such ability combination descriptions of skills (or more typically of global job performance) proceeds at a snail's pace and is almost outdated when completed. The cost in both time and money of such empirical studies is perceived by many to be too high relative to the benefit. A more promising and much more financially appealing substitute might lie in the estimation of ability requirements for jobs and for skills as well (Paterson, Gerken, and Hahn, 1953; Desmond and Weiss, 1973, 1975). The U.S. Employment Service has tried this approach with its General Aptitude Test Battery variables in its estimates of worker trait requirements (U.S. Department of Labor, 1956).

Even if estimation of ability requirements is found to be an acceptable methodology, the proposed approach is still problematic unless the full range of abilities can be specified. Again, one is faced with the quandary that empirical identification of abilities, while the most dependable procedure, is also very slow and very expensive. Hence, a taxonomy of abilities that is an extrapolation of current knowledge might serve not only to enable the use of the ability-requirement-estimation methodology, but also to facilitate the empirical identification of abilities and the development of measures of them. A proposal for such a taxonomy, a refinement of an earlier proposal (Dawis, 1977) and drawing much upon Fleishman's (1975) ideas, is given below.

Taxonomy of Abilities

The proposed taxonomy makes use of Guttman's notion of facets (Schlesinger and Guttman, 1969) and identifies three facets. Two of these are usually identified as content and process. Content refers to the nature of the test material (all ability measures are called tests here, following common practice), while process refers to the nature of the subject's response. More precisely, these two facets might be called simply stimulus and response (after Torgerson, 1958). These terms will be used here in lieu of content and process. A third facet, which recognizes an aspect of psychological testing that has not been accorded its due, is identified as observability. This facet underscores the fact that some abilities are more accessible to observation than others.

The stimulus facet consists of two contrasting categories — namely, concrete and abstract, which might be thought of as designating two ranges in the continuum of representationality. Toward one end of the continuum (concrete), the stimulus stands for itself; toward the other end (abstract), it stands for other content or other stimuli (for example, words representing facts). A more descriptive set of terms might be immediate and symbolic or mediating. We shall use them instead of the more familiar concrete versus abstract.

The immediate stimulus category may be subdivided further into stimuli that are passive as contrasted with stimuli that are active and, indeed, interactive with the subject. Ordinary objects (things) are examples of passive stimuli, while people are examples of active stimuli. A quantitative difference is presumed between an ability that deals with active stimuli and an ability that deals with passive stimuli. It is worth noting that this categorization of the stimulus facet into mediating stimulus, active immediate stimulus, and passive immediate stimulus corresponds approximately to Fine's and the U.S. Employment Service's categories of data, people, things, and to Thorndike's earlier (1920) proposal of three kinds of intelligence — abstract, social, and concrete.

The mediating stimulus category may be subdivided further according to types of symbols, of which three stand out — words, numbers, and pictures or graphic representations. It is also worth noting that these three correspond to the three areas that psychological test research has found to be relatively distinct, as well as to be major components of general intelligence — verbal, numerical, and spatial abilities.

Borrowing from basic psychology, the response facet may consist of three categories — afferent response (sensation and perception), central process (memory and reasoning), and efferent response (psychomotor and physical abilities). Thus, the proposed taxonomy has at least five divisions for the stimulus facet (immediate passive, immediate active, mediating verbal, mediating numerical, mediating graphic) and at least six for the response facet (sensation, perception, memory, reasoning, psychomotor abilities, physical abilities). These are shown graphically in Figure 1-2. The third facet, observability, is shown as having two categories, observable and inferred. Figure 1-2 represents the taxonomy as a cube; however, certain cells in the cube may not be filled. For example, central process responses will always be inferred, never observed; physical abilities may rarely or never be involved with mediating stimuli.

As might be inferred from Figure 1-2, all extant ability tests can be categorized within the proposed taxonomy. In addition, abilities are identified for which no adequate measures have been developed,

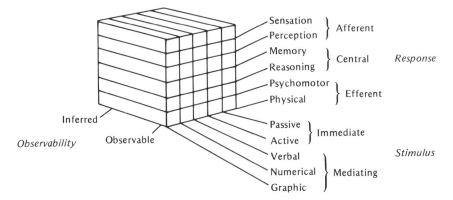

Figure 1-2. Graphic representation of a proposed ability taxonomy.

such as memory for or about people and reasoning about people (immediate active, central process). It is worth noting that abilities in the immediate active area, specifically those known as "people abilities" (e.g., negotiating, persuading), are some of the very abilities required at the higher echelons of the organization. Management potential, in particular, would appear to stem from these abilities. Yet most assessment of management potential today persists in using abilities from other areas, especially those of mediating stimuli. Thus, the proposed taxonomy can explain in part why previous efforts at the assessment of management potential have not been as successful as assessment of some skilled trades.

It is also worth noting that according to the proposed taxonomy, many assessment procedures used in the areas of skilled crafts and trades, benchwork, and other occupations requiring primarily "thing abilities" are probably misdirected efforts because of their undue emphasis on mediating stimulus abilities and their lack of coverage of immediate stimulus abilities. The low validities obtained for paper and pencil tests and the higher validities obtained with performance or apparatus tests in this area are indirect evidence in support of the present contention.

Assuming that the proposed taxonomy contains the full range of human abilities, estimation procedures can be used to identify ability combinations for the description of any skill. Having identified the requisite abilities, assessment of abilities might then proceed using the best available instruments and methodologies. For example, when psychological tests are not available, interviews or questionnaires might be used to elicit biographical information that might in turn provide adequate bases for estimation of ability levels.

Training, Education, and Experience

The use of biographical information for the assessment of abilities (and ultimately of competence potential) is a particularly promising alternative to psychological tests (Owens, 1976). This should not be surprising, since skill acquisition (hence, ability level determination) is presumably the result of experience. Unless one has experience, unless one were exposed to certain stimuli and had occasion to make (and practice) certain responses, particular skills are not acquired, and presumably the abilities underlying such skills suffer in development. Providing for experience is an important condition for skill — and ability — development. Because not everyone has the opportunity to acquire certain skills, training programs are designed, in effect, to provide the requisite experience in a short period of time. Training, then, might be viewed as compressed experience. Training is an important part of education, if by the latter is meant the "bringing out" of the person's potential. Education, however, transcends training, since it includes, among other things, appreciation, enjoyment, broadened perspective, rationality, values, and especially, a philosophy of life. Nonetheless, skills and skill acquisition are an important and necessary part of education.

Unfortunately, in recent years, educational attainment has been equated with skill acquisition to the extent that in some situations, one's experience counts for much less than one's certificates. Perversely, in other situations, the opposite might be true, where one's certificates — which indicate potential — may count for nothing because it is experience that is demanded and it is experience that the individual does not have. These possibilities indicate the contradictions to which the assessment of competence potential is subject.

A final added complication to the assessment of competence potential is introduced by the subculture. To begin with, subcultures may identify and define tasks differently. Even when the same tasks are involved, people from different subcultures may evolve essentially different skills to accomplish these same tasks — that is, the middle of the skill sequence may be different even if the beginning and end points are the same. If different subcultures emphasize different skills, it is obvious that assessment at the level of skills may "discriminate" against or in favor of one subculture over another. If the present formulation is correct, it is theoretically possible for assessment at the level of abilities to discriminate less among and to be more fair across the different subcultures.

CONCLUSION

Competence potential, defined in terms of a person's aptitude for each skill required for the job or particular work role, can be related to organizational functioning. We have discussed organizational functioning in terms of the structure of the organization, the mechanism of design of organization, and organizational performance. Competence potential influences the structure of the organization through its effect upon the work role. The match between the demands of the work role and the competence potential of the role holder is the essence of the task of those engaged in selection and staffing for the organization. Roles defined restrictively will limit the expression of competence potential. But such restriction may be necessary for purposes of coordination of the tasks to be performed in order to meet the organization's goals. Therefore, the individual differences in competence potential need to be assessed and individuals differentially allocated to jobs and roles according to the role demands.

Other aspects of structure such as the functional grouping of roles into jobs, work units, departments, and divisions indirectly influence the degree to which the individual's role is restricted and therefore the way in which competence potential is expressed. But even with hierarchically arranged and specialized roles and departments, the development and expression of competence potential may be great if the task is sufficiently complex and the technology of the task sufficiently high (as discussed above in connection with decision-making in the individual-organization-environment relationship).

Policy development and the nature of the policies required by organizations are influenced by the skill level of the organization members who determine the policies and ought to be related to the skill level of those to be guided by policy. The lower the level of skills represented by the role holders, the more policy will be elaborated and practices specified. This in turn constrains the individual role holder to continue performing the prescribed tasks in the same way, thus reducing the probability of developing the person's competence potential.

The design of the organization influences the use of the individual's skills through the mechanism of participation. To the extent that there is involvement of the individual in defining his or her work situation, there is likely to be greater commitment to task performance.

Competence potential is most often thought of in connection with organizational performance. Perhaps this is due to the direct linking of individual output to organizational output. To this linkage, there is the more focused realtionship of decisionmaking skill level to the direction of organizational action and the handling of environmental and organizational interchange.

The complexity of the interrelationship between an individual's competence potential, organizational action, and environmental demand is what makes the study of complex organizations greatly frustrating. Yet it is that very complexity and diversity that makes the topic immensely challenging to the individual investigator's own competence potential.

REFERENCES

Argyris, C. 1964. *Integrating the Individual and the Organization.* New York: Wiley.

Burns, T., and G. M. Stalker. 1961. *The Management of Innovation.* London: Tavistock.

Buss, A. R. 1973. "Learning, Transfer, and Changes in Ability Factors." *Psychological Bulletin* 80: 106-12.

Dawis, R. V. 1977. "A Model, Method, and Taxonomy for the Selection of Tests as Predictors." In S. Mussio (proj. dir.), *A Training Manual for Personnel Selection Specialists,* vol. I. Minneapolis: City of Minneapolis Civil Service Commission Research Division and Great Lakes Assessment Council.

Dawis, R. V.; G. W. England; and L. H. Lofquist. 1964. *A Theory of Work Adjustment.* Minnesota Studies in Vocational Rehabilitation No. XV. Minneapolis, Industrial Relations Center.

Desmond, R. E., and D. J. Weiss. 1973. "Supervisor Estimates of Abilities Required in Jobs." *Journal of Vocational Behavior* 3: 181-94.

———. 1975. "Worker Estimation of Ability Requirements of Their Jobs." *Journal of Vocational Behavior* 7: 13-27.

Dunnette, M. D. 1976. "Aptitudes, Abilities, and Skills." In M. D. Dunnette, ed., *Handbook of Industrial and Organizational Psychology.* Chicago: Rand McNally.

Ferguson, G. A. 1954. "On Learning and Human Ability." *Canadian Journal of Psychology* 8: 95-112.

———. 1956. "On Transfer and the Abilities of Man." *Canadian Journal of Psychology* 10: 121-31.

Fine, S. A. 1955. "A Structure of Worker Functions." *Personnel and Guidance Journal* 34: 66-73.

———. 1963. *A Functional Approach to a Broad Scale Map of Work Behaviors.* McLean, Virginia: Human Sciences Research.

Fleishman, E. A. 1972. "On the Relation Between Abilities, Learning, and Human Performance." *American Psychologist* 27: 1017-32.

———. 1975. "Toward a Taxonomy of Human Performance." *American Psychologist* 30: 1127-48.

French, J. W. 1951. "The Description of Aptitude and Achievement Tests in Terms of Rotated Factors." *Psychometric Monographs* No. 5.

Galbraith, J. R. 1977. *Organization Design.* Reading, Mass.: Addison-Wesley.

Gibson, J. L.; J. M. Ivancevich; and J. H. Donnelly, Jr. 1976. *Organizations Structure, Process, Behavior.* 2nd ed. Dallas: Business Publications, Inc.

Guilford, J. P. 1967. *The Nature of Human Intelligence.* New York: McGraw-Hill.

Hackman, J. R. 1970. "Tasks and Task Performance in Research on Stress." In J. C. McGrath, ed., *Social and Psychological Factors in Stress.* New York: Holt, Rinehart, and Winston.

Heller, F. A. 1976. "Decision Processes: An Analysis of Power Sharing at Senior Organizational Levels." In R. Dubin, ed., *Handbook of Work Organization, and Society.* Chicago: Rand McNally.

Katz, D., and R. L. Kahn. 1978. *The Social Psychology of Organizations.* 2nd ed. New York: John Wiley and Sons.

Lawrence, P. R., and D. W. Lorsch. 1967. *Organization and Environment.* Boston: Harvard Business School.

Lofquist, L. H., and R. V. Dawis. 1969. *Adjustment To Work.* New York: Appleton-Century-Crofts.

McCormick, E. J. 1976. "Job and Task Analysis." In M. D. Dunnette, ed., *Handbook of Industrial and Organizational Psychology.* Chicago: Rand McNally.

McCormick, E. J.; P. R. Jeanneret; and R. C. Mecham. 1972. "A Study of Job Characteristics and Job Dimensions as Based on the Position Analysis Questionnaire." *Journal of Applied Psychology* 56: 347-68.

Miller, R. B. 1962. "Task Description and Analysis." In R. B. Gagne, ed., *Psychological Principles in System Development.* New York: Holt, Rinehart, and Winston.

Owens, W. A. 1976. "Background Data." In M. D. Dunnette, ed., *Handbook of Industrial and Organizational Psychology.* Chicago: Rand McNally.

Paterson, D. G.; C. D. Gerken; and M. E. Hahn. 1953. *Revised Minnesota Occupational Rating Scales.* Minneapolis: University of Minnesota Press.

Schlesinger, I. M., and L. Guttman. 1969. "Smallest Space Analysis of Intelligence and Achievement Tests." *Psychological Bulletin* 71: 95-100.

Steers, R. M. 1975. "Problems in the Measurement of Organizational Effectiveness." *Administrative Science Quarterly* 20: 546-58.

Terreberry, S. 1968. "The Evaluation of Organizational Environments." *Administrative Science Quarterly* 12: 590-613.

Thompson, J. D. 1967. *Organizations in Action.* New York: McGraw-Hill.

Thorndike, E. L. 1920. "Intelligence and Its Uses." *Harper's Magazine* 130: 227-35.

Thorsrud, E.; B. Aase; and B. Gustavsen. 1976. "Sociotechnical Approach to Industrial Democracy in Norway." In R. Dubin, ed., *Handbook of Work, Organization , and Society.* Chicago: Rand McNally,

Torgerson, W. S. 1958. *Theory and Methods of Scaling.* New York: Wiley.

U. S. Department of Labor. 1956. *Estimates of Worker Trait Requirements for 4,000 Jobs.* Washington, D. C.: U. S. Government Printing Office.

———. 1970. *Manual for the USTES General Aptitude Test Battery Section II:*

Norms, Occupational Aptitude Pattern Structure. Washington, D. C.: U. S. Government Printing Office.

Vollmer, H. M. 1968. *Organizational Design — Process and Concepts.* Menlo Park, California: Stanford Research Institute.

Weber, M. 1947. *The Theory of Social and Economic Organization.* New York: The Free Press.

Woodward, J. 1965. *Industrial Organization: Theory and Practice.* London: Oxford University Press.

Chapter 2

Abstractness, Conceptual Systems, and the Functioning of Complex Organizations

Hal W. Hendrick

During the past decade, public and private organizations in the United States and elsewhere have come under increasing attack. Consumer groups have become progressively more organized and vocal in expressing alarm over the high costs to maintain organizations and the resulting inadequate services and low quality products. Increasingly, the consumer public is pressuring for greater governmental intervention and managerial initiative to change organizations and make them more effective. As Argyris (1974), in reflecting on this increasing public dissatisfaction, has noted, however, before we can change organizations, we need to understand why they are becoming less dependable.

Concomitant with the increasing symptoms of organizational problems has been a growing body of literature exploring the causes of organizational deterioration. Argyris (1971) has summarized the findings of a number of these researchers (Argyris, 1964; Bennis, 1966; Golembiewski, 1969, 1967; Hertzberg, 1966; Katz and Kahn, 1966; Tannenbaum, 1968; Whyte, 1969) with respect to both the lower level and managerial worlds.

* University of Southern California.

CHARACTERISTICS OF THE LOWER LEVEL WORLD

At the lower level these researchers frequently found that (1) work is highly specialized or fractionalized; (2) responsibility for planning the work, defining production rates, and maintaining control over speed is placed in the hands of management and not in the hands of those actually producing; and (3) responsibility for hiring employees, issuing orders, changing work, shifting employees, evaluating performance, and defining and disbursing rewards and penalties is vested in top management. Argyris (1974) notes that to the extent that organizations attempt to follow the consequences of these characteristics, they will tend to create a work world for the lower level employees having the following conditions.

1. Few of their abilities will be used, particularly those more central to self-expression and psychological success such as cognitive and interpersonal abilities.
2. Employees will tend to experience a sense of dependence and submissiveness toward their superior and feel that they have little control over the crucial decisions about their organizational life.
3. Workers will tend to experience a decreasing sense of responsibility and self-control.
4. The more rigidity, specialization, tight control, and directive leadership the worker experiences, the more he or she will tend to create antagonistic adaptive activities.
5. Administrative controls tend to be based on the assumptions that (a) management plans and controls human effort, (b) the control of human effort is manageable by logic and the use of quantitative techniques, and (c) this latter is achieved by the use of the principle of exception. These assumptions tend to result in control systems little influenced by and rarely mirroring the reality experienced by those whose behavior is being controlled. Control systems thus tend to create fear of being trapped by logic and the principle of exception, create group rivalries, force groups to think of their own and not other's problems, rarely reward an overall point of view, and place groups in win-lose situations in which they are competing with each other for scarce resources.
6. The underlying philosophy of most managements tends to be to appoint leaders whose styles are similar to and consonant with what Likert calls "production centered," McGregor calls "theory X," and Argyris calls "directive leadership." The re-

search has shown that such leadership results in a decrease in (a) the individual's experience of psychological success and essentiality, (b) the likelihood that the employee will give valid information to those above or to peers, and (c) the involvement of employees in improving or maintaining the health of the system. These findings are further supported by my own more recent research (Hendrick, 1980).

7. Policies and practices will create binds for the lower level employee. On the one hand management tells employees they are important and are to be trusted and respected, emphasizes participation, and claims to be open to change. On the other hand, management usually maintains control, allows only pseudo-participation, and resists any substantial change to organizational structure and functioning.

CHARACTERISTICS OF THE MANAGERIAL WORLD

Assuming technical competence, the biggest barriers to change at the managerial level are the interpersonal relationships, the group and intergroup relationships, and the system's norms. These barriers rarely cause problems when dealing with routine, programmed, and nonthreatening information, but become difficult to identify and overcome when dealing with innovative, nonprogrammed, or threatening data. In his research to identify why this occurs, Argyris (1968) identified aspiration for power and three specific values ingrained during the individual's educational upbringing — values that he sees as an integral part of the engineering-economic-technological world that dominates our lives. They are (1) that significant human relations are those that have to do with achieving the organization's objective; (2) that cognitive rationality is to be emphasized and feelings and emotions played down, if not denied; and (3) that human relationships are most effectively influenced through unilateral direction, coercion, and control, as well as by rewards and penalties that sanction all three characteristics. This third value is implicit in the chain of command and in the managerial control systems of most organizations. The impact of these values is to create a pattern of behavior that Argyris has identified simply as "pattern A." This pattern is characterized by a tendency to emphasize the value of rationality and getting the job done. An organizational norm tends to develop that coerces individuals to hide their feelings or to bring them up disguised as rational, technical, or intellectual problems. Ideas or values that, if explored, might expose suppressed feelings are not considered. Thus, innovation and risk taking that benefit the organization become limited.

Maccoby (1976), in a recent in-depth study of 250 managers in high technology organizations, obtained results highly consistent with those summarized by Argyris. Using psychoanalytic and social anthropological techniques, Maccoby identified four psychosocial character types of managers, including the new corporate executive type that has emerged during the last two decades, which he has labeled descriptively as the "gamesman." The gamesman is somewhat more open minded and more skilled in using human relations approaches to manipulate others than the more autocratic executives of the past. However, the gamesman's interpersonal values mirror those noted by Argyris in his literature summary. Maccoby has further enriched our knowledge by identifying the psychological costs of this value system to the managers themselves — particularly that of cognitive rationality and resultant restricted human interactions. Maccoby refers to this as the dichotomy of the head and the heart. Like Argyris, Maccoby identifies the lack of integration of the two as limiting interpersonal competency.

THE FAILURE OF CHANGE STRATEGIES

Given the disfunctional nature of much of both employee and managerial life, both Argyris and Maccoby address the issue, Why have sincere attempts to bring about fundamental change not worked? Maccoby notes that the gamesman is open to trying any new innovation that offers promise of increasing organizational effectiveness and that during the past decade managers have tried a myriad of formulas for improving morale and efficiency. From his study, Maccoby concluded that while these approaches have led to some improvement in work, on the whole they have been disappointing, largely because they ignored the real forces that determine the corporate psychostructure.

Argyris (1974) reviewed the literature on organizational change strategies and their results and also concluded that the track record was not very encouraging. In exploring the question "why," he noted that the basic assumption implicit in all of these strategies is that present employees, if given the opportunity, cannot be trusted to change the system. A related assumption is that the first one, even if valid, need not be tested publicly with those concerned. Because of these factors, employees experience change processes that are no different from the managerial processes they have experienced for many years. Argyris (1974), like Maccoby (1976) concluded that structural change must be preceded by changes in values, psychological sets, and the development of new competencies by the employees.

STRUCTURAL COGNITIVE STYLE – CONCRETENESS—ABSTRACTNESS

During the past two decades there has been a growing body of research data, largely outside the areas of organizational psychology and sociology, that I believe to be relevant to our understanding of the following:

1. The organizational problems described in the literature reviewed by Argyris and in the recent psychosocial study of high technology organizations by Maccoby, summarized above.
2. Why it is that these disfunctional aspects of organizational life have progressively surfaced during the past decade.
3. Why it is that organizational norms, structures, and values historically came to exist and persist in their present form.
4. What can be expected in terms of fundamental organizational change within the next several decades.
5. How fundamental change can be effected through intervention.

This research had its roots in the classical work of Piaget (1948) on child development. It has to do with structural cognitive style or cognitive complexity — more specifically, with the higher order predispositional personality dimension of concreteness-abstractness of thinking. Two groups of researchers have extended the study of concreteness-abstractness into the adult range — Harvey at the University of Colorado and colleagues at various institutions in the area of conceptual functioning or conceptual systems and behavior and Kohlberg and his colleagues at Harvard with respect to moral reasoning.

Conceptual Systems and Concreteness-Abstractness

A common phenomenon noted in attitude research worldwide is that persons holding a particular attitude about one thing also tend to hold similar attitudes about many other things — that is, they have a common pattern of attitudes. Similarly, other groups of people can be identified with different attitudinal patterns. During the 1950s, several prominent social psychologists hypothesized that these pattern differences might be more than just attitudinal.

Specifically, these differences might be reflective of fundamentally different ways in which people structure or organize, categorize, integrate, and interpret their knowledge of the world about them — differences in how they conceptualize reality. If indeed this was the case, it would be reasonable to expect a person's attitudes and behavior to be affected by how he or she conceptualized reality and in predictable ways. Similarly, a group's conception of reality should affect how they structure or organize their social world.

In 1961, Harvey, Hunt, and Schroder published a book summarizing the results of their research. They concluded that there appear to be at least four fundamentally different ways in which people organize or structure and integrate their experiences of reality. Further, these four ways appear to lie along an invariant developmental continuum. The underlying bipolar continuum identified was concreteness-abstractness of thinking — the same dimension Piaget had identified, but extended into the more abstract adult range. Persons who are highly concrete thinkers tend to use minimal differentiation within concepts and little integration among them. Conversely, abstract thinkers utilize a high degree of differentiation and integration.

Measuring Abstractness Level and Conceptual Stage. Aside from systematic observation of actual behavior, both abstractness level and conceptual stage can be assessed by paper and pencil instruments. Several types of instruments have been used and shown to be both valid and reliable (e.g., Harvey, Hunt, and Schroder, 1961; O'Connor, 1971; Kaats and Thompson, 1968). The method that has been the most accurate for assessing both primary and secondary conceptual functioning requires the individual to write a short paragraph to a series of topical statements that begin with the words "this I believe about . . . ." These statements then are content analyzed by trained evaluators. Interrator reliability for three or four trained judges consistently has been .90 or above (Harvey, Hunt, and Schroder, 1961; Harvey, 1966).

Moral Reasoning and Concreteness–Abstractness

When Lawrence Kohlberg set out to study moral reasoning, he was looking for structures, forms, and relationships that are common to all societies and languages (Kohlberg, 1969). Over the years he has gradually elaborated a topological scheme for describing the general structure and forms of moral reasoning that he and his colleagues have found throughout the world. Of particular importance was the finding that moral thought could be defined independently of the specific moral content of moral decisions and actions. As with the research on conceptual systems, Kohlberg found that there are stages of moral reasoning that lie along the concreteness-abstractness continuum. Kohlberg identified three developmental levels of moral reasoning that he labeled preconventional, conventional, and postconventional moral thinking. Within each of these levels he identified two related stages. Each stage can be viewed as a separate moral philosophy or conceptualization of the social-moral world. In Kohlberg's words, "moral thought, then seems to behave like all other kinds of thought. Progress through the moral levels and stages is characterized by increasing differentiation and integration" (Kohlberg, 1969: 186). As with conceptual systems, each level of moral reasoning represents an invariant developmental sequence. Whether or not the specific stages within each level are invariant is questionable (Kohlberg, 1969; O'Connor, 1971). All researchers working in this area appear agreed that about 50 percent of most people's reasoning will be at a single stage, regardless of the moral dilemma involved.

Kohlberg's primary method of investigation is to present the individual with a series of moral dilemmas. The individual's stage of moral reasoning is determined by content analysis of the individual's reasoning about these dilemmas. One limitation of this methodology has been a lack of reported reliability data, standardized number and type of dilemmas used, and published scoring procedures (see Kurtines and Grief [1974] for a review of these and other limitations). The specific levels are as follows (Kohlberg, 1969):

Preconventional or First Level of Moral Reasoning. This level is oriented around concepts of good and bad that are interpreted in terms of physical concepts (punishment and reward) or in terms of the physical power of those who make the rules (i.e., might is right). Within the preconventional level are the first two discernable stages. Stage 1 is an orientation toward punishment and unquestioning deference to superior power. Here, the goodness or badness of a decision is based on the anticipated physical consequences (i.e., a good decision leads to avoidance of punishment). Stage 2 is an orientation toward personal need satisfaction and, occasionally, the needs of others. Elements of fairness, sharing, and reciprocity are present, but it is a "you scratch my back and I'll scratch yours" kind, rather than a reciprocity based on loyalty or justice.

Conventional or Second Level of Moral Reasoning. This level can be described as conformist in the sense of maintaining the expectations and rules of one's family, group, culture, or nation. The maintenance of the existing ways is perceived as a valuable end in itself. The concern is not only with conforming to the existing social order, but also in maintaining, supporting, and justifying it. Stage 3 is referred to as the good boy–good girl orientation. Here, the goodness of an action is based on whether it pleases or helps others and is approved by them. Stage 4 is an orientation toward authority, fixed rules, regulations, and the maintenance of the existing social order. The goodness or rightness of behavior is judged by the extent to which a person is doing one's duty, showing respect for authority, and maintaining the existing order as an end in itself.

Postconventional or Third Level of Moral Reasoning. The postconventional level is characterized by autonomous, universal moral principles. These principles are seen as existing independent of the authority of the particular groups or individuals who hold them and apart from one's personal identifications with these groups or persons. Stage 5 is a social contract orientation with legalistic overtones. The rightness of action tends to be evaluated in terms of respecting the general individual rights of persons and the standards that have been critically examined and agreed upon by the whole society. Stage 5 is the "official" morality of the American government and the U.S. Constitution. Stage 6 is an orientation of universal moral and ethical principles. Morality is not defined by rules and laws of a given society but by one's own conscience in accordance with self-determined ethical principles. These are not concrete rules like the Ten Commandments; rather, they are broad and abstract and often include universal principles of justice and of the reciprocity and equality of human rights.

THE CONCEPTUAL SYSTEMS

Having considered some of the background research on the underlying dimensions of concreteness-abstractness and on moral reasoning, we now are prepared to consider the specific characteristics of the four conceptual systems. Except where noted, and for the moral reasoning data already cited, the primary source for the research on which the characteristics of the conceptual systems were determined is Harvey, Hunt, and Schroder (1961). As we consider these characteristics, keep in mind that we are dealing with tendencies of people holding a given conceptual orientation when compared with individuals holding other conceptual orientations. Also, any single individual usually will not possess all the characteristics associated with a given conceptual system.

System 1: Conventional Thinking and Behavior

As an overview to System 1 functioning in adults, we can note that their thinking and behavior tend to be highly conventional. The more concrete System 1 persons tend to utilize preconventional moral reasoning as the basis of their behavior; the less concrete System 1 individuals place greater reliance on conventional moral reasoning. The specific characteristics of System 1 functioning are as follows.

Need for structure and order. To some extent, the System 1 world resembles a giant bureaucratic organizational chart. All elements are arranged in a neat hierarchical fashion. This tends to be true of human relationships, beliefs, rules, rights, and privileges. What is important, therefore, is to learn where in this hierarchy one fits. System 1 persons have a dislike for things that are uncertain or unpredictable. They express a preference for a well-ordered, structured mode of life with a minimum of change.

High need for simplicity and consistency. System 1 persons tend to prefer working on problems where there is a possibility of coming out with a clear-cut solution. In literature, they show a preference for simple rather than complex themes. In addition, they demonstrate a low tolerance for ambiguity.

High absolutism. System 1 persons tend to see things in absolute rather than relative terms. Values, behavior, and issues are judged as "good" or "bad," "right" or "wrong." Thus, there is a right way to think, believe, behave, and be. Other ways are wrong, or at least inferior.

High authoritarianism. When in positions of authority, System 1 individuals expect subordinates to show respect and deference. When in positions of subordination, these persons are themselves deferent and seldom question or challenge the decisions or actions of those in authority.

Closedness of beliefs. System 1 persons tend to hold their beliefs so strongly that they are not very open to new input that might cause them to alter or modify their views.

High ethnocentrism. This characteristic refers to viewing one's own way of thinking, behaving, and being as "right" and anything else as inferior. Implicit in this tendency is the belief that one's own way should be instituted for everyone.

Paternalism. This is a logical extension of ethnocentrism. Behaviorally, paternalism may be seen in the interaction of System 1 persons with others who are viewed as different or subordinate.

High acceptance of prevailing rules, norms, traditions, and social roles. Not only do System 1 persons tend to hold positive attitudes about and have a high dependence on these things, but they are seen as relatively static and unchanging.

Low creativity. A major outcome of System 1 conventionalism is a lack of unique or creative thought and action. Davis (1966), using Scott's Scale of Values, has found that System 1 persons score significantly lower than others on "creativity" and "independence." For System 1 individuals, being "normal" and conforming appear to be more important than being different and creative.

High belief in external fate control. System 1 persons believe that what happens in their lives primarily is controlled by luck or other factors over which they have little control.

Rigidity. System 1 persons consistently have been found to be more rigid than persons holding other conceptual orientations.

Distribution of System 1 persons. Based on research to date, about 60 percent of the American population appear to be operating primarily from a System 1 conception of reality. However, because no survey of conceptual functioning based on a large representative sample has been conducted, this and other percentages to be presented should be regarded as approximate. Although 60 percent appear to fall in the System 1 category, the proportions differ greatly by age group: Among those in their twenties and early thirties, less than half appear to be functioning at the System 1 stage; among those in their mid-fifties or older, over 80 percent may hold a System 1 orientation. Although age related, a person's conceptual stage is not age caused; those who are System 1 now always have been.

System 2: Negativism and Self Assertion — The Transitional Stage

For many persons, the System 1 reality eventually "breaks down." The individual reacts by becoming focused on and sensitized to what is "wrong" with the "system," its institutions, its leaders, and others who exercise authority in one's life, including parents. As an essential part of this reaction, the individual also appears to learn more about oneself as distinct from the generalized cultural standards that had been applied to both self and others during Stage 1. Hunt (1966:

282) has noted from his research that "the major developmental work of Stage 1 is that of defining the external boundaries and learning the generalized cultural standards which apply to both self and others." He has further noted that this generalized standard serves as the anchoring basis for self-delineation, the major work of the System 2 stage. This self-delineation occurs through a process of "breaking away" from the standard. This initial expression of independence often appears exaggerated, but nonetheless marks the first awareness of one's feeling as cues for differential action.

In their moral decisionmaking, System 2 persons often seem in a kind of psychological vacuum. They tend to see the external norms, which heretofore they had relied upon, as having let them down and thus as no longer reliable. As yet, the individual has not replaced this external basis for one's moral thinking with an internalized basis. Thus, about all the System 2 person can do is react in a distrustful, negative manner. Kohlberg notes from his research in colleges that those students who kick conventional morality search for their own thing, for self-chosen values. But they have difficulty distinguishing between autonomous morality and justice (postconventional reasoning) and one of egoistic relativism, exchange, and revenge (preconventional, Stage 2 reasoning). As in the case of conceptual systems research, Kohlberg has found this phase to be temporary, and the students developed from this confusion to more principled moral reasoning (Kohlberg and Kramer, 1969). Whereas historically the transition to System 2 thinking has been observable internationally on college campuses, it appears to be occurring with increasing frequency during the high school years — a factor that may account for some of the increased troubles in our public schools (e.g., see Gilligan, Kohlberg, and Lerner, 1972). The specific characteristics of System 2 functioning follow:

Need for structure and order. System 2 persons demonstrate a fairly high need for structure and order, but usually show less discomfort in unstructured situations than System 1 individuals.
Need for simplicity and consistency. This need appears moderately high in System 2 individuals and often can be seen in their superficial conceptions of societal institutions and problems.
Low authoritarianism. This is consistent with the generally negative attitude toward institutional constraints and authority figures previously noted.
Absolutism. System 2 persons score fairly high on measures of absolutism, but not as high as System 1 persons.
Closedness of beliefs. System 2 individuals are fairly closed

minded, but less strongly than those with a System 1 orientation.

Low creativity. Although lacking in creativity, it is during the System 2 stage that individuals first place high value on creativity (Davis, 1966). This appears to help set the stage for greater actual creativeness as persons become more abstract.

Rigidity. For much the same reason as for System 1 persons, but to a lesser extent, System 2 individuals are personally rigid.

Distribution of System 2 persons. At any given time, about 10 percent of the population is at the System 2 stage. Since for most persons this is a transitional stage, the percentage is considerably greater among young adults and older teenagers and considerably smaller among older adults.

System 3: The World Is People

As we have seen, the essential developmental occurrence during the System 2 stage is a "breaking away" from the standard and learning about how one is distinctively oneself. Hunt (1966) points out that this self-delineation provides the empathic basis for understanding the feelings and experiences of others as being similar to or different from one's own. With development of this more abstract realization about others from this realization about self, the individual moves into the third stage of conceptual functioning.

As an overview to System 3 functioning, we can note that it is characterized by a strong, empathic people orientation. Instead of seeing differences in values, culture, beliefs, lifestyles, and institutions as deviant or "less than," as do System 1 persons, System 3 individuals tend to value these differences and to see them as enriching their personal lives and the human condition. With this increase in empathy, valuing of individual differences, and strong people orientation comes a shift to postconventional moral reasoning.

Low need for structure and order. One of the major distinctions between System 3 and more concrete conceptualizing has to do with the need for structure and order. The structure of reality is seen as looser, ambiguous, and less vertically oriented. Further, much less reliance is placed on the hierarchical aspects of structure.

Low need for simplicity and consistency. System 3 persons do not exhibit a need for simplicity and consistency. In fact, often they will express a preference for just the opposite, and they demonstrate a high tolerance for ambiguity.

Authoritarianism. System 3 persons score moderately high on measures of authoritarianism. However, there is not the tendency toward a blind acceptance of authority, nor are authority figures held in awe, as was the case in System 1 functioning. Hence, System 3 persons are more likely to view authority figures as persons like themselves and to see questioning of their opinions as legitimate.

Low absolutism. Unlike more concrete functioning, System 3 individuals view the world from a relativistic, rather than absolutist perspective. Instead of assessing differences in a judgmental manner, they tend to view differences more in terms of their functionality or disfunctionality to the individual and to society.

Openness of beliefs. Whereas System 1 persons see their beliefs as rather absolutist and unchanging, System 3 persons see their beliefs as relativistic and expect them to be modified as part of one's life-time of continual personal growth.

Low ethnocentrism. Since System 3 persons tend to see differences simply as differences, they neither view their way as superior nor expect others to be like themselves.

Moderate acceptance of the prevailing rules, mores, traditions, and social roles. Unlike System 1 functioning, these social prescriptions are viewed as dynamic, and what is important is to periodically review them to see if they still are functional in the light of change.

High need to be with people. System 3 persons tend to be motivated toward meeting new people and establishing new friendships, show a strong desire to affiliate with people, and much prefer the company of others to being alone.

Need to help people. System 3 persons, more than others, show a strong need to help people.

Creativity. When compared with more concrete functioning, System 3 individuals are more creative in their thinking and behavior. This tends to be particularly true in social realm.

Personally flexible. In contrast to concrete functioning, System 3 persons actually perform better under moderately stressful or changing situations than when under "normal" or static conditions.

Distribution of System 3 persons. About 25 percent of the American population appear to be operating primarily from a System 3 conception of reality. As with the distribution of System 1 persons, there are striking differences by age group, and they are the reverse of those for System 1: Among those in their mid-fifties or older, less than 15 percent are operating from a System 3 perspective; among those in their early thirties or younger, about one-third are operating from a System 3 orientation.

System 4: Autonomous, Creative Functioning — Conceptual Maturity

Hunt (1966) point out that the major developmental work at the fourth conceptual stage is the integration of standards that apply to both self and others. This integration enables the individual to understand both self and others as occupying different positions on the same transcendent dimension, rather than seeing self and others simply as being on different standards. In accomplishing this integration task, the individual develops greater autonomy in thought and action. System 4 persons are characterized by:

Highly internalized postconventional value system. To an even greater extent than System 3 persons, System 4 thinkers rely on postconventional moral reasoning as the basis of their actions.

Low need for structure and order, simplicity and consistency. Like System 3 conceptualizers, System 4 individuals can operate comfortably without a high degree of structure and simplicity. However, unlike System 3 persons, System 4 thinkers usually will provide adequate structure for others who need it, such as System 1 children.

Very low authoritarianism. System 4 individuals score low on measures of authoritarianism. They tend to lead from a strong sense of self-worth rather than from reliance on their formal authority.

Very low absolutism. The more abstract a person's functioning, the less absolutist and more relativistic he or she becomes.

High perceived self worth. While others may possess this characteristic, it seems universal among System 4 functioning persons.

Very open belief system. The more abstract one's functioning, the more open one's belief system tends to be.

Creativity. The more abstract a person's conceptual functioning, the more likely that person is to exhibit unique thinking and behavior.

People oriented. Like System 3 persons, System 4 individuals have a capacity to be empathic with others. Unlike System 3 thinkers, System 4 conceptualizers do not share the strong dependent need for others and thus are more autonomous in their functioning.

Highly flexible. To an even greater extent than System 3 persons, System 4 individuals are highly flexible and perform relatively better under conditions of stress than nonstress.

Distribution of System 4 persons. The conceptual system research has identified about 8 percent of the population as System 4 individuals.

Characteristics Unrelated to Conceptual Systems

At this point it may be useful to note several important characteristics that might seem highly related to conceptual stage, but that are not. First, only a weak relationship has been found between conceptual systems and intelligence, although some minimal level appears required for highly abstract functioning. Some of the most brilliant persons in all walks of life have been and are System 1 functioning individuals. Second, conceptual functioning does not appear related to generosity, friendliness, or numerous other valued personality characteristics that have not been mentioned.

Value Differences among the Four Conceptual Systems

Davis (1966), using Scott's Scale of Values, has obtained theoretically consistent differences in the strength of eight important value dimensions among the four conceptual systems. System 1 persons scored higher than all others in their valuing of self-control, honesty, kindness, loyalty, religiousness, and the desire for power and influence; they scored lowest on creativity and independence. System 2 persons valued self-control, honesty, kindness, loyalty, and religiousness less than all others and creativity and independence more highly than System 1 persons. System 3 individuals were relatively low in their valuing of self-control and independence, as high as System 1 persons on kindness, and intermediate on the other dimensions. System 4 conceptualizers valued creativity and independence highly, gave low value to self-control and religiousness and were intermediate on the other four dimensions.

Using other instruments, Davis (1966) also found System 3 persons to be high and System 2 persons low on need for affiliation; System 2 individuals also scored higher than all others on Machiavellianism.

Differences in Problem-solving Behavior

Several dimensions of problem-solving behavior related to abstractness and conceptual functioning also have been identified. These include cue utilization, change of set, novelty and appropriateness of responses, and teamwork behavior.

Cue Utilization. The data presented suggest that more abstract persons would have a greater sensitivity to minimal cues in a given situation and should better utilize available cues. Harvey and his colleagues (1966) have found this to be the case both in complex task situations and in concept formation and attainment. I have been able to demonstrate similar results with respect to utilizing behavioral cues of others to predict their future behavior (Hendrick, 1979b).

Change of Set. Harvey, Hunt, and Schroder have summarized the results from seven studies, utilizing a broad spectrum of tasks and contexts in which performance depended on the readiness and ability of the subjects to relinquish previous assumptions or approaches in order to complete the task. In all seven studies, System 1 persons were the poorest performers and System 4 individuals were the most effective.

Novelty and Appropriateness of Responses. In studies on role playing (Harvey, 1963) and concept formation and attainment (Felknor and Harvey, 1964), System 4 persons scored the highest on measures of both the novelty and the appropriateness of their responses, and System 1 individuals scored the lowest.

Teamwork Behavior and Effectiveness. One of the most striking differences that I have been able to demonstrate experimentally has been in the teamwork of concrete, as compared with abstract, managerial task groups (Hendrick, 1979a). In contrast with the behavior of abstract teams, concrete teams took twice as long to successfully complete the task, worked at a slow pace, made poor use of available cues, and did minimal testing of the rules to determine their true limits.

ETIOLOGICAL DETERMINANTS OF CONCRETENESS-ABSTRACTNESS

As previously noted, adults attain plateaus at different points along the concreteness-abstractness continuum. Research has identified at least some of the determinants of abstractness development, and inherent in all of them is an active exposure to diversity.

Active Exposure to Diversity

As Harvey (1966: 63) has noted, "from the vast amount of work done on early simulation and experience, there seems little doubt that exposure to diversity is probably the most central prerequisite of differentiation and integration." The research on moral growth lends both support and refinement to this conclusion. These studies have shown that passive exposure is not a sufficient condition for further development, but that active exposure does result in children becoming abstract and progressing to higher stages of moral reasoning (Holstein, 1969). These studies also indicate that the nature of the child's training environment at home and school with respect to providing or not providing this active exposure is critical to fostering or inhibiting abstractness and moral development. Harvey, Hunt, and Schroder (1961) also came to the conclusion that these training environments appeared to contain important determinants; in particular, the nature of the trainer role (e.g., parent, teacher, school administrator) appeared critical.

Nature of the Trainer Role

Harvey, Hunt, and Schroder (1961) proposed that reaching a plateau at a particular stage of conceptual functioning is related to exposure to a particular dominant trainer pattern during one's childhood. The essential characteristics of the four trainer patterns identified are as follows.

System 1 Trainer Pattern. Trainers of System 1 adults were hypothesized to have been authoritarian, absolutist, ethnocentric, and closed minded and to have relied on external sources in their moral reasoning. By the trainer's behavior, conformity rather than creativity of thought and action was emphasized, and the child was given little opportunity to explore values or power relationships.

System 2 Trainer Pattern. System 2 adult's trainers were hypothesized to have characteristics similar to those of System 1 trainers, but also to have been arbitrary and inconsistent. Consequently, the child learned not to trust authority figures or the institutions of social control that they represent.

System 3 Trainer Pattern. System 3 persons were hypothesized to have had trainers who were permissive, overprotective, indulgent, and somewhat socially dependent on the trainee. This enables the child, by taking advantage of the dependency relationship, to develop skill in socially manipulating others and, through this, to avoid facing the world alone. The permissive atmosphere also allowed the child greater freedom to explore ideas, values, and relationships.

System 4 Trainer Pattern. System 4 adults had trainers who themselves functioned in an abstract manner. They tended to relate to the child as an older, experienced adult to a younger, developing adult. The child was rewarded for exploring and trying the different rather than for overt responses that matched narrowly prescribed standards of the trainer and was intrinsically valued by the trainer as a person in his or her own right.

Parental Child-rearing Pattern

Research by Adams, Harvey, and Heslin (1966) using hypnotically induced parental child-rearing patterns conforming to the four trainer patterns outlined above has provided additional verification of the influence of these patterns on conceptual functioning. In a recent study (Hendrick, 1979c), I compared several hundred managers' descriptions of their childhoods with their stages of conceptual functioning. The four trainer patterns emerged from the content analysis of these descriptions and were highly related with stage of conceptual functioning as hypothesized by Harvey, Hunt, and Schroder (1961).

It is interesting to note that the System 1 trainer pattern was characteristic of American families prior to World War II and that the System 3 pattern has become progressively more common during the last three decades. When we consider that over 80 percent of those raised prior to World War II are System 1 oriented and that more than half of those raised since World War II are functioning beyond System 1, we see still further support for the strong influence of parental training patterns in determining abstractness and conceptual development.

Education

Although level of abstractness is not strongly related to intelligence per se, it is to education. As already noted, the trainer pattern appears to be an important determinant. In addition, there is a direct relation between abstractness and amount of education (Kaats, 1970; O'Connor, 1971). Also, data from Kohlberg's studies throughout the world have shown a strong relationship between education and moral development. In general, for any given population, the higher the educational level, the greater the proportion reasoning at the postconventional level (Kohlberg, 1969). Since formal education is a means of structuring one's exposure to diversity, these findings are not surprising.

Culture

Given the research on active exposure to diversity, the extent to which a given culture provides this exposure — through its institutions, trainer patterns, and availability of well-developed communications and transportation systems — should determine the general level of abstractness and conceptual maturity within that culture. Kohlberg's (1969) data also support this assumption.

Traumatic Event

During the past decade I have interviewed many persons who experienced the System 1 trainer pattern while growing up, yet have made the transition to System 3 or 4 functioning. The one common characteristic that these persons seem to possess, and to which they personally attribute their breaking away from the System 1 mold, is having undergone a traumatic event in their adult lives (e.g., divorce, near death, death of a loved one, combat in Viet Nam).

While it appears that traumatic events can lead to development of greater abstractness, it often is not the case. Harvey (1966) and Hunt (1966) have emphasized that exposure to diversity can be superoptimal as well as suboptimal and thus not facilitate conceptual growth. This may in part explain why traumatic events often do not facilitate abstractness development.

ABSTRACTNESS AND THE FUNCTIONING OF COMPLEX ORGANIZATIONS

The dimension of concreteness-abstractness and the levels of conceptual functioning have demonstrated considerable individual stability and generality across situations, and some of the key determinants have been identified. However, this is a comparatively young and complex area of research, and much remains to be done to further define the nature of conceptual systems and related behavior. Much also remains to be done in gaining a more precise understanding of how differences in levels of abstractness and conceptual functioning affect dyadic, small group, and intergroup relationships. Nevertheless, what has been done has significant implications for understanding the functioning of complex organizations and should be considered when investigating the impact of more macrocosmic organizational variables.

Present Organizational Structure, Norms, and Processes

As noted earlier, in reflecting on the disfunctional aspects of organizational life Argyris (1974) and Maccoby (1976) drew attention to the one set of factors common to the broad spectrum of organizations — those related to how they are designed. When we consider that about 80 percent of the older persons — those occupying most of the positions of power and influence in our complex organizations — are operating from a System 1 conception of reality, this is understandable. The bureaucratic, scientific management basis of present organizational design is directly reflective of a System 1 conception of the world. The bureaucratic structure models the relatively unambiguous and hierarchal structuring of reality that forms the very core of System 1 conceptualizing. Any other organizational form would be inconsistent with Stage 1 reality and thus unnatural and unreal.

From his review of the literature, Argyris (1974) cited managerial aspiration for power, Maccoby (1976) cited "careerism," and both cited a set of management values common to most organizations as the basis of present organizational structure and managerial practices. Argyris also noted from the research that an oversimplified view of man was implicit in this common organizational structure and managerial functioning. The conceptual systems and moral-reasoning research indicates that underlying and embodying all of these factors is a relatively concrete level of differentiating and integrating experience. Concreteness-abstractness, then, appears to be a transcendent human dimension that helps integrate and explain the commonality of present organizational structure, norms, and practices.

Why Present Organizational Functioning Has Become a Problem

Argyris (1974) notes that it has been during the 1960s and 1970s that the symptoms of organizational deterioration have become obvious. Assuming that structure and managerial practices have not changed drastically, and the research indicates they have not (Argyris, 1971, 1974; Yankelovich, 1978), why have these symptoms become more evident than before? When we look at the pre-1965 period, we can note that the heavily predominant mode of conceptualizing reality among both employees and managers was System 1. Thus, even though subordinates might not have liked its effects on employee life, both employees and managers accepted the bureaucratic, scientific management form of organizational functioning as natural. For both groups, it was consistent with their conception of reality.

During the post-1965 period, the children of the "baby boom" following World War II began entering the work force in progressively larger numbers. As noted earlier, many of these children were raised in a System 3 training environment. This group also grew up in a period of affluence and of vastly improved transportation and communications systems, which provided greater opportunity for exposure to diversity during their development. This exposure was further enhanced by their being more highly educated than their predecessors. Consequently, for the first time an age group entered American organizations in which the majority was not operating from a System 1 conception of reality.

Yankelovich's (1978) survey research of organizations also supports these observations. He particularly notes the shift in worker values to "recognition as an individual person" and "opportunity to be with pleasant people with whom I like to work" as now the most important in American organizations. These reflect a shift to a more abstract orientation, and Yankelovich refers to those holding this new orientation as the "New Breed." For this majority, the traditional form of organizational functioning was not consistent with their conceptual reality. They therefore have been less accepting of present organizational structure and managerial practices than were their predecessors.

When this younger, more abstract group began to clamor for greater participation in decisions that affect their lives and to progressively insist that they be treated with respect as adults, management resisted. As Agyris (1974) notes, these responses were experienced by management as disloyal acts or signs that more direct controls were needed, backed up by increasingly belligerent or paternalistic power on the part of top administrators. These managerial responses in turn triggered further resistances, which triggered more controls. As the number of more abstract persons entering the work force grew, direct confrontation occurred, and employees began to act out their frustrations by progressively greater withdrawal, displacement of hostility, and passive aggressive acts. In response to this organizational deterioration, management, as Argyris (1974) and Maccoby (1976) noted, attempted to utilize numerous human relations and other intervention strategies to appease the employees and get their organizations "back on track." However, true to a System 1 conception of reality, substantial restructuring of the organization or of managerial practices only rarely took place.

In summary, the surfacing of organizational problems and the occurrence of organizational deterioration during the 1960s and 1970s can in part be explained in terms of the entry of progressively greater numbers of more abstract persons into the work force — a trend that is continuing and that promises to profoundly affect organizational functioning as these individuals enter power positions.

Organizations of the Future

Until recently, organizations have been dominated by managers with a relatively concrete System 1 orientation. More recently, a new psychosocial personality type of manager has emerged and moved into the upper managerial positions, which type Maccoby has labeled the "gamesman." From Maccoby's (1976) description and from my own ongoing research, the gamesman most frequently exhibits a primary System 1, secondary System 3 conception of reality — a pattern I have found among approximately one-third of my graduate management students. This pattern tends to be held by persons raised in a System 1 trainer environment, who through higher education, travel, active use of the media, and managing culturally diverse groups have become more abstract, less absolutist, less ethnocentric, somewhat more people oriented and are more interpersonally skillful in their behavior. Yet the System 1 reality never has truly broken down for them. They remain fairly conformist in their thinking and behavior, rely primarily on conventional moral reasoning, and usually do not have the strong empathic people orientation of primary System 3 functioning.

During the next decade, the gamesmen should in turn begin being replaced in substantial numbers by primary System 3 (and 4) conceptualizers. Given their low need for structure and order, relativism, open-mindedness, people orientation, and greater capacity for empathy, dramatic changes in organizational functioning should result. Such changes are likely to include the following:

> *Managerial value system.* A change in the dominant managerial interpersonal value system to one based on more complex and empathic assumptions regarding the nature of human beings.

Included will be an integration of the emotional with the rational aspects of interpersonal and group problem-solving behavior.

Structure and process. A relegation of less routine aspects of organizational life that significantly affect employees or their work to more democratic and participative management practices, including looser, more ambiguous, and flexible organizational structuring.

Organizational goals. Improving the quality of work life will become an internalized organizational goal. External pressure from a progressively more abstract public will further insure the acceptance of this as a fundamental managerial and corporate responsibility.

New organizational problems. The above changes will create their own unique organizational problems. For example, almost half of the labor force still will be functioning at the System 1 level. Time spent on concerns that are not clearly task oriented will seem wasteful, threatening, and therefore frustrating to these more concrete employees and managers. This frustration will be compounded by the tendency of System 3 managers to not provide adequate structure for these more concrete functioning persons, who need it.

Decisionmaking. Based on the research by Harvey, myself, and others, as the organizational membership becomes more abstract, more effective teamwork and group decisionmaking can be expected. Given the anticipated greater reliance on these processes and the evidence for the superiority of consensual processes over other decisionmaking modes (e.g., Holloman and Hendrick, 1970, 1971, 1972), the end result should be more accurate and effective organizational decisions.

Effecting Change Through Intervention

The limited success of past intervention strategies, noted by Argyris (1974) and Maccoby (1976), was discussed earlier. When considered in the light of conceptual systems research, this historical outcome is not surprising: no strategy for fundamental change is likely to succeed if those in power have a System 1 conception of reality. Accordingly, the only intervention strategy that does offer the potential for real change is one that increases the abstractness level of the managerial group, for unless change fits with the conceptual functioning of those in the power positions, substantial change will not occur. Aside from replacing the present managers with a more abstract cadre, an educational intervention strategy to increase the abstractness of the present managers would appear to be the most feasible alternative. The validity of an educational intervention approach has been demonstrated with children by both moral reasoning (Blatt, 1971) and conceptual systems (Hunt, 1966) researchers. In a pilot project, I recently was able to effect a change in abstractness level among experienced managers through use of a formal training program. Based on these findings, further exploration of educational intervention strategies to increase the abstractness level of managers appears worthy of pursuit.

Beyond the 1980s

In what Levinson (1977: 97) has called "the single most significant contribution to this field," Jacques (1976), in his book *A General Theory of Bureaucracy*, concludes that there is a systematic psychological structure that underlies the bureaucratic work system as it has evolved across the spectrum of economic and political systems throughout the world. He goes on to say that this underlying structure leads to a sense of "felt fair pay" and to systematic levels of organizational hierarchy that in turn are a function of the "time span of discretion" — the largest period a person can work on any task without having to report to one's superior. Jacques has identified five levels of hierarchy and associated time spans. He further contends that there are individual differences in the length of time span in which persons can be comfortable without feedback and that these depend on one's level of abstractness and conceptual thinking. In summary, the hierarchical bureaucratic work system results from individual differences in the underlying psychological structure, and that structural dimension is abstractness and conceptual functioning.

Taking Jacques' conclusion to its logical extension, as the abstractness level of the work force becomes higher, the shorter "time spans of discretion," and thus their related bureaucratic level(s), will no longer be needed. The result should be the evolution of fewer hierarchical levels and more autonomously functioning workers and work groups. The notion of flatter, more autonomously functioning, complex organizations often has been posited as the ideal model for humanizing bureacratic systems. The abstractness and conceptual systems research, like Jacques' theory of bureaucracy, suggests that this model was not ideal or even practical for the past, but that we may be in transition to a future when it will be. If this is the case, as the working population becomes more abstract, it will evolve naturally and inevitably as a reflection of this new reality.

REFERENCES

Adams, D. K.; O. J. Harvey; and R. E. Heslin. 1966. "Variation in Flexibility and Creativity as a Function of Hypnotically Induced Past Histories." In O. J. Harvey, ed., *Experience, Structure, and Adaptability.* New York: Springer.

Argyris, C. 1974. "Organizations of the Future." In D. Howley and D. Rogers, eds., *Improving the Quality of Urban Management,* vol. 8, *Urban Affairs Annual Review.* Beverly Hills, Calif.: Sage Publications.

———. 1971. *Management and Organizational Development.* New York: McGraw-Hill.

———. 1968. "On the Effectiveness of Research and Development Organizations." *American Scientist* 56, 344–55.

———. 1964. *Integrating the Individual and the Organization.* New York: John Wiley.

Aronfreed, J. 1971. *Developmental Psychology Today.* DelMar, Calif.: CRM Books.

Bennis, W. G. 1966. *Changing Organizations.* New York: McGraw-Hill.

Blatt, M. 1971. "The Effects of Classroom Discussion upon Children's Moral Judgment." In L. Kohlberg and E. Turiel, eds., *Moral Research: The Cognitive-Developmental Approach.* New York: Holt, Rinehart and Winston.

Davis, K. 1964. "Some Correlates of Responses to the 'This I Believe' Test." Manuscript, University of Colorado, 1964. Summarized in O. J. Harvey, "System Structure, Flexibility and Creativity," in O. J. Harvey, ed., *Experience, Structure, and Adaptability.* New York: Springer.

Felknor, C., and O. J. Harvey. 1964. "Some Cognitive Determinants of Concept Formation and Concept Attainment." Technical Report 10. Boulder: University of Colorado.

Gilligan, C., L. Kohlberg, and J. Lerner. 1972. "Moral Reasoning about Sexual Dilemmas: A Developmental Approach." In L. Kohlberg and E. Turiel, eds., *Recent Research in Moral Development.* New York: Holt, Rinehart and Winston.

Golembiewski, R. T. 1969. "Organization Development in Public Agencies." *Public Administration Review* 29: 367–77.

———. 1967. "The Laboratory Approach to Organizational Development: The Schema of a Method." *Public Administration Review* 27: 211–20.

Harvey, O. J. 1966. "System Structure, Flexibility and Creativity." In O. J. Harvey, ed., *Experience, Structure, and Adaptability.* New York: Springer.

———. 1963. "Cognitive Determinants of Role Playing." Technical Report 3. Boulder: University of Colorado.

Harvey, O. J.; D. E. Hunt; and H. M. Schroder. 1961. *Conceptual Systems and Personality Organization.* New York: Wiley.

Hendrick, H. W. 1980. "Relation of Leadership Behavior, Subordinate Reactions, and Perceptions of Organizational Climate and Effectiveness as a Function of Abstractness." *Journal of Applied Psychology.* In press.

———. 1979a. "Differences in Group Problem Solving Behavior and Effectiveness as a Function of Abstractness." *Journal of Applied Psychology.* In press.

——. 1979b. "Effectiveness of Interpersonal Cue Utilization as a Function of Abstractness." Manuscript submitted for publication.

——. 1979c. "Some Determinants of Abstractness and Conceptual Functioning." Manuscript submitted for publication.

Hertzberg, F. 1966. *Work and the Nature of Man.* New York: World.

Holloman, C. R., and H. W. Hendrick. 1972. "Adequacy of Group Decisions as a Function of the Decision-making Process." *Academy of Management Journal* 15: 175-84.

——. 1971. "Problem Solving in Different Sized Groups." *Personnel Psychology* 24: 489-500.

——. 1970. "Individual versus Group Effectiveness in Solving Factual and Nonfactual Problems." *Proceedings of the 78th Annual Convention of the American Psychological Association* 5: 673-74. Summary.

Holstein, C. 1969. "The Relation of Children's Moral Judgment to that of Their Parents and to Communication Patterns in the Family." Dissertation, University of California, Berkeley.

Hunt, D. E. 1966. "A Conceptual Systems Change Model and Its Application to Education." In O. J. Harvey, ed., *Experience, Structure, and Adaptability.* New York: Springer.

Jaques, E. 1976. *A General Theory of Bureaucracy.* New York: Halstead Press.

Kaats, G. R. 1970. "Belief Systems and Person Perception: Analysis in a Service Academy Environment." Doctoral dissertation, University of Colorado, 1969.

Kaats, G. R., and E. A. Thompson. 1968. "The Use of Air Academy Cadets for the Validation of Personality Scales." *Proceedings of the 76th Annual Convention of the American Psychological Association* 3: 637-38. Summary.

Katz, D., and R. L. Kahn. 1966. *The Social Psychology of Organizations.* New York: John Wiley.

Kohlberg, L. 1969. "The Child as a Moral Philosopher." In Barbara Henker, ed., *Readings in Psychology Today,* pp. 180-86. DelMar, Calif.: CRM Books.

Kohlberg, L., and R. Kramer. 1969. "Continuities and Discontinuities in Childhood and Adult Moral Development." *Human Development* 12: 93-120.

Kurtines, W., and E. B. Grief. 1974. "The Development of Moral Thought: Review and Evaluation of Kohlberg's Approach." *Psychological Bulletin* 81: 453-70.

Levinson, H. 1977. Review of Elliott Jaques, *A General Theory of Bureaucracy. The Columbia Journal of World Business* (Fall): 96-100.

Maccoby, M. 1976. *The Gamesman.* New York: Simon and Schuster.

O'Connor, J. 1971. "Developmental Changes in Abstractness and Moral Reasoning." Doctoral dissertation, George Peabody College for Teachers, 1970. *Dissertation Abstracts International* 32: 4109A. Order No. 72-3831.

Piaget, J. 1948. *The Moral Judgement of the Child.* Glencoe, Ill.: Free Press.

Tannenbaum, A. S. 1968. *Control in Organizations.* New York: Basic Books.

Whyte, W. F. 1969. *Organizational Behavior.* Homewood, Ill.: Richard D. Irwin.

Yankelovich, D. 1978. "The New Psychological Contracts at Work." *Psychology Today* (May): 46-50.

Chapter 3

An Integrative Model of Job Satisfaction and Performance

Thomas A. Mahoney*

Schwab and Cummings (1970) reviewed a variety of models relating job satisfaction and performance and concluded that:

> We are frankly pessimistic about the value of additional satisfaction-performance theorizing at this time. The theoretically inclined might do better to work on a theory of satisfaction *or* a theory of performance. Such concepts are clearly complex enough to justify their own theories. Prematurely focusing on relationships between the two has probably helped obscure the fact that we know so little about the structure and determinants of each.

The point made by Schwab and Cummings to the effect that job satisfaction and performance are individually worthy of conceptualization is well taken; each is a complex concept. At the same time, consideration of potential relationships between the concepts need not be disregarded, and other things being equal, conceptualizations of each with potential links to the other ought to be favored given the long-standing interest in job satisfaction and performance. A reformulation of job satisfaction models is developed here, a refor-

* University of Minnesota.
    An earlier version of this paper appears in T. A. Mahoney, *Compensation and Reward Perspectives* (Homewood, Ill.: Richard D. Irwin, 1979).

mulation that might be proposed independent of any consideration of job satisfaction-performance relationships. Additional support for the reformulation of job satisfaction is provided in a suggestive model of job satisfaction-performance relationships.

JOB SATISFACTION

Various reviews of the job satisfaction-performance literature have been published over the past twenty years, the most recent being Locke's (1976). This review by Locke serves as a starting point in the analysis presented here. Locke defines job satisfaction as "a pleasurable or positive emotional state resulting from the appraisal of one's job or job experiences" (p. 1300) and notes that since a job is not a single entity, it must be analyzed in terms of its constituent elements. Job satisfaction, then, is some function of appraisals of these different constituent elements often termed facets or factors of job satisfaction. These elements have been the subject of more empirical analysis than conceptual formulation, and typical formulations of job elements are to a large extent functions of scaling techniques employed by researchers.

Locke distinguishes between what he terms "causal" and "content" models of job satisfaction, with causal models specifying the nature of appraisals of job elements and their combination into a concept of overall satisfaction and content models specifying the characteristic elements that comprise job satisfaction. Three classes of causal models are identified — expectancy models, need models, and values models. Briefly, expectancy models conceptualize job satisfaction as a function of the discrepancy between one's attainments and one's expectations, with satisfaction varying inversely with the degree of discrepancy. Job satisfaction is conceptualized in the needs models as a function of the degree to which the job fulfills or allows fulfillment of the individual's needs, needs being "objective requirements" of an organism's survival and well-being" whether recognized consciously or not. Values models are illustrated by Locke's conceptualization of job satisfaction: job satisfaction is a joint function of the discrepancy between what a person perceives himself as receiving and what he desires and of the importance of what is desired. In an attempt to integrate the needs and values models, Locke argues further that the values model is appropriate "providing and to the degree that . . . values are congruent with one's needs" (p. 1307).

Two major content models of job satisfaction are analyzed, Maslow's need hierarchy model and Herzberg's motivator-hygiene theory, both of which are subjected to critical analysis. Locke finds little logical or empirical support for either model and concludes merely that "needs are of two separable but interdependent types: bodily or physical needs and psychological needs, especially the need for growth. Growth is made possible mainly by the nature of the work itself" (1976: 1319). The remainder of Locke's review focuses primarily upon major findings from empirical research into job satisfaction and performance.

Locke observed, as have others, that much of the confusion regarding satisfaction-performance research is the result of inadequate conceptualization and excessive reliance upon empirical instrumentation. Job satisfaction has been defined implicitly in too many studies as "whatever my instrument measures," with the consequence of contradictory and misleading findings. Conceptualization of job satisfaction also has suffered in recent years because of controversy over Herzberg's motivator-hygiene model, much of the controversy relating to methodological issues rather than conceptual issues. The model developed here is a conceptual formulation of job satisfaction based upon concepts drawn from a variety of motivational and job satisfaction models. It is integrative in so far as it accommodates the needs, expectancies, and values causal models of job satisfaction. Elements of the Herzberg formulation also are incorporated in the model, although the primary focus of the model is causal rather than content in orientation.

Job Facet Satisfaction

We begin with Locke's depiction of satisfaction as an emotional response to a judgment regarding an element or characteristic of the object of concern, a judgment involving comparison of perceptions of that element with some standard. Most conceptualizations of job satisfaction employ this same framework: perceptions of different elements of job satisfaction are evaluated relative to standards of desirability, and overall job satisfaction is a function of these summed evaluations. Locke also noted that the relationship between satisfaction and the percept-value comparison may vary among different elements or facets of job satisfaction; he noted for illustration that any percept-value discrepancy (deficiency or excess) regarding length of work week is dissatisfying, while only deficiency percept-value discrepancies regarding amount of pay are dissatisfying. These relationships are depicted as functions A and D in Figure 3–1. Function A is drawn with a maximum value of the function corresponding to percept-value congruence, whereas no maximum

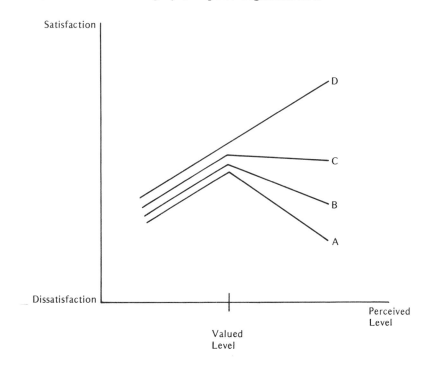

Figure 3-1. Satisfaction as a function of percept-value congruence.

value is associated with function D. Satisfaction and dissatisfaction are conceived as poles of a continuum of a single construct. While no zero point is indicated on the satisfaction scale, such a point has conceptual meaning and is not merely a scaling issue: conceptually, this zero point is the point at which one begins to speak of degrees of dissatisfaction rather than degrees of satisfaction.

While a number of functions are depicted in Figure 3-1 for comparative purposes, imagine a zero point on the satisfaction scale for each function, that point on the satisfaction scale corresponding to percept-value congruence on the perception scale. In this context, function A applies to those elements of job satisfaction with which a concept of optimality is associated, elements such as hours of work, temperature and humidity of the workplace, and closeness of supervision. The degree of dissatisfaction experienced by the individual declines as perceptions of the level of these elements approach the optimal value assigned them, and any discrepancy, deficiency, or excess is experienced as dissatisfaction. It is unlikely that the calculus of satisfaction is so precise that there is a single zero point on the satisfaction scale associated with percept-value congruence, however. Rather, there more likely is a zero range associated with a range of percept-value congruence, dissatisfaction being experienced only as the percept-value discrepancy approaches some threshold value.

Satisfaction, conceived as the upper range of the satisfaction-dissatisfaction continuum, is achieved through percept-value congruence but is not capable of increase beyond that point for job elements to which function A applies. Function D applies to those elements of job satisfaction for which no concept of optimality is appropriate, elements such as interesting work, skill development, and personal growth. The valued level of these elements is minimal rather than optimal. Percept-value deficiencies, in this instance, are dissatisfying while percept-value excesses are satisfying. The optimality value of function A implies an equilibrium concept of need, with a specific value of the job element being necessary for well-being, while the valued level of function D implies a concept of minimal needs. Satisfaction values associated with function A merely connote the absence of need discrepancies, while satisfaction, connoting a positive affect state with a range of values, is more easily associated with function D, where percept-value excesses are pleasurable.

Two other functions, B and C, are illustrated in Figure 3–1. Like function A, functions B and C break at the point of percept-value congruence, but they are not symmetrical functions as is function A. Function B is drawn to indicate that the relevance of percept-value discrepancies may depend upon the direction of the discrepancy, with deficiencies being more disturbing that excesses; and function C is drawn to indicate that only percept-value deficiencies are relevant to the satisfaction-dissatisfaction continuum. Function B might apply, for example, to elements judged against equity norms, elements such as relative severity of discipline. Function B suggests that inequitable treatment disadvantageous to the individual is more dissatisfying than inequitable treatment advantageous to the individual, although equitable treatment is most satisfying. Function C is drawn to illustrate the concept of satiation — namely, percept-value deficiencies are dissatisfying, while percept-value excesses are of no relevance to the individual. Function C might apply to elements such as cleanliness of the workplace or amount of information provided through communication policies. Lack of cleanliness or information is dissatisfying, but levels of these elements beyond the desired value are meaningless to the individual's satisfaction.

Importance of Facets

Most models of job satisfaction view overall satisfaction as a summed function of satisfaction with various job elements, the elements varying in terms of importance. Locke suggests that the importance

Figure 3-2. Relative importance of job facets to satisfaction.

of any job element to overall satisfaction is not easily separated from the evaluative judgment of that element and that importance of an element is reflected in the range of satisfaction values associated with the element. This concept is illustrated in Figure 3-2 in terms of the different slopes associated with functions X and Y: function X describes a job element more important to overall job satisfaction than the job element associated with function Y. Percept-value discrepancies in function X occasion a wider range of satisfaction-dissatisfaction values than do identical percept-value discrepancies in function Y. This concept of importance also figures in the functions illustrated in Figure 3-1: function B, for example, indicates that percept-value deficiencies are more important than percept-value excesses. Importance thus may vary from job element to job element and from one form of percept-value discrepancy (deficiency) to another (excess).

Need Values and Aspiration Values

Basic distinctions among the functions depicted in Figure 3-1 relate to the nature of the valued level of the element implied in the relationship of percept-value discrepancies and satisfaction. Functions A, B, and C all imply an optimal value of job element; function D does not. Optimality, in this context, connotes equilibrium, a connotation not associated with function D. This distinction parallels the distinction between satisfying job elements and dissatisfying job elements in the two factor model of Herzberg, Mausner, and Snyderman (1959), with dissatisfying elements being characterized by functions A, B, or C and satisfying elements being characterized by function D. Percept-value discrepancies in functions A, B, and C are associated with dissatisfaction, and percept-value excesses may be associated with increasing levels of satisfaction only in function D. It is not necessary to conceptualize two independent factors of job satisfaction and dissatisfaction, however: we can employ concepts of satisfaction and dissatisfaction as poles of a single continuum and note that only certain job elements have relevance for the range of satisfaction values. The concepts of optimal value associated with functions A, B, and C and of minimal value associated with function D also parallel Maslow's (1955) distinction between deficiency motivation (functions A, B, and C) and growth motivation (function D).

Two related concepts or dimensions of job satisfaction are suggested by the different functions in Figure 3-1 and by the difference between needs and expectancy models of job satisfaction. These concepts relate to deprivational and aspirational dimensions of job satisfaction. Needs models of job satisfaction view satisfaction as a function of the degree to which needs are met and dissatisfaction as a function of need deprivation. We hypothesize need levels for different facets of job satisfaction, levels of job facet stimuli that if not experienced occasion dissatisfaction. These need levels may be optimal in nature (functions A, B, and C) or minimal in nature (function D). Need levels of job facets probably are in most instances unrecognized as specific levels of stimuli until discomfort is experienced. Need values for job elements probably vary among individuals (e.g., temperature, noise level, cleanliness) and from one cultural setting to another (e.g., equity of compensation, interaction with co-workers, and degree of supervision) and are relatively stable and resistant to change over time. Percept–need value deficiencies are dissatisfying and are suggestive of deprivation, a state most easily identified with functions A, B, and C in Figure 3-1, although also related to percept–need value deficiencies in function D. Percept–need value excesses in function D, however, occasion increasing values of satisfaction. These excesses acquire meaning from some source other than need; they are valued for reasons other than relationship to need and suggest desires or expectancies rather than needs. The concept of aspiration rather than need is suggested by those job elements with which minimal needs values are associated (function D) and where percept-need value excesses are related to increasing values of satisfaction.

Aspirational concepts connote desires or goals, values likely to vary with an individual's experience and current achievement levels, unlike need values, which are relatively more stable over time. Following the conceptualization of March and Simon (1958), as well as concepts of need achievement motivation, aspiration values for job elements are conceived as varying with current achievements and generally as exceeding current achievements by some slight amount. Aspiration values indicating desired or goal values as well as need values can be associated with job elements. Thus, we can conceive of two separate dimensions or components of job satisfaction, one related to percept-need value judgments (needs) and the other related to percept-aspiration value judgments (aspirational).

Aspiration values for job elements are likely to coincide with needs values, given percept-need value deficiencies, and the distinction between needs values and aspiration values is largely irrelevant for job elements with optimal needs values (functions A, B, and C). Aspiration values will be relevant for job elements with minimal needs values, particularly under conditions of percept-need value excesses (function D). Percept-aspiration value deficiencies, like percept-need value deficiencies, are dissatisfying. Unlike need values, however, aspiration values vary with recent achievements, and so extreme values of aspirational dissatisfaction as well as satisfaction probably are short lived. The normal range of measures of aspirational satisfaction also probably is more restricted than the range of measures of need satisfaction.

The concepts of needs and aspirational satisfaction associated with percept-value judgments are illustrated in Figure 3-3. Perceived job element measures are indicated on the horizontal scale and needs and aspirational satisfaction measures on the left and right vertical scales, respectively. Need value for the job element is indicated at point N and will be relatively invariant with respect to perceived value of the job element; the zero point on the needs satisfaction scale is indicated at the intersection of need value and the functional relationship between needs satisfaction and percept-value judgments. Two different perceived measures of the job element, P_1 and P_2, occasion needs dissatisfaction and satisfaction, respectively. Aspiration value varies with perceived level of the job factor, given needs satisfaction, and thus is indicated only for the perceived level P_2; aspiration value varies with the achievements, and thus the aspiration value A_2 exceeds the perceived level P_2 by some slight amount.

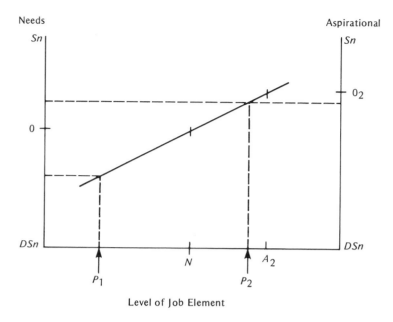

Figure 3-3. Needs and aspirational satisfaction as functions of percept-value judgments.

The zero point on the aspirational satisfaction scale is indicated at the intersection of aspiration value and the functional relationship between aspirational satisfaction and percept-value judgments, O_2. An experienced level of the job element, P_1, occasions needs dissatisfaction; aspiration value is irrelevant or indistinguishable from needs value, and so aspirational dissatisfaction is indistinguishable from needs dissatisfaction. Change in the perceived level from P_1 to P_2 occasions needs satisfaction and momentary aspiration satisfaction. Given needs satisfaction, aspiration values become relevant to the individual, and an aspiration value A_2 develops, occasioning aspirational dissatisfaction. Needs satisfaction continues, however, as need level N remains relatively constant. The individual thus experiences needs satisfaction and aspirational dissatisfaction at the same time.

To summarize, we propose two concepts of satisfaction, needs and aspirational, associated with job elements. Needs satisfaction is a function of percept–need value discrepancy and aspirational satisfaction is a function of percept–aspiration value discrepancy. Need values take the form of both optimal or equilibrium values and minimal values, each being appropriate for different job elements.

A range of values of needs dissatisfaction is associated with percept-need value discrepancies where need value takes the form of an optimal or equilibrium value; needs satisfaction in those instances is limited in range around the zero point of needs satisfaction. A range of both needs dissatisfaction and satisfaction values is associated with percept-need value discrepancies where value takes the form of a minimal value, with percept-need value excesses being satisfying.

Aspirational satisfaction is distinguishable from needs satisfaction only as associated with job elements characterized by minimal need values and under conditions of minimal needs dissatisfaction. Aspiration values reflect past achievements and tend to exceed perceptions by some amount. Thus, extreme values of aspirational satisfaction and dissatisfaction are likely to be short lived, and the range of aspirational satisfaction values is likely to be small, with a mean value indicating minor dissatisfaction.

Overall satisfaction with any job element is a function of both needs and aspirational satisfaction associated with that element. Overall job satisfaction is a summed function of satisfaction with the various job elements and, given the conceptualization of needs and aspirational satisfaction, will be influenced most by needs satisfaction levels. The possible levels of aspirational satisfaction are restricted both in range and in terms of the number of elements for which aspirational values are appropriate. Nevertheless, the needs and aspirational dimensions of job satisfaction are maintained as separate dimensions since, as noted later, they have different motivational and behavioral connotations.

The distinction made between concepts of needs and aspirational satisfaction relates specifically to distinctions made between needs and expectancies models of job satisfaction, the needs models relating to needs satisfaction and the expectancy models relating to aspirational satisfaction. The distinction between aspirational and needs satisfaction assumes different value standards for the percept-value judgments in job satisfaction and different functional relationships between satisfaction and percept-value discrepancies. A range of needs dissatisfaction may be experienced with any job element, while a range of needs satisfaction is conceivable only for job elements characterized with minimal need values. Aspirational satisfaction and dissatisfaction are relevant only relative to job elements characterized with minimal need values and in the absence of significant needs dissatisfaction. While a wide range of aspirational satisfaction levels is conceivable, extreme levels of aspirational satisfaction and dissatisfaction are likely to be short lived.

This formulation is consistent with data reported by Herzberg, Mausner, and Snyderman (1959) although the formulation differs from their interpretation. They asked individuals to recall moments of extreme satisfaction and dissatisfaction and to recount those events. Events were classified into a structure of facets of job satisfaction or elements of jobs relevant to job satisfaction and were tabulated to indicate frequency of association with extremely satisfying and dissatisfying moments. Every element was mentioned in association with both satisfying and dissatisfying events, although certain elements were more likely to be mentioned in association with either satisfying or dissatisfying events. Achievement, recognition, work itself, responsibility, and advancement were more frequently associated with extreme satisfaction; and interpersonal relations, supervision, company policy and administration, and working conditions were more frequently associated with extremely dissatisfying events. Salary, growth possibility, and status were mentioned less frequently and were associated equally with satisfying and dissatisfying events. The elements most frequently associated with dissatisfying events are those for which optimal need values appear appropriate: percept-need value discrepancies will be dissatisfying and percept–need value congruence is associated with the zero point of needs dissatisfaction. The elements associated with extremely satisfying events are those for which minimal need values appear most appropriate and where percept–need value excesses will be associated with extreme levels of needs satisfaction. The elements of salary and status are somewhat more complex; both minimal and optimal need values can be associated with each. Thus, for example, equity concepts implying optimal need values can be associated with salary, as can minimal standard of living need values: any given salary may be needs satisfying compared with one need value and needs dissatisfying compared with the other.

While Herzberg, Mausner, and Snyderman inferred two independent dimensions of satisfaction and dissatisfaction from their findings, the findings can as easily be interpreted within the context of the different minimal and optimal need value concepts of our model. Similarly, their distinction between satisfying and dissatisfying events of long and short duration parallels our distinction between needs and aspirational satisfaction, with extreme levels of aspirational satisfaction and dissatisfaction being short lived and extreme levels of needs satisfaction and dissatisfaction being capable of longer endurance.

Overall Job Satisfaction

The concept of overall job satisfaction is not uniquely determined in this formulation. Overall job satisfaction is conceived as some summary function of satisfaction with job elements, but at least two different functions are conceivable. Following Locke's logic, we view importance of the job element as incorporated in the assessment of the element rather than as an independent judgment to be combined with the assessment. However, we have specified two dimensions of satisfaction — needs and aspirational — involved in the assessment of job elements. The job element judgments that combine in overall job satisfaction can be illustrated with the three dimensional diagram in Figure 3-4, associating the two dimensions of satisfaction with every job element. Two alternative formulations of overall job satisfaction are illustrated in equations (3.1) and (3.2),

$$S = \sum_j (a + n)_j \qquad (3.1)$$

$$S = \sum_j a_j + \sum_j n_j \qquad (3.2)$$

where j refers to job element, a_j refers to aspirational satisfaction, and n_j to needs satisfaction with element j. Identical measures of overall satisfaction are obtained from both formulations, whether the aspirational and needs measures are combined and summed across job elements or aspirational measures and needs measures are summed individually across job elements and then combined.

We prefer the second formulation (3.2), which maintains the distinction between aspirational and needs satisfaction until the final operation because of different behavioral implications associated with these concepts; each individual can be characterized with aspirational, needs, and overall satisfaction levels, not merely an overall satisfaction measure. Given the logic of the model developed earlier, we would anticipate, for any individual, distributions of needs and aspirational satisfactions with job elements as indicated in Figure 3-4. The distribution of needs satisfaction measures will be positively skewed due to the fact that minimal need values are associated with only a subset of job elements. Aspirational satisfaction measures will be distributed more normally, but with restricted range and variance due to the adaptation of aspiration values to perception values.

The combination of aspirational and needs satisfaction concepts at the level of job element as in equation (3.1) would obscure any possible significance of overall aspirational satisfaction. We prefer to

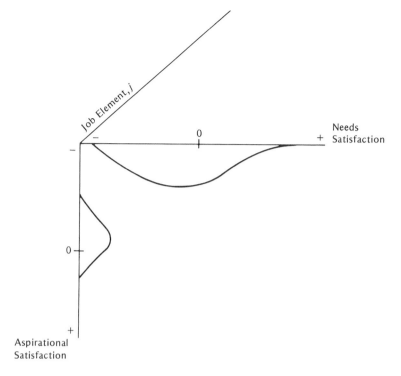

Figure 3-4. Distributions of aspirational and need satisfaction measures over job elements.

consider aspirational and needs satisfaction as related, but distinctively different, components of overall satisfaction, each implying different behavioral consequences. At any given time, each individual might be characterized in terms of both aspirational and needs satisfaction, there being no necessary relationship between these two dimensions of overall satisfaction.

SATISFACTION-PERFORMANCE RELATIONSHIPS

The Schwab and Cummings (1970) review of satisfaction-performance models identified three formulations of satisfaction-performance relationships and analyzed specific models supportive of each. One formulation hypothesized that performance is a function of job satisfaction, and Herzberg's (1959) model was considered illustrative of this formulation. Another formulation hypothesized that satisfaction is a function of performance, and the Porter-Lawler model was considered illustrative of that formulation (Lawler, 1971). Last, several models (e.g., March and Simon, 1958; Dawis, Lofquist, and Weiss, 1968) were considered where the relationship between satisfaction and performance is moderated by a variety of influences. Empirical analyses of relationships between job satisfaction and performance measures typically have been correlational in nature and thus do not demonstrate causality. Even so, these analyses tend to reveal consistent relationships between job dissatisfaction and turnover and absenteeism and negligible relationships between job satisfaction and measures of productivity.

Given the variety of measures employed in empirical investigations and a common lack of conceptualization in these studies, it is difficult to determine the extent to which the reported findings are a function of research design rather than underlying relationships. For that reason, Schwab and Cummings urged improved conceptualization of both job satisfaction and performance. Having developed a conceptualization of job satisfaction in the preceding sections, we now turn to a consideration of performance. The conceptualization of performance developed here is related to the earlier conceptualization of job satisfaction and is intended for application in the analysis of satisfaction-performance relationships, not necessarily as conceptualization of performance to be applied in other contexts.

Conceptualizations of performance in models of satisfaction-performance relationships have been even more ad hoc in nature than conceptualizations of job satisfaction. Performance has been conceived as both behavior and output and has been measured as turnover, absenteeism, and amount and quality of output. Performance behavior and output are distinctly different concepts, however; performance behavior is more easily conceptualized as a direct function of personal motivation than is performance output. Performance output is more realistically viewed as a function of task requirements and ability as well as performance behavior. Because of this, it is not surprising that more consistent empirical relationships have been observed between job satisfaction and behaviors such as absenteeism and turnover than between job satisfaction and output measures; relationships with output are moderated by more contributing influences than are relationships with personal behavior. Conceptualizations of performance relevant to investigation of satisfaction-performance relationships thus probably ought to focus upon behavioral dimensions of performance subject to individual control rather than on output dimensions, which often are controlled by other factors.

A variety of behaviors relevant to the general concept of job performance can be identified, behaviors such as seeking and/or accepting employment, termination of employment, absenteeism or work attendance, following directions, registering complaints, submitting suggestions, exerting effort, and the pacing of behavior. It is by no means obvious that all of these behaviors ought to be subject to the same motivational influences; indeed, treatments by March and Simon (1958) and Katz (1964) suggest that different work behaviors are subject to different motivational influences. Thus, relationships between job satisfaction and work behavior probably vary with the dimension of work behavior considered. Further, work behavior is conceptualized as behavior relevant to job performance whatever the motivational source, and certain work behaviors probably are influenced more by motivational influences outside the workplace than are others. Absenteeism on the first day of fishing season, for example, is influenced less by work motivations than by nonwork motivations. It seems unlikely for these reasons that job satisfaction is consistently related to all work behaviors, and investigations of relationships ought to focus upon those behaviors linked conceptually with job satisfaction.

One approach to the conceptualization of performance behavior might differentiate behaviors on the basis of relevance to output. An alternative conceptualization distinguishes between habitual behavior and choice behavior. Elements of habitual behavior in work performance include pattern or sequence of task performance, timing of rests, time of reporting for and leaving work, and habitual level of effort expended in performance — behaviors that are repetitive and relatively standardized over time. Choice behavior in work performance includes behavior exhibited in relatively infrequent circumstances as well as changes from habitual behavior patterns — behaviors such as termination of employment, occasional absenteeism and tardiness, and change in level of effort expended at work. Habitual behavior is associated with concepts of satisfaction, whereas change in behavior involving choice is more easily associated with dissatisfaction. An individual might be expected to continue to appear for work and perform at a usual level of effort as long as reasonably satisfied: given dissatisfaction beyond some threshold level, however, the individual might be expected to be alert to and seek out behavior changes that ought to prove more satisfying. Dissatisfaction, in this context, serves as the arousal stage in the motivational process: dissatisfaction motivates change, but does not determine the nature or direction of change.

Dissatisfaction with a job element in the earlier formulation is a function of discrepancy between the perceived and valued levels of the job element. Given some experienced level of dissatisfaction, the individual seeks a means of reducing dissatisfaction and/or of achieving satisfaction. Consistent with expectancy models of motivation, choice among alternative behaviors is based upon perceived contingencies and expected outcomes (Vroom, 1964; Lawler, 1971). The perceived or experienced level of any job element is more or less variable as a function of different behavior alternatives, however, and different behavior choices ought to be associated with dissatisfaction occasioned by different job elements. Thus, for example, certain job elements such as working conditions, company policies and practices, and closeness of supervision appear relatively constant for a particular job, and the only behaviors that alter the level of those elements are behaviors such as termination and absenteeism, which alter the level of the job elements actually experienced by the individual. The level of other job elements, such as experienced fatigue, fun, and sense of achievement, appear variable and controllable by individual behavior on the job. Needs dissatisfaction with job elements having variable levels is unlikely to persist over time since the individual is able to determine the achieved or experienced level of those job elements; persistent and continuing needs dissatisfaction is likely only as related to job elements with constant levels.

Reported empirical relationships between job satisfaction and performance are consistent with the conceptualization of job satisfaction and the conceptualization of satisfaction-performance relationships developed here. Reported relationships between job dissatisfaction and turnover and absenteeism, for example, would be hypothesized by the model. Persistent needs dissatisfaction is expected only where job element levels are perceived as relatively constant and variable only insofar as the individual absents himself or herself from the job situation. The lack of consistent relationships between satisfaction and level of performance also is consistent with the conceptualization of job satisfaction and also is explained partly by the fact that most investigations of satisfaction-performance relationships have been cross-sectional. Assuming the nature of needs and aspirational satisfaction developed earlier and traditional measures of job satisfaction as summed over all assessments of individual job elements, the resulting measures most likely reflect needs rather than aspirational satisfaction. Typical performance measures probably also reflect habitual levels of task performance. Thus, for any given level of job satisfaction, we might observe quite different levels of task performance, each habitual for different individuals.

Given these traditional measures, about all we might hypothesize is that individuals habitually performing at or above some minimal level of task performance would not express significant dissatisfaction with their jobs. This formulation of satisfaction-performance relationships is not unlike that of Herzberg where he suggests that dissatisfaction is associated with absenteeism and turnover and that elimination of dissatisfaction is a necessary but not sufficient condition for achieving high levels of task performance. The job elements he classed as dissatisfiers are elements with which we associate concepts of optimal need value, elements where the range of dissatisfaction measures exceeds the range of satisfaction measures and where concepts of aspirational satisfaction are least relevant. They also are job elements for which perceived levels are least controllable by the individual and where appropriate behavioral responses to persistent dissatisfaction involve absenting oneself from the job situation. Persistent needs dissatisfaction, in our context, is associated with avoidance and rejection behaviors such as termination and absenteeism that vary directly with dissatisfaction. The presence of needs satisfaction ought be associated with behaviors of staying with the organization, appearing for work each day, and performing at some habitual level, but we have no basis for inferring a direct relationship between these behaviors and different levels of needs satisfaction.

Change in work behavior is conceived as a joint function of dissatisfaction and perceived contingency relationships between behavior and job element levels. Needs dissatisfaction, which is persistent over time, is conceivable only as related to job elements with relatively constant levels; needs dissatisfaction related to job elements with variable levels can be eliminated through appropriate behavioral choices to achieve a changed level of the job element. Continued motivation to change behavior following the achievement of needs satisfaction can be inferred from the concept of aspirational dissatisfaction. Aspirational dissatisfaction is conceived as independent of needs satisfaction only relative to job elements with minimal need values and only under conditions of minimal needs dissatisfaction. Under these conditions we urged that aspiration values adapt to perceived levels and tend to exceed perceived levels: thus, some minimal aspirational dissatisfaction is normal in the presence of needs satisfaction. Job elements where this condition is likely to occur are associated with minimal need levels, elements not unlike Herzberg's satisfier or motivating elements, achievement, sense of responsibility, and intrinsic fun of the work itself. These job elements also are characterized by variable levels directly related to individual behaviors such as level of effort expended. In a longitudinal analysis, we might expect aspirational dissatisfaction to be predictive of changed behavior and needs satisfaction to be a function of changed levels of job elements resulting from this behavior.

This model of job satisfaction-performance relationships is summarized in Figure 3–5. Job elements are present for every form and level of performance behavior. The levels of some job elements, such as working conditions, minimal task requirements, and membership rewards, are relatively constant for a given job. The levels of other elements, such as incentive compensation, fatigue, and elements intrinsic to task performance, vary within a given job contingent upon performance or some other variable. Job satisfaction, an emotional response to all job elements, takes the form of needs and aspirational satisfaction and dissatisfaction. Needs satisfaction is a function of judgment of perceived level of job elements relative to need value, with the importance of the element being reflected in the functional relationship. Need value of a job element may take the form of an optimal value, a satiation value, or a minimal value. Aspirational satisfaction is a function of judgment of perceived level of the job element relative to aspiration value, with the importance being reflected in the functional relationship. Aspiration value probably will be identical with need value for job elements with optimal or satiation need values and for job elements with minimal need

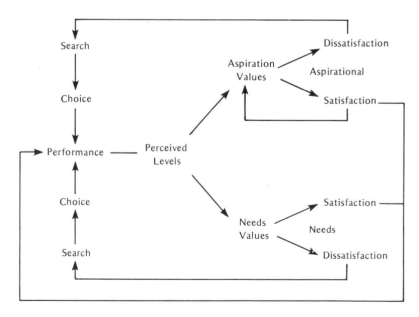

Figure 3–5. Model of job satisfaction-performance relationships.

values when there exists a percept–need value deficiency. Aspiration value will exceed need value for those job elements with minimal need values when no percept–need value deficiencies exist. Aspiration value in this instance will be a function of perceived value, always tending to exceed perceived value by some minimal amount. Summing across job elements, any individual will experience both needs and aspiration satisfaction or dissatisfaction with the job.

Given a lack of needs or aspirational dissatisfaction, habitual or customary job performance will be repeated: there is no motivation to change behavior. Experiencing needs dissatisfaction, alternatives will be sought as a means of reducing or avoiding that dissatisfaction. Job elements where the level experienced is variable and contingent upon job performance offer opportunities for reducing needs dissatisfaction, and we would anticipate changes in performance necessary to eliminate needs dissatisfaction. Needs dissatisfaction with job elements that have a constant level or that are not contingent upon job performance offer no such alternatives, and dissatisfaction is likely to persist and to be accompanied with escape behaviors such as absenteeism and turnover. Aspirational dissatisfaction with a job element where needs dissatisfaction is experienced is likely to be indistinguishable from the needs dissatisfaction; aspirational dissatisfaction will be a significant independent motivating influence only under conditions of minimal needs dissatisfaction.

Assuming some minimal needs dissatisfaction, any experienced aspirational dissatisfaction will occasion search for alternatives capable of achieving aspirational satisfaction. This dissatisfaction will be experienced relative to job elements characterized by minimal need values — job elements such as growth, fun, skill development, and achievement. Behaviors will be sought that are expected to increase the experienced level of these elements. Behavior alternatives might include job transfer or promotion, higher level of task performance, or innovative behavior capable of producing greater achievement. Given the adapting level of aspiration values, extreme levels of aspirational satisfaction and dissatisfaction are likely to be short lived. Some minimal level of aspirational dissatisfaction is more common, assuming needs satisfaction. This aspirational dissatisfaction keeps the individual alert to opportunities for change, but is not associated with the escape behaviors associated with extreme or persistent needs dissatisfaction.

The model of satisfaction-performance relationships developed here is consistent with and builds upon a variety of models of satisfaction-performance formulations as well as models of motivation. Job dissatisfaction is viewed as an arousal or energizing element in the motivational process: it does not provide an explanation of choice behavior. Choices made among alternatives are a function of path-goal expectancies expressed either as conditioned associations or in cognitive terms. Job satisfaction is a function of experienced levels of job elements — elements associated with performance in a job but that may be invariant for any specific job. In this sense, job satisfaction is a consequence of experience in job performance, not a cause of job performance.

Overall job satisfaction is a function of two separable, although not independent, dimensions or components of job satisfaction, needs and aspirational job satisfaction. Experienced job satisfaction on either component is pleasing and conducive of repetition of habitual job performance; experienced dissatisfaction is displeasing and motivates effort to eliminate the dissatisfaction. As in the March and Simon (1958) model, dissatisfaction motivates search for alternatives. Dissatisfaction, rather than satisfaction, is predictive of change in behavior or performance consistent with empirical findings regarding relationships between dissatisfaction and absenteeism and turnover. Consistent with Locke's (1976) formulation, satisfaction is conceived as an emotional response to judgment of the perceived amount of a job element present relative to some standard, with the importance of the element being included in the functional relationship rather than figuring as a separate judgment.

The distinction between needs and aspirational satisfaction relates to the distinction between needs and expectancy models of job satisfaction. Need values, in this context, are relatively invariant with respect to recent experience while expectancy or aspirational values are a function of recent experience. Consistent with Herzberg's (1959) early findings, extreme values of aspirational satisfaction tend to be short lived while values of needs satisfaction tend to be longer lived, the change in needs satisfaction being more a function of perceptions than of comparison levels. Need values that take the form of optimality values are distinguished from need values with the form of minimal values analogous with Maslow's (1955) distinction between lower order and higher order needs. Lower order needs with optimality need values are capable of satiation; higher order needs, where aspirations beyond the minimal need values are relevant, are incapable of satiation. Aspirations, however, rather than need values, account for the continuing relevance of higher order needs in this formulation. The distinction between job elements for which optimal need values are appropriate and those for which minimal need values and aspiration values greater than need values are appropriate corresponds generally to the distinction between Herzberg's hygienic and motivator factors. Similarly, the behavioral implications he attributes to his dimensions of dissatisfaction and satisfaction correspond to the behavioral implications we attribute to needs dissatisfaction and aspirational dissatisfaction. The distinction between needs and aspirational satisfaction, however, permits us to attribute behavioral change to dissatisfaction mediated by motivational choice models rather than implying that performance is a direct function of satisfaction. High levels of needs satisfaction may be correlated with high performance, but performance level in this instance is a function of aspirational dissatisfaction and behavioral choices.

RESEARCH IMPLICATIONS

The conceptualization of job satisfaction and performance developed here is tentative in nature. While supported by prior conceptualizations, which tend to appear conflicting, and consistent with empirical findings, considerable conceptual refinement and empirical investigations are required before the model can be accepted as a basis for application. It does, however, offer a framework for redirection of research into satisfaction-performance relationships—redirection that we hope will be more productive than much of the past research in this area. Following are some of the research questions posed by this formulation.

The most immediate research questions relate to the structural aspects of the conceptualization of job satisfaction. No specific structure of content elements of job satisfaction has been proposed, although the proposed distinction between job elements characterized by optimal and by minimal need values is critical to the model. The hypothesized existence of optimal and minimal need levels might be investigated directly. The consistency with which specific job elements are characterized by optimal and minimal need values might also be investigated as a function of cultural, individual, and experiential influences: this observed consistency or inconsistency might influence significantly the design of instruments to measure needs and aspirational satisfaction. Suggested parallels between elements characterized by optimal and by minimal need values and elements characterized as satisfiers and motivators in the Herzberg model might also be investigated. We anticipate that job elements classified as dissatisfiers in the Herzberg model will be characterized by optimal need values and job elements classified as motivators will be characterized by minimal need values. Aspiration values might also be investigated over time to determine if aspiration values are more variable as hypothesized.

The constructs of aspirational and needs satisfaction might be investigated. These constructs probably ought to be measured directly rather than in terms of a "have-desire" framework; relationships between satisfaction measures and need and aspiration values might then be investigated as well. We hypothesize that aspirational satisfaction is distinguishable from needs satisfaction only as related to job elements with minimal needs satisfaction; this might be investigated for supportive evidence. Overall job satisfaction, measured independently of needs and aspirational satisfaction, might be analyzed as a function of the two dimensions of satisfaction to determine if it is influenced predominantly by needs satisfaction as hypothesized. We also hypothesized relatively greater variance in needs satisfaction measures than aspirational satisfaction measures, an hypothesis that might easily be investigated in cross-sectional analyses. The relative duration of aspirational and needs satisfaction might be investigated through analysis of reported experiences as in the Herzberg methodology or through longitudinal investigation; we hypothesized that needs satisfaction was more enduring than aspirational satisfaction.

Other research questions relate to the hypothesized relationships between job satisfaction and work-related behavior, some of which might be investigated in cross-sectional analyses, while others would require longitudinal analyses. Measures of work behavior in cross-sectional analyses tend to reflect recent behavior, whether habitual or a change from previous behavior. Since we associate habitual behavior with at least minimal satisfaction and change with prior dissatisfaction, relationships between satisfaction and performance observed in cross-sectional analyses will not be as easily interpreted as relationships observed in longitudinal analyses. Nevertheless, we would expect cross-sectional analyses to indicate stronger relationships between those behaviors and aspirational or overall job satisfaction. Further, we would hypothesize stronger relationships between these behaviors and needs satisfaction with job elements with invariant levels (working conditions, organizational practices, supervision, and membership rewards) than with needs satisfaction with job elements having variable levels (incentive compensation, achievement, skill utilization).

We have hypothesized that performance change is a function of experienced dissatisfaction and perceived contingency relationships between performance and job elements. Needs dissatisfaction with variable level job elements is less likely to persist over time than needs dissatisfaction with constant level job elements. Specific performance changes depend upon perceived contingency relationships. In general, however, we would anticipate the association of rejection or escape behaviors and persistent needs dissatisfaction with constant level job elements and productive performance changes with needs dissatisfaction with variable level job elements. Behavior changes associated with aspirational dissatisfaction are expected to be changes in productive performance rather than rejection and escape behaviors.

The models of job satisfaction and of satisfaction-performance relationships outlined here have been related to other conceptualizations and research, but no exhaustive search of the prior literature has been conducted. One of the first attempts to assess the validity of the model might take the form of application of the model to findings of the full range of research into job satisfaction. We would anticipate that many of the seemingly contradictory findings reported in reviews of this research would appear compatible when interpreted in this new formulation. Also, the suggested integration of the Herzberg model and more traditional models of job satisfaction ought to contribute to relaxation of controversy regarding the Herzberg model and to more refined conceptualizations of job satisfaction and performance.

REFERENCES

Dawis, R. V.; L. H. Lofquist; and D. J. Weiss. 1968. *A Theory of Work Adjustment.* A revision. Minnesota Studies in Vocational Rehabilitation XXIII. Minneapolis: University of Minnesota.

Herzberg, Frederick; Bernard Mausner; and Barbara Bloch Snyderman. 1959. *The Motivation to Work.* New York: Wiley.

Katz, Daniel. 1964. "The Motivational Basis of Organizational Behavior." *Behavioral Science* 9: 132-46.

Lawler, Edward E. 1971. *Pay and Organizational Effectiveness: A Psychological View.* New York: McGraw-Hill.

Locke, Edwin A. 1976. "The Nature and Causes of Job Satisfaction." In M. D. Dunnette, ed., *Handbook of Industrial and Organizational Psychology.* New York: Rand McNally.

March, James G., and Herbert A. Simon. 1958. *Organizations.* New York: Wiley.

Maslow, A. 1955. "Deficiency Motivation and Growth Motivation." In M. R. Jones, ed., *Nebraska Symposium on Motivation.* Lincoln: University of Nebraska Press.

Schwab, Donald P., and Larry L. Cummings. 1970. "Theories of Performance and Satisfaction: A Review." *Industrial Relations* 9: 408-30.

Vroom, Victor H. 1964. *Work and Motivation.* New York: Wiley.

Chapter 4

Theories of Organizational Motivation

John B. Miner*

The field of organizational motivation or energy has probably spawned more theories than any other aspect of organizational study. To some extent, these theories represent alternative attempts to explain the same phenomena. However, the theories often operate in separate domains, serving to supplement each other and thus covering different segments of the total organizational behavior terrain.

This review takes as its primary task the delineation of what this mapping process has produced up to the present. Where are the gaps, the unexplored areas? Where are the conflicting explanations the different maps produce as different individuals explore the same territory? The focus is on theories — on theories that have been in existence long enough to accumulate a respectable number of research investigations and on theories that have at least at some specific time · achieved a considerable degree of scientific acceptance. There are nine theories that appear to meet these requirements — need hierarchy, achievement motivation, managerial role motivation, motivation hygiene, equity, expectancy, goal setting, behavior modification, and job characteristics.

* Georgia State University

To cover the theories of organizational motivation and their related research fully in a short study such as this is clearly impossible. Accordingly, the approach taken is to summarize the current status of each theory within a standard framework of eight questions that may appropriately be asked of any organizational motivation theory (Miner, 1977). All but one of the theories are discussed in much greater detail in a forthcoming book dealing with major theories of organizational behavior in general (Miner, 1980), and the reader is referred to that source for a fuller coverage.

The eight questions that provide the framework for analyzing the theories are:

1. What methods of measurement are available to measure the constructs of the theory effectively?
2. Does the theory predict performance levels, or more particularly their motivational components, within the theory's domain?
3. Does the theory predict work satisfaction within the domain?
4. What are the limits of the theory's domain, and exactly how does it overlap other theoretical domains?
5. What is the real nature of the constructs of the theory?
6. How and to what extent can the motivational processes specified by the theory be externally influenced?
7. Are the motivational processes specified by the theory involved in organizational and vocational choice?
8. What is the talent supply of the motivational components posited by the theory in the population at large and in relevant subgroups?

NEED HIERARCHY THEORY

Need hierarchy theory is developed in a series of publications by Abraham Maslow (1943, 1954, 1962, 1967). A more recent variant of the theory has been presented by Alderfer (1972). A major review of the theory and the current evidence bearing on it is provided by Wahba and Bridwell (1976).

Measurement

A lack of theoretically relevant measuring procedures operated as a block to evaluative research for almost twenty years, during which time need hierarchy theory received a considerable amount of uncritical acceptance. When measures were developed, they often suffered from unreliability and response bias, although in recent years there have been improvements on these scores. A major problem still remaining is that Maslow defined his need categories to include a sizable unconscious component, yet all measurement techniques to date have operated entirely at the conscious level, being self-report rather than projective in nature. Furthermore, measures have been devised only for needs falling within the hierarchy running from physiological to self-actualization. Needs of a cognitive and aesthetic nature, which were also part of the theory, remain unmeasured and thus have received no research attention.

Prediction of Performance

Very little research has been conducted to test the theory's predictions regarding performance. One would anticipate that the particular needs that are independently established as providing the predominant motivational force for an individual at a given time would be most closely associated with performance and that, generally, higher order needs would be better predictors than lower ones. The sparse evidence available in this area tends to be nonsupportive, but it is insufficient.

One tangential approach to the problem is through the research on theory X and theory Y (McGregor, 1960), a theoretical framework that incorporates aspects of the Maslow formulations. The performance-related research here is also quite limited, but what there is has not produced significant results. Another tangential approach is through the research on job characteristics theory (Hackman and Oldham, 1976), which uses higher order need strength as a moderator variable. That theory, however, has consistently proven least effective in predicting performance outcomes.

Predictions of Work Satisfactions

In contrast with performance, the theory has spawned a sizable amount of research dealing with satisfaction variables. The results of this research are quite mixed, but the tendency in many studies to utilize measures of higher order needs that are not yet engaged or activated for the subjects raises questions regarding the theoretical relevance of a number of the investigations. On the other hand, more appropriately designed longitudinal studies focusing directly on the prepotency of need categories in the hierarchy have consistently failed to support the theory. In general it would appear that need satisfaction can be an important contributor to satisfaction at work, but not necessarily in accordance with the hierarchic processes specified by Maslow.

Theoretical Domain

Need hierarchy theory was originally put forth as a general psychological theory of motivation, and in fact it was only very late in his life that Maslow became interested in applications in the organizational area at all. McGregor (1960), however, did focus on these applications somewhat earlier. In any event, insofar as the organizational behavior field is concerned, this is a broad theory having few boundary-determining criteria. The research evidence does not permit a more limited, empirically determined domain definition; there is nothing that would indicate that the theory works only with certain kinds of people, under certain environmental circumstances, or the like. Within the limitations of the measures and research designs used, the theory has characteristically failed of consistent support in any domain studied.

Construct Validity

The self-actualization construct is often described by Maslow in philosophical — even mystical — terms, which makes it very difficult to determine what the real nature of this variable is. There is reason to believe that many of the measures developed have not coincided with what Maslow meant, but on the other hand, Maslow's own efforts at measurement in this area were singularly unsuccessful, in part at least because there are some logical inconsistencies among his own statements regarding it. One of the key variables of the theory thus remains very uncertain in meaning even now.

A major approach to the construct validity problem has been to factor analyze various instruments to determine whether they yield a structure matching the constructs of the theory. Early efforts of this type were unsuccessful. Recent efforts have on several occasions provided quite good matches. It now is apparent that whether one does or does not obtain a factor structure approximating the Maslow need categories depends upon the items originally introduced into the analysis and upon the particular mathematical technique utilized.

External Influences

The theory would predict that the needs operating to influence a person's behavior can be influenced by systematically varying the levels and types of need satisfaction provided. With the exception of some research related to theory X and theory Y, there is no evidence of this kind that can be explicitly tied to need hierarchy theory. The research that can be so traced is not sufficiently well controlled to reach conclusions. Efforts have been made to design sensitivity training programs in a manner intended to develop higher needs, but data to evaluate their success are nonexistent.

Vocational Choice

Studies explicitly designed to investigate the implications of need hierarchy theory for vocational choice are lacking, in spite of the fact that the theory has been used as a factor in the classification of occupations. On the other hand, the theory has generated a considerable amount of research that, although often not providing a test of theoretical hypotheses, does indicate how the variables relate to such factors as managerial level, line staff status, company size, and the like. This research can prove useful entirely independent of the theory itself.

Talent Supply

It is clear that Maslow considered self-actualization to be a variable that society needs badly and that is in very short supply. Ultimately he came to the position that operating out of self-actualization motivation for any meaningful period of time is practically impossible for young people and very rare below the age of fifty. One of the difficulties with the various measuring instruments developed is that they consistently yield a much greater incidence of self-actualization than either Maslow's own research or his theory would anticipate. At this point, therefore, the talent supply question cannot be considered to be adequately answered.

Conclusions

In general need hierarchy theory in its original form has not demonstrated a high level of performance in the various areas where a motivational theory would be expected to contribute. Although these conclusions may be modified by subsequent research using more theoretically appropriate measures and designs, the current situation is not encouraging. The major problems appear to be inherent in the attempt to create a grand theory, often moving across the boundary into social philosophy, and in the consequent failure to incorporate the full complexity of individual differences.

ACHIEVEMENT MOTIVATION
THEORY

In actuality, achievement motivation theory deals not only with the achievement construct, broadly defined to include both hope of success and fear of failure, but also with need for power in its various manifestations and need for affiliation. The major theoretical formulations have come from McClelland (1961, 1975) and McClelland and Winter (1969). In the area of achievement motivation, reformulations and extensions derive from Atkinson (1977), Atkinson and Raynor (1974), and Weiner (1972); in the area of power motivation, from Veroff and Veroff (1972) and Winter (1973). A major review has been contributed by Heckhausen (1967).

Measurement

Achievement motivation theory has consistently acquired measures of its major variables in close parallel with the theoretical developments themselves. Thus, there has been a constant interactive relationship between research and theory. The primary measures have utilized the Thematic Apperception Test (TAT), which being projective in nature does tap the unconscious motives incorporated in the theory. However, a self-report index of fear of failure has been used to measure that particular theoretical construct, contradicting the strong arguments presented for the use of projective approaches.

In general the scorer reliabilities reported for the TAT measures have been entirely satisfactory; the test reliabilities themselves have not been. In spite of some basic problems in demonstrating reliability for the TAT measures, the failure to produce any solid evidence of adequate reliability does cause concern. In all probability longer tests, requiring a greater number of stories, would prove more reliable. In spite of the low reliabilities, however, significant discriminations often have been made with the TAT measures.

Prediction of Performance

The theory has proved quite effective in guiding research on the relationship between achievement motivation and entrepreneurship, entrepreneurial success, and societal economic development. Consistent evidence of positive relationships with organizational and societal performance criteria has been developed. The record with regard to the hypothesized role of socialized power motivation in business management performance is less strong, in part because the theoretical differentiation between personalized and socialized power is of recent origin, and sufficient research has not evolved yet. The theory overall has not yielded good predictions for females, but this can be explained on the grounds that these predictions have been attempted outside the domain.

Prediction of Work Satisfactions

The major thrust of the theory has been toward performance rather than satisfaction, and the accumulated research reflects this emphasis. However, there are some data indicating that satisfaction measures may be predicted from the variables of the theory. For instance, the limited confirmatory research in the area of power motivation has dealt primarily with measures related to work satisfaction.

Theoretical Domain

Although McClelland has extended his formulations quite broadly (to the study of alcoholism, for instance), the theory is separately stated as applied to organizations. Actually there are two such theories, each with its own limited domain. There is first a theory of entrepreneurial effort and performance at both the organizational and societal levels, and there is also a theory of more recent origin dealing with the management of corporations. At both a theoretical and operational level, the entrepreneurial theory holds for males only; the managerial theory is less explicit on this point. In general the evidence from research supports the theoretically stated boundary limitations.

Construct Validity

Although some questions have been raised regarding the achievement motivation construct based on the lack of correlation between TAT and other measures, there is good reason to believe that the non-TAT measures may indeed fail to tap the construct as set forth in the theory. However, research does not support the hypothesized roles of either independence training for male children or Protestantism in the development of achievement motivation, thus introducing a need for some modification in the overall concept of the construct itself.

Other constructs of the theory receive considerable support, especially the specification of the factors inherent in an achievement-motivation-arousing situation — medium risk, feedback, self-attribution, future goals, and the like. On the other hand, research on the various types and stages of power motivation has not yet progressed to the point where the exact nature of these variables can be specified. There is better evidence as to the fear of failure–achievement motivation differentiation.

External Influences

The theory deals at some length with the processes of motive development and how management development programs may be used for this purpose. Achievement motivation training clearly does accomplish its goals and foster entrepreneurial activity. This has been demonstrated with regard to black capitalism in the United States, economic growth in the developing countries, and motivational development among disadvantaged school children. Power motivation training also gives some evidence of promise, especially as regards shifting from personalized to socialized manifestations, although the evidence is insufficient in this area. It is clear from all of this research that an explicit effort to change motives is necessary if results are to be obtained: mere exposure to organizational climates of various kinds is not sufficient.

Vocational Choice

The primary data involve relating achievement motivation scores to occupational choice, such as the choice of an entrepreneurial role. There also is evidence that high achievement motivation people make quite realistic occupational decisions, whereas high fear of failure individuals do not; the latter carry their avoidant tendencies into the choice process itself and do not obtain needed information. There is other evidence that children from entrepreneurial families tend to develop high achievement motivation, which in turn conditions their own occupational decisions. All in all, considerable research has been done in the vocational area.

Talent Supply

One of the major approaches used in research related to achievement motivation theory is to plot measures of motivation against economic indexes for countries and cultures. This has been done for the United States, and the curves are remarkably congruent. Achievement motivation rose steadily from 1800 to 1890, peaked, and has been declining since. There is, however, some reason to believe that in the present world of large multinational firms, a decline in achievement motivation may not necessarily bring economic downfall as it has in the past, if the motives, such as, perhaps, socialized power needs, required to manage the corporations remain in good supply.

There is also evidence that achievement motivation, or at least achievement motivation as it has been traditionally measured, is lower among females. At the same time, fear of success is high among females and in fact appears to be almost nonexistent among males.

Conclusions

Achievement motivation theory as it relates to the entrepreneurial domain, and this includes certain enriched jobs within corporate organizations, appears to have demonstrated good validity. Data related to most of the major questions have been generated in considerable abundance. However, the original developmental theory of achievement motivation has not been supported.

The theory's status in the second domain of corporate management is less secure. There are clearly conflicting theories of power motivation proposed by individuals who remain generally identified with achievement motivation theory as a whole, and the available evidence does not yet permit one to choose among them. It would appear that the socialized power formulations may contain elements of fact and still be inadequate to explain managerial motivation as a whole.

MANAGERIAL ROLE MOTIVATION THEORY

The primary statement of managerial role motivation theory is contained in Miner (1965), and much of the research related to the theory is described in that volume and in Miner (1977). A major review article has also appeared recently (Miner, 1978b), as well as two treatments of the measures used (Brief, Aldag, and Chacko, 1977; Miner, 1978a). The theory as a whole has now been extended to additional domains, including the professional role, the role of group-centered systems, and the entrepreneurial or task-centered role (Miner, 1975; 1979). However, there is insufficient research evidence to evaluate these extensions as yet.

Measurement

The primary measurement technique used is projective in nature and utilizes the sentence completion approach. Scorer reliabilities of an entirely satisfactory nature have been reported with some consistency, although it is also evident that considerable learning time may be required to achieve these levels and that some people have great difficulty becoming reliable scorers. Test reliability, once scorer reliability is attained, does not appear to present a problem with this type of measure, although the coefficients for subscales are well below the level obtained with the overall measure of the theory's constructs.

Prediction of Performance

A number of studies, utilizing both concurrent and predictive designs, have indicated positive relationships between the variables of the theory and organizational performance criteria within the theory's domain. Criteria utilized include management appraisal ratings, promotion rates, compensation data, and the like. Predictions have been equally good for male and female managers.

Prediction of Work Satisfactions

The theory would anticipate that satisfaction, narrowly defined in terms of intrinsic reactions to the work itself, would result when an individual with high motivation to manage works in a truly managerial position. Research bearing on this hypothesis has not been conducted, however, nor has there been any study of the reactions of high managerial motivation people to jobs that do not permit behavior consonant with their strong motives. The area of work satisfaction is one in which tests of the theory have been markedly deficient.

Theoretical Domain

The specified domain consists of managerial work in hierarchic organizations of the bureaucratic form that are large enough so that it is not feasible to rely entirely on face-to-face communication. Within this domain the theory has worked well; outside the domain the theory fails to predict as would be anticipated. Studies have been conducted in professional organizations, with jobs below the managerial level, and in very small hierarchic systems. In all these cases falling outside the domain, significant results have not been obtained.

Construct Validity

There is consistent evidence that managers have higher motivation to manage than nonmanagers. In addition, the constructs of the theory are related to such factors as personal dominance, expressed interest in occupations having a sizable managerial component, decisiveness, and the like that would be expected to show a relationship. Several different instruments have been developed directly from the theory, and all correlate closely. The support for the overall motivation to manage construct is thus quite strong. On the other hand, the individual components of the theory, such as favorable attitudes to authority, competitiveness, and the like, have not been studied as extensively, and their exact nature is less certain. They do, however, appear to be only minimally correlated with each other, and thus each contributes unique variance to the overall index.

External Influences

Managerial role motivation training has been shown to increase motivation to manage in a variety of contexts, including the college classroom and the company management development program. It appears to work equally well with males and females. There are also some findings extending beyond motivational change to job behavior, indicating that promotions are more likely to accrue to those who have experienced the training. The degree of motivational change produced varies from individual to individual, and a number of people seem totally unresponsive. This is particularly true of passive and dependent people.

Vocational Choice

Research on vocational choice indicates that young people with strong managerial motivation do tend to select managerial careers. However, this relationship is conditioned by the level of knowledge of what managerial work entails. Without such knowledge, there is much less likelihood that the strong motives will be tied to a specifically managerial choice. Typically, persons with high motivation to manage will prefer line to staff management and highly discretionary positions such as are often found in the sales field. A major lack in the research in this area is the failure to conduct longitudinal studies relating preexisting motivational patterns to career data.

Talent Supply

Motivation to manage appears to be declining in the younger age groups of the population, at least among those who go to college. Coupled with the decline in achievement motivation, this situation represents a severe barrier to economic growth. Research has also been conducted comparing male and female college students, and the data indicate a general tendency to lower levels of motivation among females. On the other hand, in the ranks of management itself sex differences are not found. Furthermore, there are data to indicate that minority managers tend to have exceptionally high levels of managerial motivation. The talent supply question has been one of the most extensively investigated, and there is a sizable literature dealing with it (Miner, 1974).

Conclusions

Within its specified domain, managerial role motivation theory has proved in some twenty years of existence to be a highly effective conceptual tool. It remains true, however, that it deals with a much more limited domain than most other theories of organizational motivation. The attempts to expand the theoretical approach to other domains would appear to offer a potential solution to this limitation, but it is too early to judge the success of these efforts.

The overlap between managerial role motivation theory and the McClelland formulations regarding the role of socialized power motivation is apparent. It would appear that the socialized power theory has somewhat less explanatory ability than the role motivation concepts. According to this view, power motivation is only one of a number of motivational constructs needed to fully understand managerial effort. Unfortunately, research directly relating the two theories has not been conducted.

MOTIVATION HYGIENE THEORY

Motivation-hygiene theory is primarily the creation of Frederick Herzberg. It is set forth in its various forms — there have been expansions and deletions — in three volumes (Herzberg, Mausner, and Snyderman, 1959; Herzberg, 1966, 1976). The latter is largely a compendium of articles published subsequent to the previous book. In addition there are at least two major reformulations of the theory (Wolf, 1970; Hackman, 1969), although neither has elicited much subsequent research. A number of major research reviews have been undertaken, including Bockman (1971) and King (1970).

Measurement

The authors of the theory did propose a measurement technique based on the critical incident method, which involves providing information regarding satisfying and dissatisfying job experiences. This technique has continued to receive Herzberg's support as theoretically relevant, and considerable research has been stimulated as a result. Scorer reliability appears to be good. However, the tendency has been to relate theoretical variables and criterion measures obtained at the same time as part of the same measure. Under these conditions response bias is almost inevitable, and it is apparent that it does occur. Thus, the preferred measure leaves much to be desired in testing the theory.

Predictions of Performance

Studies of performance relationships have all included a potential for response bias; independent measures of performance have not been employed. Furthermore, even these relationships are better explained in terms of direct satisfaction-dissatisfaction associations rather than through the introduction of the motivator and hygiene constructs. Studies of job enrichment interventions are often invoked in favor of the performance relatedness of the theory, but it is not at all clear how job enrichment ties back to the theory, and in any event it has nothing to do with the hygiene aspects. Overall, it is apparent that the theory has not demonstrated a capacity to predict performance.

Prediction of Work Satisfaction

In many respects, motivation hygiene theory appears much stronger as a predictor of satisfactions. The results obtained using the incident technique often support the theory. However, opportunity for growth, which should be a self-actualizing motivator, is as often a source of dissatisfaction. Pay, interpersonal relations, status, and security are not just sources of dissatisfaction. They are often just as frequently contributors to satisfaction, and in certain groups some of them may well be predominantly so. Achievement and the work itself are repeatedly found to be sources of dissatisfaction as well as satisfaction.

Furthermore, there is considerable reason to believe even the confirmatory results are method bound. Defensiveness clearly contributes to the tendency to attribute dissatisfaction to hygiene factors. Given the findings, it is not possible to conclude that the two factor concept provides a valid formulation even of the work attitude relationships that are generally considered to be the central focus of the theory.

Theoretical Domain

Motivation hygiene theory, like need hierarchy, extends broadly across organizational behavior, even into the realm of mental illness and pathological behavior. It deals not just with job attitudes and satisfaction, but with needs, performance effects, and behavior in enriched jobs. Furthermore, there is no basis for restricting its domain utilizing the research evidence, except perhaps to incident measurement. To do the latter, however, would be theoretically meaningless.

Construct Validity

The use of the self-actualization concept and the tendency to describe aspects of the theory in vague, philosophical, often biblical terms tend to cloud the meanings of constructs. In addition, there is some equivocation on the true position of pay in the theory. However, the major problems of a construct validity nature relate to the fact that the incident method and other approaches do not yield the same results. As a result, one must seriously question whether the motivators and hygienes operate in the manner specified by the theory.

External Influences

The major external influence process studied is the enrichment of jobs by building in motivators — what Herzberg calls orthodox job enrichment. There is some evidence that this approach can yield positive outcomes, particularly in areas related to work satisfaction. However, its relationship to motivation hygiene theory is tangential at best. It involves motivators only, not hygienes and, among the latter, the so-called generators — the work itself, responsibility, opportunity for growth, and advancement. Achievement and recognition, which based on the research evidence one would expect to see emphasized, are in fact downplayed.

Even in the best of circumstances, 10 to 15 percent of the participants do not respond to job enrichment, and in some contexts, particularly those of a blue collar nature, the results are frequently nil. Yet the theory provides no basis for predicting these failures and in fact pays practically no attention to individual differences in any form.

Vocational Choice

Consistent with the lack of concern with individual differences, neither the theory nor its related research has contributed to our understanding of vocational choice.

Talent Supply

Like vocational choice, the talent supply issue has not concerned motivation hygiene theory advocates. The general position has been that most people will respond to motivator and hygiene factors in accord with the theory and that if they do not, they are often mentally ill. However, data bearing on the actual frequency of this kind of mental illness in the population have not been developed in a systematic manner.

Conclusions

To date motivation hygiene theory has not accumulated a solid base of research support. Perhaps more elegant designs would provide this, and there is in fact some basis for arguing that research tests to this point, whether carried out by the theory's authors or others, have often been lacking in one respect or another. On the other hand, the sheer mass of nonconfirming research appears to have had its effect, and consequently, interest in the theory is definitely on the wane in the scientific community. Many aspects of the theory as originally stated have never been adequately tested, perhaps because the authors subsequently ignored them also. Now, very little by way of tests of any aspect are to be found in the literature.

EQUITY THEORY

Equity theory has been most fully propounded by Adams (1963, 1965). A related formulation, also dealing primarily with pay, has been proposed by Jacques (1970). Weick (1966) introduced a number of logical and empirical criticisms of the theory at an early point, many of which have continued validity today. The most recent major critical review is by Goodman and Friedman (1971), although Adams and Freedman (1976) provide a thorough update on research related to the theory.

Measurement

Much of the research on equity theory has been conducted in laboratory settings with manipulation of independent variables and measurement of dependent variables. The result has been that key constructs of the theory remain unmeasured. None of these studies has included indexes of inequity tension, prevailing strength of equity motivation, inequity thresholds, and inequity tolerances. These measures are needed if the theory is to be useful beyond its current somewhat marginal status. The experimental approach has provided data on validity, but not on importance, and measures of theoretical variables are needed to accomplish the latter.

Prediction of Performance

The evidence that both overreward and underreward inequity can have the hypothesized effects on the quality and quantity of performance is quite convincing. There is a question as to how long these effects typically last before being corrected by cognitive manipulations, but the data indicate that they can last at least a week, and in all probability, under appropriate circumstances, they can last much longer. There certainly are studies that have failed to obtain the hypothesized performance effects, but inadequacies of conceptualization and design are sufficiently apparent in these instances to explain the results. On balance, the theory does seem to predict performance, at least over short periods of time.

Prediction of Work Satisfactions

Overreward inequity has been shown to produce dissatisfaction as a continuing state. The same is true of underreward inequity; in addition, underreward has been found to contribute to a propensity to separate from the organization — and in subsequent studies, to actual separation — and also to increased absenteeism. There are even instances where inequities have resulted in refusal to participate in laboratory studies and in severely disruptive behavior within the context of such studies. All in all, the data give strong support to the theory in the area of work satisfaction.

Theoretical Domain

The scope of equity theory's domain is not entirely clear, although some of the boundary constraints have been established. There must be a definite perception of the input dimensions and of the individual's position on these dimensions for equity motivation to be mobilized. It is apparent that the ambiguities of many work situations tend to muddy these perceptions, but we do not know how often. It is for this reason that the real practical significance of equity theory remains an enigma and that the extent of its domain is uncertain. We do not know how often equity motivation actually becomes engaged outside those laboratory settings where it is intentionally induced.

Construct Validity

It seems increasingly apparent that the central construct of the theory is equity motivation — or perhaps two constructs, involving guilt or shame reduction and anger or hatred reduction. Essentially, the theory deals with a content motive, much the same as achievement motivation, even though it has typically been classified as a process theory.

There has been considerable controversy over whether the experimental results obtained are a consequence of inequity or insecurity, and studies by Adams and others have adduced evidence on this point. It now appears that inequity alone can produce the hypothesized results, although insecurity may well have been an added factor in the early studies.

Some attention has been given to individual differences in responsiveness to inequitable circumstances, primarily pay inequity. Those strongly responsive to inequity stimuli turn out not to be risk takers and gamblers; they may be high on achievement motivation. The need for greater knowledge of such people, and thus of the construct, is apparent. Furthermore, the theory lacks precision regarding what factors operate as inputs and what factors as outputs under what circumstances and on how different individuals come to reduce inequity ·in a given instance. Without direct measures of equity-related variables, the central constructs of the theory remain cloudy.

External Influences

Although the laboratory studies have typically manipulated pay inequity externally, there is no research where this has been done in an organizational setting and certainly no instance where effects on equity motivation have been determined. There is a need for this kind of research. Can equity motivation be stimulated or aroused in ongoing organizations? Can it be increased or diminished? The answers to these questions do not exist.

Vocational Choice

Theoretically, equity motivation might well emerge as a major factor in job and career choice — the choice of a legal career, for instance, or of a role as a union steward. However, neither the theory nor the research have extended into this area.

Talent Supply

The question of talent supply also remains unanswered and will remain so until adequate measures of equity-related constructs are developed. On the existing evidence, it would appear that equity motivation is a dominant motive for many people and that it is often activated in the work context, but data on these points are totally lacking. Accordingly, we do not know how significant the theory as a whole really is.

Conclusions

Overall equity theory has considerable support, especially as regards the prediction of performance and work satisfaction. There is a problem, however, regarding who will respond to inequity stimulation and who will not — the problem of individual differences. And there are additional problems as to how inequities will be handled, what reference sources will be utilized, how factors come to be viewed as inputs and outputs, and so on. The theory appears to offer considerable potential. It is a limited domain theory, and within that domain it can work well. But there are still a great many unanswered questions.

EXPECTANCY THEORIES

The first formal statement of expectancy views as applied specifically to the organizational context appears in an article by Georgopoulos, Mahoney, and Jones (1957). Subsequently, various conceptualizations utilizing the expectancy framework have been presented by a number of individuals including Vroom (1964),

Galbraith and Cummings (1967), Porter and Lawler (1968), Lawler (1973), and Graen (1969). In general these statements of the theory do not differ sharply; in many cases a subsequent formulation either adds new variables or defines previously proposed variables and processes more precisely. However, Deci's (1975) theory regarding the relationships among intrinsic and extrinsic motivational processes is at variance with the earlier views. Major reviews have been provided by Campbell and Pritchard (1976), Mitchell (1974), and Wahba and House (1974), and a detailed logical critique has been written by Locke (1975).

Measurement

There are no standard or accepted measures of expectancy theory variables. Different investigators have developed or adapted their instruments according to their understandings of the theoretical constructs. In general the measures are of a self-report nature and relatively short. In many cases reliability has not been determined; when it has been, the coefficients are often low. Yet every variable of the theory has been measured with good reliability on occasion. In most studies the reliabilities for measures of different constructs vary widely, but the pattern of this variation shifts from one study to the next. Probably this is why different components of the theory prove to contribute the most to the predictions in different studies.

Prediction of Performance

A large number of investigations have attempted to predict performance criteria, or their precursor effort or force, from expectancy theory variables. The early research produced support for the theory, but not very strong support. More recently, with certain improvements in design and measurement, much more impressive results have been obtained. These improvements include the use of short lists of outcomes generated individually by subjects, within-subject rather than between-subjects analyses of the data, and conducting research that falls squarely within the domain of the theory using consistently reliable measures.

Prediction of Work Satisfactions

What has been said regarding performance prediction holds equally for the prediction of satisfaction. The research on expectancy theory has tended to emphasize performance or direct measures of the motivational force behind performance more than it has work satisfaction, but when satisfaction has been studied, it often has been effectively predicted.

Theoretical Domain

Early statements of expectancy theory gave little attention to the matter of domain, and the tendency was to view it as a broad, general theory of work motivation. Subsequent research findings have altered this situation dramatically. It is apparent that for expectancy theory to work, contingencies must be established in a concrete manner between effective job performance and attaining favorable role outcomes (Graen, 1969). The theory deals with conscious motivation only, and thus self-report measurement is appropriate. It is a theory for situations involving highly rational, maximizing, hedonistic decisionmaking. This would suggest that it is a theory for certain kinds of people who think this way, much more than for others. From an organizational standpoint the domain is one where people are rewarded relative to performance levels; merit increases are based on performance; promotions go to the best people; salary increases are clearly seen as due to performance; recognition is given for good work; and people with ability are seen as having a promising future.

This domain is not the same as that of formal decision theory since some of the boundary-determining criteria of that normative theory are not required by expectancy theory, which is descriptive. Transitivity is required, and the research results indicate that this condition is typically met. Some theorists have attempted to fit equity theory within the expectancy theory domain, but to do so requires considerable ad hoc extrapolation. The data indicate that the two are best viewed as complementary, operating in different domains and often with different kinds of people.

Construct Validity

Construct validity does present a problem for expectancy theory. Different measures of what is supposed to be the same construct often do not correlate well. The problem may derive in part from the multiple versions of the theory, but it is also due to a general tendency to rather loose formulations that often make it possible to bend the theory to handle unexpected results. There is a need for more precise theoretical definitions of constructs, especially that of expectancy itself.

External Influences

The ideal way to activate or influence the processes of expectancy theory is through the design of a highly rationalized reward contingent organization, with rewards tailored to individual wants, sizable opportunities for both extrinsic and intrinsic rewards available to good performers, and considerable opportunity to see that performance really matters. Cafeteria compensation systems and the elimination of pay secrecy are consistent with these objectives. Unfortunately, we know little about what effect instituting a comprehensive influence system of this kind has; the needed field research has not been done. Deci's (1975) theory and research suggest that the consequences would be disastrous, because intrinsic motivation would be undermined. However, given that high levels of intrinsic motivation tend to be impervious to extrinsic effects and that the phenomena described by Deci do not appear to operate where there is an implicit inducement contributions norm, as there is in the employment context, the relevance of his theory can be questioned.

Vocational Choice

Vroom's (1964) original theory contained explicit propositions dealing with vocational choice, as well as performance and satisfaction. The research on vocational choice has not only been sizable in volume, but it has yielded predictions more consistently and generally at a higher level than either performance or satisfaction. Often nonexpectancy theory variables such as peer and family pressures have been added into the predictor sets in these studies with quite favorable results. This very fact, however, appears to underline the limited scope of expectancy theory itself.

Talent Supply

The implication of the theory is that given a suitably rationalized reward contingent organization, one would want to employ people as high on the various expectancy theory measures as possible. Although knowledge of such individuals is far from complete, it is apparent that they tend to be internals who view events in their lives as subject to their own control. Direct data on talent supplies for the expectancy constructs are lacking, but there is evidence that external thinking is widely prevalent in the younger generations. Thus, as with achievement motivation and managerial motivation, expectancy motivation (effort) appears to be in relatively short supply at the present time.

Conclusions

With improvements in measurement and experimental design, expectancy theory has clearly emerged as one of the most powerful theories of organizational motivation. However, contrary to some of the early thinking, it has proved to be very much a limited domain theory. What is most needed now is to study the operation of the theory in field settings, manipulating both organizational environments and individual differences. The resultant contribution to our knowledge of organizational functioning and effectiveness could be sizable.

GOAL-SETTING THEORY

Locke's theory of goal setting emerged gradually through a long series of research publications. However, in the late 1960s and early 1970s, he made several attempts to formalize his theoretical thinking (Locke, 1968, 1969, 1970; Locke, Cartledge, and Knerr, 1970). These publications represent his major theoretical contributions. Throughout, Locke has been strongly influenced by the work of Ryan (1970). Reviews of goal-setting research generally have been published by Latham and Yukl (1975) and Steers and Porter (1974) and of the relevant management by objectives literature by Carroll and Tosi (1973).

Measurement

Probably because of the initial focus on laboratory research, goal-setting theory has elicited little attention to measurement issues. The only major concern of this kind has been with whether management by objectives does indeed "take" and result in significant goal setting. Measures to determine the facts in this regard have been developed. In general, the central concepts of the theory, such as the goals set and performance relative to them, are relatively clear-cut. Other constructs, such as values and emotional reactions, are not: they typically have not generated measures, and accordingly, research related to them is practically nonexistent.

Prediction of Performance

Goal-setting theory does predict performance levels relatively well, but not for everyone and under all circumstances. In a general sense, goal specificity, goal difficulty, and participation in goal setting are related positively to performance. Yet goal specificity works best with people having strong higher order needs and achievement motivation; goal difficulty, with individuals having strong achievement motivation, more confidence and self-assurance, greater maturity and better education, as well as among whites rather than blacks; and participation with the less well educated, blacks, those with low achievement motivation, and among those used to participation. It would appear that Locke obtained consistently positive results in his studies largely because he used college students as subjects. Typically, Locke used assigned rather than participative goal setting.

There is also evidence that the positive performance effects are contingent on independent rather than interacting tasks, where coordination of effort is not required. Individual goal setting in a top management team can create problems. Also, the motivating effects of difficult goals have a distinct tendency to dissipate over time, and specific efforts are required to reactivate them.

Prediction of Work Satisfactions

Although the theory is explicit in its statement that dissatisfaction is a consequence of discrepancies between performance and either goals or values, relatively little research has been done on these hypotheses. What has been done has been done by Locke and is confirmatory, but there is a need for more investigation, especially since the studies have been entirely of a laboratory nature.

Theoretical Domain

Locke notes explicitly that his theory does not deal with how goals are developed or how goal acceptance occurs, in spite of the fact that it applies·to accepted goals only. It is probably for this reason that individual differences are not incorporated in the theory nor utilized to establish its domain. Yet it is apparent that the theory is applicable only to certain kinds of people, probably those with an underlying need structure placing competitive striving high in their motivational hierarchies.

Attempts have been made to ally the domain of goal-setting theory with that of expectancy theory in one manner or another. Locke (1975), however, rejects this and with considerable cogency. The theories differ strongly on such matters as unconscious motivation, hedonism, and expectancy-performance relationship. There may be a certain degree of overlap, but it appears likely that each occupies considerable independent territory.

Construct Validity

The theory predicts that the performance effects of knowledge of results, time limits, and monetary incentives can be accounted for in terms of implicit goal setting: such predictions of related phenomena give considerable meaning to the goal-setting construct. Overall, the research results tend to support the idea that goal setting often is implicit in these phenomena. On the other hand, it does not account for all of the variance, once again suggesting a more limited domain for the theory than Locke originally posited. In any event, the fact that these extrapolations work at all gives greater confidence in the underlying validity and power of the goal-setting construct.

External Influences

The major approach currently used to activate motivation based on goal setting is a formal management by objectives program, although this technique actually antedates modern goal-setting theory. The research on the technique is far from universally favorable. Difficulties appear to arise because of the interactive nature of much managerial work, the tendency for the motivating effects of difficult goals to dissipate over time, and the failure of certain individuals to be responsive to goal setting at all. The evidence suggests that isolated goal setting in the dyadic superior-subordinate relationship can be much more effective than a comprehensive management by objectives program, which shortly loses its legitimacy. In this context, whether goals should be assigned or influenced strongly by the subordinate appears to depend on the subordinate, the nature of the relationship, and the question at issue.

Vocational Choice

Goal-setting theory has not concerned itself with vocational choice to date, although it might well make a contribution in predicting the occupational level that a person would strive for and achieve. There is a potential here that has not been realized.

Talent Supply

Because individual differences have not been of concern, the talent supply question has also been neglected. It would be useful to have data on such matters as the proportion of the population likely to accept hard goals and the proportion really responsive to goal setting at all. The thrust of the theory and of the research to it has not been such as to delve into this type of question.

Conclusions

Goal-setting theory has considerable explanatory and predictive power — of that there can be no question. Yet like so many other theories considered, it appears to operate with maximum effectiveness within a much narrower domain than originally envisioned. How this domain relates to that of other theories is difficult to specify, in part at least because the whole matter of how individual differences determine boundary conditions is not clear. In any event, the earlier complaint that goal-setting theory was a completely unknown entity outside the laboratory settings where it originated is now outdated. The theory has been shown to possess validity in the organizational context.

BEHAVIOR MODIFICATION THEORY

Behavior modification theory as applied to organizations owes a strong debt to Skinner (1953, 1971, 1974), but it has actually been developed by others. The initial statement was that of Nord (1969). However, the currently most fully developed versions are those of Hamner (1974), Luthans and Kreitner (1975), and Goldstein and Sorcher (1974). Critical reviews from varying perspectives, some of them dealing with ethical issues as well, have been provided by Locke (1977), Mitchell (1976), Schneier (1974), and Stolz, Wienckowski, and Brown (1975).

Measurement

The basic measurement need is to obtain precise behavioral measures of the central performance variables during a baseline period and under conditions of contingent reinforcement. This is much easier to accomplish for manual than for professional and managerial work, and it is primarily for that reason that applications and research have tended to focus on lower level positions. In any application of the theory, there is always a risk that ease of measurement rather than centrality of the variable will determine what performance factor is reinforced, with the result that little if any job-related change is produced.

Prediction of Performance

There is ample evidence that contingent reinforcement influences performance. However, this finding is equally derivable from expectancy theory. Where the two theories depart, with expectancy theory emphasizing continuous reinforcement and behavior modification theory variable — and especially variable ratio — reinforcement, the data support the expectancy theory formulations. In the organizational context, continuous reinforcement is much more powerful than behavior modification theory would lead one to expect.

In general, behavior modification techniques appear to work best in improving performance in highly controllable contexts and with variables of an independent and separate nature, such as absenteeism. In more complex situations, involving quantity-quality interactions and interdependent tasks, they work less well. Efforts to use them in quality control have not been successful. There is also evidence from a number of broad-scale applications in organizations that performance effects tend to peak and then taper off over time.

Prediction of Work Satisfactions

The theory does not view internal, mental states such as satisfaction as appropriate for scientific study; at least this is the view of the radical behaviorists, following Skinner. Such mental states are merely collateral products of prior reinforcement histories and have no explanatory force. It is not surprising, given this theoretical orientation, that behavior modification theory has not been used to predict work satisfaction per se.

Theoretical Domain

There is a serious question as to whether behavior modification theory has any unique domain extending outside the boundaries established for expectancy theory and goal-setting theory; probably it does not. A certain amount of comparative research involving both of these other theories has been conducted, generally indicating no predictive power for behavior modification approaches above and beyond the approaches derived from other theories.

Construct Validity

The problems of unique domain raise further problems related to construct validity. According to radical behaviorism, there are no internal constructs. Yet one can ask whether this black box approach is not a misinterpretation of the facts, whether the nonconstructs are not really constructs. In a number of respects, the research results from behavior modification parallel those from intentional goal setting very closely — the fall off in performance effects over time and the negative effects on performance in interacting jobs, in particular. Furthermore, a number of the reported performance effects from behavior modification programs occur in a considerably shorter time span than that required for operant learning. Expectancy theory or goal-setting theory can explain these rapid changes; behavior modification theory cannot.

Finally, when dealing with complex organizational contexts, behavior modification theorists, even some who profess a radical Skinnerian orientation, often do invoke internal constructs. This occurs particularly in dealing with modeling or imitation and self-control. Such constructs are introduced to deal with the fact that full reinforcement histories are in a practical sense impossible to obtain for mature working adults, and yet some alternative method of representing these forces is required. All in all, it appears that frequently the nonconstructs of the radical theory are indeed constructs after all and that in this highly unusual sense, construct validity (or is it nonconstruct validity?) is not obtained.

External Influences

Since behavior modification theory is strictly speaking a theory of learning processes, not motivation, we are dealing entirely with effects of external influences. This is particularly evident in the case of shaping and modeling techniques and in the whole process of applied learning as a management development procedure. These approaches, when utilized with managers to teach them to manipulate contingencies of reinforcement for their subordinates, do appear promising. Positive results relating to both subordinate absenteeism and supervisory behavior are reported. However, the whole theory requires a large element of environmental control for adequate utilization. The nonorganizational applications have been with children (often school children), hospitalized mental patients, prisoners, and of course, originally animals. Organizational applications have involved either lower level jobs or the highly controlled context of a formal management development program. Although the domain of the theory may extend to relatively noncontrollable situations, it cannot actually be applied there.

It is also evident that teaching managers to utilize behavior modification techniques is not easy. A major component of this teaching is the use of behavior modeling through role playing. However, evidence from achievement motivation and managerial role motivation training indicates that mental modeling in a person's mind can be at least as effective and perhaps, because it is less threatening, even more effective. It seems likely, therefore, that other techniques could be used to the same ends if the theory incorporated the necessary internal constructs.

Vocational Choice

The very term "choice" is antithetical to the theory. Thus, the lack of research in this area is not surprising.

Talent Supply

Talent for behavior modification theory is a product of genetic and environmental histories. In order to truly measure talent, therefore, one would have to obtain a complete picture not only of a person's history of reinforcement, but of his or her genetic background as well. The impracticalities of doing this have in fact stifled research on talent supplies, as might be anticipated.

Conclusions

Behavior modification theory has stimulated certain practical applications and an approach or set with which managers can approach relationships with subordinates that appear to be useful. However, as theory it does not offer any advantages over other theories, especially expectancy and goal-setting theories, which appear to cover and often extend beyond its total domain. There are a number of areas in which the theory simply does not venture because of its limitation on the use of cognitive variables, and these are often important areas. Whatever its value in other contexts, the theory of behavior modification appears to have little unique value in the organizational setting.

JOB CHARACTERISTICS THEORY

Job characteristics theory is an alternative approach to motivation hygiene theory as an explanation of the motivating effects of job enrichment. The original statement of the theory (Hackman and Lawler, 1971), has been followed by a number of revisions and extensions (Hackman and Oldham, 1976; Oldham, Hackman, and Pearce, 1976; Hackman, 1977). The theory has been strongly influenced by the earlier formulations and research of Turner and Lawrence (1965). Research reviews have been published by Pierce and Dunham (1976) and by White (1978) and related theoretical discussions by Salancik and Pfeffer (1978) and by Schwab and Cummings (1976).

Measurement

Measurement procedures for job characteristics theory variables have evolved slowly from the Turner and Lawrence (1965) study to the Hackman and Lawler (1971) study and finally to the Job Diagnostic Survey (Hackman and Oldham, 1975). The final measures have good reliabilities and discriminate well between jobs. In addition, entirely independent measures have been developed by other investigators that yield very similar results. Overall, the measurement question has been well answered. As a result, it is possible to say with some certainty whether a job enrichment program has actually "taken" in a given situation.

Prediction of Performance

Predictions from the theory to actual job performance have been relatively ineffective. Quantity of output is not incorporated in the theory, although it has been included in actual tests. It makes little difference; the performance results are not impressive. On the other hand, if one moves back a level to intrinsic motivation (force), the findings are much more encouraging, although in some cases they may be enhanced by a bias produced by common method variance.

Prediction in general appears to be better when the core job characteristics are combined on an additive basis than when the partially multiplicative formula of the theory is utilized. In addition, task identity does not appear to be an important factor in the theory. Also, there is a clear need for more experimental studies to untangle the causal web. Much of the research is correlational, and it is not at all clear whether it is the enriched nature of the job or some other factor associated with being enriched that causes the result.

Prediction of Work Satisfaction

Predictions of satisfaction measures have been much more successful than those for performance, and although common method variance is on occasion a problem, there are a number of instances where it is not. Satisfaction-related variables such as actual absenteeism statistics are predicted less well. Turnover, which is included in the theoretical statement, has hardly been studied at all. It appears that when dissatisfaction is really pervasive, not even job enrichment can alleviate it. The hypothesized organizational climate moderator (organic-mechanistic) has only been studied in relation to satisfaction and has not produced results matching the theory.

Theoretical Domain

The domain of the theory is circumscribed by jobs containing some degree of enrichment. Within this context it deals with both people who are and those who are not motivated by the enrichment and thus is more comprehensive within this domain than motivation hygiene theory. The origins of job characteristics theory are in expectancy theory, but in its current form these ties are so loose as to be almost meaningless. Furthermore, the use of need hierarchy theory relates only to the specification of a moderator variable. There is no incorporation of prepotency, for instance. Thus, the theory appears to be very much a limited domain theory of enriched work and its motivational effects.

Construct Validity

Even with the satisfaction outcome, the growth need moderator does not operate to produce clean-cut predictions. However, the characteristics of enriched jobs and of the achievement situation are so similar that one would expect that the use of a component of the global growth need variable, achievement motivation, might produce more substantial differentiations. The data that are available tend to support this conclusion, suggesting that growth need strength works primarily because it incorporates the achievement construct.

Of the job satisfaction moderators, satisfaction with co-workers and perhaps supervision appear to receive the greatest support, apparently because they contribute to the disruption of the enrichment-outcome relationship. If so, direct measures of socially stimulated anger and anxiety might yield cleaner moderating effects and a more precise construct definition.

Finally, there is a serious question as to whether autonomy is an adequate representation of the psychological state of experienced responsibility and whether it really differs from skill variety. The existence of skill variety almost guarantees autonomy from supervision, and thus the two constructs may not be meaningfully separable. Experienced responsibility would probably be better represented by a dimension concerned with the opportunity to attribute results to one's own efforts.

External Influences

One of the strengths of job characteristics theory is that it makes specific predictions as to when job enrichment as an external influence will actually affect motivation. The theory is very specific as to how jobs should be redesigned to achieve motivational effects. The findings suggest that one does best to be very selective in applying the technique, picking people and situations with considerable care, based on findings from some instrument such as the Job Diagnostic Survey.

Vocational Choice

Although research on job choice is not extensive, there is evidence that those with high, as yet unsatisfied growth needs do prefer enriched jobs, rather than job change per se. Job characteristics theory seems to offer considerable potential as a basis for research on vocational choice, but this potential remains unexploited at the present time.

Talent Supply

There is no basis for concluding that a strong desire for more meaningful, challenging, enriched work permeates the population. Most individuals, even in the younger age groups, appear to find jobs with a scope adequate to their needs. Thus, overall there is no reason to conclude that a large reservoir of talent for enriched jobs exists in the population. This conclusion is supported by reference to relevant talent data for need hierarchy theory and achievement motivation theory.

Conclusions

Job characteristics theory appears to be on the right track. There are certain changes that recommend themselves, but these do not in any sense invalidate the theory as a whole. In particular, a closer association with achievement motivation as opposed to need hierarchy theory seems called for. Again, we have an instance of a limited domain theory that works with at least some degree of precision within its home environment. The theory clearly moves in the right direction and performs more effectively within its domain than motivation hygiene theory, but the exact form that it will finally take is not yet fully visible.

ATTEMPTED SYNTHESIS

As an overall generalization, it appears that the broader, grand theories have either failed of research support or settled into a much smaller domain than originally anticipated. Need hierarchy theory and motivation hygiene theory do not have sufficient research support. Behavior modification theory appears to fit into a theoretical space already occupied by expectancy theory and goal-setting theory and to perform less effectively than either within that space.

The other six theories meet the research and other tests sufficiently often to justify considerable optimism regarding them. However, several have had to settle for a smaller domain than might have been expected. This is particularly true of expectancy theory, which appears now to apply only to conscious, rational choice situations and to people who are motivated by such choices. Goal-setting theory also appears to be constrained by individual differences and probably is a theory most appropriate to the competitive context.

The achievement motivation, managerial role motivation, and job characteristics theories all deal with domains defined on the basis of position types or roles. It is thus relatively easy to relate them to each other, and this has been done in the preceding discussion.

Equity theory appears to be like goal-setting theory in that it relates to a specific motivational context, that where equity motivation is aroused. However, in neither case is it apparent what specific external abstraction should be used to define the domain.

It is evident that the motivational terrain map used here does not fall along a single scale. The theories, arising from diverse origins, have carved out domains using different and probably overlapping conceptual dimensions. As a result, there is no systematically constructed map to fill in. The theories, although of limited domain, deal with apples and oranges, and perhaps with pineapples, too. It is not yet possible to sort them out appropriately. On the other hand, it is clear that when the multidimensional puzzle falls together, it will provide a high level of scientific understanding; the diversity of approaches guarantees this.

REFERENCES

Adams, J. Stacy. 1963. "Toward an Understanding of Inequity." *Journal of Abnormal and Social Psychology* 67: 422-36.
——. 1965. "Inequity in Social Exchange." In Leonard Berkowitz, ed., *Advances in Experimental Social Psychology*, vol. 2, pp. 267-99. New York: Academic Press.
Adams, J. Stacy, and Sara Freedman. 1976. "Equity Theory Revisited: Comments and Annotated Bibliography." In Leonard Berkowitz and Elaine Walster, eds., *Advances in Experimental Social Psychology*, vol. 9, pp. 43-90. New York: Academic Press.
Alderfer, Clayton P. 1972. *Existence, Relatedness, and Growth: Human Needs in Organizational Settings.* New York: Free Press.
Atkinson, John W. 1977. "Motivation for Achievement." In T. Blass, ed., *Personality Variables in Social Behavior*, pp. 25-108. Hillsdale, N.J.: Erlbaum Associates.
Atkinson, John W., and Joel O. Raynor. 1974. *Motivation and Achievement.* Washington, D.C.: Winston.
Bockman, Valerie M. 1971. "The Herzberg Controversy." *Personnel Psychology* 24: 155-89.
Brief, Arthur P.; Ramon J. Aldag; and Thomas I. Chacko. 1977. "The Miner Sentence Completion Scale: An Appraisal." *Academy of Management Journal* 20: 635-43.
Campbell, John P., and Robert D. Pritchard. 1976. "Motivation Theory in Industrial and Organizational Psychology." In Marvin D. Dunnette, ed., *Handbook of Industrial and Organizational Psychology*, pp. 63-130. Chicago: Rand McNally.
Carroll, Stephen J., and Henry L. Tosi. 1973. *Management by Objectives: Applications and Research.* New York: Macmillan.
Deci, Edward L. 1975. *Intrinsic Motivation.* New York: Plenum.
Galbraith, Jay, and Larry L. Cummings. 1967. "An Empirical Investigation of the Motivational Determinants of Task Performance: Interactive Effects between Instrumentality-Valence and Motivation-Ability." *Organizational Behavior and Human Performance* 2: 237-57.
Georgopoulos, Basil S.; Gerald M. Mahoney; and Nyle W. Jones. 1957. "A Path-Goal Approach to Productivity." *Journal of Applied Psychology* 41: 345-53.

Goldstein, Arnold P., and Melvin Sorcher. 1974. *Changing Supervisor Behavior.* New York: Pergamon.

Goodman, Paul S., and Abraham Friedman. 1971. "An Examination of Adams' Theory of Inequity." *Administrative Science Quarterly* 16: 271-88.

Graen, George. 1969. "Instrumentality Theory of Work Motivation: Some Experimental Results and Suggested Modifications." *Journal of Applied Psychology Monograph* 53, no. 2.

Hackman, J. Richard. 1977. "Work Design." In J. Richard Hackman and J. Lloyd Suttle, eds., *Improving Life at Work: Behavioral Science Approaches to Organizational Change,* pp. 96-162. Santa Monica, Calif.: Goodyear.

Hackman, J. Richard, and Edward E. Lawler. 1971. "Employee Reactions to Job Characteristics." *Journal of Applied Psychology* 55: 259-86.

Hackman, J. Richard, and Greg R. Oldham. 1975. "Development of the Job Diagnostic Survey." *Journal of Applied Psychology* 60: 159-70.

——. 1976. "Motivation through the Design of Work: Test of a Theory." *Organizational Behavior and Human Performance* 16: 250-79.

Hackman, Ray C. 1969. *The Motivated Working Adult.* New York: American Management Association.

Hamner, W. Clay. 1974. "Reinforcement Theory and Contingency Management in Organizational Settings." In Henry L. Tosi and W. Clay Hamner, eds., *Organizational Behavior and Management: A Contingency Approach,* pp. 86-112. Chicago: St. Clair.

Heckhausen, Heinz. 1967. *The Anatomy of Achievement Motivation.* New York: Academic Press.

Herzberg, Frederick. 1966. *Work and the Nature of Man.* Cleveland, Ohio: World.

——. 1976. *The Managerial Choice: To Be Efficient and To Be Human.* Homewood, Ill.: Dow-Jones-Irwin.

Herzberg, Frederick; Bernard Mausner; and Barbara S. Snyderman. 1959. *The Motivation to Work.* New York: Wiley.

Jacques, Elliott. 1970. *Equitable Payment.* London: Heinemann.

King, Nathan. 1970. "Clarification and Evaluation of the Two-Factor Theory of Job Satisfaction." *Psychological Bulletin* 74: 18-31.

Latham, Gary P., and Gary A. Yukl. 1975. "A Review of Research on the Application of Goal Setting in Organizations." *Academy of Management Journal* 18: 824-45.

Lawler, Edward E. 1973. *Motivation in Organizations.* Monterey, Calif.: Brooks/ Cole.

Locke, Edwin A. 1968. "Toward a Theory of Task Motivation and Incentives." *Organizational Behavior and Human Performance* 3: 157-89.

——. 1969. "What Is Job Satisfaction?" *Organizational Behavior and Human Performance* 4: 309-36.

——. 1970. "Job Satisfaction and Job Performance: A Theoretical Analysis." *Organizational Behavior and Human Performance* 5: 484-500.

——. 1975. "Personnel Attitudes and Motivation." *Annual Review of Psychology* 26: 457-80.

——. 1977. "The Myths of Behavior Mod in Organizations." *Academy of Management Review* 2: 543-53.

Locke, Edwin A.; Norman Cartledge; and Claramae S. Knerr. 1970. "Studies of the Relationship between Satisfaction, Goal-Setting, and Performance." *Organizational Behavior and Human Performance* 5: 135-58.

Luthans, Fred, and Robert Kreitner. 1975. *Organizational Behavior Modification*. Glenview, Ill.: Scott, Foresman.

Maslow, Abraham H. 1943. "A Theory of Human Motivation." *Psychological Review* 50: 370-96.

——. 1954. *Motivation and Personality*. New York: Harper and Row.

——. 1962. *Toward a Psychology of Being*. Princeton, N.J.: Van Nostrand.

——. 1967. "A Theory of Metamotivation: The Biological Rooting of the Value-Life." *Journal of Humanistic Psychology* 7: 93-127.

McClelland, David C. 1961. *The Achieving Society*. Princeton, N.J.: Van Nostrand.

——. 1975. *Power: The Inner Experience*. New York: Irvington.

McClelland, David C., and David G. Winter. 1969. *Motivating Economic Achievement*. New York: Free Press.

McGregor, Douglas. 1960. *The Human Side of Enterprise*. New York: McGraw-Hill.

Miner, John B. 1965. *Studies in Management Education*. Atlanta: Organizational Measurement Systems Press.

——. 1974. *The Human Constraint*. Washington, D.C.: BNA Books.

——. 1975. "The Uncertain Future of the Leadership Concept: An Overview." In J. G. Hunt and L. L. Larson, eds., *Leadership Frontiers*, pp. 197-208. Kent, Ohio: Comparative Administration Research Institute, Kent State University.

——. 1977. *Motivation to Manage: A Ten-Year Update on the "Studies in Management Education" Research*. Atlanta: Organizational Measurement Systems Press.

——. 1978a. "The Miner Sentence Completion Scale: A Reappraisal." *Academy of Management Journal* 21: 283-94.

——. 1978b. "Twenty Years of Research on Role-Motivation Theory of Managerial Effectiveness." *Personnel Psychology* 31: 739-60.

——. 1979. "Limited Domain Theories of Organizational Energy." In C. C. Pinder and L. F. Moore, eds., *Middle Range Theory and the Study of Organizations*. Leiden, Netherlands: Martinus Nijhoff.

——. 1980. *Theories of Organizational Behavior*. Chicago: Dryden.

Mitchell, Terence R. 1974. "Expectancy Models of Job Satisfaction, Occupational Preference, and Effort: A Theoretical, Methodological, and Empirical Appraisal." *Psychological Bulletin* 81: 1053-77.

——. 1976. "Cognitions and Skinner: Some Questions About Behavioral Determinism." *Organization and Administrative Sciences* 6, no. 4: 63-72.

Nord, Walter R. 1969. "Beyond the Teaching Machine: The Neglected Area of Operant Conditioning in the Theory and Practice of Management." *Organizational Behavior and Human Performance* 4: 375-401.

Oldham, Greg R.; J. Richard Hackman; and Jone L. Pearce. 1976. "Conditions Under Which Employees Respond Positively to Enriched Work." *Journal of Applied Psychology* 61: 395–403.

Pierce, Jon L., and Randall B. Dunham. 1976. "Task Design: A Literature Review." *Academy of Management Review* 1, no. 4: 83–97.

Porter, Lyman W., and Edward E. Lawler. 1968. *Managerial Attitudes and Performance.* Homewood, Ill.: Irwin.

Ryan, Thomas A. 1970. *Intentional Behavior: An Approach to Human Motivation.* New York: Ronald.

Salancik, Gerald R., and Jeffrey Pfeffer. 1978. "A Social Information processing Approach to Job Attitudes and Task Design." *Administrative Science Quarterly* 23: 224–53.

Schneier, Craig E. 1974. "Behavior Modification in Management: A Review and Critique." *Academy of Management Journal* 17: 528–48.

Schwab, Donald P., and Larry L. Cummings. 1976. "A Theoretical Analysis of the Impact of Task Scope on Employee Performance." *Academy of Management Review* 1: 23–35.

Skinner, B. F. 1953. *Science and Human Behavior.* New York: Macmillan.

———. 1971. *Beyond Freedom and Dignity.* New York: Knopf.

———. 1974. *About Behaviorism.* New York: Knopf.

Steers, Richard M., and Lyman W. Porter. 1974. "The Role of Task-Goal Attributes in Employee Performance." *Psychological Bulletin* 81: 434–52.

Stolz, Stephanie B.; Louis A. Wienckowski; and Bertram S. Brown. 1975. "Behavior Modification: a Perspective on Critical Issues." *American Psychologist* 30: 1027–48.

Turner, Arthur N., and Paul R. Lawrence. 1965. *Industrial Jobs and the Worker: An Investigation of Response to Task Attributes.* Boston: Harvard Graduate School of Business Administration.

Veroff, Joseph, and Joanne B. Veroff. 1972. "Reconsideration of a Measure of Power Motivation." *Psychological Bulletin* 78: 279–91.

Vroom, Victor H. 1964. *Work and Motivation.* New York: Wiley.

Wahba, Mahmoud A., and Lawrence G. Bridwell. 1976. "Maslow Reconsidered: A Review of Research on the Need Hierarchy Theory." *Organizational Behavior and Human Performance* 15: 212–40.

Wahba, Mahmoud A., and Robert J. House. 1974. "Expectancy Theory in Work and Motivation: Some Logical and Methodological Issues." *Human Relations* 27: 121–47.

Weick, Karl E. 1966. "The Concept of Equity in the Perception of Pay." *Administrative Science Quarterly* 11: 414–39.

Weiner, Bernard. 1972. *Theories of Motivation: From Mechanism to Cognition.* Chicago: Markham.

White, J. Kenneth. 1978. "Individual Differences and the Job Quality-Worker Response Relationship: Review, Integration, and Comments." *Academy of Management Review* 3: 267–80.

Winter, David G. 1973. *The Power Motive.* New York: Free Press.

Wolf, Martin G. 1970. "Need Gratification Theory: A Theoretical Reformulation and Job Motivation." *Journal of Applied Psychology* 54: 87–94.

Chapter 5

Decisionmaking in a Complex Organization

Roger I. Hall*

In searching for a theory to explain organizational decisionmaking, first, the evolutionary theory of organizing is interpreted in terms of short-run planning and budgeting behavior. Second, the behavioral theory of the firm is summarized and updated to supply the missing pieces concerning the cognitive and political processes used by policy elites to resolve complexity and uncertainty. A model of organizational decisionmaking that combines the evolutionary and behavioral principles is presented. Arguments are put forward for integrating different levels of analysis — the individual, the group, and the organization — into a model of the organization as an entity with its own "organizational mind." Finally, some implications are drawn concerning future research.

* University of Manitoba

The author wishes to thank his colleague Dr. W. T. Notz for directing his attention to the literature on evolutionary principle of organizing, and, similarly, his colleagues Dr. N. R. Roos and Dr. L. L. Roos, Jr., for directing his attention to the literature on cognitive maps of policy elites. Without their generous and stimulating sharing of ideas this study would not have materialized.

This study was supported in part by a Bronfman Faculty Fellowship and a Department of External Affairs (Government of Canada) travel grant.

INTERPRETING THE EVOLUTIONARY
THEORY OF ORGANIZATIONAL
DECISIONMAKING

Weick (1969) has postulated a theory of organizing that is based upon amendments to Campbell's (1965) sociocultural evolution model. This theory offers a framework for modeling the period decisionmaking behavior of a firm concerned with its annual planning and budgeting activities. An interpretation of Weick's theory for this limited purpose follows.

Weick's Theory

An organization evolves enactment, selection, and retention processes that enable it to handle ambiguous information resulting from the interaction of the organization's actions with its environments. In this way, the organization adapts to its complex enacted environments in a way that enhances survival and allows it to build upon successes. The theory is illustrated in diagrammatic form in Figure 5-1.

The enacted environments consist of an external environment created, to a large extent, by the actions of the firm when it offers its goods and services to potential customers and an internal environment created when the organization hires people and organizes them into a hierarchy to accomplish its purposes. These environments are also subject to uncontrollable external events such as changing economic conditions, the behavior of competitors, and shifts in societal norms. The variation, arising from the reaction of the environments to the firm's policy decisions, is handled by a series of equivocality-reducing procedures emanating from the organization's retained storehouse of knowledge.

Removing Equivocality

The enactment, selection, and retention processes seek to remove equivocality in the information so that the organization has a solid base from which to take action. Removing informational equivocality, for example, allows the organization to make sense of its environments, recognize problems, diagnose their cause, decide which problem to tackle first, and choose a policy to solve a clearly recognized problem. Without such a mechanism, the organization would be paralyzed by its inability to recognize whether it has a problem and to decide what action it should take, and without such

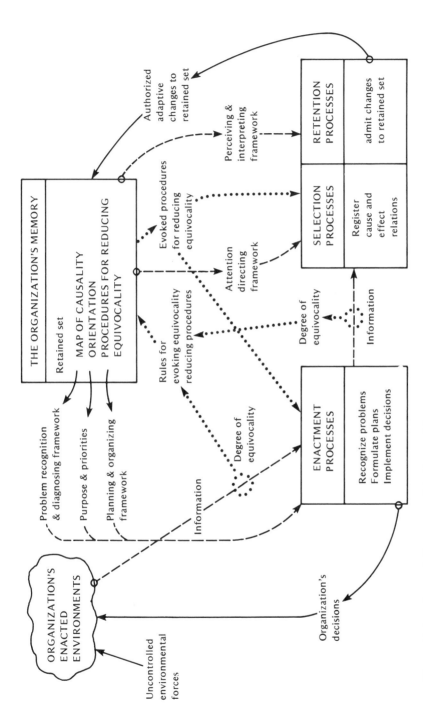

Figure 5-1. An evolutionary model of organizing.

a planning and organizing structure, its actions would be purely random.

An organization may start out its life by making random trials or, more likely, by choosing actions based on a very rudimentary map of causality. The choice of action will result from the enactment processes, which are derived by the planning and organizing procedures retained in the organization's memory.

Information, discernible from the organization's actions upon its environments, will be registered by the selection processes. These processes are governed by the perceiving and interpreting framework supplied by the retained set. Those relationships selected for attention are now available for retention in the organization's map of causality and hence may influence future decisions.

The retention process is used to admit the relationships, thus selected, to the organization's storehouse of knowledge — its memory, so to speak. It may reject or edit that which is selected to fit the existing set of retained knowledge or modify the existing set in light of the new information or even discredit the existing set and adopt its converse.

For example, the selection system of a firm may register that the sales of its products appear to be price elastic. If this coincides with the retained belief, the latter may be modified by incorporating the latest information on the sensitivity of the price-demand relationship. If it conflicts with the retained belief and is not clearly established, because the firm made other moves that confounded the results, then the selected information may be rejected. On the other hand, if the newly selected relationship is clearly demonstrated to hold, then the old retained set may become discredited and its opposite established. The retained set is now available for influencing both the enactment process (e.g., relationships to be used in choosing action) and the selection and retention process (e.g., retained procedures for selecting relationships to be retained).

Interlocking Behavioral Cycles

Each of the processes of enactment, selection, and retention comprise interlocking behavioral cycles or procedures learned from experience and retained for reducing equivocality and assembly rules or criteria for evoking these cycles. For example, "avoid conflict" might be an enactment process criteria for evoking procedures (behavioral cycles) for choosing among contending acts or policies (an equivocal situation) for solving a particular problem. This will result in a search for a subset of available policies that will rectify the unsatisfactory situation, yet does not violate the achievement of other goals and hence incur the wrath of the coalitions in the organization that identify themselves with these other goals. This would give rise to an equivocal situation. The behavioral cycles are therefore interlocking in that the actions proposed by one part of the organization has to take into account the reactive behavior of another part. This double play has been noted by Crozier and Thoenig (1976) for a public administration system and also forms the basis for the quasiresolution of conflict concept in Cyert and March's (1963) *A Behavioral Theory of the Firm*. It becomes institutionalized in rules such as: look for a solution that is acceptable to other parts of the organization.

Yet another attribute of this interlocking process concerns the number of behavioral cycles evoked for choosing, say, among contending alternative solutions. In order to reduce the number of available alternatives (an equivocal situation), several retained procedures may be invoked. For example, the aforementioned enactment process rule "avoid conflict" might result in, say, two or three equally attractive policies being available to solve a pressing problem. The choice can be further narrowed by applying another rule, such as "frequently used." One policy may now appear clearly better than the others because it has been used successfully before and, at the same time, avoids organizational conflict.

The same procedures apply to the selection and retention process — namely, rules or criteria are used to evoke interlocking cycles of behavior for removing equivocality. The information resulting from the implementation of the behavioral cycles evoked by the assembly rules will now become available for the selection and retention processes. Certain parts of the information will be perceived and selected to modify the organization's retained set. This knowledge then becomes available for controlling the enactment and selection processes and so forth. In this way, past successful cycles are retained to influence future actions.

These intuitive processes seek to minimize informational equivocality so that the organization can make sense of its environment, learn from its experience, and order its actions. It has similarities to human learning (Piaget, 1966), which is perhaps not surprising, since organizations consist of people! It enables the organization to deal with an environment that may be several orders of magnitude more complex than the cognitive abilities of the organization, or the people in it, can comprehend. Weick's theory of organizing is very rich in conceptual material, and this brief interpretation cannot do it justice. However, it does provide a framework for viewing the short-run planning and budgeting activities of a firm as a set of enactment, selection, and retention processes comprising interlocking procedures evoked from the organization's memory to reduce equivocality. What are these procedures for reducing equivocality, and what are the criteria used to evoke them? Cyert and March's (1963) behavioral theory of the firm seems to be directed at answering these questions, and we shall now turn our attention to this theory.

SUMMARIZING AND UPDATING THE BEHAVIORAL THEORY OF THE FIRM

Much of the insight into the organizational decisionmaking process derives from the original work of Cyert and March (1963). To this must be added the subsequent findings of other researchers in this field. This section attempts to interpret the theory as it pertains to periodic short-run policy decisions.

The authors of the theory describe organizational decisionmaking in terms of four interrelated concepts: (1) quasi-resolution of conflict, (2) uncertainty avoidance, (3) problemistic search, and (4) organizational learning.

Quasi-Resolution of Conflict

It appears that decision makers find ways of avoiding, where possible, the conflict arising from the interrelatedness of goals and the opposing actions often required for achieving these goals. Take, for example, the situation where more profit may be obtained for a firm by reducing sales promotion expenditure, but only at the expense of its sales goal. The conflict inherent in this kind of situation is sidestepped by such strategies as delegating goal setting to subunits in the organization, which then attempt to obtain their own goals independently. In proposing actions to further its goals, each subunit views the goals of the others as constraints on its actions and tries to avoid conflict by putting forward decisions that are acceptable to the other coalitions — that is, that do not violate the achievement of the other subunit goals. Furthermore, the conflict inherent in trying to satisfy irreconcilable coalition goals simultaneously is avoided by attending to the goals one at a time.

The conflict often present in organizational decisionmaking is not always suppressed, and in some instances, power becomes the criterion for making decisions. The results of a longitudinal study conducted by Pettigrew (1973) of an important decision in a company suggests that the past evolutionary processes, by which the various specialist activities in the organization interacted with each other and the organization's changing environment, will have determined the formation of coalitions and their relative power and status. It will also have determined the social structure through which demands on the organization's resources are processed. Power and status enable a coalition to make demands on the organization's resources. A successful power strategy depends on (1) accuracy of the coalition's (or its leader's) perceptions of how the structure for processing demands works; (2) maintaining of political credit with superiors (for example, failure of recommendations to achieve the promised results can ruin the credibility of the coalition with superiors; and (3) threats or opportunities offered by the environment that undermine one coalition's power base and increase another's.

Important decisions affecting the relative status and power of coalitions will be a source of hostility and conflict. Coalitions will try to marshal enough power to turn the decisions in their favor. Decisions characterized by a number of feasible alternatives, a degree of uncertainty about the nature of the problem or task for which the decision is needed, and a number of conflicting or differing criteria that cannot be reduced to a single index for evaluating the alternatives will be decided on the basis of power. The coalition with the most successful power strategy will force the decision that is most inline with its interests — that is, it will help its members to maintain or enhance their relative status and power position in the organization.

A corollary to this proposition is that when resources are in short supply and goals are not being met, the decision as to whose goals should remain unsatisfied and whose excess resources are to be absorbed or diverted into meeting goals will be largely political — the dominant coalition will decide. Similarly, the dominant group can exercise its right to the exclusive use of newly created organizational resources.

Uncertainty Avoidance

Decisionmakers find ways of avoiding the uncertainties arising from their general inability to correctly anticipate future events, such as the reaction of the organization's environment to its decisions, by such exigencies as crisis management and trying to control the environment. Crisis management involves waiting for problems to arise on a day-by-day basis and then reacting to them. If there is uncertainty or argument about whether a problem is imminent, it is obviously easier to wait until there is no doubt about it — for example, a perceptible deviation from a planned or budgeted target.

The uncertainty associated with the organization's environment can be reduced if the environment can be controlled. This taming of the environment can be achieved in a number of ways. If companies in an industry all use the same price markup procedures, then the relative prices of their products remain fairly stable over time and the market share of each company becomes much more predictable. So one way of effecting this control is by using standard industry practices. The internal environment can be mastered in a similar way by employing standard company practices embodied in planning rules.

Planning and budgeting can be viewed as activities for reducing ambiguity. Meeting the plan or budget becomes the focus of management decisionmaking, rather than grappling with an uncertain environment with its tendency to indecision. To some extent the plan or budget can be made self-fulfilling by manipulating the slack resources in the organization, thus removing another source of uncertainty. The slack in the system is built up during good times, when the organization's goals are oversubscribed, and used up in hard times, when its goals are not being met. The organization effectively irons out the unevennesses of the external environment.

In addition, Lindblom (1968) has observed that decisionmakers prefer to make small incremental decisions and to wait for some feedback of results before proceeding further. This is yet another way of avoiding the uncertainty inherent in predicting outcomes in a complex environment.

The participants in an organization use simplified models of causality for their policy determinations until driven to use more complex ones (Cyert and March, 1963). It would seem that although participants bring a variety of skills to bear on the organization's tasks, the converse is true for the cognitive processes of interpreting how the environmental system works and interfaces with the organization's actions. Axelrod (1976) has puzzled over this for public policy decisions, and in studying the cognitive maps or mental models used by policymakers to guide their actions, he has come to the conclusion that the maps are simplified to help the decisionmakers keep track of a large number of causal assertions. As he put it: "The picture of a decision maker that emerges from the analysis of cognitive maps is one who has more beliefs than he can handle, who employs a simplified image of the policy environment that is structurally easy to operate with, and who then acts rationally within the context of his simplified image" (p. 112).

One simplification of cognitive maps is the absence of feedback loops. Axelrod argues that not only is it hard to recognize spontaneously, because we conceptualize causation as flowing in one direction and not turning back upon itself, but also it is difficult to learn as an abstract principle readily generalizable from one instance to another. Forrester (1968:3.3) comes to a similar conclusion:

> Our experience comes from observing the simplest, usually first-order, system. When the same expectations are applied to more extensive systems the wrong results are often obtained. . . . Because we cannot mentally manage all the facts of a complex system at one time, we tend to break the system into pieces and draw conclusions separately from the sub-systems. Such fragmentation fails to show how the sub-systems interact.

The inability to spontaneously recognize feedback loops in complex systems seems, then, to be a general human failing. In large bureaucracies with departmental barriers to communication among organizational members, one would expect each subunit to possess only a fragment of the entire map of systemic cause-and-effect and never to see the recursive relations among the fragments.

A second simplification of the cognitive maps of policymaking elites put forward by Axelrod concerns the lack of indeterminancy. Indeterminancy occurs when there are two or more sides to an argument about the effectiveness of a policy. A simple example might involve the desirability of increasing a firm's revenues by increasing the price of its products. On the one hand, if there is no loss of customers, increasing prices will increase revenues, but on the other hand, if customers are lost or buy less as a result of the price increase, then the issue is not so clear. In the absence of precise economic or marketing data, which is often the case, decisionmaking groups, it appears, will come to believe that, for example, the product is price inelastic and from then on will ignore one side of the price-demand-revenue argument. Thus the cognitive map is made determinant. The determinancy in many instances cannot be verified in complex policy situations and therefore rests on belief born of practice or disseminated through the organization's culture or guiding ideology (Pettigrew, 1977). It greatly simplifies the decisional task of a group if they have a common, albeit simplified, map of their world. The maps then become integrated in the set of beliefs comprising the organization's internal culture and thence remain remarkably stable over long periods of time.

A third simplification of these cognitive maps noted by Axelrod concerns the reduction in the number of causal links in the various paths through the map from action to supposed outcome. Each path represents an argument — such as more promotion expenditure brings in more customers, which increases unit sales, which raises revenues and profits. If there are a number of paths, some containing a small and some a large number of links, then it appears that policymakers either subjectively reduce the number of links in the long paths to some manageable proportion or prefer paths or arguments with the fewest links. To summarize Axelrod's findings, decisionmakers subjectively simplify their cognitive maps or causality by reducing the number of links in the paths through the maps and by ignoring some paths to resolve indeterminancy. They seem to be totally blind to recursive paths of causality that produce feedback loops.

Steinbrunner (1974:112-24) summarizes the cognitive processes for subjectively resolving complexity as the principle of reinforcement and weight of information in memory, inconsistency-management mechanism, and the effects of small group interactions. The reinforcement principle states that the strength of a belief is a function of the number of times that its use has been followed by rewards. Also, the amount of stored information organized under a given belief will determine in part its strength and resistance to change. The strength of a belief also derives from the structural configuration in which it is manipulated and stored in human memory. Mechanisms of the brain attempt to maintain a coherent interlocking set of beliefs by rejecting inconsistent ideas. Last, social interactions among members of a group under pressures of inconsistency can result in convergence to a uniform belief, which Steinbrunner (1974:121) refers to as follows: "The well-known tendency in informal social groupings for individual members to agree on important salient beliefs and even to purge apostates from their midst seems in all likelihood both cause and effect of the cognitive consequences of such social interactions."

An explanation for this phenomenon is supplied by Weick (1969:11), who suggests that groups form around primitive issues, are predominantly emotional, but vacillate less over issues than individuals. We might surmise that an individual joins a group for the "primitive" purpose of surviving in the organization and pursuing his or her own career objectives. He or she associates with people of like mind who form a coalition. Those professional activities of common interest (be it production, marketing, or whatever) that bring pleasure and fulfillment to the members (feelings of emotion) become enshrined as goals. Group cohesion is formed by accepting the lowest common denominator of belief to maintain group membership. A consistent pattern of interlocking and reinforcing beliefs becomes established. Thereafter, any new members are carefully screened and socially conditioned to accept the official system of beliefs, which becomes self-perpetuating. Last, new information is accepted only within the structural configuration of beliefs; it does not change the beliefs.

Problemistic Search

Search behavior by organizations, it seems, is stimulated only when a problem appears and is suppressed when the first satisfactory solution is obtained. The pattern of search is simpleminded and, as we have seen, proceeds on the basis of elementary models or maps of causality until driven to more complex ones. The pattern of search also proceeds in ever widening circles from solutions suggested by the symptoms, to solutions that worked for this problem before, to solutions that absorb the slack of excess resources in the system. This pattern of search is biased by the particular local expertise of the unit undertaking the search and usually commences among the variables within the control of the problem solvers. This implies that a sales department, for example, when faced with a dissatisfied goal such as poor sales growth, first looks to the symptoms of the problem, say loss of customers, and the alternatives this suggests, such as reduce prices or increase promotion efforts. Second, if one of these alternatives has been used successfully before, it will be the preferred one. Third, if neither of these alternatives is satisfactory, a search may be undertaken into areas where slack exists.

Thus, for instance, if it transpires that the production department has excess resources, pressure will be brought to bear to divert these to the sales goal by forcing the department to give better customer service, to improve quality, or simply to reduce the production budget and expend the savings so made on promotional activities. In searching for a solution, the marketing department would be biased toward decisions within its direct control such as promotion expenditure. The search process, therefore, attempts to avoid uncertainty and conflict and becomes progressively more political if satisfactory and acceptable decisions are not easily found.

An addition or modification to this concept has been supplied by Rados (1972). He observed that when several alternative solutions are available or easily evoked — as for a repetitive management decision — a more exhaustive search is made for the best solution, rather than choosing the first satisfactory solution that arises.

Organizational Learning

The fourth and last concept of Cyert and March's theory concerns the way organizations learn to accommodate themselves to a changing environment. One adaptive process concerns adjusting aspiration levels for goal achievement in the light of experience. There is a rapid upward adjustment of aspirations when hopes and achievement are coincident (when performance is improving) and a less rapid downward adjustment when performance is deteriorating. The aspiration level is affected also by the performance of comparable organizations.

Organizations learn to pay attention to some parts of their comparative environment and to ignore others. The attention changes over time as comparisons do or do not produce results satisfactory to important coalitions in the organization. In evaluating performance by explicit measurable criteria, organizations learn to attend to some criteria and ignore others, and there are long-run shifts toward indexes that produce generally satisfactory results. The organization's orientation toward the comparative statistics and performance measures that it attends to is therefore a product of those activities at which it was most successful in the past or the activities of interest to the dominant coalition. Managers manage organizational meaning and purpose by emphasizing certain criteria and discrediting others (Pettigrew, 1977).

There is also an adaption in rules for searching for solutions. When the organization discovers a solution by searching in a particular way, it will be more likely to search in that way for problems of the same type arising in the future. Also, a code or language for communicating information in decisionmaking is developed. This code helps classify all possible states of the environment into a smaller number of categories. Learning consists of changes in the classification system dictated by experience. Simple examples of codes might be the performance indexes "profit margin" or "return on investment" that unite in a single ratio differing items of revenue and expense or of profit and capital investment. It helps to resolve indeterminancy in the organization's map of causality.

The cognitive maps of causality, mentioned in the uncertainty avoidance concept, also, it appears, adapt to experience in a limited way. Steinbrunner (1974:136-37) refers to this as a system of beliefs that adapts to new information and experience by incorporating the latter within the already established conceptual structure. This is accomplished without causing any general adjustments or alterations to the structure. For example, new information may cause the belief about the effect of prices on sales in an uncertain environment to strengthen or weaken but not to change radically from, say, a negative correlation to a positive one. Managers tend to look only for confirming results and hardly ever for disconfirming information (Einhorn and Hogarth, 1977).

Turner (1976) suggests that it takes a major crisis before organization undertakes a "cultural readjustment," presumably resulting in a structural realignment of its members' cognitive maps of causality. This change in beliefs appears to coincide with a change in the nature of the uncertainty facing the organization, which if severe enough, triggers a change in the dominant coalition (Pettigrew, 1973). This new coalition can presumably provide the services to cope with this new form of uncertainty. It can now advance its goals by manipulating meaning and purpose to add credit to some goals and discredit others (Pettigrew, 1977). However, the organization can be remarkably resistant to change (Roberts, 1975; Ackoff and Emshoff, 1975), and a substantial change in personnel may be necessary to bring about this restructuring (Nystrom, Hedberg, and Starbuck, 1976). The past is reinterpreted in light of the new set of goals and beliefs (Weick, 1969) to produce new policies to overcome the uncertainty. In this rather disjointed way, organizations adapt their goals and maps of causality to a changing environment.

In summary, organizations accommodate a changing environment by adjusting their aspiration for goal attainment to experience, by learning to pay attention to parts of the comparative environment of interest to important coalitions and ignoring others, by using search procedures that have been proved successful, by developing a code to help classify many possible states into a smaller number to resolve indeterminancy, and by incorporating new environmental information into an established cognitive map of causality. It takes an obvious breakdown of policies heralded by a crisis or sequence of critical problems or substantial change of personnel before a review is undertaken to alter the structure of the organization's map of causality and reformulate its goal priorities.

Interrelationships among the Concepts

As Cyert and March point out, these concepts are heavily interrelated. For example, a problem only becomes recognized (uncertainty avoidance) when an aspiration level for a goal (organizational learning) is not attained. Search for a solution commences from the symptoms of the problem (problemistic search) and proceeds in ever widening circles among available alternatives, variables within the control of the coalition performing the search, and so on, until a satisfactory solution is found. At this time, search activity stops (uncertainty avoidance). The solution itself must not violate the attainment of the goals of other coalitions (quasi-resolution of conflict), and similarly, the solutions proposed by others must not hinder the attainment of the goals of this coalition. This interrelated behavioral theory of organizational decisionmaking can be viewed from Weick's previously defined evolutionary framework as a set of interlocking behavioral cycles evoked by equivocality-reducing criteria or assembly rules. The behavioral theory suggests that these criteria are to reduce conflict, avoid uncertainty in both recognizing problems and finding solutions, and reduce uncertainty and ambiguity in learning to adapt to a complex environment using a simple organizing structure and learning process.

There would appear to be some contradictions among the findings of the researchers of organizational decisionmaking. When will conflict be avoided according to Cyert and March's quasi-resolution of conflict concept, and when will decisions be based on a naked show of power, as described by Pettigrew? Also, when will the organization settle for the first available solution (Cyert and March, 1963), and when will they search more deliberately for a best solution (Rados, 1972)? It is hoped that these enigmas will be resolved later in this chapter.

A BEHAVIORAL MODEL OF PERIODIC ORGANIZATIONAL DECISIONMAKING BASED ON EVOLUTIONARY PRINCIPLES

We shall now attempt to construct a model of periodic organizational decisionmaking by uniting the evolutionary and behavioral theories of decisionmaking. Figure 5–2 shows, in diagrammatic form, the framework for planning and organizing according to Weick's theory, together with the equivocality-reducing procedures based on the extended Cyert and March theory. The decisions of concern here are limited to changes in policy variables, such as prices of products or services, in order to overcome short-run problems associated with the budgeting cycle. Decisions of a longer run nature, concerning such strategic variables as launching new products or services, seeking new markets, or investing in new technologies, are excluded from consideration here.

The model illustrated in Figure 5–2 comprises enactment processes (box B), selection and retention processes (box C), and a retained set of relations and procedures subject to short-run and long-run adaptive learning that represent the organization's memory (box D). The system of interactions among these components can be described as follows.

The organization's enacted environments (box A), which repre-

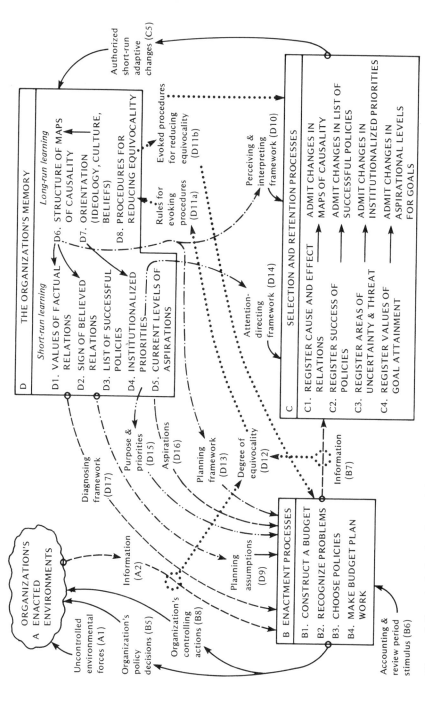

Figure 5-2. A behavioral model of periodic organizational decisionmaking based on evolutionary principles.

125

sent such things as its markets, production technologies, and internal industrial relations, react to the organization's decisions (B5), controlling actions (B8), and uncontrollable environmental forces (A1). The organization's decisions, concerning such policy decisions as changing prices, emanate from the organization's enactment processes (box B). The environmental forces comprise such things as changes in customers' tastes, technological factors, and industrial relations that are outside the control of the firm.

Enactment Processes

The information about the organization's environments will contain ambiguous elements. As we have seen, ambiguity invites inaction and is, therefore, an anathema to the organization that seeks ways of reducing the equivocality in the environmental signals that it receives. According to the degree of equivocality (D12) present in the information, the organization assembles rules or criteria to guide the effort to remove the offending uncertainty. These rules (D11a) serve the purpose of evoking equivocality-reducing procedures (D11b) from the organization's memory (D8). The equivocality-reducing enactment processes routinely evoked by the accounting review period stimulus (B6) are constructing a budget (B1), recognizing problems (B2), choosing policies (B3) to enable a satisfactory budget to be struck, and making the budget plan work (B4). We shall examine these processes in more detail.

Constructing a Budget (B1). We are concerned here with how a firm decides to manipulate those variables within its immediate control for the purpose of meeting its short-run goals. This latter type of decisionmaking takes place at intervals associated with the firm's accounting and review periods — usually an annual event. The core of the process is the formulation of a budget, which once agreed upon forms the basis of the firm's plan of action for the next period. The budget itself is an analogue of the firm's set of reported accounts. This device alone reduces equivocality considerably, since achieving the budget will automatically guarantee the acceptability of the financial statement at the end of the year.

Each line in the budget is computed using planning assumptions (D9) about causality taken from stored past experiences (D1 through D6). Where a clear causal relationship does not exist (e.g., the relationship of demand to price may not be known with the required precision), then simple forecasts, based on extrapolating past trends, are used.

Table 5-1. Enactment Procedures for Constructing a Budget (B1)

Rules for Evoking a Retained Procedure	*The Procedure Evoked*
Reduce the uncertainty of producing unsatisfactory financial results at year end	Construct a budget plan using the structure of the financial accounts as the basis of the plan
Reduce ambiguity about the assumptions to be used for computing each line of the budget	Estimate each budget item using clearly established relationships retained from past experience. If these relationships are unclear, use simple forecasts based on extrapolating past results

The construction of the budget can be considered from the evolutionary viewpoint as comprising a set of procedures assembled from the organization's storehouse of knowledge using rules that minimize ambiguity and uncertainty (behavioral theory of the firm concepts). Table 5-1 summarizes the set of evoked procedures for constructing a budget.

Recognizing Problems (B2). The achievement of each organizational goal, computed by the budget, is compared with the aspiration level for that goal. These aspirations (D16), based on past achievements, are evoked from the organization's memory (D5). The organization's problems are identified by shortfalls or surpluses in meeting these expectations. Both are equivocal situations requiring policies to be found to eliminate the shortfall or divert surpluses into the activities best able to advance the survival and success of the organization, as determined by the institutionalized purpose and priorities (D15) of the organization.

Where shortfalls are found, it is usual to diagnose the cause of the problem by standard financial management diagnosing procedures (D17) evoked from the organization's memory, such as computing operating ratios and growth rates for each budget item and comparing these with previous years' figures. A set of symptoms is generated thereby that forms the first step in searching for a solution. These evoked procedures are summarized in Table 5-2.

Choosing a Policy (B3). In undertaking to look after its own goals, each subunit in the organization evokes policies to dispel the symptoms of its dissatisfied goals as identified in the budgeting process. This is done by referring to the subunit's map of causality — the structure of beliefs in cause and effect in its policy domain — and

Table 5-2. Enactment Procedures for Recognizing a Problem (B2)

Rules for Evoking a Retained Procedure	The Procedure Evoked
Reduce ambiguity of disagreement in recognizing problems	Compare the results computed by the budget with the organization's expectations for each goal. Identify shortfalls and supluses in achieving the goals (organization's problems)
Reduce uncertainty and disagreement in diagnosing the cause of problems	Use standard financial procedures to compute operating ratios and growth rates of items in the proposed budget. Compare with previous year's figures to identify cause of problems (symptoms of the problem)

putting forward remedial policies suggested by the diagnosing framework (D17).

The process may lead to conflict, since departments in the organization may vigorously push their preferred policy solutions to each of several problems that occur concurrently. A policy chosen to solve one problem may undo the achievement of a goal in some other part of the organization, which can create tension and division among departments. To avoid possible internal disharmony, each subunit searches, first, for acceptable policies that do not violate the goals of others.

If such acceptable policies cannot be found, political procedures are evoked whereby the powerful coalitions ensure that their goals are met at the expense of the weak coalitions. The purpose and goal priorities (D15) of the organization have been established and institutionalized (D4), because in the past they helped the organization to survive and flourish. Servicing these goals should therefore minimize the uncertainty facing the organization from its external environment.

If an acceptable policy cannot be found to satisfy conflicting goals by a political process, then the goals are attended to sequentially. This kind of situation is typical of cost versus quality arguments. The policies to improve the quality of a product or service may increase its cost and vice versa. The irreconcilable goal situation can be circumvented by dealing with the goals one at a time. It can lead, obviously, to unstable situations of alternating policies.

Conversely, the search for a solution may uncover a number of acceptable policies; the problem (an equivocal situation) is which one to choose. More rules or criteria have to be brought into play to reduce the choice to one. One procedure that will accomplish this is to choose the policy previously used most frequently to solve this problem. This will also minimize the uncertainty of the outcome, since the policy must obviously be a successful one. The impact of the proposed policies on the organization's environment may be problematic, in which case the organization will need to proceed in a cautious manner to minimize the unforeseen impact of its policy decisions. This can be accomplished by making only small conservative incremental changes to the policy variables chosen for implementation. Last, the policy proposals screened by the above procedure are coordinated by plugging them into the budget, recomputing the shortfalls and surpluses, searching for policies to ameliorate the problems still existing, and so on, until all goals are satisfied, all slack is absorbed, or no solution can be found. Mintzberg, Rasinghani, and Théoret (1977) have observed such a cyclical pattern of search for discrete policy decisions. These procedures for choosing a policy based largely on the problemistic search concept, are laid out in Table 5-3.

Table 5-3. Enactment Procedures for Choosing a Policy (B3)

Rules for Evoking a Retained Procedure	*The Procedure Evoked*
Minimize inconsistency	Each subunit evokes the policies to dispel the symptoms of its dissatisfied goals using its retained map of causality
Minimize internal conflict	A search is made for acceptable policies that do not violate other subunit goals
Minimize uncertainty facing the organization	If an acceptable policy cannot be found, select policies that meet the goals of the politically powerful subunits at the expense of the politically weak
Minimize conflict in satisfying important goals with conflicting policies	If an acceptable policy still cannot be found for important goals, attend to the dissatisfied goals one at a time
Minimize uncertainty in choosing among several contending policies	If several policies exist for a dissatisfied goal, choose the one most frequently used before
Avoid uncertainty concerning the reaction of the organization's environment to its actions	Make only small conservative incremental changes to the policy variables chosen for implementation
Reduce conflict in planning and coordinate the proposals of several subunits	Plug admitted changes to policy variables into the budget and recompute the shortfalls and surpluses. Repeat until all problems are solved or no solution can be found

The rules, however, on closer examination seem to evoke procedures for handling two quite different types of equivocality. The first type deals with the situation described by Cyert and March (1963), where no solution exists initially. Procedures are evoked for widening the search until one solution is found — at which event, search is terminated. The second type of equivocality is generated by having too many acceptable alternatives. For example, a rule used to stimulate search for a solution may result in uncovering several competing solutions. The dilemma now facing the organization is how to reduce this choice — a situation constituting the more traditional view of decisionmaking as a choice among contending alternatives (Simon, 1945). Rados (1972) views this process as a deviation from Cyert and March's basic concept, but this study suggests that they are both subordinate to Weick's theory. An organization may alternate between rules to evoke a solution to a pressing problem and procedures to reduce the number of competing solutions, so discovered, to one.

Making the Budget Work (B4). The agreed upon budget is then implemented, and deviations from it are computed on a quarterly or monthly basis. Corrective changes to externally related policy variables, if made too frequently, may create more problems than they solve. For example, customers may become angry and confused over continuously changing prices. The organization is, therefore, left with the option to manipulate internally related variables.

Cyert and March (1963) suggest that organizations attempt to make their plans self-fulfilling by manipulating "slack." When the plan is being overachieved, the organization finds ways of absorbing the surplus — salesmen visit fewer customers, production quotas are reduced, executives' suites are redecorated, more staff is hired than is really necessary, and so forth. When the plan is underachieved, the reverse takes place, and the "slack" is squeezed out of the organization. The outcome of this process is that a primary source of equivocality (i.e., deviations from the organization's plan) is suppressed. Because these procedures are internally controllable, they will be invoked more frequently — say, on a monthly basis — than those procedures concerning the external environment. These procedures, also based on the problemistic search concept, are laid out in Table 5-4.

Selection and Retention Processes (Box C)

The results of the enactment processes become available for the selection and retention processes. Equivocality in the information

Table 5-4.   Enactment Procedures for Making the Budget Plan Work (B4)

Rules for Evoking a Retained Procedure	*The Procedure Evoked*
Reduce ambiguity and uncertainty arising from failure to meet the budgeting targets	Manipulate only internally controllable variables. If the target is undersubscribed and slack exists, invoke a slack reduction program. If the target is oversubscribed, invoke a slack absorption program

(B7) about the success or failure in meeting the organization's budget will evoke procedures for trying to reduce the equivocality. These selection and retention processes involve, first, registering cause and effect relations and then admitting changes in the official map of causality (C1); second, registering the success of policies and then admitting additions and deletions to the list of frequently used policies (C2); third, registering areas of uncertainty facing the organization and then admitting changes to the institutionalized priorities (C3) that raise the status and associated goals of coalitions best able to handle the uncertainty; and fourth, registering the goal achievement of the organization and comparable organizations and then admitting changes to the aspirations for goal achievement (C4). A more detailed examination of these processes follows:

Cause and Effect Relations (C1). Cause and effect interactions among the significant variables describing the organization's environments are required as planning assumptions (D9) for constructing the budget and as a diagnosing framework (D17) for problem solving. The planning, perceiving, and interpreting frameworks (D10 and D13) are supplied by the structure of the map of causality (D6) retained in the organization's memory. The map is fragmented into a number of subunit maps describing the causal paths that lead from policy achievement of subunit goals. It has already been argued that these maps will be simplified structurally to exclude feedback loops, resolve indeterminacy, and reduce the number of causal links through long causal paths (uncertainty avoidance concept). The maps of causality comprise three sorts of relations:

1. Simple logical or accounting relations, such as more unit sales, subject to price remaining unaltered, will cause sales revenues to increase;
2. Relations that are a matter of observable fact from the feedback of the results of controlled policies (e.g., from the closely monitored activities of salesmen, the promotional cost of acquiring an extra unit of sale might be estimated quite precisely); and

3. Relations subject to belief and environmental conditioning, where the necessary evidence of proof is not available or is confused.

The latter relation represents points of indeterminancy in the maps of causality. An example is the effect of price on sales, which may be clouded by changing economic conditions, the behavior of competitors, and changes in the design and quality of the product. This kind of situation, it has been argued, is usually resolved by believing in one argument or the other — for example, that the demand for the product is or is not price elastic. If the result of raising prices is an increase in revenue without a loss of unit sales, then the belief in price-inelastic demand (a zero sign of correlation) is established, and raising prices becomes a viable policy for raising revenues and profits.

The different types of relationships would seem to call for different treatments by the organization's selection and retention mechanism. First, the simple logical and accounting relations are considered to be part of the structure of the maps of causality and hence immutable. They do not come up for conscious consideration, even though vital links crossing departmental boundaries might be missing: only relations that accord with the maps of causality are perceived. Second, the factual relations, whose values can be estimated with reasonable precision from unconfounded results of the interaction of the organization's actions with its environments, are selected to update the currently retained values of these parameters. Third, relations of the "belief" kind become part of organization's interlocking set of beliefs that describe its internal culture and are not readily changed in spite of disconfirming evidence. The beliefs in the signs of correlation between cause and effect are not changed until an evaluation, following a crisis, suggests that the believed in relation no longer holds. So a price-inelastic demand belief might be held in the absence of unconfounded evidence until a crisis or critical problem occurs and an analysis of the problem disproves the belief. At this time, the belief in the sign of causality is changed, and the demand is now held to be price elastic until another crisis causes a reversal in belief, and so on. The rules and evoked procedures that might be used for selecting and retaining relationships for budgetary purposes are shown in Table 5-5.

Successful Policies (C2). Once a particular policy has been used, its success in ameliorating the problem for which it was evoked can be registered. If it is successful, it becomes a candidate for retention. A precedent has been created so that, when that particular problem

Table 5-5. Procedures for Selecting and Retaining Cause and Effect Relationships for Use in Budgeting (C1)

Rules for Evoking a Retained Procedure	The Procedure Evoked
Minimize internal conflict	Each subunit maintains its own causal map independent of the others. The map describes the path of causality leading from policies to achievement of subunit goals
Reduce uncertainty and disagreement over perceiving and interpreting results of enacted policies	Accept the logical and accounting cause and effect relations as immutable
	Retain the relations, whose values can be estimated from unconfounded trials, by updating the values of these relations stored as budgeting assumptions
	Retain the results that reinforce a currently held belief in the direction of causality
Reduce uncertainty in retaining spurious results	Admit changes in belief only if the investigation following a policy failure or crisis suggests that the currently held belief no longer holds

arises again, the policy is a prime candidate for reconsideration. This reduces the uncertainty about the outcome, and the work of selecting a policy becomes a matter of organizational stimulus response.

The attention-directing framework (D14) sensitizes the organization to those explicitly measurable criteria at which it has been most successful in the past and that are held to be important by the dominant coalition. We can posit that the belief in the efficiency of a policy will increase every time it is used successfully, decrease when results are ambiguous, and become extinguished when it clearly does not work. The rules and evoked procedures that could be used for selecting and retaining successful policy variables are shown in Table 5-6.

At first glance, the mechanism seems similar to that used to select and retain cause and effect relations, except that success and failure (both feelings of emotion) form the basis for the selection process. In a complex environment, the organization could be conditioned to correlating actions and results that do not exist. This kind of misattribution of causality has been referred to as "superstitious learning" (Lave and March, 1975). As an example of this phenomenon, Ackoff and Emshoff (1975:12) detail the time, effort, and large

Table 5–6. Procedures for Selecting and Retaining a Successful Policy for Solving Problems (C2)

Rules for Evoking a Retained Procedure	The Procedure Evoked
Reduce uncertainty of obtaining satisfactory results	Pay attention to those explicitly measurable criteria of a policy's success that are of importance to the dominant coalition
	Register the success of a policy in ameliorating the problem for which it was evoked
	If a policy is successful, increase the belief in it
	If a policy is not successful, but the evidence is clouded, decrease the belief in it
	If a policy is clearly unsuccessful, abandon it only after a major crisis and review

number of trials it took to discredit the belief that "more advertising brings more sales" for a firm. As they put it: "The strength of the opposition to the results of our early experiments is less surprising in retrospect than it was at the time. These results contradicted the strong beliefs of people who had good reason to believe they understood advertising and who had the success of the products involved to prove it."

Institutionalized Priorities (C3). Although the profit goal is of overriding importance to survival for a private firm, there are many other goals that can be pursued in parallel with producing a satisfactory profit. Roberts (1975) has noted that the internal structure and ideology of utility companies can give a better account of their overt behavior than the distinction between public and private ownership of these same companies.

Pettigrew (1973), as we have seen, suggests that the coalitions vie with each other for status and power, which enables them to make demands on the organization's resources to pursue their own subculture goals. At the same time, the changing environment fosters or retards the formation and growth of coalitions by creating or reducing the organization's need for their services. Thus, the enhancement of the power of one coalition vis-à-vis its rivals will be determined largely by the external environment.

Izraeli (1975) has documented the tactics used by a new manager to expand his power over his department's resources and comments that a benign environment increases the chances of success of these tactics. It would seem that a coalition's power is to a large extent dependent upon the organization's need for its services in removing the equivocality or threats facing the organization. When such needs exist, the coalition can demand that a greater priority be accorded its goals. The formation and priority ordering of goals by the organization's power and status system facilitates its adaption to a changing environment, albeit in a crude and sometimes disjointed way, by giving it a direction or orientation that, at least in the past, allowed it to survive and flourish. This phenomenon has been described by Roberts (1975:418):

> Over time, the structure of an organization, its control system, and the beliefs and values of its members often change in response to changes in the external environment. The degree to which such internal features have an independent explanatory role depends on how rapidly they alter in response to such external changes and on how much discretion the organization has once such readjustments have taken place. In an imperfectly coercive environment, the internal features of an organization will be partially self-determining. The current structure of an organization, its incentive system, and the beliefs and values of its personnel will all reflect its responses to past problems. Hence, an organization's immediate response to current problems, as well as its subsequent reactions if those efforts should prove unsuccessful, will tend to reflect its past history and development.

The priorities of the organization, so derived, can now influence the enactment processes by providing purpose for the organization's plans to attain and priorities for attacking problems (D15). Similarly, they provide an attention direction framework (D14) for the selection and retention processes.

This system is not perfectly adaptive, since a coalition, once entrenched in a position of power, is able to use delaying tactics against rival coalitions seeking to displace it and to promote their own goals. Changing the organization's culture and orientation is not easily achieved (Silverzweig and Allen, 1976). To some extent this is desirable, because changing goals too frequently could produce chaos. It would seem that the organization has to experience a crisis before the dominant coalition or leader is displaced (Hall, 1976; Nystrom, Hedberg, and Starbuck, 1977) and the organization adjusts to a new orientation (Turner, 1976). The rules and evoked procedures based on the organizational learning concept for selecting and retaining the precedence ordering of goals are summarized in Table 5-7.

Table 5-7. Procedures for Selecting and Retaining the Precedence Ordering of Goals (C3)

Rules for Evoking a Retained Procedure	The Procedure Evoked
Reduce the uncertainty and threats facing the organization	Register the nature of the uncertainty or threat facing the organization, and attempt to advance the status, and hence the goals, of the subunit whose services are required for removing the uncertainty
Reduce the confusion and conflict associated with changing goal priorities too frequently	Admit changes in subunit dominance, and hence goal ordering, only after a period of recurring uncertainty or after a survival crisis

Aspiration Levels for Goals (C4). It has been argued that goals aspiration levels adapt to experience. When achievement of a goal rises, so does the expectation for future achievement. When achievement falls, so does the expectation or aspirational level for that goal. Aspirations seem to adjust more quickly in the direction of hopes than away from them. Aspirations can also be affected by the performance of competing organizations. This process, couched in terms of the organizational learning concept, is shown in Table 5-8.

The aspiration level is used to define problems for an organization. When the results or budget forecast fall below the aspiration level for a goal, the organization has a problem. The threshold for perceiving a performance gap for an organization does not seem to have been

Table 5-8. Procedures for Selecting and Retaining the Achievement Level for Goals (C4)

Rules for Evoking a Retained Procedure	The Procedure Evoked
Reduce uncertainty about the level of achievement possible in the circumstances	Register the current achievement for the goal
	Register the current achievement in competing organizations
Reduce the ambiguity gap between what organization members hope to achieve and what they can expect	If achievement has risen over expectation, raise the expectation to the amount achieved. If achievement has fallen, reduce the expectation by a fraction of the shortfall. Wider deviations in performance are not retained

studied. If it conforms to human perception, then a 3 percent relative difference is of the order of magnitude to be expected, although this may be dependent upon the precision of measurement of the goal achievement level: the more precise the measurement, the smaller the relative difference required to recognize a problem. Conversely, wild deviations of achievements due to exceptional circumstances are not retained.

The Organization's Memory (Box D)

The organization's memory comprises two parts — those items subject to short-run learning and those items subject to long-run learning. Short-run learning occurs as the adaptive changes (C5) authorized by the organization's retention processes pass into the organization's memory. It results in updated values of factual cause and effect relations (D1) and changes in the beliefs in causality (D2) for relations subject to environmental conditioning. As the list of successful policies is amended (D3) and changes in the order of goal priorities (D4) due to the effect of political processes in the organization become institutionalized, the organization may take on a new orientation. Last, the current levels of aspirations (D5) for these goals are adjusted in the light of immediate past performance and the performance of comparable organizations. These items provide the planning assumptions (D9) for the enactment processes — the figures to use to compute each budget line, the criteria for recognizing problems, the acceptable policies for ameliorating the problems and controlling actions for making the plan work. The institutionalized priorities also provide the framework for directing attention (D14) to information to be considered by the selection and retention processes.

Long-run learning affects the structure of the maps of causality and the retained procedures for reducing equivocality in the enactment, selection, and retention processes. The structure of the maps of causality (D6) supplies the framework for perceiving and interpreting organizational information (D10) and for organizing the values and beliefs in cause and effect relations (D1 and D2). It has been argued that these maps are simplified structurally and remain remarkably resistant to change. They are influenced by the organization's internal culture, which supplies the missing relations at points of indeterminacy through beliefs in causality that key in with the dominant coalition's ideology and orientation (D7). Hence, they require crises, or substantial turnover in personnel, to bring about a change.

Since each subunit keeps its own map, major changes in the organizational structure, such as amalgamating several subunits, presumably would bring about similar structural changes to the maps of causality. This could be a key factor in determining the need for organizational restructuring, an idea requiring further research.

Procedures for reducing equivocality (D8), such as discovering new procedures for searching for solutions, are also considered to be subject to long-term organizational learning. The nature of these long-term learning processes is excluded from this study. The procedures are evoked for reducing equivocality (D11b) in the enactment, selection, and retention processes by rules (D11a) that are subject to the degree of equivocality (D12) in information about the results of the organization's decisions on its environments.

We have now turned a full circle in describing organizational periodic decisionmaking as a feedback system of interlocking behavioral procedures based on evolutionary principles that is self-directing and self-learning.

IMPLICATIONS OF THE STUDY

So, What Is New?

The model of decisionmaking developed for this study attempts to integrate the behavioral theory of the firm, the politics of organizational decisionmaking, and the cognitive processes used by policymakers. An evolutionary learning framework serves to organize these pieces of the jigsaw puzzle into a more coherent whole at the level of organizational decision making. Whereas Cyert and March (1963) argue that the concepts of the behavioral theory of the firm are heavily interrelated, the studies of the political and cognitive aspects of organizational learning previously stood more or less alone. Now these are interwoven with the other concepts to show how the organization acquires purpose, meaning, and orientation and a quasi-official map of causality. These attributes of the organization's retained set guide its subsequent actions and attention to items in its stream of experience that it will select for retention and so on in a closed loop form. The model provides insights into the underlying causes of pathologies of decisionmaking that aid prescription. The confusion about the level of search undertaken to solve a problem (Will the organization choose the first available alternative, or will it search more thoroughly among contending alternatives?) can now be resolved in terms of the nature of the equivocality facing it and the interlocking procedures evoked. The question of the use of "power" versus "acceptability" as the criteria for choice behavior can be resolved similarly. What we have previously seen as dichotomous issues are now seen as subsets of a more all-embracing theory.

However, this all-embracing theory is an integration of studies made at different levels of decisionmaking behavior — the individual, the group, and the organization. Perhaps we should attempt to justify this approach. Implicit in our model is the existence of a corporate mind, although in reality, decisions are being made by individuals either singly or in groups.

The Existence of a Corporate Mind

For an organization to function as an entity with its own mind and organizing processes, the actions of the individual within the organization must be heavily constrained and quite predictable. This flies in the face of some research studies about individual and group behavior (e.g., groups will make riskier and, by implication, more random decisions than individuals — see for example Wallach, Logan, and Bern, 1962). The justification for the corporate mind concept lies in the heavy influences and constraints placed upon the individual decisionmaker in an institutional setting.

Simon (1945) has argued that organizations seek to influence their members' decisions through the means of structure, unity of command, training and selection, sanctions and rewards, and formal communications. These devices circumscribe the member's decisionmaking discretion by inculcating her or him with the facts and values for making organizationally "correct" decisions in a narrow area defined by the structured division of decisionmaking work. This is further reinforced with sanctions and rewards aimed at increasing the "zone of acceptance" of authority and by an authority system providing both a stimulus to decisionmaking activity and a mechanism for resolving conflicting directives.

In a similar vein, Roberts (1975) argues that the external environment, the organizational structure, the control system, and the set of objectives and beliefs held by the individual will determine his or her choices. The external environment determines the consequences of an individual's actions and, hence, to some extent the rewards. The organizational structure defines the tasks and the resources he or she controls. The control system, which includes all personnel promotion and compensation practices, metes out rewards and punishments as a result of those actions. The ideal control system from the point of view of top managers would so shape the individual's actions as to lead to corporate outcomes desired by those top managers. The individual objectives and beliefs, which include those personal and professional norms and beliefs distinctly characteristic of the organization members (the organization's ideology) and/or the top management's strategy imparted by the particular recruitment, socialization, and promotion practices of the organization, will account for the discretionary remnant of the individual's choice.

From another standpoint, the person with a vested interest in her or his own survival and career prospects within the organization cannot usually (if ever) make unilateral decisions. Such an individual has to interlock his or her actions with those of others in the working group(s). Similarly, the various coalitions and departmental groups have to interlock their behaviors. Mumford and Pettigrew (1975) have illustrated the political origins of this interlocking behavior. The phenomenon has been described by Coser (1964:405): "The parties must agree upon rules and norms allowing them to assess their respective power position in the struggle. Their common interest leads them to accept rules which enhance their mutual dependence in the very pursuit of their antagonistic goals. Such arguments make their conflict, so to speak, 'self-liquidating.'"

This "self-liquidation" of conflict provides, perhaps, the explanation for the observed convergence of beliefs among members of a group in an organization (Steinbrunner, 1974) and the reduced vacillation over issues (Weick, 1969). It is the aggregated effect of all these influences on the individual members that determines the pattern of organizational behavior and leads to the notion of the "corporate mind." If one could document the current state of the determinants of the corporate mind and if one could understand the processes by which these states are changed from one state to another, then one could explain and perhaps even forecast the organization's responses to environmental and self-imposed problems. This study purports to do this for a limited set of short-run budget-related decisions.

Some Research Questions

No mention has been made as to where the enactment, selection, and retention processes reside in the organization. Where would one look for them? Some of the processes seem to be formalized in standardized written procedures, but most seem to be hidden in an amorphous cloud of customs, norms, rules of thumb, conventional ways of doing things, expectations, informal communications, and reward and punishment systems that provide the laboratory for the cultural anthropologist and sociologist. The fact that they cannot readily be seen does not deny their existence or mean that they have no real impact on organizational decisionmaking. It does, however, create problems in validating a model of this nature.

Given that these processes do exist, how do they evolve, and how are they related to, say, organizational structure? It might be supposed that an unacceptable amount of equivocality at one level will drive the process to another level. For example, the selection of a new departmental head might be a contentious and confusing issue. A committee may be struck for deciding on the criteria to be used by another committee that will interview and screen applicants. This is akin to a procedure for selecting a procedure. This subject may warrant further exploration as a possible basis for explaining how a hierarchy of equivocality-reducing procedures grows. If the equivocality concerns the organization's day-to-day operations, then the result of the process may become institutionalized in the organization's structure — a new level of management is born. Do we have here the beginning of a theory of how organizational structure grows and adapts to experience? This could lead to a better understanding of the long-run adaptation of an organization.

It has long been recognized that structure is a tactic of strategy, but it is usually assumed that the reassignment of responsibilities is the prime cause of the observed change in behavior (see, for example, Texas Instruments Inc. cases, discussed in Learned et al., 1969). This study suggests that the restructuring of the departmental cognitive maps of causality may have an equally important effect on organizational decisionmaking. How could we test this?

A more fundamental question concerns the formation and adaptation of the organization's maps of causality. It has been argued that the departmental maps were formed around an accounting model of the firm with beliefs coincident with the dominant coalition's strategy substituted for indeterminant relations. Is this the way it really works?

We have also stretched Pettigrew's (1973) concepts of the politics of organizational decisionmaking to encompass any significant organizational problems — not just major innovations. It is posited that the political activities surrounding the solution of organizational problems will result in the goals of the strong coalitions being serviced at the expense of the weak and that the strong have the right to divert organizational slack to their purposes. The annual budget provides the battle ground for these decisions. Would someone care to validate this?

REFERENCES

Ackoff, Russell L., and James R. Emshoff. 1975. "Advertising Research at Anheuser-Busch, Inc." *Sloan Management Review* 16 (Winter): 1-16.

Agenti, John. 1976. *Corporate Collapse: the Cause and Symptoms*. London: McGraw Hill.

Ashby, W. R. 1956. *An Introduction to Cybernetics*. New York: John Wiley.

Axelrod, R. 1976. *The Structure of Decision: the Cognitive Maps of Political Elites*. Princeton, N.J.: Princeton University Press.

Beck, P. W. 1977. "Strategic Planning in the Royal Dutch/Shell Group." Paper presented to TIMS/ORSA Conference, New Orleans.

Bossel, Hartmut. 1977. *Concepts and Tools for Computer Assisted Policy Analysis*. Basle: Birkhauser.

Brown, Wilfred. 1971. *Organization*. London: Heinemann.

Campbell, Donald T. 1965. "Variation and Selective Retention in Sociocultural Evolution." In H. R. Barringer, G. I. Balnksten, and R. W. Mack, eds., *Social Change in Developing Areas*. Cambridge, Mass.: Schenkman.

Churchman, C. W. 1971. *The Design of Inquiring Systems: Basic Concepts of Systems and Organization*. New York: Basic Books.

Coser, L. A. 1964. "The Termination of Conflict." In W. J. Gore and J. W. Dyson, eds., *The Making of Decisions*. Glencoe, Ill.: Free Press.

Coyle, R. G. 1977a. *Management System Dynamics*. London: John Wiley.

——. 1977b. "Modeling the Future of Mining Groups." *Dynamica* 3, no. 3 (Summer): 132-71.

——. 1978. "System Dynamics — the State of the Art." Bradford, England: University of Bradford, System Dynamics Research Group, working paper.

Crozier, Michel, and Jean-Claude Thoenig. 1976. "The Regulation of Complex Organized Systems." *Administrative Science Quarterly* 21:547-70.

Culligan, Matthew J. 1970. *The Curtis-Culligan Story*. New York: Crown Publishers.

Cyert, Richard M., and James G. March. 1963. *A Behavioral Theory of the Firm*. Englewood Cliffs, N.J.: Prentice-Hall.

Einhorn, Hillel J., and Robin M. Hogarth. 1977. "Confidence in Judgement: Persistence of the Illusion of Validity." London Graduate School of Business Studies, working paper.

Forrester, Jay W. 1968. *Principles of Systems*. Cambridge, Mass.: Wright-Allen Press.

——. 1970. "Counterintuitive Behaviour of Social Systems". *Technology Review* 3:52-68.

Friedrich, Otto. 1970. *Decline and Fall*. New York: Harper and Row.

Gray, Jerry L., ed. 1976. *The Glacier Project, Concepts and Critiques: Selected Readings on the Glacier Theories of Organization and Management*. New York: Crane Russak.

Hall, Roger I. 1976. "A System Pathology of an Organization: the Rise and Fall of the Old Saturday Evening Post." *Administrative Science Quarterly* 21 (June): 185-211.

————. 1977. "Simple Techniques for Constructing Explanatory Models for Policy Analyses." *Dynamica* (in press).

Izraeli, Dafna Nundi. 1975. "The Middle Manager and the Tactics of Power Expansion." *Sloan Management Review* 16: (Winter) 57–70.

Jacques, Elliott. 1956. *Measurement of Responsibility.* London: Tavistock Publications.

————. 1961. *Equitable Payment.* London: Heinemann.

Kuhn, Arthur J. 1976. "Organization Design and General Motors versus Ford Motors, 1918–1937." Paper presented at joint TIMS/ORSA conference, Miami.

Lave, C. A., and J. C. March. 1975. *An Introduction to Models in the Social Sciences.* New York: Harper and Row.

Learned, Edmund P.; C. Roland Cristensen; Kenneth R. Andrews; and William D. Guth. 1969. *Business policy: Tests and Cases.* Lev. ed. Homewood, Ill.: Irwin.

D. Guth. 1969. *Business Policy: Tests and Cases.* Homewood, Ill.: Irwin.

Lindblom, Charles E. 1968. *The Policy Making Process.* Englewood Cliffs, N.J.: Prentice-Hall.

Mintzberg, Henry; Duru Rasinghani; and André Théoret. 1977. "The Structure of Unstructured Decision Processes." *Administrative Science Quarterly* 21 (June): 246–75.

Mumford, Enid, and Andrew M. Pettigrew. 1975. *Implementing Strategic Decisions.* London: Longman.

Nystrom, Paul C.; Bo L. T. Hedberg; and William H. Starbuck. 1976. "Interacting Processes as Organization Designs." in R. H. Kilmann, L. R. Pondy, and D. F. Slevin, eds., *The Management of Organization Design.* New York: Elsevier North-Holland.

Pettigrew, Andrew M. 1973. *The Politics of Organizational Decisionmaking.* London: Tavistock.

————. 1974. "Learning from Extreme Situations." Brussels: European Institute of Advanced Studies in Management, working paper no. 74-33.

————. 1977. "The Creation of Organizational Cultures." Brussels: European Institute of Advanced Studies in Management, working paper no. 77-11.

Piaget, Jean. 1966. *The Psychology of Intelligence.* Totowa, N.J.: Littlefield Adams.

Pugh, A. L. 1970. *Dynamo Il User's Manual.* Cambridge, Mass.: MIT Press.

Rados, David L. 1972. "Selection and Evaluation of Alternatives in Repetitive Decision Making." *Administrative Science Quarterly* (June) 196–206.

Ratnatunga, A. K., and C. J. Stewart. 1977. *Dysmap User's Manual.* Bradford: University of Bradford: System Dynamics Research Group.

Roberts, Marc J. 1975. "An Evolutionary and Institutional View of the Behaviour of Public and Private Companies." *American Economic Review* (May): 415–26.

Roos, Leslie L., and Roger I. Hall. 1978. "The Organizational Power Game: Evaluators, Garbage Cans and Cognitive Maps." Winnipeg: University of Manitoba, Faculty of Administrative Studies, working paper.

Sharp, J. A. 1977. "System Dynamics Applications in Industrial and other Systems." *Journal of the Operational Research Society* 28, no. 3: 489-504.

Silverzweig, Stan, and Robert F. Allen. 1976. "Changing the Corporate Culture." *Management Review* 17 (Spring): 33-49.

Simon, Herbert A. 1945. *Administrative Behaviour.* New York: Free Press.

Steinbrunner, J. D. 1974. *The Cybernetic Theory of Decision.* Princeton, N.J.: Princeton University Press.

Turner, Barry A. 1976. "The Organizational and Interorganizational Development of Disasters." *Administrative Science Quarterly* 21 (September): 378-97.

Wallach, Michael A.; Natham Logan; and Dave J. Bern. 1962. "Group Influence on Individual Risk Taking," *Journal of Abnormal and Social Psychology* 65, no. 2: 75-86.

Weick, Karl E. 1969. *The Social Psychology of Organizing.* Reading, Mass.: Addison-Wesley.

———. 1977. "Organization Design: Organizations as Self Designing Systems." *Organizational Dynamics* (Autumn): 31-46.

Winter, Sidney G. 1970. "Satisficing, Selection and the Innovating Remnant." Ann Arbor: University of Michigan Institute of Public Policy Studies, discussion paper no. 18.

Chapter 6

Leadership and Organization Structure: A Critique and an Argument for Synthesis

John L. Kmetz*

INTRODUCTION

"The concept of leadership has an ambiguous status in organizational practice, as it does in organizational theory" (Katz and Kahn, 1978:256 — first sentence of the first paragraph in their chapter on leadership). It would be difficult to find a more appropriate sentence to describe the state of our knowledge of the relationship between leadership and organization structure in present theory.

A Twofold Omission

Both the general process of management and the specific phenomenon of leadership have been subject to years of study. Despite being one of the few social processes to be investigated through a systematic and cumulative program of research (Calder, 1977), leadership still remains a poorly understood aspect of organizational functioning (Calder, 1977; McCall, 1977; Katz and Kahn, 1978). Miner (1975) suggests abandoning the concept in favor of research into control, which he contends is the real issue.

* University of Delaware

Within recent years there has been a burgeoning literature on organization structure. Much of this work has attempted to describe relationships between structure and "context" variables (environment, technology, interdependence, size, and others) that are hypothesized to explain variations in structure. In the vast majority of this literature, however, little or no attention has been given to the role of the leader or any human actor.

Nevertheless, theoretical linkages between leadership and organization structure have long existed. Almost all reviews of the "classical" school of management (Filley, House, and Kerr, 1976) indicate a responsibility for the design or structure appropriate to the goals of the organization. More recently, Katz and Kahn (1978) explicitly treated leadership as the design and application of structure, where "application" refers to both the use of structure and the departure from structure prescriptions as the case may require. Despite a large amount of research stimulated by the overall work of Katz and Kahn, little direct research into this hypothesized leadership-structure relationship is to be found. Other, albeit less detailed, linkages may be found in the work of Worthy (1950), Urwick (1943), Argyris (1964), and others.

Purpose

The purpose of this chapter is to address this omission, to give a critique of existing work, and to suggest needed future research. It is hoped that an integration of the two bodies of work may be stimulated, not only for the purposes of investigating these relationships per se, but because it is argued that the two organizational processes are inextricably bound together. If this is true, then study of the interaction between leadership and organization structure will assist us in understanding each of the two variables as individual entities.

Several points should be noted before initiating the review:

1. It is the intention of the author to review the literature in these fields only from the perspective of the theoretical and empirical relationships between the two major variables of leadership and organization structure.

2. It should be noted that the author does not presume that all leadership functions through, or is manifested through, structure. Nor is it presumed that all structure is a function of leadership alone, especially with respect to secondary effects of structure or decisions affecting structure. There are important components of variance in both leadership and organization structure that cannot be explained by the other variable.

3. An overview of research on both leadership and structure illustrates that each area of investigation has proceeded largely without reference to the other. Consideration of structure in the leadership literature and consideration of leadership in the structure literature are both most notable by their absence. Much of the inconclusiveness in the two literatures is believed to be attributable to these omissions.

STRUCTURE FROM THE LEADERSHIP PERSPECTIVE

Theoretical Models

Several theories of leadership incorporate a variable termed "structure." However, almost without exception, the "structure" referenced has been task structure. While the leadership literature suggests awareness of organization structure and its effects, it is typically treated as a background factor — statistically, it becomes a component of error variance.

Most of the models or theories that have examined the interaction between organization structure and leadership have been derived from work at the University of Michigan. Prior to the first edition (1966) of Katz and Kahn's book *The Social Psychology of Organizations*, Mann (1965: 70) discussed this linkage:

Structurally, the organizational role of the supervisor at any level is primarily one of linking together different parts of the organizational structure of work groups and integrating the specialized performances of these units. This is the role on which the *entire system* depends to achieve and maintain unity and coherence. Specifically, at the structural level, the role of the supervisor entails the following functions: (1) directing and coordinating the tasks and activities of the subordinates within the supervisor's work group; (2) relating these activities to those of other work groups at the same organizational level within which his group interacts; and (3) relating the activities of his group and his own activities to those of other organizational units operating at the next higher, as well as the next lower level in the organization. The role of the supervisor may be viewed as that of a structural coordinative "linking pin," involving social psychological functions to coordinate individual member needs and goals with organizational objectives. [Emphasis added.]

Likert (1967) has argued that the role of the manager is that of a "linking pin," fulfilling interests of both the organization and its members. Likert argues that structure is one of the "causal variables" in an organization, where causal variables are definitionally restricted to those that the leaders have some power to change or control (p. 29). Further, in his discussion of system change in Weldon Manufacturing Co., Likert suggested that leader styles at one level seemed constrained by the styles of leaders at higher levels (p. 45). Thus, Likert proposes that leaders influence the structure of the organization and therefore the behavior of leaders and members at lower levels.

Katz and Kahn (1978) similarly argue that the role of the leader is to create and use structure for the accomplishment of organizational objectives. They argue that the relationship between leadership and structure varies depending on the hierarchical position of the leader. Top echelon leaders originate (create, change, and eliminate) structure. They must have an overview of the entire system and must be charismatic leaders to be identifiable to lower level members. Intermediate echelons interpolate (supplement and piece out) structure. They must have a subsystem perspective and must possess good human relations skills to succeed. Lower echelons are administrators, using existing structure. They need technical skills and must be conscientious in fair administration of rewards and penalties.

Along with being one of the few conceptual schemes to link leadership with structure in any systematic fashion, the Katz and Kahn framework also attempts to relate the research on leader behavior to the various role requirements. It is disappointing to see how little further work has been stimulated by this ambitious concept.

Much more attention has been devoted to task structure. However, since the focus of this chapter is on organization structure, only three major concepts will be briefly reviewed. First, research at Ohio State (Stogdill, 1974) identified two major factors of leader behavior — initiating structure and consideration. Initiating structure refers to leader behavior directed toward identification and clarification of goals, setting work and performance standards, enforcing rules, and requiring a task-focused mode of behavior on the part of subordinates. Consideration measures the extent to which the leader is approachable, supportive, and consultative-participative with members of the work group.

In terms of the Katz and Kahn framework, the initiating structure scale principally measures the use of existing structure, not the creation or interpolation of it. The theory is concerned with the immediate interaction between leader and subordinates, not the overall structure of the organization. In this sense, the Ohio State work is reflective of the origins of most of the leadership research — namely, early social psychology and small group studies (McCall, 1977).

Second, Fiedler's (1967) leadership studies identified task structure as one of the three major variables affecting "situational favorableness" for the leader. The other two variables were position power and leader-member relations. Fiedler's conceptualization also included a measure of leader supportiveness, measured through his ASo or LPC scales. Interpretation of the LPC scale has been somewhat problematic, in that it is uncertain whether it measures personality or motivation (Stinson and Tracy, 1974). In general, Fiedler's theory attempts to differentiate between situations where optimum group performance will be obtained through the use of task-directed methods or supportive leader behavior.

Like the Ohio State work, Fiedler focuses primarily on the relationship between leader and group. Fiedler (1976) suggests that optimum performance will be obtained by matching the leader to the situation, a process that may entail changing either the style of leadership employed, the nature of the situation, or both. His theory does not address broader issues of organization structure theory.

Third, House's (1971) path-goal theory argues that leaders in unstructured situations should use a task-oriented style of leadership and a supportive style in structured situations. The major focus of this theory is, as with others, on leader-group relationships. The role of the leader in House's theory is to create work-directed motivation by clarifying behaviors and consequent outcomes desirable to the subordinate. Structure factors to be considered by the leader are the degree to which rules, procedures, and policies govern the subordinate's work, although these play a minor role in the theory. The leader also examines other task and background factors in determining style. However, once these characteristics of the task and organization have been examined, they appear to be treated as fixed by the theory.

Thus, with the exception of the Michigan scholars, the treatment of structure in leadership concepts has been limited to concern with task structure and has in the author's view been unnecessarily limiting. Even more recent formulations, such as Calder's (1977) attribution theory of leadership, still reflect a primary concern with the leader-led relationship within the immediate task context.

Empirical Research Linking Leadership and Structure

Only a few studies have directly investigated the relationship between leadership and organization structure, but the results are tantalizing. Bass and Valenzi (1974) studied the effect of four categories of system inputs (organizational characteristics, work group characteristics, task characteristics, and personalities of subordinates) to the use of managerial styles. Managerial styles, in turn, were related to work group effectiveness and satisfaction with the job and the supervisor. When the sample was split into high- and low-scoring groups on system input measures, it was found that three organizational characteristics (degree of organization, external environment influence, and management planning and coordination) were related to satisfaction with directive management styles. Directive supervision was more satisfying when the organization was disorganized, the external environment strongly influenced work activities, and tasks required planning and coordination (p. 147). Participative styles of supervision were satisfying when the organization was disorganized and organizational constraints were loose (p. 148). Group effectiveness was highest for participative managers in disorganized settings and for directive managers in tasks requiring much planning and coordination. Thus, leader style was shown to be related to broader characteristics of the organization, among which were structure.

In a study of sixty college fraternity chapters, Osborn and Hunt (1975) found strong support for the effects of organization environment on leadership. All of the chapters were organized around the same "mechanistic" model (Burns and Stalker, 1961), as required by the national headquarters. Osborn and Hunt measured (1) the chapter president's perception of environmental complexity — that is, external unit interaction and dependency on external units; (2) the members' perception of the president's leader behavior; and (3) member satisfaction.

Both leader-initiating structure and consideration were significantly related to the degree of environmental complexity. They argue that the leader is constrained by both the external reality in which he or she operates and by necessary reactions to subordinates' influence on the leader. While Osborn and Hunt did not directly study the effect of structure on leadership, their model did test relationships between leadership and variables related to structure. Within the framework of a single form of structure, these environmental variables are shown to influence leader actions. Finally, Osborn and Hunt postulate that it is not the behavior of the leader per se, but his or her discretionary behaviors (nonexternally determined), that have the greatest impact on group members.

Bowers (1975) examined data from 1683 work groups from twenty-one organizations, measured using the University of Michigan *Survey of Organizations* (Taylor and Bowers, 1972). He examined the relationship between four measures of supervisory leadership, four measures of peer leadership, and two criterion variables, satisfaction and group process (group coordination, facilitation, and the like).

Bowers found that while supervisory leadership was not related to satisfaction in the same way across hierarchical levels (supporting the Katz and Kahn theory), group process was less affected by hierarchical level. Peer leadership was the predictor most strongly related to group process; peer leadership varied somewhat with the nature of supervisory leadership, indicating an indirect relationship between structure (hierarchy) and group process. Bowers concludes that while leadership is contingent, it is "not widely so" (1975: 80).

Franklin (1975) found that measures of group process (also measured with the *Survey of Organizations*) at hierarchically higher levels of the 246 work groups he surveyed were the primary predictors of organization climate at hierarchically lower levels. Within any group, organization climate was the primary predictor of supervisory leadership, which in turn was the primary predictor of peer leadership. Peer leadership, finally, was the primary predictor of within group process. Franklin's findings lend support to the argument that higher level structures have significant impact on the functioning of leaders at different levels in the hierarchy, consistent with the observations of Likert (1967). His findings are of particular interest since they are the result of a two wave longitudinal study separated by somewhat more than one year.

Both Bowers' and Franklin's results are only weak support for the effects of structure on leadership, however, since the only structural variable is the level of hierarchy. However, this would indicate that research designs should control for this variable. Further, Kerr (1976) argues that many of the structural and other properties of organizations serve to direct member behavior in lieu of, and sometimes in conflict with, appointed leaders. A number of organizational characteristics (formalization, inflexibility, highly specified activities, and spatial difference between leaders and subordinates) were suggested as substitutes for leadership. Kerr argues that other characteristics of the task, some of which are likely to be designed into the tasks by managers, and characteristics of the subordinates both serve to limit the influence of the leader. Overall, "structure," in general terms, can be argued to exact significant influence over leader behavior.

Critique of Structure from the Leadership Perspective

Five major criticisms of the treatment of structure in the leadership literature are warranted. First, the potential impact of organization structure on leadership has not gone unrecognized, and this makes it difficult to justify its absence in theoretical formulations. Worthy (1950) noted that the effect of centralization and complexity on leadership was extremely detrimental to leader-subordinate relations and argued that until structure was changed, little could be done to improve leadership. Dubin (1965) argued that although supervisors could exert some influence on productivity, they were nevertheless strongly limited by other organizational factors such as technology and structure.

It is the author's contention that conceptualizations of leadership that do not consider the role of the organization are deficient. As it is, most conceptualizations of leadership place the leader in an organizational vacuum. Thus, results such as those reported by Mott (1972), showing that nearly any theory of leadership predicts organizational effectiveness as well as any other but that none predict it very well, should not be unexpected.

The second criticism has been widely noted — the definition of leadership. As many reviewers have noted (Bennis, 1959; and Stogdill, 1974, to name only two), leadership has never been adequately or generally defined. But leadership is a process that must enact itself in a social structure; if that structure is a formal structure, as Katz and Kahn (1978) suggest, a leader must create it. That structure may itself become either a limitation on the discretion of the leader (or other leaders) or a tool that defines the power of the leader (French and Raven, 1960). From a definitional perspective, then, which is the "real" act of leadership — creation of the structure that limits and/or defines power or use of structure following its creation? Existing definitions of leadership are generally too restrictive to address this question, although most empirical investigations of leadership theories implicitly assume that leadership is the use of structure after its creation.

This suggests a third criticism. An implicit assumption of most leadership research is that if some "formula" for leadership were to be discovered, not only would researchers be able to prescribe leader choices (of methods, styles, etc.), but it would make a significant difference in the functioning and effectiveness of the organization. Such evidence has never been convincingly demonstrated, and there is evidence to suggest that it would not make a difference. Argyle, Gardner, and Ciofi (1958) concluded that "good" supervision, as identified by the Michigan theories, might yield little more than a 15 percent increase in subordinate productivity. In a study of leadership rotation, Rosen (1969) could not clearly identify the effect of leadership styles on productivity. There have been many studies showing a relationship between leadership and other criteria, particularly job satisfaction, but even for these outcomes, the direction of relationships is open to question (Lowin and Craig, 1968; Greene,

1975). The underlying issue in this criticism, therefore, is the question of whether the intense study of leadership as leader-group interaction is justifiable either in terms of results achieved or potential future benefits to organizations and their members.

A fourth criticism concerns the nature of the contingencies considered by the contingency theories of leadership. Specifically, contingencies at the level of the leader, especially the personality and preferences of the leader, have not been included to a sufficient degree. Leader preferences and personality variables have not been studied in what would seem to be a perfectly logical context, the way they manifest themselves in organization designs. Early research using personality measures to predict managerial potential was not very fruitful (Campbell et al., 1970), but little of this work has used criterion measures other than individual work performance. Research by the author, although still in incomplete form, has shown a very strong relationship between leader preferences and self-reported levels of centralization, formalization, and standardization in units led by the respondents (Kmetz, 1978a).

A final criticism is that many leadership theories implicitly presume a homogeneity of leadership actions in controlling task behavior. This should not be misconstrued to mean that leaders all behave the same way: research has established that leader behavior varies (Hill and Hughes, 1974). Rather, it is argued that the theories presume that once contingencies have been identified, a given style of leadership appropriate to that situation will be chosen by all effective leaders faced with a similar situation. The theories tend to overlook the possibility of relativism — that is, that supportiveness, directiveness, or other leader behaviors may be defined by either leader or subordinates with respect to a limited degree of leader discretion. Such limited discretion, and its significance to the leader, are suggested by Calder's (1977) attribution theory and the empirical work of Osborn and Hunt (1975). A study of perceived effectiveness differences between centralized and decentralized units showed that supportiveness was indeed much more important in centralized units (Kmetz, 1978b).

LEADERSHIP FROM THE STRUCTURE PERSPECTIVE

Just as the study of organization structure is relegated to an inferior status in the leadership literature, the concept of leadership is largely ignored in the organization structure literature. This lack of convergence with the leadership literature can be traced to two major roots: (1) traditionally, organization theory has evolved from a more sociological perspective; and (2) much of the investigation of structure and variables related to it was stimulated by the work of Woodward (1965), which postulated a "technological imperative" determining organization structure. Much subsequent theoretical and empirical work has focused on the predictive powers of various "context" variables — particularly size, technology, and environmental variables — for organization structure.

The principal thrust of organization theory in recent years has been toward refinement of the contingency theory of organization. As Child (1974) has noted, these studies implicitly treat the human participants of the organization, leaders included, as a form of mythical "average man." He notes that these studies have concentrated on the development of the best contingency response to a given set of circumstances, seemingly ignoring the possibility that multiple responses to a defined environment might be available (Miles, Snow, and Pfeffer, 1974; Miles and Snow, 1978). The major shortcoming of this contingency work, in short, is that it fails to acknowledge that while contingencies may constrain design choices and structural forms, they do not singularly determine the structural form.

Empirical Research Linking Structure and Leadership

As one of the early contributors of the Aston scholars, Pugh et al. (1968) concluded there are two basic structure alternatives — (1) direct supervisory intervention in the process of work ("line control of workflow") and (2) use of structure to control worker discretion ("structuring of activities"). As one of these is an "active" mode through leader behavior and the other a "passive" mode through structural prescriptions, the results imply a relationship between leader activity and organization structure.

Another early study, and perhaps one of the cornerstones of the contingency theory of organization, is the work of Lawrence and Lorsch (1967). They showed that increased unit differentiation required increased leader action to integrate the units of the firm. Both differentiation and integration were conceptualized and operationalized as having both psychological and organizational properties.

Reeves and Turner (1972) reported an interesting relationship between the activities of foremen and the process of dealing with uncertainty in the production process. Much of organization theory argues that organizations will attempt to buffer the technical core of the organization from disturbances emanating from the environment in order that production may proceed with minimal interruptions (Parsons, 1960; Thompson, 1967). Reeves and Turner's work, however, indicated that the activities of the foremen may be a significant source of unintended task uncertainty. The foremen had to act as "glorified progress chasers," continuously monitor production progress of various orders, and make immediate decisions regarding the sequence of processing of these orders. This was frequently done at the expense of prior production plans.

Contemporary organization theory would view this as the "organization" attempting to functionally deal with environmental contingencies. But it is possible to reverse this argument and to contend that reported departures from scheduled production are an unplanned source of disturbances from within the system. Leaders at the production level, for very defensible reasons, are one of the principal disruptors of higher management's plans. In this sense, contingency theory fails to explain the functional equilibrium between leaders on different levels and organizational outcomes that they must achieve on their respective levels.

Most theoretical structure formulations are ill-prepared to contend with the dynamics of a situation so turbulent as this. And most organizations are turbulent. While such formulations might prescribe a high level of formalization to report on the status of production, along with a decentralized system of production decisionmaking, the actions of the leadership cannot be interpreted without reference to the nature of the organization structure, any more than the structure can be described without reference to leader actions. As Burns and Stalker (1961) clearly indicated, the decision to adopt or abandon an "organic" structure was not purely a response to context variables.

Much structure literature assumes that structure exerts control on the behavior of organization members. Ouchi and Maguire (1975) found some support for this effect, but they also found that direct personal surveillance of behavior (behavior control) was not replaceable by output control — this is, by impersonal structural mechanisms. They concluded that these two forms of control are independent of each other. Following this work, Ouchi (1977) concluded that structure and control are not the same thing and that this distinction has not been made in the literature. He found that only about 33 percent of the variance in control in the earlier study could be explained by structure variables.

These findings would disagree with Miner's (1975) contention that we should abandon the leadership concept and apply our efforts toward understanding the control process. Ouchi and Maguire's work clearly suggests that control is effected partially through direct leader action, as well as through structure, and that the two cannot be used as substitutes for each other.

Numerous other studies have suggested a relationship between leadership and either organization structure or one or more of the "macro" variables frequently related to structure. Mahoney and Weitzel (1969) showed that managers develop models of organizational effectiveness consistent with their functional responsibilities and that these serve as the criteria for judgment of their unit's performance. Duncan (1972, 1973) showed that the effects of the environment are enacted through managers' perceptions of environmental uncertainty. These perceptions in turn lead to differentiation, which depends on both perceived uncertainty and perceived influence over the environment as well as the leader's model of effectiveness. Hrebiniak (1974), in a study of thirty-six hospital units, showed that both task technology and style of leadership are related to work unit structure. Leadership was measured using the Ohio State dimensions, and while Hrebiniak's findings were limited to work units, they show that leadership and structure are certainly not independent of each other. Meyer (1975) measured leadership by the degree to which it was "entrenched" in the organization and found that structure-environment relationships were moderated by the extent that leadership was entrenched: structure-environment relationship strength varied directly with degree of entrenchment. The effects of size were also attenuated with entrenched leadership. Meyer's study is particularly interesting specifically because it does differentiate between leadership as a personality trait and as a condition of the organization.

In their study of strategic and work decisionmaking in Belgian city governments, Bacharach and Aiken (1976) reported that process variables (such as the level of decision autonomy and communication) had different effects, and asymmetrical effects, from structure variables across levels of hierarchy. For middle echelon managers, the strongest predictors of strategic decisionmaking were lower work groups' autonomy and communication within middle echelons; the only structure variable to predict significantly was the middle level span of control. In lower echelons, decisions were most strongly predicted by communication (for strategic decisions) and routinization (for work decisions).

In examining the relationship between perceived environmental uncertainty (PEU) and structure through boundary-spanning activity, Leifer and Huber (1977) found that structure may predict PEU better than the reverse relationship. The role of boundary spanners is critical in this relationship, suggesting that leaders may have an important interpretive role. While the sample in the Leifer and Huber study was not restricted to the unit leaders, Ford (1976b) demonstrated this clearly as a function of the leader role. Using the Ohio State dimensions of leadership, he showed that the relationship between perceived structure and intended structure was moderated by the leader's behavior, principally in initiating structure. The apparent lack of relationship between these two types of structure measures (Pennings, 1973; Sathe, 1975), according to Ford, can be largely explained by the behavior of the leader as an intervening variable.

Critique of Leadership from the Structure Perspective

The first criticism refers to the presumed determinism that exists between context variables and organization structure. Pfeffer and Salancik (1978) demonstrate this form of implied determinism in their analysis of organizational reactions to environmental pressures — particularly, dependence on the environment for resource acquisition. The literature frequently refers to the "actions" of organizations as a convenient aggregation for the responses of the decisionmakers. The specific reasons for those actions go unquestioned and unexamined and result in the kind of mechanistic bias noted by Child (1974). This determinism continues to characterize much of the present work in organization theory despite findings that severely question it.

A second criticism refers to three particular points of convergence that have been demonstrated but not integrated in macrotheories of organization: (1) the relationship between leadership, task structure, and broader organization design variables that has been shown in the studies on job enlargement and job enrichment; (2) the relationship between structure and leadership actions in the literature on centralization and decentralization; and (3) a similar relationship in the literature on matrix organization. An illustrative case of the relationships between these variables in job redesign is that of General Foods (Walton, 1972). The changed job designs directly and positively affected supervisor-subordinate relationships and work performance. However, the perceived reduction in higher management power resulted in management's resistance to the program and in some degree of reversion back to the form of structure employed in other General Foods plants. While a negative example, this nevertheless shows the relationship between job redesign and leadership preferences for organization structure.

Decentralization is widely recognized as a discretionary leader style (Worthy, 1950; Tannenbaum, 1968; Galbraith, 1977). Decentralization has emerged as a factor of organization structure in many studies of the dimensions of structure and in relationship to context variables (see Ford [1976a] for a review). Centralization has also been found to be related to task structure at the level of the supervisor (Pheysey, Payne, and Pugh, 1971). In view of such findings, centralization and decentralization should logically be treated as discretionary variables in organization theory.

Matrix structures clearly link leader decisionmaking with organization theory (Davis and Lawrence, 1977; Galbraith, 1977; Lawrence, Kolodny, and Davis, 1977). They affect the distribution of power, leader style, and task structure. They have been shown to influence variables at the microlevel, including the levels of conflict (Butler, 1973) and satisfaction, job involvement, and role ambiguity for workers (Joyce and Garber, 1975). In sum, it is disappointing to see the extent to which the work in macrotheory fails to either integrate or learn from phenomena that exist so clearly.

A third criticism is the presumed homogeneity of structure — namely, that dimensions of organization structure are the same and have the same meaning at all levels of the organization. If one accepts the argument that structure follows context variables, then this is a sensible assumption. However, if one assumes that design and decision processes intervene between the context variables and structure, the assumption quickly loses merit. Only two studies have directly examined the question of the effect of context variables on subunit structure, which is the major question posed. Neither the author's research (Kmetz, 1977) nor the work of Mendenhall and Delbecq (1977) supported the argument that context variables directly affected the structure of the subunits.

AN INTEGRATED MODEL OF LEADERSHIP AND ORGANIZATION STRUCTURE

Figure 6-1 is a model proposing an integration of theory and research into organization context, organization structure, and leadership. The model integrates both bodies of research reviewed above and illustrates necessary research direction.

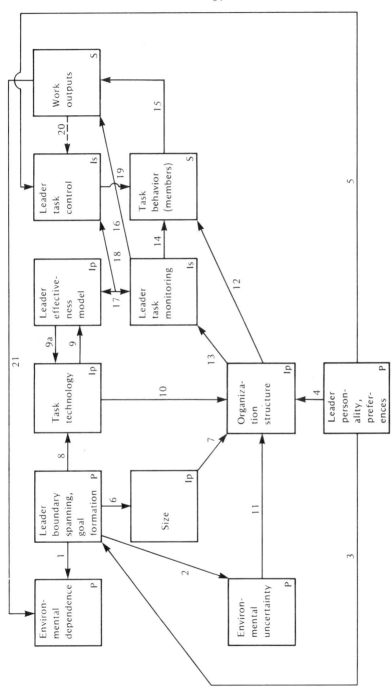

Figure 6-1. An integrated model of organization environment, organization structure, and leadership.

Several general points about the model should be noted prior to discussion of it. First, the model is simplified in a number of important respects. Leadership is partitioned into five distinct components that encompass, in aggregate form, all the major leadership variables studied — namely, functions, behavior, and personality. Structure has similarly been treated as a single aggregate variable. It is recognized that detailed study of relationships between leader variables and structure variables in some cases would require decomposition of these aggregates into their respective components, but this is not incompatible with the model. Relationships between the aggregate variables, on the other hand, are hypothesized to be those shown.

Second, the model is a closed loop model, but not a closed system model. If it is true that dependence on the environment is a critical contingency of organizations, then one of the tasks confronting leaders is that of effectively relating organization outputs to the demands and expectations of the environment. The integration of these must be achieved through leadership actions, since the leadership must sense what the environment expects, on the input side, and determine that the organization fulfills these expectations as completely as possible, on the output side. The latter function requires monitoring of work processes and corrective action if deviations from the required behaviors occur. Thus, organizational outputs close the loop between the organization and its environment, and between a number of internal processes and the demands of the environment, where leadership is one of the crucial internal processes.

Third, the model is consistent with what we know of relationships between context and structure at the macrolevel and leadership and organizational activities on the microlevel. It thus permits these two levels of functioning to be combined. The model assumes that the leader is the link between organizational processes and context variables. The leadership functions shown are thus categorized by this intermediary role, not as variables defined by other research. For example, leader boundary-spanning behavior and leader task monitoring are really both forms of monitoring (Mintzberg, 1973). Since they are focused on different organizational processes, however, they are decomposed here.

Variables in the Model

The model consists of twelve aggregate variables. Table 6-1 shows the names, conceptualizations, and possible operationalizations of these. If one were to examine the flow of an identified work process from beginning to end in an organization, there would be a sequence

Table 6-1. Variables in the Integrated Model

Variable	Conceptualization	Operationalization
Environmental dependence	Extent to which organization is dependent on outside agencies for supply, output disposal, sanctions	Autonomy to make operating decisions without approval; perceptions of boundary-spanning managers
Environmental uncertainty	Extent to which task environment is changeable, unknowable, unpredictable, possibly threatening	Rate of change of task environment elements; perceptions of boundary spanners
Leader boundary spanning and goal formation	External monitoring and information-processing role behavior	Percent of time performing this role; number of contacts with internal and external persons concerned with same issues
Organization size	Dimensions of organization and/or unit	Number of employees, volume of throughput
Leader personality and preferences	Relevant dimensions of total personality that specify or suggest normative aspects of control	Values, theory X versus theory Y orientation, preferences for control modes; actions taken in situations where action can be taken
Task technology	Knowledge and mechanization required to transform inputs to outputs	Knowledge and training required, skill specificity; sophistication of mechanization used; extent of man-machine interface (ratio measure); *caution* — easily confounded with structure
Leader effectiveness model	Criteria of performance for unit or organization	Perceived outcomes that organization or unit must attain to be effective; operational requirements and expectations
Organization structure	Pattern or planned, formal relationships; centralization, standardization, formalization, functional specialization, interdependence, reward system	Perceptions of each structure component; various objective measures too numerous to mention here; *caution* — easily confounded with technology (see Stanfield, 1976)

Table 6-1. (continued)

Variable	Conceptualization	Operationalization
Leader task monitoring	Observance and measurement of work behavior and/or outputs	Reporting (oral and written), personal surveillance, visitations, inquiries
Leader task control	Specific leader behaviors intended to influence level of output, quality of output, member behavior	Initiating structure with respect to task performance; standard enforcement and giving of task-related feedback
Task behavior (members)	Actual work performance and its functional utility	Various measures of compliance with requirements of workflow and other performance parameters
Work outputs	Results-outcomes of task performance	Quantity, quality, efficiency, and so forth of outputs

in which different groups of these variables would enter into the workflow. It is on this basis that the variables are grouped.

1. *Logically prior variables (P)* — environmental dependence, environmental uncertainty, leader personality, and leader boundary-spanning and goal formation. These variables are considered to be "logically prior," since they constitute the precedent conditions for any episode of organization-environment interaction. The conditions of the environment must be perceived and interpreted by the leader for their transformation into meaningful information for the organization.

2. *Intervening variables (I)* — As a group, these variables intervene between the initiation and completion of an episode between the organization and its environment. These are further divided into two groups:

   a. *Primary intervening (Ip)* — task technology, the leader's effectiveness model, organization size, and organization structure. These variables in a sense constitute the organization's "internal givens." All variables in this group are characterized as having relationships with logically prior variables as moderated through leader perceptions and prior decisions. The one partial exception to this statement is the relationship between structure and environmental uncertainty.

   b. *Secondary intervening (Is)* — leader task monitoring and leader task control. Both of these variables are elements of discretionary leader behavior, where the discretion is bounded by prior decisions and actions such as the creation of specific structures.

3. *Logically subsequent variables (S)* — task behavior of members and work outputs. These variables are considered "logically subsequent" because the parameters that define and constrain them are all of the variables described above. They represent the organization's closure with the environment, since the outcomes of these processes determine the extent to which the organization fulfills the demands imposed on it by its environment.

Description of the Model

Although the model is a closed loop, it is convenient and theoretically appropriate to begin examination of it at the point of environment-leader interaction. It is hypothesized that the selective perceptions of the leaders (boundary spanning) determine what is sensed in the environment and not that the environment somehow indicates automatically the appropriate response to contingencies it poses. As Weick (1969, 1977) argues, the "enacted environment" is more a function of leader creation than of environmental dictum. Pennings (1975) showed that structure did not vary with the environment as organization contingency theory would predict. Meyer (1975) showed that leadership was a function of the organization and was able to function independently of environmental demands. Finally, Leifer and Huber (1977) showed that perceived environmental uncertainty was predicted by structure rather than the reverse. However, consistent with Galbraith (1977) and Pfeffer and Salancik (1978), the model hypothesizes that environmental uncertainty may have some direct effects on organization structure. These effects are shown by arrows 1 and 2 in Figure 6-1.

The specific aspects of environment sensed are partly determined by leader perceptions, values, and preferences (personality), shown by arrow 3. Thus, unless the leaders regard an environmental variable as significant, the organization does not respond to it in its goal formation processes. Negandhi and Reimann (1973) have shown that "objective" environmental characteristics and managers' perceptions of these are not necessarily the same.

Leader preferences also affect structure by design choices (arrow 4). Research into this relationship has been largely absent from the literature, despite arguments from McGregor (1960) and Argyris (1964, 1973) and some empirical work suggesting that the relationship exists (Stanton, 1960; Bowers, 1975; Franklin, 1975). For this reason, Galbraith cautions against simple interpretation of relationships between environment and centralization (1977: 80). Research by the author (Kmetz, 1977) has shown that system level and unit level structures do not covary with context variables, as contingency theory suggests: they are nearly independent of each other.

Structure is also influenced by size (arrow 7), although the effect is hypothesized to vary with leader perceptions and preferences. This is argued for two reasons: (1) leaders may choose to define goals and work technologies that restrict variation in size; and (2) leaders may choose to vary directly the size of organizations and/or subunits (Filley, House, and Kerr, 1976). In sum, while it is accepted that size influences structure (Hickson, Pugh, and Pheysey, 1969), it is hypothesized that prior leader decisions influence size.

Arrow 8 indicates that goal definition partially determines the task technology to be used. This choice also influences structure, as shown by arrow 10 (Woodward, 1965; Van de Ven and Delbecq, 1974).

It should be noted that structure, up to this point, has been defined as the macrolevel structure of the organization — that is, centralization, formalization, standardization, span of control, horizontal and vertical differentiation, and so on. Task structure, on the other hand, is conceived to be a joint function of organization structure and leader control.

Organization structure is hypothesized to have two principal relationships to task behavior and control. Once a goal has been defined and a technology to achieve it chosen, task structure partially depends on the technology (arrow 12). The other effect is to create measurable characteristics of task behavior and/or work output, which are then monitored (Ouchi and Maguire, 1975; Lawler and Rhode, 1976).

Whether the leader exerts direct personal control over the work depends on the "effectiveness model" of the leader, and this must be discussed. There are two considerations. First, managerial models of effectiveness are hypothesized to be a function of goal definition and task technology, as shown by arrow 9 (Mahoney and Weitzel, 1969; Mahoney and Frost, 1974). However, these effectiveness models may influence choice of task technology (arrow 9a).

The second consideration involves task-monitoring behavior (arrows 14 and 16). Information from both task behavior and work outputs is monitored, the proportion of each depending on the extent to which performance processes are understood (Ouchi and Maguire, 1975; Ouchi, 1977). This information is then compared to the effectiveness model (arrow 17). Depending on the extent to which the effectiveness model is satisfied (arrow 18), the leader may choose to directly intervene in task behavior or work processes.

There is one additional element of this choice process that has yet to be considered. The personality or preferences of the leader may also directly influence the decision to intervene. Much research into Fiedler's (1967) model has demonstrated that leader perceptions of subordinates as measured by ASo or LPC scores may be a dimension of leader personality.

Therefore, this model hypothesizes control of task behavior to be a joint function of organization structure and direct leader intervention. Work control is partially designed into the structure and task technology; exceptions require leader decisionmaking and intervention to maintain control. These functions interact, since many of the monitored elements of work performance are a function of structure (e.g., information that must be recorded). Much of the leader's monitoring ability is similarly a function of prior decisions by higher management. The leader at any hierarchical level is not completely constrained by the structure of the organization, however, as the model indicates.

Task behavior leads to work outputs (arrow 15), although relationships among various work outputs are more complex than shown in aggregate form here (Porter and Lawler, 1964; Schwab and Cummings, 1970). From the perspective of this model, the most relevant outputs are those that directly affect environmental dependency (arrow 21). The significance of arrow 20, which is dashed to indicate that these outputs do not always occur, is twofold. Some work outputs may directly affect leader task-monitoring behavior — for example, outputs of staff units or higher management. The other effect may be from the work group, where outputs from the group may influence task-monitoring behavior (Lowin and Craig, 1968).

The loop between the organization and environment is closed by the outputs shown by arrow 21. If these satisfy relevant elements of the task environment (Hirsch, 1975), the organization receives positive cues. Those that are not satisfactory result in negative cues, and the leaders can either (1) ignore them for the short term, (2) attempt to change them (arrow 1), or (3) attempt to change the outputs of the organization (goal formation and control).

CONCLUDING COMMENTS: THE POTENTIAL FOR THE FUTURE

Throughout this chapter it has been argued that both the leadership and organization structure theories and research have been inadequate because they ignore each other. It is proper to ask the potential benefit of using an integrated model such as the one proposed here. Several clarifications and theoretical advances may accrue to the use of such a model.

In general, we may be able to resolve many of the inconsistencies found in much of the research in both fields. Examining leadership as a choice mechanism may help us understand how and why the leader chooses his actions, the context of his choices, and the effects of those choices on the behavior of others. We may also be able to understand the processes by which limited aspects of the environment affect the leader, structure, and work behavior.

Such an approach may also help to define leadership in meaningful terms. This has not yet been achieved and is still a major stumbling block in understanding leadership. The leader may, in fact, be "acting out a script" determined by these broader organizational factors, where we now assume complete or nearly complete discretion. If personality manifests itself within a defined environment, we may be able to learn how the leader's personality affects the functioning of the organization and its members. It is commonly observed that leader personality does have this effect, but present theories have failed to indicate how or why it is manifested in formal organizations.

The model also specifies leader actions that are directly related to other, logically prior organizational variables. The assumption that consideration or initiating structure may be used solely at the discretion of the leader has limited the explanatory power of not only the Ohio State model, but others as well. One significant variable that these theories have never really defined is the "task structure" of the leader himself. The present model indicates what this task structure may be and how it may be formed.

Many authors have argued that we need longitudinal studies to really determine causation between variables in our theories. This is still the case, and it applies to this model as well. However, it is possible to trace the progression of effects through a meaningful sequence of variables that functionally affect the leader. Longitudinal studies of previous leadership theories have reported largely ambiguous and inconclusive results. It is this author's contention that these disappointing results have been obtained not only because the data were inadequate, but because the basic models themselves were. Longitudinal data on the wrong questions does not yield understanding.

The approach suggested by this model should help us to understand more than simply the derivation of leadership and organization structure, but also how this actually results in control of an organization. Control is a major issue in both lines of research, but it is not the only issue. However, much previous work has implicitly been directed toward understanding of methods for achieving reduction in behavior variance. While this is necessary both for prescriptions of leader behavior and in the design of structures, both leadership and structure also serve as mechanisms to define and redefine organizational goals. In this sense they are "focusing" devices, not controlling devices, and this role of these processes has been largely ignored.

Finally, an integrated approach to studying leadership and organization structure should help to both define organizational effectiveness and understand more fully how to achieve it. Most present research on leadership assumes that "better" group performance, defined in various ways, is the objective of good leadership. Most theories of organization structure proceed with no criterion variable at all. Neither of these approaches is satisfactory. Complex organizations have complex goals, and the contribution of both leadership and organization structure should be toward optimization of objective attainment. This requires that our theories be able to cope with goal complexity and the common phenomenon of goal conflict, which none of them really do at present. By examining the system as a system within a broader context and using this as a model for all levels of analysis, it may be possible to approach understanding of not only the relationships between these processes, but the meaning of them as well.

REFERENCES

Argyle, M.; G. Gardner; and F. Ciofi. 1958. "Supervisory Methods Related to Productivity, Absenteeism, and Labour Turnover." *Human Relations* 11: 23-40.

Argyris, C. 1964. *Integrating the Individual and the Organization.* New York: Wiley.

———. 1973. "Personality and Organization Theory Revisited." *Administrative Science Quarterly* 18: 141-67.

Bacharach, S. B., and M. Aiken. 1976. "Structural and Process Constraints on Influence in Organizations: A Level-Specific Analysis." *Administrative Science Quarterly* 21: 623-41.

Bass, B. M., and E. R. Valenzi. 1974. "Contingent Aspects of Effective Management Styles." In J. G. Hunt and L. L. Larson, eds., *Contingency Approaches to Leadership.* Carbondale, Ill.: Southern Illinois University Press.

Bennis, W. G. 1959. "Leadership Theory and Administrative Behavior: The Problem of Authority." *Administrative Science Quarterly* 4: 259-301.

Bowers, D. G. 1975. "Hierarchy, Function and the Generalizability of Leadership Practices." In J. G. Hunt and L. L. Larson, eds., *Leadership Frontiers.* Kent, Ohio: Kent State University Press.

Burns, T., and G. M. Stalker. 1961. *The Management of Innovation.* London: Tavistock.

Butler, A. 1973. "Project Management: a Study of Organizational Conflict." *Academy of Management Journal* 16: 84-102.

Calder, B. J. 1977. "An Attribution Theory of Leadership." In B. M. Staw and G. R. Salancik, eds., *New Directions in Organizational Behavior.* Chicago: St. Clair.

Campbell, J. P.; M. D. Dunnette; E. E. Lawler; and K. E. Weick. 1970. *Managerial Behavior, Performance, and Effectiveness.* New York: McGraw-Hill.

Child, J. 1974. "Managerial and Organizational Factors Associated with Company Performance — Part I." *Journal of Management Studies* 11: 175-89.

Davis, P. M., and P. R. Lawrence. 1977. *Matrix.* Reading, Mass.: Addison-Wesley.

Dubin, R.; G. C. Homans; F. C. Mann; and D. C. Miller. 1965. *Leadership and Productivity: Some Facts of Industrial Life.* San Francisco: Chandler.

Duncan, R. 1972. "Characteristics of Organizational Environments and Perceived Environmental Uncertainty." *Administrative Science Quarterly* 17: 313-27.

———. 1973. "Multiple Decision-Making Structures Adapting to Environmental Uncertainty: the Impact on Organizational Effectiveness." *Human Relations* 26: 273-91.

Fiedler, F. E. 1967. *A Theory of Leadership Effectiveness.* New York: McGraw-Hill.

Fiedler, F. E., and M. M. Chemers. 1976. *Leadership and Effective Management.* Glenview, Ill.: Scott, Foresman.

Filley, A. C.; R. J. House; and S. Kerr. 1976. *Managerial Process and Organizational Behavior.* 2nd ed. Glenview, Ill.: Scott, Foresman.

Fleishman, E. A. 1973. "Twenty Years of Consideration and Structure." In J. G. Hunt and L. L. Larson, eds., *Current Developments in the Study of Leadership.* Carbondale, Ill.: Southern Illinois University Press.

Ford, J. D. 1976a. "Contingency Models and Organization Structure." Paper Presented at the 13th annual Easter Academy of Management meetings, George Washington University, Washington, D.C.

———. 1976b. "The Interaction of Size, Technology, and Environment on Dimensions of Intended Structure." Paper presented at the 36th annual Academy of Management meetings, Kansas City, Mo.

Franklin, J. L. 1975. "Down the Organization: Influence Processes Across Levels of Hierarchy." *Administrative Science Quarterly* 20: 153-64.

French, J. R. P., and B. H. Raven. 1960. "The Bases of Social Power." In D. Cartwright and A. Zander, eds., *Group Dynamics: Research and Theory.* 2nd ed. New York: Row, Peterson.

Galbraith, J. 1977. *Organization Design.* Reading, Mass.: Addison-Wesley.

Greene, C. N. 1975. "The Reciprocal Nature of Influence between Leader and Subordinate Performance." *Journal of Applied Psychology* 60: 187-93.

Hickson, D. J.; D. S. Pugh; and D. C. Pheysey. 1969. "Operations Technology and Organizational Structure: an Empirical Reappraisal." *Administrative Science Quarterly* 14: 378-97.

Hill, W. A., and D. Hughes. 1974. "Variations in Leader Behavior as a Function of Task Type." *Organizational Behavior and Human Performance* 11: 83–86.

Hirsch, P. M. 1975. "Organizational Effectiveness and the Institutional Environment." *Administrative Science Quarterly* 20: 327–44.

House, R. J. 1971. "A Path-Goal Theory of Leader Effectiveness." *Administrative Science Quarterly* 18: 321–32.

Hrebiniak, L. 1974. "Job Technology, Supervision, and Work-Group Structure." *Administrative Science Quarterly* 19: 395–409.

Joyce, W. F., and D. M. Garber. 1975. "The Matrix Structure and its Impact on Organizational Behavior." *Proceedings of the 12th Annual Eastern Academy of Management* (Pennsylvania State University, College Station, Pa.).

Katz, D., and R. L. Kahn. 1978. *The Social Psychology of Organizations.* 2nd ed. New York: Wiley.

Kerr, S. 1976. "Substitutes for Leadership: Some Implications for Organizational Design." *Organization and Administrative Sciences* 6/7: 135–46.

Kmetz, J. L. 1977. "System Level and Unit-Level Structures: an Empirical Appraisal." *Proceedings of the 37th Annual National Academy of Management Meetings.*

———. 1978a. "Organization Design: Slack, Preferences, and Unappreciated Variables." Working paper, University of Delaware.

———. 1978b. "Decentralization and Unit Effectiveness." Working paper, University of Delaware.

Lawler, E. E., and J. G. Rhode. 1976. *Information and Control in Organizations.* Pacific Palisades, Calif.: Goodyear.

Lawrence, P. R., and J. W. Lorsch. 1967. *Organization and Environment.* Cambridge, Mass.: Harvard University Press.

Lawrence, P. R.; H. F. Kolodny; and S. M. Davis. 1977. "The Human Side of the Matrix." *Organizational Dynamics* 6 (Summer): 43–61.

Leifer, R., and G. P. Huber. 1977. "Relations Among Perceived Environmental Uncertainty, Organization Structure, and Boundary-Spanning Behavior." *Administrative Science Quarterly* 22: 235–47.

Likert, R. 1967. *The Human Organization.* New York: McGraw-Hill.

Lowin, A., and J. R. Craig. 1968. "The Influence of Level of Performance on Managerial Style: an Experimental Object-lesson in the Ambiguity of Correlational Data." *Organizational Behavior and Human Performance* 3: 440–58.

Mahoney, T. A., and P. J. Frost. 1979. "The Role of Technology in Models of Organizational Effectiveness." *Organizational Behavior and Human Performance* 11: 122–38.

Mahoney, T. A., and W. Weitzel. 1969. "Managerial Models of Organizational Effectiveness." *Administrative Science Quarterly* 14: 357–65.

Mann, F. C. 1965. "Toward an Understanding of the Leadership Role in Formal Organization." In Dubin et al., *Leadership and Productivity: Some Facts of Industrial Life.* San Francisco: Chandler.

McCall, M. W. 1977. "Leaders and Leadership: of Substance and Shadow." In J. R. Hackman; E. E. Lawler; and L. W. Porter, *Perspectives on Behavior in Organizations.* New York: McGraw-Hill.

McGregor, D. 1960. *The Human Side of Enterprise.* New York: McGraw-Hill.

Mendenhall, J. S., and A. Delbecq. 1977. "The Axiomatic Theory — A Partial Test." Paper presented at the 37th Annual National Academy of Management, Orlando, Florida.

Meyer, M. W. 1975. "Leadership and Organization Structure." *American Journal of Sociology* 81: 514-42.

Miles, R. E., and C. C. Snow. 1978. *Organizational Strategy, Structure, and Process.* New York: McGraw-Hill.

Miles, R. E.; C. C. Snow; and J. Pfeffer. 1974. "Organization-Environment: Concepts and Issues." *Industrial Relations* 13: 244-64.

Miner, J. B. 1975. "The Uncertain Future of the Leadership Concept: an Overview." In J. G. Hunt and L. L. Larson, eds., *Leadership Frontiers.* Kent, Ohio: Kent State University Press.

Mintzberg, H. 1973. *The Nature of Managerial Work.* New York: Harper & Row.

Mott, P. E. 1972. *The Characteristics of Effective Organizations.* New York: Harper & Row.

Negandhi, A., and B. C. Reimann. 1973. "Task Environment, Decentralization, and Organizational Effectiveness." *Human Relations* 26: 203-14.

Osborn, R. N., and J. G. Hunt. 1975. "An Adaptive-Reactive Theory of Leadership: The Role of Macro Variables in Leadership Research." In J. G. Hunt and L. L. Larson, eds., *Leadership Frontiers.* Kent, Ohio: Kent State University Press.

Ouchi, W. G. 1977. "The Relationship between Organizational Structure and Organizational Control." *Administrative Science Quarterly* 22: 95-113.

Ouchi, W. G., and M. A. Maguire. 1975. "Organizational Control: Two Functions." *Administrative Science Quarterly* 20: 559-69.

Parsons, T. 1960. *Structure and Process in Modern Societies.* New York: Free Press.

Pennings, J. 1973. "Measures of Organizational Structure: a Methodological Note." *American Journal of Sociology* 79: 686-704.

———. 1975. "The Relevance of the Structural-Contingency Model for Organizational Effectiveness." *Administrative Science Quarterly* 20: 393-410.

Pfeffer, J., and G. R. Slancik. 1978. *The External Control of Organizations.* New York: Harper & Row.

Pheysey, D. C.; R. L. Payne; and D. S. Pugh. 1971. "Influence of Structure at Organizational and Group Levels." *Administrative Science Quarterly* 16: 61-73.

Porter, L. W., and E. E. Lawler. 1964. "Properties of Organization Structure in Relation to Job Attitudes and Job Behavior." *Psychological Bulletin* 64: 23-51.

Pugh, D. S.; D. J. Hickson; C. R. Hinings; and C. Turner. 1968. "Dimensions of Organization Structure." *Administrative Science Quarterly* 13: 68-89.

Reeves, T. K., and B. A. Turner. 1972. "A Theory of Organization and Behavior in Batch Production Factories." *Administrative Science Quarterly* 17: 81-97.

Rosen, N. 1969. *Leadership and Work-group Design: a Rotation Experiment.* Ithaca, N.Y.: Cornell University Press.

Sathe, V. 1975. "Measures of Organizational Structure: A Conceptual Distinction Between Two Major Approaches." *Proceedings of the 35th Annual Academy of Management Meetings.* New Orleans, La.

Schwab, D. P., and L. L. Cummings. 1970. "Theories of Performance and Satisfaction: A Review." *Industrial Relations* 9: 408-30.

Stanfield, G. G. 1976. "Technology and Organization Structure as Theoretical Categories. *Administrative Science Quarterly* 21: 489-93.

Stanton, E. S. 1960. "Company Policies and Supervisors Attitudes toward Supervision." *Journal of Applied Psychology* 44: 22-26.

Stinson, J., and L. Tracy. 1974. "Some Disturbing Characteristics of the LPC Score." *Personnel Psychology* 24: 477-85.

Stogdill, R. 1974. *Handbook of Leadership*. New York: Free Press.

Tannenbaum, A. 1968. *Control in Organizations*. New York: McGraw-Hill.

Taylor, J.; and D. M. Bowers. 1972. *The Survey of Organizations*. Ann Arbor: Institute for Social Research, University of Michigan.

Thompson, J. D. 1967. *Organizations in Action*. New York: McGraw-Hill.

Urwick, L. F. 1943. *The Elements of Administration*. New York: Harper.

Van de Ven, A. H., and A. Delbecq. 1974. "A Task Contingent Model of Work-Unit Structure." *Administrative Science Quarterly* 19: 183-97.

Walton, R. E. 1972. "How to Counter Alienation in the Plant." *Harvard Business Review* 14: 70-81.

Weick, K. E. 1969. *The Social Psychology of Organizing*. Reading, Mass.: Addison-Wesley.

———. 1977. "Enactment Processes in Organizations." In B. M. Staw and G. R. Salancik, eds., *New Directions in Organizational Behavior*. Chicago: St. Clair.

Woodward, J. 1965. *Industrial Organization Theory and Practice*. London: Oxford University Press.

Worthy, J. C. 1950. "Organizational Structure and Employee Morale." *American Sociological Review* 15: 170-79.

Chapter 7

Governance of Organizations: Leader-Led Roles

Raymond E. Miles*

Role change is a constant, recognizable, usually unsettling fact of life. Over time role shifts occur among nations, across and within large-scale institutions, and at the level of the family and the small face-to-face group. While the process of role change is complex and only partially understood, it is identifiable by shifts in attitudes, expectations, and behaviors of role holders. Whatever the process, changes in roles frequently produce major concern and pervasive consequences. Such is clearly the case with the changes that have occurred over the past three decades in the roles of leaders and led in formal organizations.

Changes in the formal leader-led roles in organizations are perhaps most visible today in Western Europe. A recent report by the American Center for the Quality of Work Life (1978:25) refers to the industrial democracy movement in Europe as a "phenomenon" and an "explosion" and suggests that future economic and social historians may view the changes of the 1970s as the "beginning of a transformation of industrial society at least as significant — in an opposite direction — as the transformation launched in Russia's violent

---

* University of California, Berkeley.

October Revolution of 1917." Across the world, the pattern of leader-led roles and behaviors in post-WWII Japanese organizations — a new "phenomenon" at least to Western observers — is also gaining increasing, though probably less intense, attention. In the United States, the major exporter of organization and managerial concepts during the first half of this century, change in leader-led roles and behavior has occurred perhaps less dramatically and over a longer time period than in other Western nations, but the ultimate effects may be equally if not more profound.

How substantive are these changes? How lasting are they likely to be? What implications do they have for organizational performance and national economic and social well-being? What further changes may be in store? The purpose of this chapter is to address these and related questions — to describe the more important changes that have occurred in leader-led roles and in the behavior of role participants in formal organizations and to analyze the current and future consequences of these shifts.

The scope of this effort is such that no attempt will be made at inclusiveness or chronological precision. I will use the U.S. experience as the focal point of my description and analysis, comparing changes in the United States with those in other nations. Focusing on the United States is in some ways inefficient: recent changes in Western Europe, as noted above, are certainly easier to define and describe. Nevertheless, my comparative advantage clearly lies with the U.S. experience.

In the following pages, I will first attempt to clarify and work my way around some of the conceptual barriers to discussing leadership in formal organizations. I will then describe and analyze leader-led roles and behaviors as they were defined, particularly in the United States, in the early 1950s and then, in the following section, use that period as the base point for comparison with current patterns. With the relatively easier tasks of description accomplished, we can then face the far more difficult process of analyzing the current and immediate future consequences of changed roles and behaviors, a task made troublesome by our lack of knowledge and/or agreement on the relationship between leadership and organizational performance. The final section will be both highly speculative and highly prescriptive — speculative with regard to the longer term consequences of present trends and prescriptive with regard to what further changes, if any, ought to occur in research, theory building, and organization practice.

CONCEPT CLARIFICATION

An only slightly caricatured summary of recent reviews (see, e.g., Pfeffer, 1977; Calder, 1977) on leadership would suggest that (1) leadership is at best an ambiguous concept, difficult, if not impossible, to operationalize as a useful research construct, and that (2) whatever leadership is, we know very little about it; (3) but neither (1) nor (2) is particularly upsetting because leadership, whatever it is, does not appear to matter much anyway.

As my tone suggests, I am not totally in agreement with the positions exaggerated in the above statements. The terms leadership and leader are frequently used in an ambiguous manner. We use the term leader to refer to an elected official, a person holding a formal post as supervisor of a work group, and an individual who emerges as an exerciser of exceptional influence in an ad hoc task group. Clearly the roles played in these three circumstances are not identical, and the forces shaping the attitudes, expectations, and behaviors of the players, both leaders and followers are widely varying. In the first instance, the political "leader" has presumably sensed and verbalized the goals and directions sought by his or her constituents and must continue to at least appear to be responsive to their wishes and needs to remain in office. In the second setting, the appointed work group supervisor usually operates within the constraints of fixed performance demands and procedures determined in part by in place technology. Moreover, he or she faces a set of at least partially formalized expectations (shared by work group members) concerning appropriate "leadership" behavior — work assignments that can and cannot be made, orders that are legitimate, requests that are acceptable under certain circumstances, and the like. Presumably an effective "leader" in such a supervisory post understands the existing constraints and expectations and operates, at the margin, to limit dysfunctions and enhance present and future contributions.

Finally, the emergent "leader" of an ad hoc task group has presumably demonstrated some ability to contribute to shared goals within the group, contributing ideas, channeling discussion, clarifying problems, and so forth, We know that a variety of "leadership" behaviors may be recognized as such by group members, some specific to a given task or setting and others that appear to be personal characteristics valued by different groups in a variety of circumstances. (Recently, "attribution" theorists have focused attention not so much on the traits and behaviors of leaders but instead on the process by which followers (subordinates, constituents, etc.) assign cause-effect power or responsibility to those in positions of formal or informal authority. I will at several points deal with subordinate desires and beliefs about their leaders' ability to influence events, to have an important impact, but I will not specifically utilize the perspective of the attribution theorists [see Calder, 1977].)

Despite the differences in the above examples, the common application of the terms leader and leadership is inappropriate (inaccurate) only if one demands conceptual consistency in degree as well as kind. That is, while the politician may be primarily engaged in maintaining a positive balance between power accumulation and expenditure, political "leadership" is usually achieved through some of the same behaviors visible in the emergence of the ad hoc task group leader — technical knowledge, the ability to articulate issues and answers, the capacity to sense the basis for agreement or compromise, and so on. The fact that some political leaders engage in such behaviors more effectively in the cloakroom than on the rostrum is of importance only in another context.

For the appointed leader, the holder of an organizational position superordinate to other members, the terms leader and leadership may be appropriate only to a portion of his or her behavior. As suggested earlier, the bulk of the manager or supervisor's interactions with subordinates may occur within what Simon referred to as the "zone of acceptance" (Simon, 1976: 116, 133, 204) — an area encompassing a set of actions, orders, requests, directives, and decisions that subordinates generally hold to be appropriate or legitimate. The zone of acceptance may be formalized by a labor contract, defined by unspoken bargaining leading to a "psychological contract," rooted in tradition, or specified by law and may be wide or narrow, highly situational, or stable or tenuous. Whatever the "width" of the zone of acceptance, leaders expect and generally obtain compliance with those requests, orders, directives, and the like that fall within its limits — that are part of what their subordinates treat as legitimate demands on their time and energies. Simon intended to specify by the zone of acceptance that arena in which subordinates do not question requests or orders but tend to follow them as a matter of course — doing what they are expected and paid to do.

However, at the margin of the core area of acceptance and extending outward to an area of unqualified rejection, is what I refer to as a "zone of conditional acceptance" (see Figure 7-1) — an area in which directives, orders, decisions, and so forth may or may not be accepted, depending on the office holder's leadership behavior (or

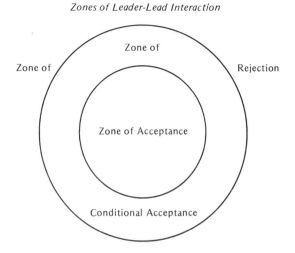

Zones of Leader-Lead Interaction

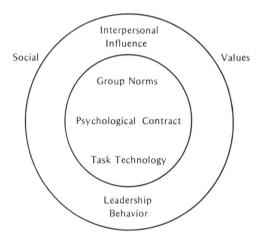

Determinants of Interaction

Figure 7-1. Incidence of leadership and management style.

lack thereof). As far as I know, the zone of conditional acceptance
has not been dealt with specifically in the leadership literature,
though its existence and limits have often been implied. Within this
arena, subordinates do not "accept" orders or directives automatically, but may do so if (1) the leader is charismatically persuasive, (2)
compelling information about the need for compliance is articulated,
(3) subordinates are involved in the decision process and thus feel

some ownership of the objectives being sought, or (4) an implicit bargain is struck with the leader.

The precise nature of the leadership behaviors that may operate in this "zone of conditional acceptance" and the efficacy of each are matters of contention and have been the primary focus of much of leadership research over time. Nevertheless, the same general set of behaviors that accrue influence for the politician or the informal leader are visible in the behavior of some organization office holders as they seek to move beyond (or prevent reduction in) the area of agreement they share with their subordinates. (Note that within the zone of acceptance, goal congruence is not assumed to exist. Nevertheless, agreement, or at least acceptance, is viewed as legitimate, even if "purchased" as part of a formal or psychological contract. Similarly, within the zone of conditional acceptance, goal congruence is not assumed to exist. Leaders may attempt to persuade or involve subordinates to achieve congruence or may "bargain" for an extension — usually temporary — of willingness to accept a goal that primarily serves organizational purposes.)

As the broader topic of this chapter is "organization governance," prime attention here will be focused on roles and behaviors of leaders and led in formal organizations and particularly in work organizations. The role of leader (and the role of led) will be examined with respect to both of the zones described above — the zone of acceptance "built in" to the post and the zone of conditional acceptance defined by the unspecified interaction of leader and led. It is my contention that characteristics of both "zones" have undergone change and that change in each zone must be analyzed separately and as an interactive process. We will return to this point in section three. First we must examine organizational leadership, the zone of acceptance, and the zone of conditional acceptance as it existed in our base period — the early 1950s.

LEADER-LED ROLES IN THE 1950s

The 1950s provide a point of comparison with today for a variety of contemporary social phenomenon — from sexual mores to market behavior. In the arena of leadership, the 1950s represent a period of strained stability, one in which formal leaders, stripped of many of their pre-WWII role sanctions, clung tightly to a precipice of paternalism and followers, while no longer worshipful, were at least still respectful.

Societal Perspective

To understand the leaders of the 1950s, one must understand the mood of the led. In the United States at least, the cry was for stability — a chance to make up for the long years of Depression and war with a period of good times unfettered by major social change. Electorates sought calm and stable leaders of unquestioned direction and integrity — the Eisenhowers, Adenauers, Macmillans, and De Gaulles. Few members of the favored nations were seeking to build a new world: most were only seeking the chance to climb a few rungs up the socioeconomic ladder toward the good life, using the accepted rules of ascension brought forward from their parents' generation. Political leaders, identified or created by their followers' desires, sought to preserve, protect, and only grudgingly change a world where order, while far from perfect, seemed to demand only strength, purpose, and perseverance. In the main, the political leaders of this period sought not to reign but to respond, traded morning clothes for business suits, and quietly sought to do as little as had to be done. (De Gaulle of course was the exception, but so was his task: he took over leadership in France in a period when not only was every aspirant free to seek the premiership, but most achieved it.) Political leaders sought to be not pontifical, but parental; not above life, but part of it; not idiosyncratic, but predictable; and a little warm, well intentioned blunder or two served to protect rather than damage their image. It is important to acknowledge that the 1950s were not without turmoil. In the United States, the period began in the grip of McCarthyism and the trauma of the Korean War and moved toward its close with troops at schoolhouse doors to help enforce the desegregation decision of the Supreme Court. Even so, the turmoil, while real and often tragic, tended to stay "in bounds." McCarthy was censored by the Senate; the war was brought to a negotiated conclusion; and the challenges to "white" schools were few enough to be dealt with at an orderly pace.

Among corporate leaders, the human relations philosophy of management was reaching full flower in the 1950s. Seeded in the 1920s and nurtured by the Hawthorne studies, the human relations philosophy focused on boosting the morale, loyalty, and cooperation of organization members through thoughtful, considerate leadership; limited involvement in decisionmaking; and improved programs of employee activities and benefits. (Throughout this chapter, I will utilize my three part categorization of managerial philosophies [and their resultant leader roles] — traditional, human relations, and human resources. These philosophies are abstracted in Appendix A.) In-house training programs designed to smooth the rough edges of supervisory practice were widespread, and university executive programs were beginning to attract audiences of middle and upper level managers. The message in all of these efforts was common: take care of your people and they will take care of you; treat them well and pay attention to their needs to feel important and a part of things.

The Zone of Acceptance

During the 1950s, the zone of acceptance narrowed perceptibly among unionized blue collar workers in the United States. In declining employment arenas (e.g., railroad crafts and the printing trades), workers fought for job security through restrictive work agreements, limiting managerial prerogatives with regard to job assignments and scheduling. Grievance machinery in many industries was increasingly formalized, and authority of lower level managers was measurably reduced not only by union agreements but by company policy and the growing power of special production and personnel staff units.

However, while the zone of acceptance was constricting in some industries among the lower ranks, in the fastest growing segments of the workforce — namely, white collar clerical and technical personnel and middle managerial ranks — compliance with managerial directives appeared little changed from earlier periods. In fact, given an expanding economy and a limited cohort of upwardly mobile organization members of prime age, young white collar workers and managers frequently identified closely with organizational goals as they sought to ascend the hierarchy. So close was the identification, so clear the conformity to organizational policies, that observers worried about the demise of individuality (see, for example, Mills, 1951; Whyte, 1966).

Not only was the zone of acceptance still broad for many organization members, but its supporting spokes were being constantly strengthened by the rapid growth of fringe benefits — vacations, pensions, holiday pay, medical benefits, and so forth — all tied to employment longevity and thus presumably to organizational loyalty. In most circumstances, managers could expect compliance with their orders and needed only to avoid excessively arbitrary behaviors, a point constantly stressed in company manuals and supervisory training classes.

In fact, by the late 1950s many managers had become competent enough interpersonally for most organization members to expect at least minimal levels of consideration of their personal needs. A major leadership research conclusion of the 1950s and early 1960s was that a lack of supervisorial consideration was associated with increased levels of member absenteeism, turnover, and grievances. Understandably, once consideration reached what were presumably expected levels, it appeared to have no further effect on member behavior (see Fleishman and Harris, 1962).

Zone of Conditional Acceptance

With the zone of acceptance apparently stable, the zone of conditional acceptance was the focal point of much organizational research and progressive organizational practice in the 1950s. The two major "experimental" studies of the period, at Prudential Insurance (Morse and Reimer, 1956) and at Harwood (Coch and French, 1948), demonstrated that employee involvement in the change of organization work practices tended to lead to higher levels of acceptance and satisfaction. It should be noted that at this time, leader and led roles in the United States were probably more conducive to gains from participative practices than was the case in other countries. Efforts to replicate the Harwood results in Scandinavia indicated that organization members there questioned the legitimacy of decision participation (see French, Israel, and As, 1960).

Looking backward, the zone of conditional acceptance in the 1950s was highly malleable, more malleable in fact than management made any attempt to test. Given the prevailing human relations philosophy, leaders tended to exercise the bulk of their influence in attempts to maintain cooperation rather than to stimulate subordinate creativity. That is, when the role of the led was enlarged to allow some involvement in the decisionmaking process, the role expansion typically was aimed at gaining acceptance for a particular, already chosen, line of action.

Managers in this period were constantly reminded that there were two parts to effective decisionmaking — (1) choosing the right alternative and (2) implementing that choice (. . . . , gaining acceptance of it). If, as it appeared, the implementation phase could be assisted by subordinate participation in helping choose ways of carrying out the plan, then by all means the manager should encourage participation. If a subordinate should, in the process of decision involvement, come up with an original idea, that creative input was treated as a bonus, an unexpected consequence of a process aimed primarily at removing resistance to the leader's ideas.

Three additional points should be made about the zone of conditional acceptance during the 1950s. First, leaders could obtain cooperation beyond "formal" lines by involving subordinates precisely because involvement, in the United States at least, was a socially valued opportunity not yet widely available. The led did not expect to be allowed to participate: it was not defined as part of their role, and for most it was not a major part of their prework experience. The situations that most had experienced in their prework worlds — in their homes, schools, churches, military organizations, and so forth — were by and large autocratically structured.

Second, it was regularly made clear to managers in the 1950s that they could expand the role of their subordinates without threatening their own role. The led could participate in the "trivial" phase of decisionmaking — implementation — without threatening the leader's prerogative to choose. It is important to note that even where participation was "formalized" (for example, in Scanlon Plan cost-savings schemes), it was focused on process improvements. The "crucial" decisions (e.g., product design, pricing, capital investment, etc.) were by and large outside the scope of subordinate involvement. Throughout the 1950s, management, even outside the unionized sector, defended its prerogatives with outspoken care. Even so progressive a management theorist as Peter Drucker (1954:310-11) was resolute on this point, arguing that employees should be aided in developing "managerial vision" (an understanding of the whys of organizational processes) but that management had sole responsibility for choosing organizational ends.

Finally, it should be noted that U.S. managers and management theorists at this point viewed themselves (perhaps appropriately) as well ahead of their colleagues in other parts of the Western world. U.S. firms were productive and were expanding abroad, and U.S. management skills were widely hailed. U.S.-based management consultants were active in Europe, spreading the word on organization designs and managerial practices. Many U.S. authors advocating participative practices were as well (if not better) known in Europe than at home.

In the United States, a growing number of management theorists and some managers were vaguely aware of the major European venture in the direction of subordinate involvement — the mandatory, highly limited (at that time) experiments in co-determination in Germany. In the main, co-determination was not viewed with alarm: it was not even considered particularly important. After all, it was (to the U.S. observer) merely a carefully structured mechanism for allowing limited minority involvement in decisionmaking. It was accepted, in the light of U.S. participatory practices, for what it appeared to be — an extremely low cost means of gaining wide-spread acceptance of organizational goals among the led. Interest-ingly, although co-determination and the awareness of U.S. managers of it have greatly expanded, it is still viewed (now somewhat cynically) as a nonthreatening, useful means of obtaining coopera-tion. The current view, and the reasons underlying it, will be explored in more detail and in better chronological perspective in a later section.

THE 1960S AND EARLY 1970S: WHAT CHANGED AND HOW?

The mid- and late 1960s were times of turmoil in the United States (and around the world) — so much so that one observer noted dramatically that "everything tied down is coming loose" (Bennis, 1966). Perhaps in broader historical perspective, the period will be viewed as far less calamitous than it appeared, but against the relative tranquility of the 1950s, the times (as Bob Dylan noted) were clearly changing.

Societal Perspective

In the United States, the 1960s began with an indictment of the self-indulgence of the 1950s and a challenge to create a new sense of national purpose and direction. The new rhetoric was quickly put to test. Internationally the confrontation began with walls in Berlin, missiles in Cuba, sputniks in the sky, and a quickening beat to the Lorelei's song in southeast Asia. Domestically, as the civil rights movement gained momentum, resistance stiffened and grew more violent, providing the first of a series of causes for a generation of rebels not yet aware of their own destiny.

From these turbulent beginnings, the United States was off on a well-chronicled roller coaster ride traveling the heights of legislative, judicial, and scientific achievements and plunging to the depths of assassinations, riots, a soul wrenching war, and domestic political embarrassment. Few institutions escaped the 1960s and early 1970s unscathed, and one of the most severely battered was formal organi-zational authority.

To understand the changes in attitudes toward authority during the 1960s and early 1970s, we must look briefly at the youth of the period — particularly during the mid- and late 1960s, when for a period at least, the led became the leaders. Many members of the middle class U.S. generation that came of age during the early 1960s were quick to accept the call to work for a better world, internationally through the Peace Corps and domestically through assisting the civil rights movement. By and large the members of this cohort had paid no dues, and they knew it. They had grown up in the midst of increasing affluence; their parents had attempted to be generous and supportive; and most of the institutions they had had contact with had been concerned with their individual and social needs. Having always known security, they could not understand their parents' concern with material gain, and many were shocked to discover a world of injustice from which they had been shielded.

This generation became, almost overnight, the searing conscience of a nation and its self-appointed saviors. They had the time, freedom, and energy to be activists in the causes of the day, including their own, and they had the money (from the parents they chastised) to promote a youth-oriented swing in the arts, fashions, and finally in the media.

Initially, the generation of the 1960s was successful — their causes in the main were right, and the institutions they challenged were malleable. Universities acceded to their demands, the civil rights movement made apparent gains, and finally their voices against the war in Vietnam began to be heard. It should be noted that a detailed and balanced commentary would stress that the 1960s generation was seldom if ever alone in their battles and that the excesses associated with their movement were many. Moreover, in the later 1960s, as a second cadre of leaders less dedicated to nonviolence moved to the fore of the youth movement, the means of revolt became ends to themselves, competing factions emerged, and the movement helped pull its political friends down to defeat.

However its history is finally written, the youth movement of the 1960s helped U.S. political and educational leaders relearn an important lesson — formal authority is useless when it is held to be illegitimate. That is, in a society reluctant to resort to ultimate force, the sanctions available to most institutions can be rendered impotent by concerted, determined, persistent resistance on the part of followers who have a moral cause supported by some meaningful segment of the population.

More importantly, the youth movement taught a lesson to the led. The 1960s generation refused to be coopted. The limited participation in decisionmaking offered by human-relations-trained leaders held little value for those who had always been "consulted" with regard to means if not ends. Manipulative techniques were seen for what they were and shrilly condemned (even when they did not exist). The battle cry of the movement — "You can't trust anyone over thirty" — helped lay a foundation of distrust and cynicism that has persisted well after the movement faded.

The U.S. youth movement in the 1960s and early 1970s did not, of course, represent the United States as a whole or the rest of the world. It did, however, embody and exaggerate many of the underlying forces for change across other age groups and cultures. And while the youth movement at the time had direct impact only on a tiny fraction of U.S. work organizations (other than political and educational institutions), it is having a direct effect today as its former members move into middle and upper organizational ranks and an indirect effect, as suggested above, as its message of cynicism permeates all institutions. To see these effects we should look at the zones of acceptance in work organizations as they changed during the 1960s and early 1970s.

The Zone of Acceptance

Nothing as dramatic as the youth revolt occurred in the U.S. work organizations during the 1960s and early 1970s. In fact, at the lowest organizational levels, among blue collar workers, the zone of acceptance may well have increased marginally as a number of industries (e.g., West Coast shipping companies, railroads, newspapers, and to a lesser extent, steel) "bought out" a number of restrictive work practices. During the mid- and late 1960s, with employment at record levels and wage and fringe gains flowing freely, blue collar workers frequently found themselves at odds with the student movement — in the position of defending the system rather than being its critics. The well-publicized Lordstown strike, viewed by some as a work demand for new freedoms and broader work roles, was probably more appropriately viewed as a very traditional response to an apparent "speed up."

Some new problems emerged in this period, notably those associated with an increased use of drugs among auto workers and company efforts, under legal pressure, to improve minority employment in traditionally "white" jobs. In the main, however, in the already tightly constrained arena of blue collar work roles, the only real narrowing of acceptance of managerial prerogatives occurred in areas where groundwork had already been laid in union contracts (e.g., restrictions on overtime scheduling, subcontracting, plant movement, etc. — extensions of traditional job protection efforts).

In other areas, however, among service workers, white collar clerical employees, governmental employees, and quasi-professionals (public school teachers, nurses, some technical specialities), zones of acceptance narrowed perceptibly, and restrictions on managerial prerogatives proliferated. The union movement began to make uneven, but overall large, gains in these areas, and the process of formalizing work arrangements brought many issues of managerial discretion under open scrutiny for the first time. In some of these areas, worker demands were exacerbated by the growing strength of the women's movement — the office coffee pot became a symbol of "liberation" from traditional female work roles and stimulated demands for role restructure that carried over into other arenas of traditional managerial discretion over work assignments for office workers of both sexes.

In sum, at lower organizational levels, the zone of acceptance narrowed overall during the 1960s and early 1970s, with the largest reductions occurring among those groups that had traditionally been the most loyal to organizational goals and the most compliant to managerial requests. This is, of course, not a surprising result in hindsight. There was clearly far more room for restrictions to occur in those arenas, and in a sense many white collar workers were merely catching up with work arrangements already achieved by their blue collar counterparts. What seems logical enough in hindsight, however, was hardly viewed with equanimity by management at the time. After all, during the 1950s, white collar and technical and professional employees were always considered essentially a part of management. Blue collar workers might have been expected to be obstreperous, but for trusted lieges to question managerial prerogatives was truly shocking.

However, if management was shocked by a shrinking zone of acceptance among white collar staff, it was even more taken aback by defections in its own ranks. With increasing frequency during the late 1960s and early 1970s, managers at various levels quietly revolted by turning down transfers designed to lead to higher office and even refusing promotions when these appeared to conflict with family and/or personal needs. Finally, the executive "dropout" began to appear. At first, it was Sunday supplement material to find a former bank executive sculpting in the village or growing organic potatoes in Idaho. Later, dropouts were not only numerous, they were organized — at least it appeared so as ex-executives formed associations to assist those colleagues taking the plunge into new lifestyles.

For most executives, the "rebellion" went no farther than an extra inch or so of hair over the collar and a wistful eye cast in the direction of the newer sexual mores. Still, even though the numbers of executives who dropped out or limited their quest for advancement were small, their actions were so out of place with expectations that the zone of acceptance in executive ranks was narrowed substantially. Many organizations began, on the surface at least, to modify their expectations that executives "marry" the firm, dropped many of their demands on executives' social lives, and began to accept a variety of lifestyles and behaviors that would in the past have been unthinkable.

The Zone of Conditional Acceptance

While the zone of acceptance was narrowing for many of those traditionally closest to the organization, management was finding that its principal means of exerting influence within the zone of conditional acceptance was also under attack. As noted above, the cries of distrust from the youth movement (in chorus with many civil rights and women's movement leaders) were echoing well beyond their ranks. Suspicion of leaders' efforts to involve subordinates in decisionmaking spread quickly from the campus to the political arena and paved the way for work organization members to express what were probably long-smouldering doubts about a variety of participative practices. Moreover, many of the concerns about leader behavior expressed by students and organization members were echoed and expanded by much of the applied leadership literature of the early and mid-1960s. First the T-group movement and later organization development (OD) consultants sought to sensitize managers to their subordinates' needs and to replace pseudoparticipative techniques with "openness," "trust," and "authentic" relationships (Miles, 1976).

While OD programs probably had significant impact on some managers, our surveys in the mid- and late 1960s still showed many managers questioning their subordinates' capacities for self-direction and self-control and viewing participation primarily as a means of obtaining cooperation (Miles and Ritchie, 1968, 1971). Not surprisingly, throughout the late 1960s and early 1970s, many managers well schooled in the human relations philosophy found that their previously successful techniques for expanding cooperation (i.e., pseudoparticipative) seemed to lead to greater resistance. While in fact most subordinates were no more skilled at exercising openness and trust than their superiors, their eyes were being increasingly opened — by organization friends (e.g., consultants) as well as foes — to sham.

Significantly, the success stories involving expansion of the zone of conditional acceptance during the late 1960s and early 1970s tended to portray much deeper levels of participation than were apparently required in the 1950s and early 1960s. Within managerial ranks, consultants who were able to structure direct manager-subordinate joint problem-solving activities (e.g., in "family" team-building sessions or with data feedback approaches) reported successes. At the rank and file employee level, the major successes of the period tended to be those in which totally new systems were designed that facilitated virtually complete work group self-direction and self-control (e.g., the Topeka dog food plant; see Walton, 1972). It should also be noted that the two "old" participative schemes that enjoyed renewed interest during this period, the Scanlon Plan and the Kelso employee stock ownership plan, both emphasize dollar payoffs for involvement. The revival of interest in these two programs was in direct contrast to the 1950s, when financial rewards for cooperation were not a major part of most human relations participative schemes; simply being consulted was viewed as valuable enough in itself.

In sum, for many managers, the 1960s and early 1970s brought frequent periods of confusion and disheartenment. Employees tended to treat as their rights conditions and behaviors that managers had always considered privileges to be traded for cooperation. Managers were now expected to be sensitive and considerate, and efforts to involve subordinates in minor decision matters, instead of being appreciated, were now frequently viewed as manipulation.

DOCUMENTING CHANGING ROLES

While it is easy enough to describe the changes that have occurred in the last two decades in the roles of leaders and led in work organizations, it is far more difficult to prove that such changes have occurred. That is, while there is little doubt in the minds of managers or organizational observers that changes have occurred, there is little comparative data. Even where, for example, one can point to increased formalization of white collar roles in the form of union contracts, there is usually no objective information available concerning preunion work practices and expectations.

The comparative data that does exist suggests, but does not document, the changes that we have described. For example, job satisfaction surveys have been undertaken regularly by the Survey Research Center in the Institute of Social Research at the University of Michigan. A careful analysis of these surveys from the 1950s into the early 1970s does not, surprisingly enough, provide proof of a major overall decline in job satisfaction among organization members. In fact, average job satisfaction scores have declined, if at all, only marginally (Quinn, Staines, and McCullough, 1974).

What is apparent is that job satisfaction remained lower and declined more among younger members, minorities, and women from the early to the late 1960s. The fact that job satisfaction appears to have declined more (though not at all dramatically) for the three groups of organization members at the forefront of the 1960s "revolt" fits with our explanation of broad role changes, but again, is not solid proof. One can, for example, infer that role changes have been limited to these groups or even that the expectations of members of the three groups have simply outraced organization practices. (However, unpublished material just becoming available suggests that major drops in job satisfaction have occurred from the late 1960s through the middle 1970s.)

One highly relevant set of data appears to point to clear changes in managers' attitudes toward their superiors. Unfortunately these data cannot be accepted as proof of change because they were not collected with attention to normal research requirements. Nevertheless, they are worth comment because they are highly suggestive.

Beginning in the early 1960s, my colleague Ritchie and I studied managers' leadership attitudes in a variety of settings, including plant and office personnel, private and public organizations, and even among health professionals and union leaders (see Miles and Ritchie, 1968, 1971). In these studies, managers were asked, among other things, to evaluate themselves, their superiors, their immediate subordinates, and rank and file employees with regard to a set of ten traits describing valued capabilities or characteristics (e.g., judgment, creativity, pride in performance, initiative, etc.). Among all the groups systematically studied, a common pattern emerged. Managers, on average, tended to place themselves well above rank and file employees and their subordinates and close to, but just below, their superiors. (Individual managers, of course, varied around this pattern, and their responses were relatable to their attitudes toward participation, the satisfaction of their immediate subordinates, etc.)

From the late 1960s on, neither Ritchie nor I collected leadership attitude data systematically. However, we did regularly employ the research instruments in leadership-training programs, collecting and feeding back attitudinal data to literally dozens of groups of managers as a pedagogical tool. In the early 1970s, we were each struck with the fact that the pattern of data collected was clearly changing on one specific dimension — managers' views of the capabilities of their superiors. Instead of rating their bosses slightly above themselves, managers at the turn of the decade were, on average, now placing themselves equal to their superiors. Moreover, the change in profiles has continued into the mid-1970s, so that it is now commonplace for groups of managers to rate themselves above their superiors across the full set of traits — a finding that never occurred in the mid-1960s. And it should be noted that during the later periods, data were "collected" from groups as varied as those in the early systematic studies — from a variety of levels in a wide range of public and private organizations.

Finally, the systematically collected job satisfaction data and our nonsystematically gathered leadership attitude comparisons fit an overall pattern of declining trust in institutions and their leaders visible in the United States and abroad. The recent work of Lipset and others makes it clear that public opinions of work organizations have declined along with opinions toward government, religious institutions, and the like (see Lipset and Schneider, 1978). Declining levels of confidence and trust do not, as suggested above, provide proof that leader and led roles have changed, but such declines are what one would expect to find if our descriptions of role changes are accurate.

EFFECTS OF ROLE CHANGES ON ORGANIZATION PERFORMANCE

If proving that role changes have occurred is difficult, it is virtually impossible to tie these changes to variations in organization performance. It is first of all difficult to document changes in organizational effectiveness or efficiency, and second, when such changes are apparent, a plethora of possible causes is readily available. Lack of evidence, of course, does not inhibit (probably promotes) speculation — there are any number of observers prepared to attribute varying degrees of national economic success to variations in managerial practices.

Similarly, one can speculate concerning relationships between leader-led role changes and variations in performance within an economy across time periods. In the United States, the 1950s and early 1960s were a period of steady growth, with productivity gains averaging 3 to 4 percent per year. Established work organizations tended to grow slowly but steadily, in line with population increases and the beginning growth of world markets. The future was bright and the course steady — all that was needed, as noted earlier, was to maintain the cooperation of organization members. The roles of leaders and led, structured in the human relations philosophy, were suited to the maintenance of loyalty and stable, though not outstanding or innovative, performance.

The mid- and late 1960s were a period where economic performance was stimulated by heavy government spending on the space program and in support of the Viet Nam war. Despite these infusions, however, weaknesses began to appear in the pillars of the U.S. economy — steel and autos — and the rapid growth of U.S. markets abroad began to slow. Following these first hints, the world of management in both public and private organizations grew tougher with each passing year into the mid-1970s.

First, economic growth slowed, productivity increases declined, population and new family formation forecasts were drastically revised downward, and foreign competition began to make major inroads domestically and in U.S. markets abroad. Simultaneously, demands for environmental improvements and the protection of worker health and safety led to legislation and new regulatory agencies. Moreover, while organizations were being urged (and sometimes forced) to restrain growth and to protect or enhance environments, demands were being made for job creation and promotional opportunities for women and minorities. Almost as a final straw, cheap fuel, the premise on which America had designed its economy and lifestyle in the 1950s, became a thing of the past.

In sum, in the established sector of the economy, management suddenly (from its perspective) had more problems than it could handle. The prevailing human relations philosophy was proving unworkable as a means of maintaining cooperation and was never intended as a means of drawing out innovation and creativity.

On the other hand, primarily in the newer areas of the economy — electronics and the service industries — newer managerial philosophies combined with new opportunities to offer new promises for the future. In companies like Texas Instruments and Hewlett Packard, something akin to what I have termed a human resources management philosophy emerged, emphasizing (though not always practicing) widespread participation in important work decisions and increased levels of member self-direction and self-control. Similarly, in a number of franchise product and service organizations (SAGA food serves as an outstanding example), managers received training in building effective work teams through meaningful participation. The fact that firms such as these were growing rapidly and could offer rapid promotions and that in the main these newer plants and operations were safe, efficient, and environmentally unthreatening were important ingredients in their success.

The fact that a new managerial philosophy — the human resources approach — was available that fit the circumstances of the newer, rapidly expanding industries was, of course, not happenstance. As Stinchcombe (1965) has noted, organization structures and processes carry the imprint of their birth period. Many of the most progressive organizations grew up in the same time period that the new philosophy was taking shape. The concept of "organismic" organizations (in which managers played facilitative rather than controlling roles, and innovative, self-directing behavior was viewed as appropriate for subordinates) emerged from studies of expanding electronics firms (Burns and Stalker, 1961). The new philosophy not only matched the personal values of many of the young leaders in the newer industries, it was readily seen to be essential to organization success.

Rapid growth could not be achieved unless managerial and technical personnel developed at an unusually fast pace (Hewlett Packard expanded from six divisions to more than thirty over roughly a ten year period). Similarly, unless virtually all organization members were kept closely informed of and involved in new technological and product advances, such organizations could not move rapidly enough to stay at the edge of the development field. And if the firms did not remain at the forefront, their products were certain to be copied and undersold. Thus, with innovation the prime ingredient for success, managers could not, even if they chose to do so, cast their roles in traditional or human relations molds.

THE PRESENT

The United States emerged from the 1960s and early 1970s tired and far less confident than it had been in the 1950s about its role in the world and its ability to manage its own destiny. Domestically, hints of progress may be even more difficult to find than in the international arena. The glamour industries of the 1960s are having growing pains, and the aging industries and the public sector have problems that appear to some to be almost insurmountable.

The progressive organizations of the 1960s and early 1970s embraced new managerial roles without undue strain in their formative stages. While such organizations were still relatively small, corporate staffs and major division managers could play facilitative roles and still be closely involved in most important organizational issues. Major growth, however, demands either increasing formalization of the management of interdependencies or else a growing tolerance for uncertainty and an increased willingness to accept apparent risks of semiautonomous, self-directed behavior. Managers are discovering that leader roles under human resources-like approaches are tough to maintain: risks do increase, and the urge to "take charge" rather than consult grows proportionally. Defections from new approaches are beginning to appear — usually in those areas where major innovations were made quickly and without a systemwide acceptance of supporting managerial philosophies.

In the aging industries, little real change has occurred since the 1950s. Bureaucratic structures and processes, despite the dire predictions of some, not only still exist but perform reasonably effectively in environments characterized by at least moderate stability.

The problem is thus not that bureaucratic organizations in older industries are in imminent danger, it is simply that no one is particularly happy with them. In steel, manufacturing, transportation, and the like, once proud "flagship" firms have lost the challenge of ever-increasing markets, and instead of being hailed for their command of managerial skills and technological advances, they are being criticized for their investment shortsightedness and their inability to keep pace with production methods and technological advances among foreign competitors. Managers complain that if their organizations were not shackled by regulatory restrictions and union contracts, they could compete effectively — at least against those competitors who engaged in legitimate tactics. Lower level organization members, facing futures with limited advancement opportunities (and for some the frightening spectre of ultimate job loss), are understandably inclined to take narrow, demanding, short-run views. In all, organizations that were once prestigious and purposeful have become cumbersome, complicated, and beset. Their members are tired and frustrated, but have not yet been pushed to the point of attempting major redirection.

However, despite the problems faced by older private sector industries and organizations, they are not the most beleaguered sector of the U.S. economy. The "prime target" distinction clearly belongs to the public sector agencies and institutions. The "great tax revolt" of the mid- and late 1970s is placing many government organizations in the center of dramatically conflicting demands — on the one hand for expanded services to a host of groups whose expectations were raised substantially in the 1960s and on the other hand by taxpayers who claim to be angered only by waste but who are also probably reacting against shifting domestic priorities, particularly increases in welfare programs. It is, of course, too early as yet to tell how deeply the tax revolt will actually cut into operating budgets of public organizations, but it is already clear that the growth of government services is highly unlikely to keep pace with demand.

WHERE DO WE GO FROM HERE?

This question implies that I expect major changes in U.S. organizations in general and in leader and led roles in particular. Such is not the case — at least in the short run. Major short-run change is unlikely first of all because existing roles and organizational arrangements are still working well enough to maintain effectiveness, if not efficiency and satisfaction. That is, they can still "get the job done" well enough to survive, though often with high costs in terms of both material and human resources. Second, short-run change is unlikely because much of the pressure generated in the 1960s is at least temporarily spent: the 1960s generation is now working within, if not for the system; the woman's movement has come up against lagging enforcement and a fundamentalist backlash; the civil rights movement has lost its easy targets; and the tax revolt has effectively blunted growth in the public sector. Third, and perhaps most importantly, major short-run changes in roles and relationships are not likely because there are no highly visible, easily assimilated models. I will comment briefly on the first two points and focus major attention on the third.

As suggested earlier, U.S. organizations and institutions came out of the 1960s and early 1970s battered, but only marginally bent. Nothing collapsed, and while service curtailments have occurred and productivity gains have slowed, the majority of people, in their life space generally and in their organizational role specifically, are better off than they were in the 1950s. The major immediate problems of unemployment and inflation hit hardest at those with the least political muscle, and for the majority, rising expectations are simply being lowered to match reality. A pattern of declining saving and investment may well be emerging in both the public and the private sectors, but the full effects may not be felt for a decade or so. In the meantime, major role strain is likely to be felt only by those most vulnerable to external demands. Most managers in internally focused organizational roles have tended to lower their standards to meet the restrictions that their subordinates have placed on their zones of acceptance.

The movements of the 1960s lost zest as their leaders aged and as the problems they addressed became increasingly more complex and intractable. Once the war was halted, the only common rallying point for many groups disappeared, and tradeoffs became more apparent (i.e., competition between women and male minority members for jobs, conflict between slow growth policies of environmentalists and demands for new jobs to benefit minorities, etc.). The most capable student leaders of the 1960s moved into government and industry and are now using their skills to climb organizational ladders; and among older progressive leaders, a willingness to accept a slower rate of change is apparent.

However, even if U.S. organizations were functionally less effective than they are and even if more energy remained in the reform movements of the last decade, there is little likelihood that major changes would occur in the short run for the simple reason that there is very little agreement concerning what to change, toward what, or how.

In contrast to portions of Western Europe where there appears to be at least an operational level of agreement among government leaders, labor spokesmen, and social scientists concerning the value of some degree of role restructure (in the form of work redesign and formal participation mechanisms), opinion in the United States is sharply divided concerning the desirability and/or efficacy of role changes. For example, in the U.S. labor movement, only a handful of top officials have taken an active role in the push for work redesign (job enrichment). And even in those unions (e.g., the UAW) where at least an interest in restructure has been voiced, job enrichment is not a bargaining goal. Similarly, there is no impetus in the U.S. union movement for demanding worker representation on corporate boards. There appears to be little likelihood in the short run that U.S. unions will drop their basic focus on economic gains or that they will demand or even support widespread experimentation with work restructure.

Without union support, government officials are highly unlikely to provide much more than lip service to major programs aimed at role restructure. Government financial support now provided to stimulate and study work restructure activities is small and currently shrinking. Political leaders are responsive to the problems of the day and inflation and unemployment have far higher priority even among blue collar workers than does work reform. Moreover, in the minds of many politicians and their advisors, work redesign is viewed as likely to raise production costs, at least in the short run.

Finally, U.S. social scientists are far from united in their views toward role restructure. In fact, there are probably more critics of job enrichment and worker participation schemes than there are supporters among active researchers and writers on organizational issues. Advocates of major work and role restructure — the human resources theorists — enjoyed major support in the mid- and late 1960s. Perhaps prescriptive theorists such as Likert, Argyris, Bennis, Herzberg, and others (myself included) promised too much. It is clear that they (we) promised more than most organizations were willing or able to put into practice and that research evidence related to experiments in job enrichment, departmental role redesign, and organization development has been open to a variety of interpretations. Today advocates tend to protect themselves from critics' barbs by designing contingency models that are viewed by most practitioners as providing little or no direction for change. Given that there is almost no chance that research can be designed that will produce unequivocable evidence concerning work or role change experiments, it appears highly unlikely that any new consensus will emerge among social scientists concerning new directions for leaders or led. No new prescriptive thrust has been offered since the mid-1960s, and none appears on the horizon.

The fact that the last decade has brought no new general prescriptions for changes in leader-led roles and, in fact, has not even produced a clear continuation of the participative management of the late 1950s and early 1960s is neither condemnable nor surprising. On the positive side, the social scientists' recent preference for descriptive, rigorously defined multivariate models and analyses represents, for many, a serious attempt to bring order and objectivity into what has remained essentially a philosophic pursuit. Earlier, loosely specified global theories have, of course, been easy targets for modern critics.

On the negative side, the king has been killed, and the bells have not tolled for the installation of a new monarch. The 1960s generation, with the help of social science theory and research, killed human relations as a viable, or at least socially acceptable, guide to managerial practice. Moreover, managers who were already finding System 4, Human Resources, and Theory Y threatening and difficult to implement are highly unlikely to be encouraged toward further, more extensive experimentation by the recent organization literature. Overly complex contingency models provide little or no guidance to the practitioner: the prescription that "it depends" is a license to maintain the status quo (or alternatively, to follow one's own rubrics). Of course, the social scientist who reports inconclusive results concerning role change experiments is only doing his or her job. For the practitioner, however, operating in a hyped world of competing claims, inconclusive or mixed results are likely to be treated as negative.

There is, in fact, in all the literature virtually no recent evidence that role changes in the form of increased subordinate involvement in actual work group decisions produce diminished overall work group satisfaction or performance. There is evidence that positive results from involvement may vary from individual to individual on the basis of personality predispositions and from group to group based on attitudinal and situational characteristics. It is, of course, incumbent on the social scientist to warn against potential dysfunctions, and it is perhaps equally important to stress the likelihood of at least marginal positive benefits from thoughtfully designed role change experiments.

WILL EUROPEAN EXPERIMENTS
PROVIDE A MODEL FOR THE
UNITED STATES?

I began this chapter by commenting on the current "revolution" in leader-led roles in Western Europe. It is appropriate as we near the end of this analysis to return to that topic and to question whether the European experience will provide a model for change in the United States. The answer, I think, is no — in the short run at least. The reasons for my position are twofold. First, the total amount of experimentation (outside of codetermination legislation) in Europe to date (if the recent Quality of Work Life Center report is indicative) is probably still less than that which has occurred, in aggregate, across U.S. companies in the past twenty or so years. Second, and relatedly, much of what is occurring in Europe is now viewed as old hat in the United States — something we tried once and found wanting. Not surprisingly, many U.S. companies and managers, jaded by one new program after another over the years, now find it impossible to differentiate between real and pseudo role change prescriptions. As noted earlier, legislatively enforced shop floor or board room participation in the United States is highly unlikely, and voluntary experimentation will probably continue with about the same scope and intensity as is occurring in Europe. Such fragmented, short-term experimentation is not likely to produce major system-wide changes in the leader and led roles.

In sum, one can argue that in the United States during the 60s and early 70s (and more recently in Western Europe), most managers have played with change in leader and led roles, but have not taken the full implications of their "experiments" seriously. That is, with few exceptions efforts to expand subordinate roles to include more involvement in decisionmaking and more self-direction and self-control have not been accompanied by total system redesign. Without an "ecologically" sound perspective, changes at one hierarchical level inevitably place role strains on adjacent hierarchical levels and laterally across the system. Unless leaders are given new things to do, role expansion for the led has been and will be limited, shallow, and subject to constant threat of reduction. It is probably the case that serious redesign of roles at lower levels would require the removal of one or more layers of management, an outcome that is likely to be resisted as fiercely as adjustments to technological redundancy at the shop floor. Moreover, jobs that are "enriched" or "humanized" to minimally meet the capabilities and expectations of today's work force will probably be impoverished again by tomorrow's standards.

There is simply nothing in current theory or practice to suggest a major continuing commitment to role restructuring in Western societies. Work organizations, for the near future at least, will probably continue to be the only arena in which most people are expected to stop growing. Almost parenthetically, the Japanese systems of participative management, which place fewer arbitrary limits on member growth, are not likely to provide operational models for U.S. leader-led role changes as those systems are supported by societal norms that are probably nonreproducible in the United States except perhaps in the long run.

THE LONG RUN?

In twenty years or so, if current developments follow earlier patterns, we will probably be able to proclaim that real changes in leader-led roles have occurred. Influence will be widely shared across roles, and a variety of structure and process changes will have emerged that promote broader arenas of self-direction and self-control among organizational members at all levels. The human relations movement took thirty or more years to produce significant systemwide changes in treatment of organization members. Future, more demanding role changes will probably take longer to become commonplace.

If such changes do occur, they will probably be responsive to two forces — (1) continuing internal pressure by increasingly more competent organization members and (2) shifting market forces, which will demand new organization strategies and structures, dependent in large measure on the wider utilization of capabilities of all organization members.

In a modified version of the famous Bennis prediction that bureaucracy is dead and democracy will rule (Bennis, 1966: ch. 1), I expect organizations to increasingly find themselves required to simultaneously pursue goals of efficiency and innovation. Arenas of more or less stable operation will be managed under the same "system" roof with short-term experimental projects. Organizations faced with this and other forms of related complexity will search for new forms of structure that promote effective, synergistic lateral relations. Decision points will abound in such operations, and the expansion of the number of members legitimately exercising influence will greatly modify traditional leader-led roles. If my expectations are correct, role change will become an economic must rather than an ethical ought and will occur as a matter of course (for an expansion of these comments, see Miles and Snow, 1978: esp. chs. 9, 10).

As is required by convention, I close with the suggestion for a redirection of research efforts. I seriously doubt that additional research on participative experiments will greatly influence the course of organizational events (though the research process — not its results — may stimulate continued, though probably limited, expansion of led roles). On the other hand, research aimed at uncovering organizational experiments with new strategy-structure-process systems may well lead to an understanding of new leader-led role arrangements.

APPENDIX A: LEADERSHIP MODELS[a]

1. The Traditional Model — This model suggests a series of management policies prescribing close supervision and tight control of subordinates performing narrowly defined jobs. These prescriptions flow out of the assumption that people are basically lazy, uncreative, and concerned only with what they earn, not what they do to earn it. This model anticipates at least minimal performance if the manager is constantly alert and exercises tight formal control.

2. The Human Relations Model — This model prescribes a limited amount of subordinate participation in decisionmaking and limited subordinate self-control based on the assumption that people are essentially loyal and dependable if their basic social needs are fulfilled — if they feel that they are important to the organization and that their work is recognized by their superiors. This model anticipates that this limited participation will improve subordinates' morale and need satisfaction and thus make them more willing to cooperate with their superior's directives.

3. The Human Resources Model — This model prescribes a continually expanding degree of subordinate participation, self-direction, and self-control based on the assumption that the creative resources

[a]Adapted from Raymond E. Miles, *Theories of Management: Implications for Organizational Behavior and Development* (New York: McGraw-Hill, 1975).

of most organization members are seldom utilized and that, given the opportunity, most people will exercise responsible self-direction in the accomplishment of goals they have helped establish. This model anticipates that subordinate participation will directly improve organizational decisionmaking and performance and will, in the process, provide deeper satisfaction of the full range of needs of most organization members.

Approaches to Management

TRADITIONAL	HUMAN RELATIONS	HUMAN RESOURCES
Assumptions	*Assumptions*	*Assumptions*
1. People dislike work	1. People want to feel important	1. People want to contribute
2. Work only for money	2. Want to be recognized	2. Can exercise broad self-direction, self-control
3. Few capable of self-control or self-direction	3. Want to be consulted	3. Represent "untapped resources"
Policies	*Policies*	*Policies*
1. Assign simple, repetitive tasks	1. Manager should discuss plans, listen to objections	1. Create climate where all can contribute fully
2. Supervise closely; maintain tight control	2. Allow self-control on routine tasks	2. Develop full participation on important problems
3. Set rules and routines; enforcement firm but fair		3. Continually broaden area of self-direction and control
Expectations	*Expectations*	*Expectations*
1. If closely controlled, people will meet standards	1. Participation increases satisfaction and morale	1. Direct improvements in decisionmaking and control
2. If firm but fair, people will respect supervisor	2. Subordinates will willingly cooperate	2. Satisfaction increases as by-product

REFERENCES

American Center for the Quality of Work Life. 1978. *Industrial Democracy in Europe: A 1977 Survey.* Washington, D.C.

Bennis, Warren. 1966. *Changing Organizations.* New York: McGraw-Hill.

Burns, Tom, and G. M. Stalker. 1961. *The Management of Innovation.* London: Tavistock.

Calder, Bobby J. 1977. "An Attribution Theory of Leadership." In Barry M. Staw and Gerald R. Salancik, eds., *New Directions in Organizational Behavior.* Chicago: St. Clair Press.

Coch, L., and J. R. P. French, Jr. 1948. "Overcoming Resistance to Change." *Human Relations* 1: 512-32.

Drucker, Peter. 1954. *The Practice of Management.* New York: Harper and Brothers.

Fleishman, Edwin A., and Edwin F. Harris. 1962. "Patterns of Leadership Behavior Related to Employee Grievances and Turnover." *Personnel Psychology* 15: 43-56.

French, J. R. P.; J. Israel; and D. As. 1960. "An Experiment on Participation in a Norwegian Factory." *Human Relations* 13: 3-19.

Lipset, Seymour M.; and William Schneider. 1978. "How's Business?" *Public Opinion* 1: 41-47.

Miles, R. E. 1976. "Organization Development." In George Strauss et al., eds., *Organization Behavior: Research and Issues.* Belmont, Calif.: Wadsworth.

Miles, R. E., and J. B. Ritchie. 1968. "Leadership Attitudes Among Union Officials." *Industrial Relations* 8: 108-17.

———. 1971. "Participative Management: Quality vs. Quantity." *California Management Review* 13: 48-56.

Miles, R. E., and C. C. Snow. 1978. *Organization Strategy, Structure, and Process.* New York: McGraw-Hill.

Mills, C. Wright. 1951. *White Collar.* New York: Oxford University Press.

Morse, Nancy C., and Everett Reimer. 1956. "The Experimental Change of a Major Organizational Variable." *Journal of Abnormal and Social Psychology* 52: 120-29.

Pfeffer, Jeffrey. 1977. "The Ambiguity of Leadership." *Academy of Management Review* 2: 104-12.

Quinn, R. P.; G. L. Staines; and M. K. McCullough. 1974. "Job Satisfaction: Is There a Trend?" Washington, D.C.: U.S. Department of Labor Manpower Research Monograph No. 30.

Simon, Herbert. 1976. *Administrative Behavior.* 3rd ed. New York: Free Press.

Stinchcombe, Arthur L. 1965. "Social Structure in Organizations." In James G. March, ed., *Handbook of Organizations.* Chicago: Rand-McNally.

Walton, R. E. 1972. "How to Counter Alienation in the Plant." *Harvard Business Review* 50: 70-81.

Whyte, William H. 1966. *The Organization Man.* New York: Simon and Schuster.

Chapter 8

Leadership, Politics, and the Functioning of Complex Organizational and Interorganizational Networks

John M. Bryson* and George Kelley**

Leadership, politics, and the functioning of complex organizations are three topics not usually considered together. In an earlier paper we presented a political perspective on leadership emergence, stability, and change in organizational networks (Bryson and Kelley, 1978). In this study we will expand that perspective in three ways. Each represents a separate major section of the present chapter. First, we will consider the major theoretical thinking in the area and critically review research studies undertaken. Second, we will consider explicitly the relationships between leadership, politics, and the functioning of complex organizational and interorganizational networks (ONs and INs, respectively). Given the paucity of theory and research relating the three topics, we have seen our principal task as the creation of a framework and series of propositions relating leadership, politics, and the functioning of ONs and INs. Such a framework and set of propositions are new and, we hope, offer a use-

*University of Minnesota
**University of Wisconsin
This chapter represents a major revision and extension of Bryson and Kelley (1978).

ful view both of what lies ahead and the promise of the area. This effort naturally leads to the third major section of the chapter, where we explicitly discuss what we feel lies ahead, as well as the promise of the area.

Before proceeding, some definitions and frame setting are in order. Leadership as a concept has been subject to considerable definitional confusion. We will do no more than define leadership as "behavior that makes a difference in the purposive behavior of others" and hope that that suffices for present purposes (Karmel, 1978:476). The approach to leadership that we will take is basically person oriented and does not focus on the various organizational design "substitutes for leadership" (Kerr, 1977).

As noted, our approach will be distinctly political. To paraphrase Wamsley and Zald (1973:18) and Tushman (1977:207), politics refers to the structure and process of the use of authority and power to affect definitions of goals, directions, and other major parameters of the ON or IN. Political in this sense refers to the broad problems of governance and their solutions — that is, to the determination of "who gets what, when and how" (Lasswell, 1936). Organizations generally do not form or enter into INs unless there is interdependence of some sort and unless goals not achievable separately are achievable jointly (Van de Ven, 1976). This implies joint decisionmaking and is precisely the situation in which Tushman (1977), for one, argues that a political approach is most useful. One of the major topics of such joint decisionmaking would be leadership — who the leaders are, how they get there, what they do while they are there, how long they stay, and what their role is in the functioning of ONs and INs.

Because a political approach is being taken, several literatures in addition to those on organization and management have proved helpful. In particular, the political science and public administration literatures have been quite helpful in developing an integrative framework of key variables and a set of testable propositions. This helpfulness is especially true of the research on legislative bodies.

The framework used to approach ONs and INs will follow that offered by Van de Ven (1976) and Van de Ven et al. (1974). They argue, following Parsons (1962), that ONs and INs are social action systems that, like all such systems, must solve four functional problems to survive — goal attainment, integration, adaptation, and instrumental pattern maintenance. They argue further that the larger INs divide the primary performance of these functions into three levels. The three levels constitute a continuous system-subsystem hierarchy, but functional orientations tend to differ qualitatively at each level.

The first level (Level I) is the member organizational level and is concerned primarily with instrumental goal attainment and pattern maintenance. The second level (Level II) is concerned primarily with the integration of the differentiated, but interdependent, member organizations. As such, the focus of the second level is on the coordination, control, and procurement of activities among member organizations. Finally, the third level (Level III) is concerned with the governance of overall goals and policies and with external legitimation, domain maintenance, and domain enhancement with other social action systems.

One salient implication of Van de Ven et al.'s (1974) framework is that things become increasingly political as one rises through the levels. This further strengthens the case for a political approach to leadership and the functioning of ONs and INs, especially at the highest level. (It will be recalled that the U.S. Congress was set up by the states as a "Level III board" to govern some of the actions of thirteen interdependent "member organizations.")

Organizational and management analysts usually look at individual processual, structural, and environmental variables (Filley, House, and Kerr, 1976; Hall, 1972; Van de Ven, 1976). Though different names may be applied, the same clusters are of interest to political scientists and public administration theorists (Lowi, 1977; Presthus, 1975; Wamsley and Zald, 1973). In this chapter, leadership emergence, activities, stability, change, and effects on the functioning of ONs and INs will be discussed in relation to these sets. In particular, our literature review led to the construction of Table 8-1, which lists specific variables that appear to have a major impact.

When speaking of the functioning of ONs and INs, three things are meant — structural arrangements, design mechanisms, and performance variables. Structural arrangements are one of the clusters of variables listed in Table 8-1. Design mechanisms, of both a structural and a processual nature, are here argued to be primarily controlled by the dominant coalition(s) in the ONs and INs. Therefore, these mechanisms will be discussed most thoroughly when dominant coalitions are discussed.

Several organizational and interorganizational performance variables will be considered here. Of primary importance from our political perspective is satisfaction of the goals of the dominant coalition (Cyert and March, 1963; Tushman, 1977). Other variables, listed in approximate order of importance from our perspective,

Table 8-1. Clusters of Variables Affecting Leadership Emergence, Activities, Stability, and Change in Organizational and Interorganizational Networks

Individual	*Processual*	*Structural*	*Environmental*
Coalition membership	Pattern of succession	Level of position	Resource depen-dence
Ideology	Nature of accession to office	Differences in ON or IN structure: com-plexity, centralization, formalization	Binding perfor-mance reviews
Constituency	Stage of leadership development		Involvement by ma-jor outside actors
Seniority		Domain similarity	
Skill and competence	Acquisition, intensity, and direction of re-source flows	Coalitions: relative strengths and weak-nesses	Interest group activ-ity
			Media influences
	Acquisition, intensity, and direction of infor-mation flows	Expectations and per-ceptions of members and member organiza-tions: commitment, awareness, consensus	General external en-vironment
	Decisionmaking		

Source: Adapted in part from Peabody (1976) and Van de Ven (1976).

include resource acquisition, profitability or satisfaction of external constituents, productivity, adaptability and flexibility, and job satis-faction of those outside the dominant coalition (Steers, 1977). The variables are listed in Table 8-2.

These variables obviously are interconnected and situationally affected, so only this rough ordering is possible. Resource acquisition is crucial to development of an ON or IN power base (Caro, 1974; Pfeffer and Salancik, 1974). Profitability or satisfaction of external constituents is important to the maintenance or enhancement of an established power base (Benveniste, 1977), as is productivity. Adaptability and flexibility can assure long-run survival. Finally, job satisfaction of those outside the dominant coalition may be neces-sary for ON or IN stability or growth (Steers, 1977).

Specifying the exact domain to which the propositions are applica-ble remains a task for empirical research. But given their primary source in the more political literatures, it seems safe to say that they will have their greatest applicability in ONs and INs where the mem-bership plays a key role in leadership selection and policymaking. Universities, cooperatives, business and professional associations, political organizations and interest groups, and labor unions would be examples of organizations where this often is the case (Bryson

Table 8-2. Organizational and Interorganizational Performance Variables

---

1. Satisfaction of the goals of the dominant coalition
2. Resource acquisition
3. Profitability or satisfaction of external constituents
4. Productivity
5. Adaptability and flexibility
6. Job satisfaction of those outside the dominant coalition

Source: Adapted in part from Cyert and March (1963) and Steers (1977).

and Kelley, 1978; Wilson, 1973). Specific qualifiers are offered at places where strategic differences between the public and private sectors appear to be especially salient.

A further qualification is based on the fact that our framework and set of propositions are drawn from a field characterized by a paucity of theory and research. Characteristically, the area consists of small sample comparative research, case studies, and/or biographies of political actors. Thus, both the framework and propositions remain quite tentative. Further, since much of the theory and research is formally intraorganizational, extensions to interorganizational networks must remain especially tentative — that is, they must be taken only as suggestions. Some propositions even appear to be in conflict with one another. Nonetheless, our framework and propositions are offered in hopes of integrating much past research within a common conceptualization and of stimulating new and different research in the area of leadership, politics, and the functioning of ONs and INs.

MAJOR THEORETICAL THINKING AND CRITICAL REVIEW OF RESEARCH STUDIES UNDERTAKEN

In reviewing the literature, we have chosen to focus primarily on leadership — rather than on politics or the functioning of ONs or INs — for two reasons. One is that while an immense amount of research has been done on the basically nonpolitical supervisory aspects of leadership, little has related leadership to the functioning of ONs and INs. The second is that little work has been done on politics in ONs and INs and even less has been done relating leadership to ON or IN politics. Thus, we are forced to concentrate on the more traditional supervisor-related leadership literature almost by default. We do make a point, however, of relating this research at a later time to our framework and set of propositions.

Leadership research falls essentially into two categories. Most of the leadership research concentrates on the microlevel of supervisory behavior and subordinate response. This literature is basically non-political. While at times this literature is rich and useful, its excessively narrow perspective has led to the elimination from consideration of a broad range of other variables and relationships relevant to the functioning of ONs and INs. Thus, it is difficult to know what to make of this literature beyond its tight confines.

At the macrolevel, to our knowledge only Pfeffer and Salancik (1978), besides ourselves (Bryson and Kelley, 1978), have presented a framework relating leadership to external and internal organizational variables. However, while their framework and our initial and revised frameworks are compatible, our initial and revised frameworks include more variables, and we speculate on more relationships than they do. Further, our revised framework considers interorganizational relationships as well.

The Microlevel of Supervisory Behavior and Subordinate Response

Three types of studies dominate microlevel research on leadership — the trait, behavioral, and situational approaches (Filley, House, and Kerr, 1976). The trait approach asserts that there are a limited number of identifiable characteristics (traits) used to discriminate between successful and unsuccessful leaders. The approach focuses on aspects of one of the clusters of variables identified in Table 8-1, skill and competence, and relates these to some of the performance variables in Table 8-2.

Ghiselli (1971) argues that intelligence level, supervisory ability, initiative, self-assurance, and individuality are significantly related to a leader's level of position and ratings of his or her performance. However, most of the evidence does not strongly support the trait approach (Filley, House, and Kerr, 1976:218-9). One reason for this lack of strong support is the approach's narrow perspective and its static nature. The perspective we present in our framework indicates that a broad concept of skill and competence is important, but in a dynamic, processual sense and in relation to the numerous other variables in Tables 8-1 and 8-2.

The behavioral approach asserts that successful leaders are characterized by specific behavior patterns. This approach also focuses on aspects of one of the clusters of variables identified in Table 8-1, skill and competence, and relates these to some of the performance variables in Table 8-2.

Four types of leadership behaviors are identified. Supportive leadership often results in improved subordinate attitudes, satisfaction, and performance. However, several situational modifiers have been found, including the degree to which the task is intrinsically satisfying to the subordinate, the extent to which the subordinate is free of supervisory control, and the extent to which the granting of performance-based rewards is independent of the leader. Further, there is the question of which comes first — supportive leadership or desirable subordinate behaviors (Filley, House, and Kerr, 1976: 219-22).

Participative leadership involves participative decisionmaking and supervision by leaders and subordinates. Several studies show that participative leadership can lead to increased subordinate satisfaction, productivity, acceptance of decisions made by superiors, quality of group decisions, and reduced resistance to change. However, numerous situational modifiers limit these findings. The leader must have the skills to use participative leadership behaviors; subordinates must be favorably inclined toward participation; the task must be complex and nonroutine; and it must require a high quality decision, subordinate acceptance, or both (Filley, House, and Kerr, 1976:229).

Instrumental leadership asserts that effective leaders structure work in a goal-oriented fashion. In particular, the initiation of psychological structure is the focus. This includes planning, organizing, coordinating, directing, and controlling the work of subordinates. Instrumental leadership has been found to be effective, but contingent upon the existence of any one of several conditions (Filley, House, and Kerr, 1976:230-67):

1. There is a high degree of pressure for output due to demands imposed by sources other than the leaders.
2. The task is satisfying to subordinates.
3. The subordinates are dependent on the leaders for information and direction.
4. The subordinates are psychologically predisposed, due to their attitudes, expectations, or personalities, toward being told what to do and how to do it.
5. The subordinates perceive that they have labor mobility — that is, there is a demand for their services in organizations other than the one where they work.
6. Subordinates' tasks are nonroutine.
7. Subordinates have high occupational level jobs.
8. Subordinates are under stress due to threat from sources other than the leaders.

9. The number of people working together for the same leaders is high (approximately twelve or above).

10. The leader is considerate.

Finally, there is the "Great Person" view — namely, that effective leaders behave in both supportive and instrumental ways. There appears to be some support for this proposition when dealing with low-skilled workers. However, it is not supported when applied to highly skilled white collar workers. There appear to be occupational level and task modifiers at work. Combining the two behaviors may reconcile the conflicting demands made on leaders, although that may be difficult for any particular leader (Filley, House, and Kerr, 1976).

Three situational approaches to leadership are Fiedler's (1967:37) contingency model, Vroom and Yetton's (1973) decisionmaking model, and House's (1971:55) path-goal theory. The basic idea behind each of these approaches is that there is a range of leader behaviors and that the appropriate choice of behavior is contingent upon the situation. Fiedler sees the choice between supportive or instrumental leader behavior as contingent on (1) the leader's personal relationship with members of the group, (2) the formal power or authority that the leader's position provides, and (3) the degree of structure in the task which the group has assigned to perform (Filley, House, and Kerr, 1976:244). Fiedler (1967:165; Filley, House, and Kerr, 1976:244) fits these elements together as follows:

> In very favorable conditions, where the leader has power, formal backing, and a relatively well-structured task, the group is ready to be directed on how to go about this task. Under a very unfavorable condition, however, the group will fall apart unless the leader's active intervention and control can keep the members on the job. In moderately unfavorable conditions, the accepted leader faces an ambiguous task, or his relations with group members are tenuous. Under these circumstances, a relationship-oriented, nondirective, permissive attitude may reduce member anxiety or intragroup conflict, and this enables the group to operate more effectively (i.e., the members would not feel threatened by the leader, and considerate, diplomatic leader behavior under these conditions may induce group members to cooperate).

Fiedler's approach is based on an attitude measure called the least preferred co-worker (LPC) scale. There is considerable doubt about what Fiedler's findings mean because of a protracted debate about what the LPC measures or means (Rice, 1978). Fiedler's findings are more of an empirical generalization than an explanation of relationships. Nonetheless, if the meaning of the LPC scale can be determined, the "theory" holds considerable promise (Filley, House, and Kerr, 1976:261).

Vroom and Yetton developed a prescriptive decisionmaking model specifying appropriate leader decisionmaking methods based on fourteen problem types and eight decision rules. Based on their studies, the model specifies a broader range of leader behaviors than most managers exhibit. Further, the model specifies that leaders should be both more autocratic and more participative than they usually are. The model's validity has not been established, although it does appear plausible and internally consistent (Filley, House, and Kerr, 1976:246-52).

Finally, House's path-goal theory relates leader behavior to subordinate motivation and satisfaction (House, 1971; House and Mitchell, 1974). The theory involves two propositions. One is that leader behavior will be acceptable and satisfying to subordinates when they see it either as an immediate satisfaction or as instrumental to future satisfaction. The second is that leader behavior will be motivational when it makes satisfaction of subordinate needs contingent on effective performance and when it complements the environment by providing the coaching, guidance, support, and rewards necessary for effective performance, which may be otherwise lacking in subordinates or in the environment (Filley, House, and Kerr, 1976:254).

Contingency factors considered in House's theory are personal characteristics of subordinates (extent of subordinates' control over their environment, authoritarianism, and perceptions of their abilities), and environmental pressures and demands subordinates must cope with — subordinates' tasks, formal structure of the organization, and task unit.

The theory considers four leadership types. The path-goal research finds that supportive leadership, as in the behavioral approaches, helps performance most when subordinates are dissatisfied or frustrated. Participative leadership is most satisfying to subordinates of all personality types when they are engaged in nonrepetitive, ego-involving tasks. When engaged in repetitive, non-ego-involving tasks, authoritarian subordinates are less satisfied with participative leadership, while nonauthoritarian subordinates are more satisfied (Schuler, 1973; Filley, House, and Kerr, 1976:258-59).

Instrumental leadership leads to higher satisfaction and motivation of subordinates when engaged in ambiguous tasks, but to less satisfaction and motivation when engaged in clear tasks. However, personality variables act as modifiers, with authoritarian types preferring more instrumental leadership with clear tasks at lower organizational levels (Dessler, 1973; Filley, House, and Kerr, 1976:259). Achievement-oriented leadership leads to higher employee motivation when facing ambiguous, nonrepetitive tasks, but has no effect when subordinates face fairly unambiguous, repetitive tasks (Filley, House, and Kerr, 1976:260).

In general, research results to date support the path-goal theory. However, numerous contingency factors appear to be at work, and the theory would be improved by articulating and testing more of these contingent relationships (Filley, House, and Kerr, 1976:261–26).

Hunt, Osborne, and Schriesheim (1978) provide an excellent critique of the state of the art in microlevel leadership research. On the theoretical side, they argue that improvements have been made. First, there are the new theoretical advances in the development of the situational models just discussed. Second, recent research using similar measures aids in comparison of studies.

On the negative side, they note that there is too much emphasis on supportive and instrumental behaviors and on the LPC scale; almost all leadership research has focused on individual characteristics, whether of leaders or subordinates, and excluded organizational and environmental variables. The low levels of explained variance indicate that many of these additional variables ought to be incorporated into leadership theory and research.

On the question of measurement application, they identify several nagging, persistent problems. The most critical one concerns the soundness of current leadership instruments. This problem is best exemplified by the continuing controversy surrounding the LPC scale (Rice, 1978). Additional problems include the use of modified scales, failure to report reliabilities, incomplete or incorrect specification of the scale used, and the use of small sample sizes.

The Macrolevel

At the macrolevel, to our knowledge only Pfeffer and Salancik (1978), besides ourselves (Bryson and Kelley, 1978), have presented a framework relating leadership to external and internal organizational variables. Our initial framework and theirs were developed independently. Both our initial and revised frameworks are compatible with theirs. However, our initial and revised frameworks include more variables, and we speculate on more relationships than they do. Further, our revised framework considers interorganizational relationships as well. Pfeffer and Salancik's framework will be discussed only briefly because of its compatibility with our own.

Pfeffer and Salancik (1978:228) take a resource dependence perspective. They are concerned principally with how environmental contingencies — particularly of a resource dependence nature — affect emergence, stability, activities, and change among top organizational leaders to make an organization more aligned with its environment. They summarize their argument as follows: (1) the environmental context, with its contingencies, uncertainties, and interdependencies, influences the distribution of power and control within the organization; (2) the distribution of power and control within the organization affects the tenure and selection of major organizational administrators; (3) organizational policies and structures are results of decisions affected by the distribution of power and control; and (4) administrators who control organizational activities affect those activities and resultant structures. Executives are a source of control, and it matters who is in control because control determines organizational activities. The environment affects organizational activities because it affects the distribution of control within the organization.

The principal causal connections in their framework are posited as follows:

Environment
(source of uncertainty, constraint, contingency)
↓
Distribution of power and control within organization
↓
Selection and removal of executives
↓
Organizational actions and structures

However, they are quick to point out that a perfect relationship is unlikely because each intermediate variable probably has other causes and because the linked nature of the process would magnify any intermediate indeterminancy. Their literature review notes two things — first, the absence of much work at this macrolevel; and second, that the literature that does exist either supports their framework or at least is not inconsistent with it.

CONVERGENCE AND DIFFERENCE IN APPROACHES AND RESULTS OF RESEARCH STUDIES AND RECONCILIATION OF THE DIFFERENCES

As indicated above, the microlevel literature on supervisory leadership behavior is making both theoretical and measurement advances. However, on both counts there is still a long way to go.

Especially problematic is that most of the microlevel research does not set the context, so that it is usually impossible to relate the theory and results to the rest of ON or IN functioning. At the macro-level only very recently have integrative frameworks been developed to help explain leadership emergence, stability, activities, and change. For one thing, at the macrolevel it is not all that clear what leadership is — except that it is much more than supervisory behavior and probably includes such skills as resource acquisition, boundary spanning, mediation of major organizational conflicts, and so forth.

The basic convergence between the micro- and macrolevels is that both focus on behavior that makes a difference in the purposive behavior of others. In other words, both types of leadership research examine the same domain of behaviors. However, the divergence is immense. Microlevel research by and large concentrates on various aspects of the twin dimensions of initiating structure and consideration in a supervisory relationship (Karmel, 1978). This is true of virtually all of the situational or contingency approaches. The micro-level research hardly ever considers macrolevel variables, or politics, or the overall functioning of ONs or INs. The macrolevel literature — to the extent that it exists — pays little attention to supervisory behavior. Macrolevel approaches typically focus on the behaviors of top level managers, including, for the most part, behaviors other than supervisory behavior.

Reconciling these differences calls for an integrative framework that merges both micro- and macrolevel perspectives. A framework is needed that merges supervisory behavior with "leader" (more broadly defined) behavior and leader behavior with a broader range of individual, processual, structural, environmental, and effective-ness variables. A framework is needed, in other words, that relates leadership to overall ON or IN functioning.

In the rest of this section we will present a framework, and a set of propositions based on the framework, that we hope are useful in performing this needed integrative task. We hope that the frame-work and propositions address the question of leadership, politics, and the functioning of ONs and INs in a way that incorporates past research and places that research in a larger and more realistic con-text. We hope that the framework and propositions indicate what we feel lies ahead and what the promise of the area is. As such, this sec-tion leads naturally to the last major section, where we discuss the future of research in the area.

Our framework and propositions represent essentially a mapping of a slice of ON and IN functioning. It is very hard to say how this slice relates to other slices, given the state of the literature. The existing literature has mainly been helpful in suggesting the importance of the task we have undertaken (Hunt, Osborn, and Schriesheim, 1978; Pfeffer and Salancik, 1978) and in providing useful clues and paths. Another difficulty in relating this slice to other slices of ON and IN functioning is that, typically, discussing leadership, politics, and the functioning of ONs and INs means discussing a very loosely coupled, indeterminate system (Child, 1977; Pfeffer and Salancik, 1978). So what we are offering is exploratory and tentative — a next step in the development of research on leadership, politics, and functioning of ONs and INs.

A New Framework

Individual Variables. Biographies of successful political actors help identify four probable prerequisites to potential candidacy for top leadership positions (Bryson and Kelley, 1978; Peabody, 1976). First, the potential leaders should be members in good standing of their home organization (Level I), Level II groupings, and the top network (Level III). Second, the leaders' ideology should be mainstream. Of course, exactly what "mainstream" means probably is affected by some of the structural variables, especially member organization expectations and perceptions regarding commitment, awareness, and consensus. Third, their position in their home organization should be safe, so it is possible to gain seniority at higher levels. Fourth, seniority in turn leads to experience and knowledge of the workings of higher level arenas.

Outlaws, mavericks, and rookies will be denied election to top level leadership posts. They will not have enough of the prerequisites to be supported by a necessary majority to take power and hold it. These four variables affect emergence primarily by reducing the field of potential candidates.

In the private sector, developing a secure home base is much more difficult than in the public sector, where, for example, "safe" voting districts, tenure, or civil service provide protection. Furthermore, in the private sector, a necessary "majority" is much smaller — for example, support of the largest single stockholder may be all that is necessary in most cases.

Logically, for the people who make the cutoff on the first four variables, two events can occur. The first is that some of the potential candidates might pull themselves out of any bids for leadership. The candidates may not want a leadership position or may have more attractive leadership opportunities elsewhere, or may feel they are not leadership material. The second option is that some of the candidates may decide to mount a campaign (Hess, 1976; Peabody, 1976).

The fifth variable, skill and competence, is crucial in determining who becomes a leader and who stays a leader, given the narrowed field of candidates (Bardach, 1972; Ilchman and Uphoff, 1969). Studies of congressional leadership indicate that the most important characteristics accounting for both stability and change are the skill, competence, and style of the incumbents (Peabody, 1976). In part, this variable (really itself a cluster of variables) includes trait, behavioral, and situational considerations and propositions that organizational and management theorists usually focus on in their leadership research. The type of behavior addressed here basically is supervisory behavior.

However, in addition to supervisory concerns, this variable cluster includes a substantial measure of political savvy as well. Level I leaders probably are most concerned with supervisory behavior; Level II leaders would be less so, and Level III leaders least so.

Key elements in this political savvy include knowing how structural arrangements and design mechanisms affect leadership emergence, activities, stability, and change, as well as how they affect the performance variables and the interactions between the two. Biographies of political actors indicate a keen awareness of how these can be used to personal advantage and to the advantage of the ON or IN to the extent it coincides with personal advantage (see esp. Caro, 1974; Rakove, 1975; Williams, 1969). Other elements of political savvy frequently include persuasiveness and lobbying skills (Haider, 1974), conflict resolution ability (Lawrence and Lorsch, 1967), statesmanship (Delbecq and Filley, 1974), mediation and negotiation skills (Holtzman, 1970), coalition management skills (Kelley, 1976), and general management skills (Filley, House, and Kerr, 1976).

Processual Variables. Four processual variables have a major impact on leadership. There is a close connection between these variables and the structural variables discussed in the next section.

The pattern of succession in the leadersip hierarchy usually is up the hierarchy one step at a time. For example, in Congress, rising stars usually become party whips, then assistant majority leaders, then majority leaders, then speakers (Peabody, 1976). This may be less true in the private sector, since there not everyone enters at the same level. For example, while everyone first enters the House of Representatives as a representative, in the private sector people often enter an organization in a top leadership post, such as manager of a major division, vice-president, or even president.

The nature of accession to office refers to how contested the struggle is. This appears to be dramatically affected by some of the structural variables, and discussion of it will take place in the next section.

The stage in leadership development is another important processual variable. This refers to the skill and competence the leader or candidate has acquired and is related to most of the important individual variables. Research in this area is very sketchy; it is not clear what the stages would be. However, reading biographies of political actors indicates that a developmental learning process occurs where skills and competencies gained in one stage prepare the actor for new and bigger tasks and responsibilities in later stages. The usefulness of the concept is supported by analogy to developmental learning in general over the adult life cycle (Erikson, 1950, 1975; Sheehy, 1976).

In general, it appears that leadership is both learned and earned. One learns to be a leader by being a leader, and one is promoted in the leadership hierarchy in increments based on past performance and promise of future performance. In other words, there appears to be a connection between the stage in leadership development and level of position.

There also appears to be a connection between the stage in leadership development and vulnerability to challenges. If a leader is prepared and if the stage of leadership development matches the level of position, the leader would be less vulnerable to challenges. Or if the leader were challenged, the leader would be in a better position to defeat the challenger (Caro, 1974; Peabody, 1976; Rakove, 1975; Williams, 1969).

The degree of leadership involvement in the internal affairs of units in the ON or IN appears to depend on who the leaders are and how involved they wish to be. Generally, as the complexity of the network or organization goes up, the likelihood of extensive involvement by top leadership in lower unit affairs would decline. Leaders would attempt to leave such involvement to other leaders lower in the hierarchy (Galbraith, 1973; Peabody, 1976). On the other hand, a top leader wishing to centralize power and to limit the emergence of potential rivals might choose to have a high degree of involvement in unit affairs (Caro, 1974; Kearns, 1976; Peabody, 1976; Williams, 1969).

Acquisition, intensity, and direction of resource and information flows are important processual variables. Van de Ven (1976) argues that resource flows involve task instrumental functions, while information flows involve pattern maintenance functions. As such, previous trait, behavioral, and situational leadership research considered both flows and show that both flows are of qualified importance (Filley, House, and Kerr, 1976; Stogdill, 1974). Both bear direct and indirect relationships to the performance variables. Implicit in our framework is the proposition that control of resource and information flows is a tremendous political resource. In general, controllers of resource and information flows gain power relative to those who lack such control (Bardach, 1972; Benveniste, 1972).

Leaders make every effort to control enough resources to meet minimum standards on key performance variables. Failure to do so seriously jeopardizes any leader's position. In addition, leaders will strive for resource independence. The more resource independence leaders have, the more they control their own actions; the more resource dependence leaders have, the more their actions can be controlled by forces outside their control (Butler et al., 1977-1978; Pfeffer and Salancik, 1978).

Control of organizational actions through control of resources is possible by using several mechanisms. Relative resource independence allows for added design control over ON and IN structure and process. This makes growth easier, easing pressures on existing leadership. For instance, pressures for a change in leadership may be eased through a successful showing on one or more of the performance variables, and potentially competing leaders can be diverted into growth sectors. Also, control of resources means more easily manipulable reward and punishment systems. These can be powerful forms of control.

Taking a somewhat broader perspective, the greater the number of leaders able to control sizable resources, the more political the processes of leadership emergence, activities, stability, and change will be. Universities frequently provide a fairly clear example of this (Butler et al., 1977-1978).

Steers (1977) presents several strategies for improving downward, upward, and horizontal communications in ONs. The same strategies are useful in INs (White, 1974). These strategies aim at improved effectiveness in relation to the performance variables. However, improved communications may not be in the best interests of the existing leadership or the dominant coalition. In particular, destabilizing rival leaders or rival coalitions depends on skillful use of conflicting, confusing, misdirecting messages (Leuchtenburg, 1963).

Top level decisionmakers do not make decisions until they are forced to or are convinced of the correctness of the decision. "Correctness" means the goals of the dominant coalition are met or at least not harmed, the decision is perceived to be technically sound, and the decision is perceived as nonthreatening to the existing mind set and value systems of the ON or IN and the dominant coalition within it (Benveniste, 1972; Kelley, 1976).

Structural Variables. Several structural variables have a major impact on leadership. Of these, level of position in the leadership hierarchy is most important, at least in a predictive sense, since one rises in the hierarchy one level at a time. However, as noted earlier, the relationship may be less strong in the private sector.

The complexity of the network in terms of the number of units in the network and the number of projects and tasks undertaken significantly affects the meaning of level of position in any organization. The greater the complexity, the greater the number of leadership posts and the greater the hierarchy of positions. The greater the complexity of the network, the greater the formalization of the network in terms of organizational agreements and contracts and the greater the centralization of the network where Level II and III decisions are binding on Level I organizations (Azumi and Hage, 1972; Filley, House, and Kerr, 1976; Hall, 1972; Ven de Ven, 1976; Van de Ven et al., 1974).

The greater the complexity, the more leadership posts there would be. Further, the posts would be arranged hierarchically, with additional carefully delineated roles and responsibilities and additional power and authority attached to each position the higher the leader goes in the hierarchy.

Complexity also has an indirect effect on the pattern of succession. The pattern usually is up the hierarchy one step at a time — the greater the complexity, the more levels leaders need to climb to the top of the hierarchy.

Complexity has a direct effect on the nature of accession to office. The general indication is that as complexity increases, so does factionalism (Tushman, 1977; Wilson, 1973). The same effect results from a decline in domain similarity (Van de Ven, 1976). We expect serious challenges to incumbents only when they are vulnerable (Caro, 1974; Gamson and Scotch, 1964; Williams, 1969), but increased factionalism tends to make any incumbent leader more vulnerable, since more diverse coalitions are possible.

Increased factionalism leads to fiercer campaigns where less is held sacred, including the incumbent (Peabody, 1976). Leadership security under these conditions appears to depend on the presence of adequate safeguards, such as an extremely powerful dominant coalition, superior conflict resolution procedures, legal insulation of top leadership posts from contest, and so forth.

Increased complexity leads to a greater number of innovative proposals, providing more opportunity for adaptability and flexibility. Where the top leadership controls the disposition of these proposals, long-term stability is enhanced. Where others control the disposition of these proposals, top leadership is threatened (Benveniste, 1972; Meltsner, 1976).

Centralization gives leaders enforcement power through the use of sanctions and rewards. Increased complexity makes it possible for leaders to accrue still more power through increased autonomy of office. At least in Congress, as complexity increases, a clear separation of the top leadership from the rest of the organization emerges — that is, there is a clearer separation in the House than there is in the Senate (Peabody, 1976).

An advantage of centralized leadership is that it appears to lead to greater stability when the leader is already in place. However, when choosing a new leader, there will be a large number of contestants battling for the position. For example, this was the case in the Soviet Union after Stalin's death (Khruschev, 1974).

The disadvantage is that it appears that more conflicts result among the leadership and the members (Rosenthal, 1974). The reason is that because power and information are less widely shared, consensual decisionmaking is limited (Filley, 1975; Mechanic, 1962; Pettigrew, 1972b; Tushman, 1977).

The greater the centralization, the more likely it is that members will take an adversary relationship with the leadership (Luttwak, 1976; Needleman and Needleman, 1974; Peabody, 1976; Wilson, 1973). Thus, ON or IN operations could turn into a wild free for all unless precautions are taken. One way to avoid this situation is to install a statesperson, or diplomatic figure, in the top leadership position. This leader, respected by all and willing to stay above the fray, could act as a calming element and could undertake a mediating role between the rest of the leadership and the ON and IN membership (Delbecq and Filley, 1974; Lawrence and Lorsch, 1967; Selznick, 1957).

Another related precaution is for the leadership to avoid violent confrontations with the membership, since a coup may become more likely as a result (Alinsky, 1971; Luttwak, 1968). To do this, one strategy is to use many boundary spanners and liaison people to strengthen fragile relationships and to resolve conflicts before they become crises (Delbecq and Filley, 1974; Haider, 1974).

One critical problem in centralized networks is that top leaders

either become inadvertently isolated from important information
(Steers, 1977) or actually are subverted by their subordinates
(Mechanic, 1962). This can destabilize top leaders, and wise incumbents avoid it, particularly through the use of multiple information
channels (Kelley, 1976).

Formalization also affects leadership emergence, activities, stability, and change. An increase in leadership stability results from
greater knowledge of the rules and regulations, the development of
the required ON and/or IN contacts and contracts, and the trappings
of power resulting from the prestige of a highly formalized leadership position (Caro, 1974; Ilchman and Uphoff, 1969).

Under these conditions, an increase in tangible and symbolic rewards increases satisfaction among the members of the network
while reducing jealousies and conflict. And this leads to ON or IN
growth as a leadership strategy for control and stability (Caro, 1974;
Ilchman and Uphoff, 1969; Sapolsky, 1972). Growth can channel
potential rivals into new domains and/or leadership posts in other
sectors. This occupies their time and energies and avoids or post-
pones direct competition with the top leadership. Growth was a
basic controlling strategy, for example, of the Roman emperors
(Luttwak, 1976). On the other hand, if not carefully controlled,
growth can have a destabilizing effect (Pfeffer and Salancik, 1978).

Domain similarity affects leadership emergence, activities, stability, and change. The variable refers to the sameness of goals, services,
staff skills, and clients in ONs and INs (Van de Ven, 1976). There is a
curvilinear relationship between domain similarity and the intensity
of organizational and interorganizational resource and information
flows. If domains are identical, a merger is likely; if they are totally
dissimilar, there would be no reason for an ON or IN (Pfeffer, 1972;
Van de Ven, 1976). For the same reasons, there is a curvilinear relationship between domain similarity and complexity. Domain similarity and complexity affect the acquisition and volume of resource
and information flows available for ON and IN performance reasons
and for use as political resources. Both lead to demands on the skill
and competence of incumbent leadership for handling these tasks
and maintenance, as well as political, activities.

Over time, organizational members and units form differing coalitions with each other around issues of mutual importance (Tichy,
1973; Tushman, 1977). The top leaders of the ONs and INs emerge
from one of the dominant coalitions (Kelley, 1976).

The strongest of the coalitions is likely to have the broadest
domain and the most resource independence. The U.S. Congress is a
Level III in that illustrates this point well. The Democrats in recent

years chose the top leadership because they have the majority in each house. They have the majority because they have the largest domain — the workers, big cities, blacks, the poor, liberals, and so forth, as well as a keen sense of what the people want from government.

On the the other hand, the Republicans have the smaller domain — businessmen, conservatives, and much of the farm belt. Because they command disproportionately more resources, the Republicans have an influence on leadership emergence, activities, stability, and change far in excess of their numbers. Their party raises more money and enjoys higher rates and intensity of citizen participation than their Democratic organizational counterparts (Verba and Nie, 1972).

The dominant coalition participates in all major decisions affecting strategic goal setting or design of ON or IN structure and process. They function primarily as frame setters, rule makers, referees, and enforcers. If the dominant coalition does not make the actual decisions, at least its views will not be excluded from consideration (Kelley, 1976).

Changes affecting the dominant coalition lead to changes in the top leadership. That is, as major setbacks afflict the dominant coalition, especially in connection with the performance variables, one result is an overthrow of the top leadership. If the leadership is successful in problem solving or pure power politics to overcome the challenges, the leadership will enjoy a more secure position (Benveniste, 1972; Hoopes, 1973; Peabody, 1976; Williams, 1969).

As the complexity of the ON or IN increases, or as domain similarity declines, the dynamics change. As the number of coalitions increases, compromising increases, and the amount of democratic decisionmaking increases (Grimes, 1964; Sennett, 1970). Strong coalitions or committees develop as a result (Galbraith, 1973; Peabody, 1976; Rosenthal, 1974). Again, as coalitions or committees take adversary relationships with the leadership, network statespersons (as opposed to politicians) become necessary to preserve order and continuity.

Over time, a stable majority coalition develops, reducing opposing coalitions to permanent minority status (Downs, 1957; Ilchman and Uphoff, 1969; Michels, 1949). The dominant coalition has privileged access to the rewards and power of the network; the minority coalitions have "privileged" access to the punishments and alienation. The result is that the minority members often finally choose to leave the network. The development of political third parties in the United States is an example of this (Leuchtenburg, 1963; Woodward, 1963).

Member expectations are considered structural because their primary manifestation is an intricate and stable set of roles attached to positions defined primarily by the other structural variables (Katz and Kahn, 1966; Wilson, 1973). The principal expectation is that actual or potential leaders strive to maintain and enhance the ON or IN and their position in it (Wilson, 1973:9). Satisfaction of the goals of the dominant coalition is especially crucial. If leaders did the opposite, they would at least be vulnerable to challenge, if they were not actually reprimanded, passed over, transferred, demoted, or fired.

At the IN level, expectations and perceptions of member organizations also involve commitment to problems, issues, or opportunities; awareness; and consensus (Van de Ven, 1976). Operationally, Van de Ven defines these as perceived commitment to resolve environmental needs or opportunities; knowledge of environmental needs, problems, or opportunities, of services and goals of member organizations, and of personal acquaintance with member organization representatives; and agreement over IN ends and means.

Van de Ven makes two points tying expectations and perceptions to other variables in Table 8-1. He hypothesizes that first, the greater the resource dependence, the greater the frequency of IN communications and the greater the awareness and consensus among the IN; and second, the greater the frequency of IN communications, and the greater the awareness and commitment, the greater the consensus. Both hypotheses increase the political importance of resource and communication control for leadership emergence, activities, stability, and change. In particular, the greater the commitment, awareness, and consensus in the IN, the greater the stability in leadership (Downs, 1957; Peabody, 1976).

Environmental Variables. Studies of legislative leadership indicate that environmental factors have a substantial effect on the leadership, but less of an effect than the internal factors (Peabody, 1976). Here a crucial difference between the public and private sectors is apparent. In the private sector, where, for example, market forces and technological changes often dramatically affect leadership stability, environmental factors frequently have more of an effect than the internal factors.

Of the environmental variables, resource dependence is the most important: there would not be an ON or IN if there were not some resource dependence on the part of each ON or IN member and on the part of each network in relation to its broader environment. Resource dependence within the ON or IN affects leadership emergence, activities, stability, and change through its effect on the nature and formation of dominant coalitions. Resource dependence on the broader environment affects the leadership, even to the point of changing the leadership (Pfeffer and Salancik, 1978).

Binding performance reviews in the form of annual elections, stockholder meetings, periodic audits, and/or evaluations influence the actions of ON and IN leadership. Reviews are especially important if they concern satisfaction of the goals of the dominant coalition, resource acquisition, profitability or satisfaction of external constituents, or adaptability and flexibility. Performance on these variables is tied most closely to survival of the dominant coalition and the leaders it chooses or ratifies. These reviews affect the stability of the dominant coalition. The decision of Lyndon Johnson not to seek reelection in 1968 anticipated a poor performance in that binding review (Hoopes, 1973; Kearns, 1976; Sherman, 1976). The subsequent election of Richard Nixon changed the dominant coalition in the executive branch.

Involvement by major outside actors (e.g., a change in law, the emergence of competing ONs or INs, or a change in resource dependence changes the continuity in leadership (Ilchman and Uphoff, 1969; Peabody, 1976). The rise of black leaders in political INs in the South after the Civil War and after passage of the Civil Rights Act of 1964 provides examples of this.

Interest group activity, including that of client groups, professional groups, unions, and so forth, affects the issues discussed and the decisions taken, especially on highly visible, emotional issues (Clark, 1968; Crain and Rosenthal, 1969; Haider, 1974; Peabody, 1976; Wilson, 1973).

Media influences in terms of features, publicity, and exposés support or damage ON or IN leadership. In restrictive regimes, the support role is clear (Brown, 1971; Khruschev, 1974), but it is used elsewhere as well as a matter of course (Hess, 1976; Ilchman and Uphoff, 1969; National Governors' Conference, 1976). In extreme conditions, media can be used against the ON or IN leadership by a savvy coalition or by a major external actor, such as a competing ON or IN (Alinsky, 1971; Bardach, 1972; Luttwak, 1968; Williams, 1969).

Finally, the general external environment, reflected by the amount of turbulence and the rate of technological and social change, can affect the ON or IN leadership (Burns and Stalker, 1961; Ilchman and Uphoff, 1969). Often the effect appears through the structural variables (Lawrence and Lorsch, 1967) and their relation to the performance variables. Table 8-3 summarizes this discussion of the hypothesized effect of individual, processual, structural, and environmental variables on leadership emergence, activities, stability, and change in ONs and INs.

Table 8-3. Hypotheses on Leadership Emergence, Activities, Stability, and Change in ONs and INs

Individual

1. Leaders will be members in good standing of both their home units and the top level network.
2. Leaders' ideologies will be centrist.
3. Leaders' positions in their home units will be secure.
4. Leaders will have substantial seniority.
5. The skill and competence of leaders will be the most important individual variable, and the most important variable overall, in explaining leadership emergence, activities, stability, and change in ONs and INs.[a]

Processual

1. The pattern of succession in the leadership hierarchy is up the hierarchy one step at a time, although in the private sector this would hold less frequently.
2. Stage in leadership development will be positively related to the level of position. The strength of this relationship will increase as complexity increases.
3. Stage in leadership development will have an inverse relationship with leadership vulnerability.
4. The greater the complexity of the ON or the IN, the less extensive will be top leadership involvement in the internal affairs of the ON or IN. The strength of this relationship will decline as the desire of the top leadership to centralize power and to truncate the development of other leaders increases.
5. Leaders who control resource flows will gain power relative to those leaders and coalitions who do not.
6. Leaders who control information flows will gain power relative to those leaders and coalitions who do not.
7. Leaders will make every effort to control enough resources to meet minimum standards on key performance variables. Failure to do so will seriously jeopardize any incumbent's position.
8. Relative resource independence by a leader allows for increased design control over ON or IN structure and process.
9. The greater the number of leaders able to control sizeable resources, the more political will be the processes of leadership emergence, activities, stability, and change in ONs and INs.
10. Top level decisionmakers will not make a decision until they are forced to or are convinced of the correctness of the decision. "Correctness" means in particular that the goals of the dominant coalition are met or at least not harmed, that the decision is perceived to be technically sound, and that the decision is perceived as nonthreatening to the existing mind set and value systems of the ON or IN and the dominant coalition within it.

Structural

1. Level of position will be the most important structural variable, at least in a predictive sense, in accounting for leadership emergence, activities, stability, and change.

[a] A fairly complete listing of propositions related to supervisory aspects of leader behavior and subordinate response will be found in Kerr (1977) and Stogdill (1974).

Table 8-3 (continued)

2. The greater the complexity of the ON or IN, the greater the centralization and formalization of the ON or IN. Thus, the greater the complexity of the ON or IN, the more leadership posts available, the more they will be arranged hierarchically, the more they will involve additional carefully delineated roles and responsibilities, and the more power will be attached to each position the higher one goes in the hierarchy.

3. The greater the complexity of the ON or IN, the more the pattern of succession will be up the hierarchy one step at a time.

4. Serious challenges to an incumbent leader will occur only when he or she is vulnerable.

5. The greater the complexity, or the less the domain similarity, the greater the factionalism. The greater the factionalism, the more contested leadership succession will be. Further, the greater the factionalism, the more insecure an incumbent leader will be in his or her position, unless adequate safeguards are built in. Safeguards might include, for example, an extremely powerful dominant coalition, superior conflict resolution procedures, legal insulation of top posts from contest, and so forth.

6. Increased complexity probably would lead to a greater number of innovative proposals, which provide more opportunity for adaptability and flexibility. To the extent that the top leadership can control the disposition of these proposals, long-term stability in that leadership will be enhanced. To the extent that others control the disposition of these proposals, top leadership stability will be threatened.

7. As centralization increases, so does the power of the top ON or IN leadership.

8. as the complexity of the ON or IN increases, the clearer the separation between the top ON or IN leadership and the leadership of the constituent units.

9. As the centralization of the ON or IN increases, the greater the leadership stability when the leader is already in place, but the greater the number of contestants when the leadership position is open.

10. The greater the centralization of the ON or IN, the greater the conflict between the ON or IN leadership and others in the ON or IN — that is, the more an adversary relationship will be likely to develop.

11. The greater the centralization of the ON or IN, the more ON or IN survival depends on statespersons holding influential positions in the hierarchy and the more it depends on boundary spanners and liaison people to avoid violent confrontations with the others in the ON or IN.

12. Leadership stability will be enhanced through the availability of multiple information channels to incumbents.

13. The greater the formalization of the ON or IN, the greater the stability in top leadership.

14. The greater the growth in an ON or IN, the greater the stability in the top leadership.

15. There is a curvilinear relationship between domain similarity, on the one hand, and intensity of ON or IN resource and information flows, as well as complexity, on the other. The greater the intensity of resource and information flows, the greater the demands on the personality and skill of ON or IN leadership.

16. Over time, members or units in the ON or IN will form differing coalitions with each other around issues of mutual importance. The strongest of the coalitions will be the one with the broadest domain and the one that is the most resource and information independent. The top leadership in the ON or IN will emerge from one of the strong dominant coalitions.

17. The dominant coalition will be in on all major decisions affecting strategic goal setting, structural arrangements, and design of ON or IN structure and process. Their role will be primarily as frame setters, rule makers, referees, and enforcers.

18. As the complexity of the ON or IN increases, or as domain similarity declines, more compromising and democratic decisionmaking will occur in ON or IN deliberations.

Table 8-3 (continued)

19. As the complexity of the ON or IN increases, or as domain similarity declines, strong coalitions or committees will develop.
20. Over time, persistent minority coalitions will leave the ON or IN.
21. The principal expectations of ON or IN member organizations would be that actual or potential ON or IN leaders would strive to maintain and enhance the ON or IN and their position in it.
22. The greater the commitment, awareness, and consensus in the IN, the greater the stability in IN leadership.

Environmental

1. In the public sector, external factors will have less of an impact on leadership emergence, activities, stability, and change than will internal factors. This will not be as true in the private sector, where environmental factors often may have more of an impact than internal factors.
2. Resource dependence will be the most important of the environmental variables in explaining leadership emergence, activities, stability, and change.
3. Binding performance reviews will have a direct effect on the stability of the dominant coalition; positive reviews will stabilize it, and negative reviews will destabilize it.
4. The more visible and emotional the issue, the greater the impact of interest group activity on ON or IN leadership decisions.
5. Media will be used either to stabilize existing network leadership by that leadership or to destabilize existing ON or IN leadership by opposition coalitions, external actors, or competing organizations.
6. The general external environment will affect ON or IN leadership primarily through its effect on ON or IN structure variables and their relation to the performance variables.

WHAT LIES AHEAD: THE PROMISE OF THE AREA

The value of integrating micro- and macroviews of leadership, politics, and the functioning of ONs and INs should be better understanding, explanation, prediction, and prescription in this important area. In order to capitalize on this promise, however, several important steps need to be taken.

First, the question of leadership should be framed far more broadly than it has been traditionally. The usual focus of leadership research has been supervisory behavior and subordinate response. This focus has captured an important component of leadership research, but there is more to the question of leadership than that. By accepting a framework such as our own, or ones likely to be developed by others, traditional leadership research can be related to the important questions of ON and IN politics and the functioning of ONs and INs. Relating traditional leadership research to these broader questions should enhance the value of microlevel approaches.

Further, by framing the question more broadly, it should be possible to create a categorization of leader behaviors in addition to those involving initiating structure and consideration. Our framework indicates that political behaviors in particular are important leadership concerns, especially as one moves to the highest ON or IN levels. Differing leader behaviors imply differing theories and instrumentation than those usually used in microlevel leadership research.

Further still, framing the question more broadly should provide the opportunity to address the question of just how important leadership is at differing levels of ONs and INs. If you only read the psychologically oriented microlevel research, you might assume that leader behaviors were the most important of all organizationally relevant behaviors. The limited research that exists based on a broader perspective indicates that while leadership makes a difference, other variables typically explain more of the variance in overall ON or IN functioning (Pfeffer and Salancik, 1978).

Second, the question of ON or IN politics needs to be addressed much more positively than it has been in the past. Up until quite recently, organizational and management researchers have viewed ON or IN politics as a nagging, though minor, problem at best or downright "dirty" at worst. Indeed, one recent attempt to define organizational politics essentially equates it with subversion (Mayes and Allen, 1977). Either view has led researchers to ignore politics, if possible. Political scientists or public administration theorists, on the other hand, would say that subversion is always a problem, though usually a minor one, when examining the question of politics. They assume that people and organizations typically behave politically or at least that the behavior of people and organizations always has political consequences. This leads to a variant of Lasswell's definition of politics: ON or IN politics is deciding who gets what, when, where and how.

Perhaps such a definition goes too far in the other direction, but we think not. For one thing, we think that our definition presents a more accurate view of what politics is. Further, to argue a priori, through a definition, that nonsubversive ON or IN behavior is nonpolitical is extremely short sighted. Most importantly, such a definition would lead one to ignore the political nature and consequences of nonsubversive behavior. But further, one is unlikely to draw upon the more politically oriented literatures, where subversion is treated as a minor problem. Such narrow disciplinary parochialism on the part of organization and management theorists most certainly would impede our understanding of leadership, politics, and the functioning of ONs and INs. Phrased differently, several leading theorists have called for a more political approach to ONs and INs; we need to make sure that in answering the call we do not unwittingly cripple our approach from the start.

Another implication of a more positive approach to ON or IN politics is the likely introduction of new concepts, methodologies, and perspectives into organizational and management research. The notion of coalition behavior was introduced from the more politically oriented literatures and has had an enriching influence. Other notions have been less well incorporated to date, including lobbying (that is, the extended process of proposal initiation, modification, blockage, and/or adoption); governance; the politics of intra- and interorganizational strategy formulation; and the politics of interorganizational behavior. Sophisticated theorizing, models, simulations, computer methodologies, and journals exist around many of these concepts in the more politically oriented literatures. Organizational and management research would be enhanced by reviewing and adapting these materials to its own purposes.

The third major necessary step is primarily methodological. The perspective we have presented on leadership, politics, and the functioning of ONs and INs is dynamic and loosely coupled — that is, it is shifting and indeterminate. "Strategic choice" plays a crucial role (Child, 1972). A major consequence of this view is that the normal quantitative analyses of ONs and INs are not adequate. We can look at initiating structure and consideration behavior, count levels and protocols, and run regressions forever and never capture the real flavor of leadership, politics, and the functioning of ONs and INs. What our view implies is that prior to such quantitative analyses, a deep and rich anthropological reconnaissance of the target ONs and INs is necessary. Only by having a deep and rich understanding of the context — including individual, processual, structural, environmental, and performance concerns — can quantitative analyses be truly meaningful. While expensive and time consuming, linking anthropological approaches with more sophisticated quantitative methodologies should greatly enhance our understanding in this area. Essentially, what is necessary is a piggybacking of methodologies to capture what is always done, what is done contingently, what is done through strategic choice, and what is never done — and the whys of each case.

We feel that the questions of leadership, politics, and the functioning of ONs and INs are important. If the steps noted above are taken, we feel certain that better understanding, explanation, prediction, and prescription should result.

REFERENCES

Aiken, Michael et al. 1975. *Coordinating Human Services.* San Francisco: Jossey-Bass.

Aldrich, Howard. 1977. "Visionaries and Villains: The Politics of Designing Interorganizational Relations." *Organization and Administrative Sciences* 8, no. 1: 135-46.

Aldrich, Howard, and Jeffrey P. Zeffer. 1976. "Environment of Organizations." *Annual Review of Sociology* 2: 79-105.

Alinsky, Saul D. 1970. *John L. Lewis, An Unauthorized Biography.* New York: Vintage Books.

———. 1971. *Rules for Radicals.* New York: Random.

Allen, Michael Patrick. 1974. "The Structure of Interorganizational Elite Cooptation." *American Sociological Review* 39: 393-406.

Azumi, Koya, and Jerald Hage. 1972. *Organizational Systems.* Lexington, Mass.: D. C. Heath.

Baldridge, J. V. 1971. *Power and Conflict in the University.* New York: John Wiley & Sons.

Bardach, Eugene. 1972. *The Skill Factor in Politics.* Berkeley: University of California Press.

———. 1977. *The Implementation Game: What Happens After a Bill Becomes a Law.* Cambridge, Mass.: MIT Press.

Barnard, Chester. 1938. *The Functions of the Executive.* Cambridge, Mass.: Harvard University Press.

Bass, B. M., and E. R. Valenzi. 1974. "Contingent Aspects of Effective Management Styles." In J. G. Hunt and L. L. Larson, eds., *Contingency Approaches to Leadership.* Carbondale: Southern Illinois University Press.

Benveniste, Guy. 1972. *The Politics of Expertise.* Berkeley: Glendessary.

———. 1977. *Bureaucracy.* San Francisco: Boyd and Fraser.

Berne, Robert, and Charles H. Levine. 1977. "Interorganizational Analysis: An Analytical Handle on the Complexity of Service Delivery Systems." *Administrative Science Quarterly* 12: 411-22.

Boissevain, Jeremy. 1974. *Friends of Friends: Networks, Manipulators and Coalitions.* Oxford: Basil Blackwell.

Bowers, David G., and Stanley E. Seashore. 1966. "Predicting Organizational Effectiveness with a Four-Factor Theory of Leadership." *Administrative Science Quarterly* 11, no. 2: 238-63.

Brown, Trevor. 1971. "Free Press Fair Game for South Africa's Government." *Journalism Quarterly* 48, no. 1: 120-27.

Brown, William P. 1977. "Organizational Maintenance: The Internal Operation of Interest Groups." *Public Administration Review* 37: 48-57.

Bryson, John M., and George Kelley. 1978. "A Political Perspective on Leadership Emergence, Stability and Change in Organizational Networks." *Academy of Management Review* 3, no. 4: 713-23.

Bucher, R. 1970. "Social Process and Power in Medical Schools." In M. Zald, ed., *Power in Organizations,* pp. 3-49. Nashville: Vanderbilt Press.

Burns, Tom, and G. M. Stalker. 1961. *The Management of Innovation.* London: Tavistock.

Butler, R. J.; D. J. Hickson; D. C. Wilson; and R. Axelsson. 1977–1978. "Organizational Power, Politicking and Paralysis." *Organizational and Administrative Sciences* 8, no. 4: 45–59.

Callow, Alexander B. 1976. *The City Boss in America: An Interpretive Reader.* New York: Oxford University Press.

Caro, Robert. 1974. *The Power Broker: Robert Moses and the Fall of New York.* New York: Knopf.

Child, John. 1972. "Organization Structure, Environment, and Performance." *Sociology* 6: 1–22.

———. 1977. "Organizational Design and Performance: Contingency Theory and Beyond." *Organization and Administrative Sciences* 8, nos. 2 and 3: 169–84.

Clark, Terry N. 1968. "Community Structure, Decision-Making, Budget Expenditures, and Urban Renewal in Five Urban Countries." *American Sociological Review* 33: 576–93.

Cohen, M., and J. March. 1974. *Leadership and Ambiguity.* New York: McGraw-Hill.

Crain, Robert, and Donald B. Rosenthal. 1969. "Community Status as a Dimension of Local Decision-Making." *American Sociological Review* 36, no. 6: 970–84.

Crozier, M. 1964. *The Bureaucratic Phenomenon.* Chicago: University of Chicago Press.

———. 1973. "Problem of Power." *Social Research* 40: 211–28.

Cyert, R., and J. March. 1963. *A Behavioral Theory of the Firm.* Englewood Cliffs, N.J.: Prentice-Hall.

Delbecq, Andre, and Alan Filley. 1974. *Program and Project Management in a Matrix Organization: A Case Study.* Madison: University of Wisconsin, Graduate School of Business.

Dessler, G. 1973. "An Investigation of a Path-Goal Theory of Leadership." Doctoral dissertation, Baruch College, City University of New York.

Deutsch, Karl. 1974. *Politics and Government, How People Decide Their Fate.* 2nd ed. Boston: Houghton Mifflin.

Downs, Anthony. 1957. *An Economic Theory of Democracy.* New York: Harper and Brothers.

Erikson, Erik. 1950. *Childhood and Society.* New York: W. W. Norton.

———. 1975. *Life History and the Historical Moment.* New York: W. W. Norton.

Fiedler, F. E. 1967. *A Theory of Leadership Effectiveness.* New York: McGraw-Hill.

———. 1971. "Validation and Extension of the Contingency Model of Leadership Effectiveness: A Review of Empirical Findings." *Psychological Bulletin* 76, no. 2: 128–48.

Filley, Alan. 1975. *Interpersonal Conflict Resolution.* Glenview, Ill.: Scott-Foresman.

Filley, Alan; Robert House; and Steven Kerr. 1976. *Managerial Process and Organizational Behavior.* 2nd ed. Glenview, Illinois: Scott-Foresman.

Fleishman, E. A. 1973. "Overview." In E. A. Fleishman and J. G. Hunt, eds., *Current Developments in the Study of Leadership.* Carbondale: Southern Illinois University Press.

Galbraith, Jay. 1973. *Designing Complex Organizations.* Reading, Mass.: Addison-Wesley.

Gamson, William, and Norman Scotch. 1964. "Scapegoating in Baseball." *American Sociological Review* 70: 47–62.

Ghiselli, E. E. 1971. *Exploration in Managerial Talent.* Santa Monica, Calif.: Goodyear.

Grimes, Alan P. 1964. *Equality in America.* New York: Oxford University Press.

Haider, Donald H. 1974. *When Governments Come to Washington: Governors, Mayors, and Intergovernmental Lobbying.* New York: Free Press.

Hall, Richard. 1972. *Organizations: Structure and Process.* Englewood Cliffs, N.J.: Prentice-Hall.

Hess, Stephen. 1974. *The Presidential Campaign: The Leadership Selection Process After Watergate.* Washington, D.C.: Brookings.

———. 1976. *Organizing the Presidency.* Washington, D.C.: Brookings.

Hickson, D.; D. Hinings; R. Lee; R. Schneck; and J. Pennings. 1971. "A Strategic Contingencies Theory of Intra-Organizational Power." *Administrative Science Quarterly* 16: 216–29.

Hinings, C.; D. Hickson; J. Pennings; and R. Schneck. 1974. "Structural Conditions of Intra-Organizational Power." *Administrative Science Quarterly* 19: 22–45.

Hollander, Edwin P., and James W. Julian. 1969. "Contemporary Trends in the Analysis of Leadership Processes." *Psychological Bulletin* 71, no. 5: 387–97.

Holtzman, Abraham. 1970. *Legislative Liaison: Executive Leadership in Congress.* Chicago: Rand McNally.

Hoopes, Townsend. 1973. *The Limits of Intervention, An Inside Account of How the Johnson Policy of Escalation was Reversed.* Rev. ed. New York: David McKay.

House, Robert J. 1971. "A Path Goal Theory of Leader Effectiveness." *Administrative Science Quarterly* 16, no. 3: 321–38.

House, R. J., and G. Dessler. 1974. "The Path Goal Theory of Leadership: Some Post Hoc and A Priori Tests." In J. G. Hunt and L. L. Larson, eds., *Contingency Approaches to Leadership.* Carbondale: Southern Illinois University Press.

House, R. J., and T. R. Mitchell. 1975. "Path-Goal Theory of Leadership." In Kenneth N. Wexley and Gary A. Yukl, eds., *Organizational Behavior and Industrial Psychology: Readings with Commentary.* New York: Oxford University Press.

Hunt, J. G.; R. N. Osborn; and C. A. Schriesheim. 1978. "Some Neglected Aspects of Leadership Research." In Charles N. Greene and Philip H. Birnbaum, eds., *Proceedings of the 21st Annual Conference of the Midwest Division of the Academy of Management.* Bloomington: School of Business, Indiana University.

Ilchman, Warren F., and Norman T. Uphoff. 1969. *The Political Economy of Change.* Berkeley: University of California Press.

Jacobs, David. 1974. "Dependency and Vulnerability: An Exchange Approach to the Control of Organizations." *Administrative Science Quarterly* 19: 45-59.

Janis, Irving, and L. Mann. 1977. *Decision Making.* Boston: Free Press.

Kahn, Si. 1970. *How People Get Power.* New York: McGraw-Hill.

Karmel, Barbara. 1978. "Leadership: A Challenge to Traditional Research Methods and Assumptions." *Academy of Management Review* 3: 475-82.

Katz, D., and R. Kahn. 1966. *The Social Psychology of Organizations.* New York: Wiley.

Kaufman, Jerome. 1978. "Intervention: A Strategy to Increase Planning Effectiveness." In R. W. Burchell and D. Listokim, eds., *Planning in the 1980's: A Search for Future Directions.* New Brunswick, N.J.: Rutgers University, Center for Urban Policy Research.

Kearns, Doris. 1976. *Lyndon Johnson and the American Dream.* New York: Harper and Row.

Kelley, George. 1976. "Seducing the Elites: The Politics of Decision Making and Innovation in Organizational Networks." *Academy of Management Review* 1: 66-74.

Kerr, Steven. 1977. "Substitutes for Leadership: Some Implications for Organizational Design." *Organization and Administrative Sciences* 8, no.1: 135-46.

Kerr, S.; C. Schriesheim; C. J. Murphy; and R. M. Stogdill. 1974. "Toward a Contingency Theory of Leadership Based Upon the Consideration and Initiating Structure Literature." *Organizational Behavior and Human Performance* 12: 62-82.

Khruschev, Nikita. 1974. *Kruschev Remembers: The Last Testament,* edited and translated by Strobe Talbott. Boston: Little, Brown.

Kochan, T.; G. Huber; and L. Cummings. 1975. "Determinants of Intraorganizational Conflict in Collective Bargaining in the Public Sector." *Administrative Science Quarterly* 20: 10-23.

Lasswell, Harold D. 1936. *Politics: Who Gets What, When and How.* Chicago: University of Chicago Press.

Lawrence, P., and J. Lorsch. 1967. *Organization and Environment.* Boston: Harvard University, Graduate School of Business Administration.

Leuchtenburg, William E. 1963. *Franklin D. Roosevelt and the New Deal.* New York: Harper and Row.

Levine, Charles. 1977. *Racial Politics and the American Mayor.* Lexington, Mass.: D. C. Heath.

Levine, Sol, and Paul E. White. 1961. "Exchange as a Conceptual Framework for the Study of Interorganizational Relationships." *Administrative Science Quarterly* 5: 583-601.

Litwak, Eugene, and Lydia F. Hylton. 1962. "Interorganizational Analysis: A Hypothesis on Coordinating Agencies." *Administrative Science Quarterly* 6: 395-420.

Lowi, Theodore. 1977. *American Politics: Incomplete Conquest.* Hinsdale, Ill.: Dryden Press.

Luttwak, Edward N. 1968. *Coup d'Etat: A Practical Handbook.* London: Allen Lane.

———. 1976. *The Grand Strategy of the Roman Empire.* Baltimore: John Hopkins.

Maccoby, Michael. 1977. *The Gamesman.* New York: Simon and Schuster.

MacMillan, I. 1975. "Organizational Politics: A Prerequisite Perspective." *Business Management* 6: 11–20.

March, J. 1958. *Organizations.* New York: Wiley.

Martin, John B. 1976. *Adlai Stevenson of Illinois.* Garden City, N.Y.: Doubleday.

Maxwell, Robert S. 1969. *LaFollette.* Englewood Cliffs, N.J.: Prentice-Hall.

Mayes, Bronson T., and Robert W. Allen. 1977. "Toward a Definition of Organizational Politics." *Academy of Management Review* 2, no. 4: 672–78.

McGinniss, Joe. 1969. *The Selling of the President 1968.* New York: Trident Press.

McMahon, J. Timothy. 1972. "The Contingency Theory: Logic and Method Revisited." *Personnel Psychology* 25: 697–710.

McNeil, K. 1978. "Understanding Organization Power: Building on the Weberian Legacy." *Administrative Science Quarterly* 23: 65–90.

Mechanic, David. 1962. "Sources of Power of Lower Participants in Complex Organizations." *Administrative Science Quarterly* 7: 349–64.

Meltsner, Arnold. 1976. *Policy Analysts in the Bureaucracy.* Berkeley: University of California Press.

Michels, Robert. 1949. *Political Parties.* New York: The Free Press.

Miner, J. B. 1975. "The Uncertain Future of the Leadership Concept." In J. G. Hunt and L. L. Larson, eds., *Leadership Frontiers.* Kent, Ohio: Comparative Administration Research Institute, Kent State University.

Mowday, R. T. 1978. "The Exercise of Upward Influence in Organizations." *Administrative Science Quarterly* 23: 137–56.

National Governors' Conference. 1976. *The Governor's Office Series, Ten Reports.* Washington, D.C.

Needleman, Martin, and Carolyn Emerson Needleman. 1974. *Guerillas in the Bureaucracy.* New York: John Wiley.

Oppenheimer, Martin, and George Lakey. 1964. *A Manual for Direct Action.* Chicago: Quadrangle Books.

Osborn, Richard N.; James G. Hunt; and Robert S. Bussom. 1977. "On Getting Your Own Way in Organizational Design: An Empirical Illustration of Requisite Variety." *Organization and Administrative Sciences* 8, nos. 2 and 3: 295–310.

Parsons, Talcott. 1962. *Toward a General Theory of Action.* New York: Harper and Row.

Peabody, Robert L. 1976. *Leadership in Congress.* Boston: Little, Brown.

Pelz, D. C., and F. M. Andrews. 1966. *Scientists in Organizations.* New York: John Wiley.

Pennings, Johannes M. 1977–1978. "Organization Environment: Antecedent for Normative Statements on Organization Design?" *Organization and Administrative Sciences* 8, no. 4: 1–14.

Perrow, C. 1972. *Complex Organizations.* Glenview, Ill.: Scott-Foresman.

Pettigrew, A. 1972a. "Information Control as a Power Resource." *Sociology* 6: 187–204.

——. 1972b. *The Politics of Organizational Decision Making.* London: Tavistock.

——. 1975. "Towards a Political Theory of Organizational Intervention." *Human Relations* 28: 191-208.

Pfeffer, J. 1972. "Merger as a Response to Organizational Interdependence." *Administrative Science Quarterly* 17: 382-95.

——. 1973. "Size, Composition, and Function of Hospital Boards of Directors." *Administrative Science Quarterly* 18: 240-64.

Pfeffer, J., and G. Salancik. 1974. "Organizational Decision Making as a Political Process." *Administrative Science Quarterly* 19: 135-52.

——. 1978. *The External Control of Organizations.* New York: Harper and Row.

Presthus, Robert. 1975. *Public Administration.* 6th ed. New York: Ronald Press.

Rakove, Milton. 1975. *Don't Make No Waves, Don't Back No Losers: An Insider's Analysis of the Daley Machine.* Bloomington: Indiana University Press.

Rice, R. W. 1978. "Psychometric Properties of the Esteem for Least Preferred Coworker (LPC Scale)." *Academy of Management Review* 3: 106-18.

Rondinelli, Dennis A. 1973. "Urban Planning as Policy Analysis: Management of Urban Change." *Journal of the American Institute of Planners* 39: 13-32.

Rosenthal, Alan. 1974. *Legislative Performance in the States: Explorations in Committee Behavior.* New York: Free Press.

Royko, Mike. 1971. *Boss.* New York: E. P. Dutton.

Salancik, G., and J. Pfeffer. 1974. "Bases and Use of Power in Organizational Decision Making." *Administrative Science Quarterly* 19: 543-73.

Sapolsky, Harvey M. 1972. *The Polaris System Development: Bureaucratic and Programmatic Success in Government.* Cambridge, Mass.: Harvard University Press.

Schmidt, S., and T. Kochan. 1972. "Conflict: Toward Conceptual Clarity." *Administrative Science Quarterly* 17: 359-70.

Schriesheim, C. A., and S. Kerr. 1977. "Theories and Measures of Leadership: A Critical Appraisal of Current and Future Directions." In J. G. Hunt and
• L. L. Larson, eds., *Leadership: The Cutting Edge.* Carbondale: Southern Illinois University Press.

Schuler, R. S. 1973. "A Path-Goal Theory of Leadership: An Empirical Investigation." Doctoral dissertation, Michigan State University.

Scott, W. E., and L. L. Cummings. 1973. *Readings in Organizational Behavior and Human Performance.* Rev. ed. Homewood, Ill.: Richard D. Irwin.

Selznick, V. 1949. *T.V.A. and the Grass Roots.* Berkeley: University of California Press.

——. 1957. *Leadership in Administration.* New York: Harper and Row.

Sennett, Richard. 1970. *The Uses of Disorder.* New York: Random.

Sheehy, Gail. 1976. *Passages, Predictable Crises in Adult Life.* New York: E. P. Dutton.

Sherman, Norman, ed. 1976. *The Education of a Public Man: My Life and Politics/Hubert H. Humphrey.* Garden City, N.Y.: Doubleday.

Sherwood, Robert E. 1948. *Roosevelt and Hopkins.* New York: Harper and Brothers.

Smart, Carolyne, and Ilan Vertinsky. 1977. "Design for Crisis Decision Units." *Administrative Science Quarterly* 22: 640-57.

Stagner, R. 1969. "Corporate Decision Making." *Journal of Applied Psychology* 53: 1-13.

Steers, R. M. 1977. *Organizational Effectiveness: A Behavioral View.* Santa Monica, Calif.: Goodyear.

Steiss, Alan W. 1972. *Public Budgeting and Management.* Lexington, Mass.: Lexington Books.

Stogdill, Ralph M. 1974. *Handbook of Leadership.* New York: Free Press.

Terreberry, Shirley. 1968. "The Evolution of Organizational Environments." *Administrative Science Quarterly* 12: 590-613.

Tichy, N. 1973. "An Analysis of Clique Formation and Structure in Organizations." *Administrative Science Quarterly* 18: 194-208.

Tushman, Michael L. 1977. "A Political Approach to Organizations: A Review and Rationale." *Academy of Management Review* 2: 206-16.

Van de Ven, Andrew H. 1976. "On the Nature, Formation, and Maintenance of Relations Among Organizations." *Academy of Management Review* 2: 34-53.

Van de Ven, Andrew H. et al. 1974. "Frameworks for Interorganizational Analysis." *Organization and Administrative Sciences* 5: 113-29.

Verba, Sidney, and Norman H. Nie. 1972. *Participation in America: Political Democracy and Social Equality.* New York: Harper and Row.

Vroom, V. H., and P. W. Yetton. 1973. *Leadership and Decision Making.* Pittsburgh: University of Pittsburgh Press.

Wamsley, G., and M. Zald. 1973. *The Political Economy of Public Organizations.* Lexington, Mass.: D.C. Heath.

Warren, R. 1967. "Inter-Organizational Field as a Focus for Investigation." *Administrative Science Quarterly* 12: 396-419.

Warwick, D., and T. Reed. 1975. *A Theory of Public Bureaucracy.* Cambridge, Mass.: Harvard University Press.

Weick, K. 1969. *The Social Psychology of Organizing.* Reading, Mass.: Addison-Wesley.

White, Paul E. 1974. "Intra- and Interorganizational Studies: Do They Require Separate Conceptualizations?" *Administration and Society* 6: 107-52.

Wildavsky, A. 1964. *The Politics of the Budgetary Process.* New York: Little, Brown.

Wilensky, H. 1967. *Organizational Intelligence.* New York: Basic Books.

Williams, Thomas Harry. 1969. *Huey Long.* New York: Knopf.

Wilson, James Q. 1973. *Political Organizations.* New York: Basic Books.

Woodward, C. Vann. 1963. *Tom Watson, Agrarian Rebel.* New York: Oxford University Press.

Yukl, Gary. 1971. "Toward a Behavioral Theory of Leadership." *Organizational Behavior and Human Performance* 6, no. 4: 414-40.

Zald, M. 1970. *Power in Organizations.* Nashville: Vanderbilt Press.

———. 1970. "Political Economy." In M. Zald, ed., *Power in Organizations.* Nashville: Vanderbilt Press.

Ziegler, Herman, and Michael A. Baer. 1969. *Lobbying: Interaction and Influence in American State Legislatures.* Belmont, Cal.: Wadsworth.

Chapter 9

Technology and Organization:
A Review and Synthesis of
Major Research Findings

Bernard C. Reimann* and Giorgio Inzerilli**

One of the most hotly debated issues in the literature of organization theory is that of "technological determinism". On the one hand, it seems eminently sensible to suppose that organization structure should depend a great deal on the technology it uses to transform inputs into outputs. As Thompson (1967:12) has suggested: "differences in technical function or 'technologies' (should) cause significant differences among organizations." On the other hand, numerous recent reviews of the literature (e.g., Donaldson, 1976; Scott, 1975; Stanfield, 1976; Gillespie and Mileti, 1977; Ford and Slocum, 1977; Miles and Snow, 1978; Fry, 1978) clearly point out that the findings of empirical studies on the relationship between technology and structure have been very inconsistent and often directly contradictory. This, of course, may simply reflect the reality that no fundamental, consistent relationship exists. It seems more likely, however, that the inconsistency of results is due mainly to substantial inconsistencies in the methodologies of different researchers.

In this chapter, research examining the relationship between tech-

* Cleveland State University
** University of Pennsylvania

nology and structure is reviewed in an effort to highlight the sources of its current state of utter confusion and disagreement. The major problem appears to be one of lack of a basic, underlying theory of the role of technology in organization, which has lead to a proliferation of noncomparable research methods and findings. When the various studies are classified according to basic similarities in type of technology and type and level of organization unit examined, it becomes apparent that most of the controversy centers around studies focusing on the impact of transformation technology at the level of the organizational system. Studies focusing on the unit level of the organization or those defining technology in terms of environmental inputs and outputs (rather than transformation processes) seem to be remarkably consistent in their support of technological determinism. It is proposed that future research should be based on a consistent theory for relating technology and structure at the system level. This theory should recognize that a given complex organization may operate with a variety of "core" — or "first order" — transformation technologies, in addition to which it will typically utilize one or more "second order" technologies to support, coordinate, and control its "first order" activities.

METHODOLOGICAL DIFFERENCES

The above-cited reviews have listed a variety of methodological differences, including (1) definition of technology and structure variables; (2) measurement techniques; (3) consideration of other variables, such as size and dependence; and (4) choice of focal organizational unit (i.e., total system versus subunit, product versus service organization). All of these methodological differences reflect the fact that there appears to be no basic underlying theoretical model for the technology-structure relationship. Rather, a variety of models have been employed, since researchers in this area apparently have used a "grounded theory" approach (Glaser and Strauss, 1967) in designing their studies. That is, they have first selected some variables that were of interest and developed operational measures for each. Then they have applied these measures to a set of organizations and analyzed the relationships between these measures. Finally, they have attempted to develop some theoretical or conceptual explanation of these relationships. As a result, their theories are "grounded" in the data.

DEFINITION OF VARIABLES

Perhaps the most direct consequence of this lack of agreement on a theoretical model has been a wide divergence in the way technology and structure have been defined and operationalized. For example, both Woodward (1965) and Harvey (1968) were concerned with the "same" variable of organizational technology, defined by Harvey as "the mechanisms or processes by which an organization turns out its product or service" (p. 252). However, Woodward actually measured the degree to which the process of input transformation was continuous or smooth (Starbuck, 1965), while Harvey measured the number of product changes to represent his technological "specificity" of the process.

It is quite clear here that these two researchers looked at very different aspects of technology. Where Woodward was concerned with the transformation process, Harvey focused on the nature (variability) of the organization's output. In this regard, Harvey's measure of "technology" was actually more of a measure of environmental variability, like those of Burns and Stalker (1961) and Lawrence and Lorsch (1969). Not surprisingly, then, Harvey's results were considerably more supportive of the latter researchers than of Woodward. In essence, he found that the greater the variability of the output, the more decentralized or organic the structure of his sample of manufacturing firms.

Another, related complication arises when the same operational measure is used to represent two different variables. For example, Fullan (1970); Mohr (1971); and Van de Ven, Delbecq, and Koenig (1976) all considered task interdependence to be an index of technology, while the Aston researchers (Pugh et al., 1969; Hickson, Pugh, and Pheysey, 1969; Child and Mansfield, 1972) treated it as a dimension of structure. Grimes and Klein (1973) considered the discretion of personnel as part of technology, while others such as Pugh et al. (1969) considered this to be an index of centralization.

The seriousness of these definitional problems was highlighted by Scott's (1975) review of literature. He counted twenty-one different definitions of the technology variable, some referring to the nature of inputs processed by the organization, some to the outputs, and others to the transformation process itself. Most studies focused on the operations involved in the process, but some looked at the nature of the materials processed, while still others examined the knowledge required to carry out the transformation process.

MEASUREMENT OF VARIABLES

As indicated above, the different conceptions of technology and structure have been reflected in different operationalizations. However, a further difficulty concerns the actual method of measuring these variables. On the one hand there is the "objective" or "institutional" (Sathe, 1978) method of interviews with managers, observation, consultation of organizational documentation, and a priori classification favored by researchers like Woodward (1965) and the Aston group (e.g., Pugh et al., 1969). On the other hand, researchers such as Hage and Aiken (1969), Mohr (1971), and Van de Ven and Delbecq (1974) have relied primarily on "subjective" instruments such as questionnaires to measure the perceptions and attitudes of organization participants.

A serious difficulty with using the perceptions of the same individuals for both technology and structure variables is that the resulting relationships may well be psychological artifacts (Mohr, 1971:447; Reimann, 1977:548). Furthermore, there is very little convergent validity between objective and subjective measures of the same organizational variables (Pennings, 1973; Sathe, 1978). Another measurement variation is that in most studies the data were gathered by researchers at the study sites, while in a few cases questionnaires were mailed to key organizational respondents such as top managers (e.g., Khandwalla, 1974).

Finally, in some studies, most notably those of the Aston group (Pugh et al., 1969, Hickson, Pugh, and Pheysey, 1969), and their various replications, researchers have constructed aggregate scales as if they were dealing with unidirectional vectors. However, Mansfield (1973) has argued that many of the Aston items are in reality scalar and not vector quantities and should therefore not be aggregated. This possibility casts considerable doubt on the validity of some of the Aston measures of technology (e.g., "Workflow Integration") and structure (e.g., "Concentration of Authority").

CONSIDERATION OF
OTHER VARIABLES

All of the above measurement problems obviously compound the difficulty of comparing and integrating the various studies of the technology-structure relationship. A further contribution to the incomparability of different research efforts is a substantial variation in the extent to which other variables that may confound the technology-structure relationship have been included in the analysis.

One such confounding factor that has been widely discussed in the literature is organization size. For example, the Aston researchers have shown that size has a strong interactive effect on the technology-structure relationship (Hickson, Pugh, and Pheysey, 1969; Child and Mansfield, 1972). Another important factor that has often been ignored is that of "dependence" or the relative autonomy of the focal organizational unit from the larger (i.e., parent) organization of which it is a part. The Aston studies, as well as those of Negandhi and Reimann (1973) and Blau et al. (1976), showed that this factor was significantly related to structural variables such as specialization, standardization, and centralization.

Still another important variable that has seldom been considered is environmental conditions (e.g., environmental uncertainty or variability). Numerous studies have demonstrated the strong relationship between environmental conditions and structure (e.g., Burns and Stalker, 1961; Lawrence and Lorsch, 1969; Negandhi and Reimann, 1973). Moreover, a recent study by Reimann (1977) demonstrated that the relationship between operations technology (degree of mass production) and structure (centralization of authority) may be substantially modified by the degree of technological change (actually productivity change) in the organization's environment. For manufacturing firms operating in an environment of relatively slow technological change, no relationship was found between technology and structure. However, for those firms facing relatively rapid technological change, a significant positive relationship was found between the degree of mass production and the amount of centralization. Freeman (1973) has also argued that environmental conditions, by permitting different degrees of "slack," can exert a strong influence over the relationship (or "fit") between technology and structure.

Finally, it seems to be often overlooked that Woodward's technological determinism hypothesis was based on a comparison of the structure-technology "fit" of high- and low-performing firms. With very rare exceptions (such as Khandwalla, 1974), subsequent studies have not included the performance variable and could not, therefore, provide a true test of technological determinism. In any event, to the extent that various studies have or have not included certain "other" variables that may influence the technology-structure relationship, their results are not strictly comparable.

CHOICE OF FOCAL ORGANIZATIONAL UNIT

Perhaps the most serious obstacle to the comparison and integration of the results of the many technology and structure studies is the fact that different researchers have focused on technology at different organizational levels. One group of scholars has concentrated on the total organization at the systems or modal level (e.g., Woodward and the Aston researchers), while another group has made the subunit or work group its primary focus (e.g., Mohr, 1971; Hrebiniak, 1974; Van de Ven, Delbecq, and Koenig, 1976).

Interestingly enough, the degree of convergence of findings is substantially greater at the work group level than at the system level. In fact, much of the controversy over the technological imperative would vanish if the findings of all of the system level studies (except Woodward's) were eliminated from consideration.

This, of course, is not very surprising when we consider the fact that the organizational system is, by definition, composed of one or more subunits and therefore will generally be far more complex than any individual subunit. Moreover, the function of the organization as a whole is likely to be different from that of its subunits, and therefore the technology-structure relationship is likely to differ between different levels of the organization.

As Reeves and Woodward (1970) have suggested, the primary purpose of structure is that of controlling the activities of the organization. For lower, work group levels these activities will consist principally of the basic "core technology" or the organization's basic transformation process. The activities at higher (system) levels are not of the same nature, since they deal with servicing, maintaining, coordinating, and (ultimately) controlling of the lower units, rather than with the transformation process (workflow) itself.

That is, in any complex organization we can identify two very different types of transformation process technologies. One is the core technology describing the activities at the lowest workflow level of turning out the organization's product or service. The other could be considered as a kind of second order technology of control that would characterize the transformation processes of higher level units. In Parsons' (1962) framework, these activities would be the managerial as opposed to the instrumental functions. Or in Thompson's (1967) conceptual scheme, the second order technology would characterize the work of the various boundary-spanning units in buffering the activities of the first order technology of the "technical core." Due to the wide disparity of their basic activities, these first and second order technologies are very likely to differ in any complex organization, and if the technological imperative holds, so are their structures likely to differ.

While we know of no research studies that have explicitly differentiated between these first and second order technologies, the study by Blau et al. (1976) provides some interesting empirical data in this regard. In their study of 110 New Jersey manufacturing plants, Blau and his colleagues focused on two types of technology. The first was the traditional kind of mechanization of the basic production process according to Amber and Amber's (1962) measure of the degree of automation. The second was a measure of the automation (i.e., computerization) of various clerical functions in supportive or boundary-spanning functions such as purchasing, accounting, production scheduling, and sales. The relationships between the mechanization of the core technology (i.e., "first order") and structural variables were quite different from those with the automation of support functions (i.e., "second order" technology). These results demonstrate that when the technology-structure relationship is examined for the entire organizational system, we must differentiate between the technologies characterizing the work at different levels of organization.

Another study that illustrates this point from a different perspective is that of Hickson, Pugh, and Pheysey (1969). These researchers measured the lower level (i.e., first order) technology of the transformation process, but measured structure both at the lower and system levels (Ford and Slocum, 1977). Not surprisingly, they found no relationship between their lower level measure of organizational technology and their system level measures of structure. Only the lower level structural variables, or those "centered on the workflow," were found to be significantly related to operations technology (Hickson, Pugh, and Pheysey, 1969:394). Organization size and dependence were much stronger "predictors" than technology for system level structural measures (e.g., centralization, functional specialization, structuring of activities).

Thus the Aston and Blau studies provide ample empirical evidence that the technology-structure relationship may depend considerably on the level of analysis in the organization. A related consideration is the fact that when focusing on the system level, there is a good chance that we will be looking at a "mix" of several first order, or workflow, technologies. Most system researchers have either attempted to identify a representative or "dominant" work-flow technology (e.g., Woodward, 1965; Zwerman, 1970) or developed some kind of aggregate measure(s) (e.g., Pugh et al., 1969; Khandwalla, 1974; Reimann, 1977). Either of these approaches is problematic, however, whenever an organization has more than one workflow technology.

For example, Woodward based much of her analysis on a sub-sample of just 80 of her 100 firms. One of the reasons for excluding some firms was that their technological systems were "mixed," in that they contained more than one of her basic technology categories. One of the reasons other systems level researchers have been unable to duplicate Woodward's findings could well be the fact that the firms in her subsample were essentially "pure" types with a single dominant transformation technology, while all the rest had highly "mixed" types.

Khandwalla (1974), in his survey of seventy-nine manufacturing firms, mailed a questionnaire to high-ranking executives asking them to indicate the relative extent to which their firms used each of five major categories, based on Woodward's scale of production continuity from unit to process production. From this he arrived at a score of "mass output orientation" as a weighted average of the five levels of increasing production continuity.

Khandwalla's aggregate measure did give him a rough indication of the overall degree of mass versus unit production in a firm, since it was strongly correlated with capital intensity. However, two firms could come up with identical mass output orientation scores and yet have very different technologies in their various subunits. Furthermore, Khandwalla's score was not only a function of the average continuity of the firms' production processes, but was also strongly influenced by the number of different technologies used in a firm. Therefore, his measure also tapped a dimension of second order technological complexity (i.e., the greater the number of different processes, from unit to continuous process, used in an organization, the more complex the second order technology of controlling, servicing, and coordinating these diverse technologies).

The above interpretation of Khandwalla's technology measure can go a long way toward explaining his otherwise very unexpected finding of a significant positive correlation ($r = .37$) between the degree of mass output orientation and decentralization of authority among his most successful firms. Rather than contradicting Woodward (1965), as well as the Aston group (e.g., Pugh et al., 1969), this result may reflect the fact that higher scores on mass output orientation also tend to mean higher technical complexity at the system level, requiring decentralization for effective coordination and control.

A related problem is that many researchers have studied manufacturing or product-processing organizations (e.g., Woodward, 1965; Freeman, 1973; Khandwalla, 1974; Blau et al., 1976), while others have studied service or people-processing organizations, such as hospitals or government agencies (e.g., Hage and Aiken, 1969; Mohr, 1971; Hrebiniak, 1974; Van de Ven, Delbecq, and Koenig, 1976).

Fuchs (1968) has argued that there is a fundamental qualitative difference between product and service industry technologies. If so, it may be difficult and even misleading to try and compare technology-structure relationships observed in manufacturing firms with those from service organizations. In fact, the Aston researchers (Pugh et al., 1969; Child and Mansfield, 1972) found substantial differences in the technology-structure relationships depending on whether or not they included service firms in their analyses along with manufacturing firms. For example, in both studies the correlation between the technology variable of "workflow integration" and specialization dropped from being significant to practically nil when the service organizations were eliminated from the analysis.

The list of methodological differences outlined above is by no means exhaustive, since it only includes the most substantial contrasts between the different studies. However, it should be quite clear that with this plethora of methodological differences, any attempt at a meaningful integration of the many studies on the technology-structure relationship is doomed to failure. However, it may still be instructive to examine certain subsets of these studies, chosen on the basis of some similarities in their methodological perspectives. The perspectives that seem most promising for making such an analysis are those dealing with the type of technology measure used and the level and type of organizational unit.

The types of technology examined can be divided into those that deal with the organizational unit's transformation process and those that deal with environmental inputs or outputs. The levels of analysis are the system versus the subunit or work group, and the type of unit is either product or service. The two categories of each of these two perspectives can be arranged in the eight cell matrix as shown in Table 9-1. Those studies that can be assigned to a particular cell should be roughly comparable, at least with respect to type and level of organization and general definition of the technology variable. We will therefore briefly summarize the results of the major studies classified in each cell and try to integrate them.

Table 9-1. Eight Cell Matrix

Organizational Process	Organizational Level	
	Unit	System
Transformation-product	Grimes and Klein (1973)	Woodward (1965) Fullan (1970) Zwerman (1970) Hickson, Pugh, and Pheysey (1969) Negandhi and Reimann (1973) Freeman (1973) Khandwalla (1974) Blau et al. (1976) Reimann (1977)[a]
Transformation-service	Bell (1967) Mohr (1971) Hrebiniak (1974) Van de Ven, Delbecq, and Koenig (1976) Van de Ven (1977)	Hage and Aiken (1969) Blau and Schoenherr (1971) Dewar and Hage (1978)
Environmental (input/output)-product	Lawrence and Lorsch (1969)[b]	Burns and Stalker (1961) Rushing (1968) Harvey (1968) Lawrence and Lorsch (1969)[b] Reimann (1977)[a]
Environmental (input/output)-service	c	c

[a] Reimann used both environmental and transformation dimensions of technology.

[b] Lawrence and Lorsch focused on both unit and system levels.

[c] None of the studies of service organizations reviewed here focused exclusively on environmental aspects. Most researchers examined both transformation and input or output characteristics, but typically they combined them into a single index (such as Hage and Aiken's "routineness"; or Van de Ven, Delbecq, and Koenig's "task uncertainty").

TECHNOLOGY AT THE SUBUNIT LEVEL

Numerous studies have been done that focus on the technology or task at the subunit or work group level. However, most of these have not concerned themselves with structure, but rather with individual attitudes toward work, supervision, and the like (e.g., Rousseau, 1977; Overton, Schneck, and Hazlett, 1977; Billings,

Klimoski, and Breaugh, 1977; Ouchi, 1977; Nemiroff and Ford, 1978). Since these studies have not considered organization structure as a primary dependent variable, they are not relevant to this discussion.

As can be seen from Figure 9-1, there have not been very many studies on the technology-structure relationship at the work group level. Moreover, all but two have dealt with service-oriented units, and all but one have focused primarily on the transformation processes.

Lawrence and Lorsch (1969) studied ten manufacturing firms and their major subunits or departments (e.g., manufacturing, sales, R&D). They focused on the relative uncertainty of the "task environments" faced by the firms as well as by their individual subunits. They found, in essence, that the more uncertain a unit's task environment, the more organic and flexible its structure. These results formed the basis of their famous "contingency theory" of organization.

Grimes and Klein (1973) studied subunits (twenty-five branch plants) of a large, "successful" manufacturing organization. Their measure of technology was based on Perrow's (1967) index of the relative "routineness" of the organization's tasks, as operationalized by Hage and Aiken (1969). That is, they assessed the degree of routineness with questionnaires given to organization members. Grimes and Klein found that (perceived) autonomy of the organizational unit increased as the (perceived) degree of routineness of tasks decreased. This relationship was considerably stronger at the work (bottom) level than at the "modal" (branch plant) level. The rest of the studies at the subunit level of analysis all took place in "people-processing" service organizations but came up with results that show remarkable agreement with each other as well as with the above studies of manufacturing subunits.

An early study by Bell (1967) of thirty departments of a general hospital revealed that the more complex the task, the smaller the span of control. Mohr (1971) studied 144 subunits of thirteen local health departments. His main indicator of technology was "task manageability," based on the uniformity, complexity, and analyzability of tasks. This definition was similar to the "degree of routineness" of Perrow (1967), Hage and Aiken (1969), and Grimes and Klein (1973).

However, in contrast to the above researchers, Mohr's technology measure was, in part at least, an "objective" one. That is, in addition to a perceptual questionnaire measure, Mohr used a priori classification of jobs by himself and by three independent "experts" to assess their relative "manageability"[1] (1971:448). His structural variable of "participativeness" was measured by averaging subordinate responses to questionnaire items in a fashion similar to previous researchers such as Hage and Aiken. However, it should be noted that this procedure reduced substantially the possibility of the artificial relationship between perceptions of the same individuals that existed in previous studies. Not surprisingly, therefore, Mohr found a considerably lower correlation between his technology and structure measures than had previous researchers. However, the relationship was still statistically significant, indicating an increase in participativeness as task manageability (equivalent to "nonroutineness") increased. Moreover, another perceptual measure of technology, task interdependence, was considerably more strongly related to participativeness, as was a rather unique indicator of technology — that of the noise level in the work group.

Hrebiniak (1974) examined the technology-structure relationship in thirty-six departments of a general hospital, but also included a possible moderating variable — the effect of supervision. He assessed four aspects of the work groups' tasks — (1) technological level, (2) predictability, (3) interdependence, and (4) manageability.

The first of these was based on independent classifications by the investigator and two "experts" according to the various jobs' general manageability (similar to Mohr, 1971). The other three measures were based on the perceptions of work group members. His structural variables of job autonomy, participation, closeness of supervision, rule usage, and unity of control were also based on worker responses to questionnaire items based on the work of Bell (1967), Mohr (1971), and Grimes and Klein (1973). Hrebiniak (1974:405) found no evidence for a "clear technological imperative" at the group level based on bivariate correlations. However, when controlling for "effects of supervision" (such as the supervisor's perception of autonomy for his group and of his participation in higher level decisions) by multiple regression, far stronger relationships between subunit technology and structure emerged.

Thus, Hrebiniak's results provide some important evidence to corroborate Mohr's (1971) contention that the technology-structure relationship must be studied in a multivariate framework. That is, Hrebiniak's results were consistent with the technological imperative hypothesis at the work group level only when controlling for the "mediating effect" of supervision. Thus Hrebiniak's results, along with those of a number of other researchers, argue quite strongly (and sensibly) against a broad technological imperative and in favor of the "contingency approach" that emphasizes the importance of considering various other organizational factors as "contingencies" (such as "supervision," size, etc.) that may influence the technology-structure relationship.

A subsequent study of 197 subunits of an employment security agency by Van de Ven, Delbecq, and Koenig (1976) has provided still further insights as to the complex relationship between work group technology and structure. These researchers examined the two dimensions of "task uncertainty" and "task interdependence." The former was a function of the variability and difficulty of the task and essentially very similar to the measures of routineness and manageability used by previous researchers. As Mohr (1971) had done, these researchers used an objective measure for each of their variables along with a perceptual one. They report good reliability and validity for each type of measure (Van de Ven, Delbecq, and Koenig, 1976: 33–36).

Van de Ven, Delbecq, and Koenig found that the two different aspects of technology had qualitatively different impacts on the way in which activities within the various subunits were coordinated. As the task uncertainty increased, there was an increasing substitution of informal horizontal communication channels and group meetings for formal, hierarchical means of coordination. This, of course, was in line with predictions of Galbraith's (1977) information-processing model of organization. On the other hand, Van de Ven, Delbecq, and Koenig found that increasing task interdependence was accompanied by an additive increase in the use of all coordinating mechanisms (both formal and informal). Most significant to the controversy about technological determinism was the fact that Van de Ven, Delbecq, and Koenig found that their technology variables were considerably more important than size in explaining variations in the structure of the work units they examined.

While qualitatively different, and considerably more sophisticated in research design, Van de Ven, Delbecq, and Koenig's research is clearly supportive of previous studies of technology and structure at the primary work group level. In fact, a careful look at the results of all of the studies summarized in this section reveals a basic convergence about the relationship between work group structure and technology. That is, as the transformation process (or task) of the work group becomes less routine, or more uncertain and complex, its structure becomes more organic, with increased participation, autonomy, and informality of relationships in the group. As suggested earlier in this chapter, when we confine ourselves to an analysis of research at the level of primary work groups, the research results consistently point to a clear technological imperative. This, of course, is no great revelation, since the nature of the transformation process is bound to play an important role in the activities at the primary work group level. It is at the system level of complex organizations that problems can be expected to arise with any effort to arrive at consistent results. It is to this problem that we now turn.

TECHNOLOGY AT THE SYSTEM LEVEL

Where the majority of studies at the subunit level were done in service ("people-processing") organizations, the most extensive system level organizational studies of technology and structure have been carried out in primarily manufacturing-oriented business firms (see Figure 9-1). Moreover, most have focused on the transformation processes rather than on the nature of environmental inputs or outputs.

The classic study in this area is, of course, the one by Woodward (1965) of some 100 manufacturing concerns in the English Midlands. Based on extensive interviews with managers, personal observations, and consultation of company documents, the Woodward study concluded that the most successful firms were those that had chosen the internal structures most appropriate for their operations technologies. Her technology measure was a scale of increasing "technical complexity" consisting of nine ordered categories that she collapsed into the following three for many of her analyses — (1) unit and small batch production, (2) large batch and mass production, and (3) process production. She found that some aspects of structure, such as vertical span, chief executive span, and ratio of indirect to direct labor, increased linearly as the degree of technical complexity increased. However, she also found a curvilinear (U-shaped) relationship with some other aspects of structure. In particular, she found that successful firms with the least and most advanced technologies (unit as well as process) had relatively "organic" structures (i.e., more informal and decentralized), while their counterparts with moderately advanced mass production technologies were relatively "mechanistic" (i.e., more formal, bureaucratic, and centralized).

Zwerman (1970) attempted to replicate Woodward's study with a sample of fifty-five Minnesota manufacturing firms and concluded that his results were in general agreement with Woodward's (1965). (However, it should be mentioned, that a careful reanalysis of Zwerman's results has led Donaldson [1976] to question some of Zwerman's conclusions.)

Fullan (1970) also used Woodward's process technology classifications in his study of twelve manufacturing firms. However, his structural variable was a subjective one — workers' perceived degree of "integration" in terms of their relationships with management and the company. He found that continuous process workers experienced the most integration, with unit production firms a close second, and mass production the least, by a substantial margin. To the degree that workers would tend to experience greater integration in organically structured firms than in mechanistic ones, Fullan's results support Woodward's curvilinear relationship between production continuity and structure.

Several major comparative research projects were carried out by researchers from the University of Aston — generally known as the Aston group. The first of these to focus explicitly on system level technology and structure was that reported by Hickson, Pugh, and Pheysey (1969), based on data gathered from extensive interviews, observation, and examination of company records in forty-six English work organizations (thirty-one manufacturers and fifteen service concerns). Where Woodward (1965) had found technology to be far more strongly related to structure than organization size, the Aston researchers reported the exact opposite (Hickson, Pugh, and Pheysey, 1969).[2] They measured two aspects of operations technology. The first, "production continuity," was essentially similar to Woodward's original "complexity" scale, while the second, "workflow integration," represented the "degree of automated, continuous, fixed-sequence operation in the technology" (Hickson, Pugh, and Pheysey, 1969:384).

The Aston researchers were able to replicate Woodward's (1965) findings only with those aspects of structure (such as number of workers per foreman or proportion of employees in inspection, maintenance, and production control) that were "centered on the workflow." For other, more general, aspects of structure (i.e., more distant from the workflow per se), such as formalization, specialization, and centralization, any relationships with the technological variables were insignificant in comparison to the relationships with other "contextual" variables such as organization size and dependence on other organizations. Hickson, Pugh, and Pheysey (1969) attempted to reconcile their findings with Woodward's (1965) by pointing out that Woodward's sample firms tended to be somewhat smaller than those studied by the Aston group. (About two-thirds had less than 500 employees as compared to about one-third in the Aston sample.) Therefore, the importance of technology in Woodward's study may simply reflect the fact that "the smaller the organization, the more completely its structure is pervaded by the immediate effects of this [workflow] technology" (Hickson, Pugh, and Pheysey, 1969:378).

A subsequent replication of the original study by Aston researchers Child and Mansfield (1972) with the "national" sample of eighty-two diverse business organizations in Britain was supportive of Hickson, Pugh, and Pheysey's basic conclusions about the technology-structure relationship (especially for their subsample of forty manufacturing firms). Child and Mansfield report that "size has a much closer relationship to the aspects of structure measured than does technology. This is particularly true of the overall measures of structure. . . " (1972:383). Moreover, they also found a generally stronger technology-structure relationship among smaller organizations than among larger ones (especially for centralization). As in the earlier Aston research, Child and Mansfield found that the strongest associations tended to occur between technology and those structural aspects most closely tied to the workflow.

Two other replications of the Aston work also were generally supportive of Hickson's conclusions about the overall technology-size-structure relationship. The first, by Inkson, Pugh, and Hickson (1970), applied abbreviated versions of the major Aston scales (Pugh et al., 1969) to a sample of forty manufacturing and service organizations. The second was a direct replication of the Aston study with seventy manufacturers in the United States, Canada, and Britain (Hickson et al., 1974). In all three countries, organization size had a considerably stronger relationship with structure (formalization and specialization) than did technology (workflow integration).

Thus, the considerable weight of the Aston research and its several substantial replications argues very strongly against a technological imperative at the level of the total organization (unless, of course, that organization is relatively small). However, while the Aston researchers did a very thorough job of analyzing the technology-structure association in relation to other possible mediating variables such as organization size and ownership, they did not focus on organizational performance. It can be argued, therefore, that the Aston studies did not provide a true test of the technological imperative, since Woodward's (1965) conclusions were clearly based on an analysis of relatively high-performing organizations. The less successful firms in her sample did not show the same pattern of associations between technology and structure. On the other hand, the Aston researchers relied heavily on sophisticated, multivariate analysis of their data, while Woodward's findings were essentially based on simple bivariate relationships.

A study by Khandwalla (1974) of seventy-nine U.S. manufacturing organizations overcame some of the key drawbacks of the above-cited research by using multivariate statistics (including path analysis) as well as a performance measure (profitability). Khandwalla operationalized his technology variable by a minor modification of Woodward's (1965) scale of production continuity. Since he (realistically) expected many of his U.S. firms to employ more than one of Woodward's categories, he created a weighted average of the relative degree of use of each major category to arrive at a score of "mass production orientation." While Khandwalla considered three "dimensions" of structure, only one of these — decentralization — is strictly comparable to previous research on technology and structure. The other dimensions were the degree of vertical integration, which is most closely related to the Aston group's contextual variable of dependence (Pugh et al., 1969), and the use of sophisticated control techniques, which has no direct parallel in either the Aston or Woodward studies.

Although Khandwalla (1974) concludes that his "study does not support Woodward's [1965] thesis of a technological imperative," (p. 96), his results do not seem to justify his conclusion entirely. For his total sample, the degree of mass production orientation had a "modest and selective impact" on structure (p. 88). More specifically, decentralization of top level decisions was only weakly correlated with mass production orientation. However, among the relatively high-performing firms, a significant positive correlation ($r = .37$) was observed between decentralization and mass production, while among the lower performing firms, the correlation was actually negative ($r = -.10$).

Therefore, Khandwalla's findings in one sense strongly support Woodward's thesis of a technological imperative. On the other hand, the linear relationship discovered by Khandwalla is quite different from Woodward's U-shaped one. One possible (but speculative) explanation for this discrepancy is that Khandwalla's sample of manufacturers may have underrepresented the lower end of the mass production scale (i.e., unit production) relative to Woodward. Moreover, as pointed out earlier, Khandwalla's technology measure may have been qualitatively quite different from Woodward's in that it reflected the complexity of the "mix" of different technologies in the organization as well as the average degree of production continuity.

Khandwalla also concluded that his results did not support Hickson, Pugh, and Pheysey's (1969) hypothesis of the absence of a technological imperative. While this is accurate, of course, his results are not really comparable to Hickson, Pugh, and Pheysey's, since the only structural measure he used is decentralization of top level decisions (roughly similar to the Aston group's "concentration of authority" scale). Moreover, Khandwalla did not explore those structural variables centering on the workflow, so his study sheds no new light on Hickson, Pugh, and Pheysey's most interesting hypothesis regarding the selective impact of operations technology only on those aspects of structure most central to the workflow.

A study by Negandhi and Reimann (1973) of thirty manufacturing companies in India revealed that environmental variables (organizational concern for task agents and dependence on parent organization) were much more strongly related to decentralization than was process technology (using Woodward's scale of production continuity).

In spite of the substantial disagreements among the various studies cited above, one general conclusion does emerge quite clearly: operations technology — in terms of the degree of complexity and/or continuity of the production system — is quite selective in its impact on organization structure. The disagreements seem to center primarily on the importance of operations technology relative to other variables such as organization size, dependence, or vertical integration (strategy). Moreover, it is only for those structural variables that are directly concerned with the organization's production system or workflow that any sort of specific convergence of findings can be detected. This convergence seems to suggest, for example, that the more highly complicated or mechanized the workflow, the higher the levels of administrative intensity (proportion of "indirect" workers, or staff, administrative and managerial personnel).

A study by Freeman (1973) of forty-one manufacturing organizations was designed to test this hypothesis. However, his measure of operations technology differed somewhat from the one used in the previous studies. He measured the degree of "mechanization" on the basis of (1) whether the substance produced was integral or dimensional, (2) whether or not automated production lines were used, and (3) the proportion of orders on automated lines.

His bivariate correlations with administrative intensity supported his hypothesis with respect to the first two measures of mechanization ($r = .39$ and $.34$, respectively), but not for the third ($r = .10$). Freeman also examined interaction effects between mechanization, administrative intensity, and environmental diversity and change. He points out that Ashby's (1956:207) Law of Requisite Variety suggests that an organization must develop a sufficient variety in its "administrative subsystem" to cope with the variety of its inputs and still maintain stability in its outputs. Therefore, Freeman proposes that the technological complexity introduced by mechanization and environmental variability will interact positively to contribute to increasing administrative intensity. His results seem to confirm this proposition and are therefore also essentially consistent with the Aston and Woodward results for administrative intensity — in spite of his different operationalization of the operations technology variable. That is, increasing mechanization (or automation) of the production process tends to increase the size of the administrative or "supportive" (in Aston terminology) component in organizations.

Another major study that focused on the degree of automation of operations technology is that of 110 New Jersey manufacturing plants by Blau et al. (1976). These researchers defined their variable of operations technology as "the substitution of mechanical equipment for human labor" (p. 21). However, as mentioned earlier, they departed from previous work by focusing on two very different dimensions of mechanization. The first of these was mechanization of production technology, of which they measured two aspects — degree of automation of equipment (Amber and Amber, 1962) and production continuity (Woodward, 1965). The second was a function of the degree of mechanization, or computerization, of clerical functions in areas like accounting, purchasing, and sales.

The structural measures examined by Blau and his coworkers (1976) consisted essentially of (1) various aspects of vertical and horizontal differentiation (including the Aston measure of functional specialization), (2) various indexes of administrative intensity of supportive (indirect) personnel, (3) spans of control of top and middle managers, and (4) decentralization — the locus of decision-making, including headquarters (i.e., one level above the plant's top management).

In one respect, Blau et al.'s results support the conclusions of Hickson, Pugh, and Pheysey (1969), while disconfirming Woodward's (1965). Organization size was far more strongly and consistently correlated with structural differentiation than was either measure of mechanization. However, both measures of mechanization were significantly related to the proportion of indirect production personnel, in keeping with the findings of Woodward (1965) and of the Aston researchers (Hickson, Pugh, and Pheysey, 1969; Child and Mansfield, 1972), as well as those of Freeman (1973).

On the other hand, Blau et al. (1976:27) were not able to confirm Hickson, Pugh, and Pheysey's (1969) conclusion that structural aspects more closely linked to the production process will have stronger correlations with mechanization (except for some curvilinear relationships with Woodward's three categories) nor the hypothesis that the effects of mechanization would be stronger for small organizations than for large ones (Blau et al., 1976:27).

In one respect Blau et al.'s results strongly confirm some of Woodward's results. Based on an analysis of the shape of the relationships between Woodward's three major categories they concluded:

> advances in production technology do not have linear, but do have curvilinear, relationships with various aspects of plant structure. As one moves from small-batch to mass production, the nature of manufacturing tasks becomes more uniform, which is reflected in an increase in routine work, a lower skill level of the labor force, and reductions in support components. The data indicate that these trends are reversed in advanced production technologies. Thus, production jobs are least standardized in process plants, since they generally involve maintenance of complex equipment or responsible monitoring functions there. Process plants usually have not only the most highly skilled blue-collar work force, but also the largest proportion of white-collar jobs requiring specialized skills. (1976:30)

Of particular theoretical and practical interest is Blau et al.'s finding that mechanization of the production process was negatively correlated with decentralization of operational (marketing and production) decisions. However, the relationship was curvilinear (inverted U-shaped) with decentralization of personnel decisions — with mass production plants being the most decentralized in this regard. The authors interpret this finding as reflecting the fact that most of their sample organizations were branch plants of much larger firms. Since increasing mechanization means larger capital investment, it follows that corporate management would be relatively more likely to keep operational decisions centralized at headquarters in relatively highly mechanized plants. On the other hand, mass production factories require less skilled and trained employees than either unit or process manufacturers. Therefore, personnel decisions may be least critical to the success of mass production plants and are therefore most likely to be delegated.

The relationships that Blau and his coworkers found between computerization and various aspects of structure were only partly supportive of previous research. For example, in contrast with Whisler's (1970) conclusions, computerization tended to increase, rather than decrease, the number of administrative levels in the plant. Blau et al. explain this result by suggesting that "a computer system serves as an impersonal mechanism of control, which makes it less disadvantageous for management to be separated from the workflow by many hierarchical levels" (1976:32).

On the other hand, Withington's (1969) observation of increases in administrative (nonproduction) workers with increasing computer use was supported (Blau et al., 1976:33). Moreover, computer use was positively associated with most of Blau et al.'s measures of structural differentiation.

Perhaps the most interesting result is that the impact of computer automation of support functions on decentralization of decision-making was the exact opposite of the impact observed for automation of the production process itself. That is, the greater the use of on site computers, the greater the decentralization or autonomy of plant management in making operational (production and marketing) decisions and, to a much lesser extent, personnel decisions. Blau et al. also found that the location and use of a computer in combination with a relatively high proportion of personnel engaged in sales exerted a very strong influence on the autonomy of plant management — lessening centralization of corporate authority. The two variables in combination explained nearly half the variance in their decentralization measure (1976:37).

Blau et al.'s finding that automation (or mechanization) of the plant's production process appeared to have an impact on decentralization that was the exact opposite of the impact found for automation (or computerization) of the support functions is very interesting as well as unprecedented. However, this unique result is largely a function of the fact that Blau et al.'s decentralization measure, like the Aston measure of "concentration of authority" (Pugh et al., 1969), reflected to a large extent decentralization *to* the organization in question, not *within* it. That is, corporate management might be, on the one hand, loath to decentralize authority to a plant that represents a very high capital investment in automated machinery. On the other, to the extent that administrative support functions are automated by computer (which typically represents a very minor capital investment relative to production equipment), corporate management may feel it has the necessary "impersonal" control over operations to permit greater decentralization of operating decisions. By the same token, as Withington (1969) has pointed out, local management in plants with computers has ready access to the information needed for operating decisions, and corporate management has less of a "monopoly" over this information.

Therefore, Blau et al.'s (1976) results appear to corroborate Withington's (1969) and Stewart's (1971) findings that increasing use of computers tends to increase the degree to which top management delegates decisionmaking authority to lower levels.[3] It should be pointed out that these results were also in keeping with Blau and

Schoenherr's (1971) finding of a strong positive relationship between decentralization and computerization in employment agencies.

It is difficult to compare Blau et al.'s (1976) decentralization results directly to the Aston group's, since the latter focused on a variety of functional decisions (Pugh, Hickson, and Turner, 1968; Inkson, Pugh, and Hickson, 1970), while the former created separate indexes for operational and personnel decisions. Nevertheless, for operational as well as combined operational and personnel decisions, Blau et al. (1976:35) concluded that decentralization of decision-making decreased with increasing mechanization. This result is at least modestly in agreement with Pugh et al. (1969), who (after controlling for size effects) report an insignificant but positive correlation between production continuity and centralization ($r = .28$, $n = 31$).

Of course Blau et al.'s results do not support Woodward's at all, since the former study suggests that process production plants would be the most centralized, while the latter found that process as well as unit production firms tended to have the least centralized (i.e., most organic) structures. However, the two studies are not directly comparable. First of all, Woodward (1965) measured delegation within her firms, while a large part of Blau et al.'s (1976) measure was a function of delegation to the local organization from parent headquarters. Furthermore, like the Aston researchers and others, Blau et al. did not consider the relationship with organizational performance, as Woodward had done. What is more, a "majority" of Blau et al.'s 110 New Jersey plants had experienced a "decline of 5 percent or more in their labor force" in the six years prior to this study (1976:22). Such a decline is likely to be an indicator of poor performance, unless, of course, it was accompanied by increasing productivity. In any event, the lack of performance data and the possibility that many of the organizations studied by Blau et al. may have been relatively low in performance make the results of this study substantially less than a conclusive test of Woodward's technological determinism thesis.

In spite of the fact that all of the studies reviewed in this section focused on the same (system) level of similar (manufacturing) organizations, their findings with respect to the technology-structure relationship are difficult to compare and, where they are comparable, often inconsistent. This, of course, was to be expected, since many of the various complex organizations studied may have been operating with several different workflow technologies (e.g., some unit, some mass, and some process production), and the aggregate measures used generally did not reflect this possible variety. Moreover, as pointed out earlier, the system level may well include first and second order technologies with widely different impacts on different aspects of structure.

It is very significant that the only area where some degree of convergence can be detected is among those structural aspects that are most central to the workflow — such as various administrative ratios or "job count variables" that do not "deal with the wider administrative or hierarchical structure" (Hickson, Pugh, and Pheysey, 1969: 388). Moreover, the findings for these structural variables tend to confirm the findings of strong and consistent technology-structure relationships at the lower level unit or task group level summarized in the previous section.

SYSTEM LEVEL SERVICE TECHNOLOGY

The system level studies described above all focused on manufacturing firms. It may be instructive to see whether those researchers focusing exclusively on service-oriented organizations have had any better success in developing consistent results. Unfortunately, we were only able to find three major studies in this area, two of them based on the same sample of organizations. However, while the studies of service organizations do not permit a good test of result convergence, they add some interesting insights with respect to the results of other research.

The first system level analysis of service concerns was Hage and Aiken's (1969) study of sixteen health and welfare agencies. These researchers assessed the degree of "routineness" of the workflow of each of their agencies from a weighted average of the responses of organization members to a questionnaire based on Perrow's (1967, 1970) technology construct. Structural variables were similarly assessed on the basis of employee and management perceptions. (The problem this methodology may have introduced has been discussed earlier.) In essence Hage and Aiken found that the routineness of the organization's overall technology was positively associated with structural aspects such as centralization, formalization, and standardization — very much in line with the results of work level unit research.

A study of fifty-three state employment agencies by Blau and Schoenherr (1971) came up with somewhat different conclusions, however. These researchers defined technology in terms of the degree of automation of tasks by means of computerization. Structural aspects considered included division of labor, vertical and horizontal differentiation, managerial spans of control, clerical ratios, and centralization of authority. Blau and Schoenherr concluded that size had a far stronger, more pervasive impact on structure than any other variable, including their technology variable. They felt that their results were in substantial agreement with those of the Aston researchers (Hickson, Pugh, and Pheysey, 1969).

However, Blau and Schoenherr do report some fairly substantial relationships between structure and their measure of transformation technology. Perhaps the most interesting of these is the relationship between automation (use of computers) and delegation of authority. They concluded (1971:125): "Automation in employment security agencies clearly promotes decentralization," since the extent of computer use was positively related to delegation of authority within the headquarters. However, the delegation from headquarters to local levels interacted with agency size. In small agencies delegation was actually negatively related to automation, but in larger agencies this relationship was strongly positive. Blau and Schoenherr interpret this result as evidence that "large size creates pressures to delegate administrative decisions to lower levels and that these pressures overcome the otherwise existing tendency in automated agencies not to decentralize responsibilities beyond the headquarters" (1971:128).

Blau and Schoenherr also found that automation was positively related to vertical differentiation, but less strongly than to agency size. Automation was also quite strongly and negatively correlated with the proportion of unskilled clerks. Increasing computerization tended to raise the average skill level of personnel due to the employment of programmers and systems analysts and to reduce the need for unskilled clerks.

The results reported by Blau and Schoenherr are not strictly comparable to those of Hage and Aiken because of considerable methodological differences. First of all, the former used objective means for assessing their variables, while the latter used subjective questionnaire methods, and the convergent validity of these techniques is not good (Pennings, 1973; Sathe, 1978). Second, their definitions of technology and structure are not strictly comparable. However, the positive relationship between automation and decentralization in Blau and Schoenherr's agency headquarters may be supportive of some of Hage and Aiken's results to the extent that increasing computer automation decreases the routineness of tasks within the agency (a distinct possibility since routine tasks should be those most likely to be automated, leaving the less routine tasks to be carried out by relatively more skilled personnel).

Blau and Schoenherr's interpretations of the positive correlation between computerization and decentralization are worth noting here. They argue that computerization serves the function of an "impersonal control mechanism," thus reducing the risk of delegation (1971:126). Another possibility they mention is that those agencies that were first to adopt computerization might have been the more decentralized ones, whose more flexible authority structures might have made them less resistant to this technological change. (Of course cross-sectional studies such as the ones considered so far cannot establish the causal direction of the relationships observed.)

The most recent system level study of service organizations by Dewar and Hage (1978) is a reanalysis of data gathered by Hage and Aiken (1969). This study is methodologically quite different from the above and will be discussed in detail later in this chapter when we consider longitudinal research designs.

"ENVIRONMENTAL" VERSUS TRANSFORMATION TECHNOLOGY

Certainly the above analysis of research in both manufacturing and service organizations suggests that it may be quite futile to look for a convergence to some basic, consistent relationship between technology and structure at the system level. Those researchers who have chosen to define system level technology in terms of the characteristics of environmental inputs or outputs rather than the transformation process itself have, however, been far more successful in this regard. These researchers have come up with remarkably consistent results.

Burns and Stalker (1961) studied twenty English firms and discovered that among firms that faced rapid changes in technologies and markets, the most successful ones had very flexible, "organismic" structures. For firms with relatively stable environments, however, a more bureaucratic or "mechanistic" structure appeared to be more successful. Lawrence and Lorsch (1969), as pointed out earlier, report similar relationships between the relative uncertainty of environmental inputs and outputs and structure at both the subunit and system levels for their ten manufacturing firms.

Harvey studied forty-three diverse manufacturing firms and used essentially the same conceptual definition of technology as Woodward and the Aston researchers — that is, "the mechanisms or processes by which an organization turns out its product or service"

(Harvey 1968:247). This, however, is where the similarity ended, since Harvey actually focused on the variability of the organization's output. He operationalized his technology variable as the number of product changes over the previous ten years, which he considered to be an indicator of the degree to which the technology was "diffuse" (many changes) versus "specific" (few changes). He concluded that his technology variable was much more strongly related to various aspects of structure (subunit specialization, levels of authority, ratio of managers and supervisors to total personnel, and degree of program specification) than were organization size or other contextual variables, such as ownership. The organizations he examined tended to be less structured on the above dimensions, the greater the rate of change in the technology.[4]

The above three major comparative studies all reached basically the same conclusion: the more variability and uncertainty an organization encounters in its environmental inputs or outputs, the more flexible or organic its internal structure will (or should) be. Moreover, these results are in line with the findings of the unit level researchers, if we consider the fact that greater uncertainty or variability of the "environmental" inputs or outputs of the unit will generally contribute to greater uncertainty and variability of the transformation process and therefore to lower task routineness.

Actually all but one (that of Lawrence and Lorsch, 1969) of the unit level studies were based on Perrow's conceptualization of technology. Perrow (1967, 1970) suggested that organizational technology could be considered in terms of two dimensions. The first of these dealt with the nature of the input — the number of exceptional cases encountered or the variability of the raw material. The second dimension focused on the knowledge aspect of the transformation technology — the degree to which the organization has developed effective "search" or analytical problem solving techniques to deal with exceptions. Perrow himself and several researchers (e.g., Hage and Aiken, 1969) have combined these two dimensions into the single dimension of degree of task "routineness." Similarly, Van de Ven, Delbecq, and Koenig (1976) combined their "task variability" and "task difficulty" dimensions into their technology variable of "task uncertainty" (roughly equivalent to nonroutineness).

Therefore, it should come as no great surprise that the major convergence between unit and system level findings comes when the focus is on the environmental aspect of technology — such as its variability. However, this convergence makes theoretical as well as empirical sense. When the impact on structure of the technology of the inputs or outputs to the transformation process is considered, we are by definition focusing on the total system in which the (total) transformation takes place. That is, the environmental inputs and outputs will tend to have an impact on the transformation system, whether it is a lower level primary work group or a complex system made up of several hierarchies of work groups. It is when the technology of the transformation process itself (i.e., "inside" the focal organization) is the primary focus that the problems of multiple types and levels of technology begin to appear at the system level.

This further illustrates the very fundamental difference between the two definitions of technology — that is, whether we focus on the environment external to the organizational unit or on the internal transformation process itself. For example, Katz and Kahn (1978: 136-37) make a distinction between an organization's "internal" technology (the one actually in use) versus the "external" technology potentially available to it.

Reimann (1977) has made a related distinction between the current form of an organization's (internal) transformation technology and the rate of change of this technology in the organization's (external) environment. As pointed out earlier, he discovered that these external and internal dimensions appeared to interact in their relationship to structure. This result demonstrates the need to distinguish between these different aspects of organizational technology and also the importance of considering them both in our research designs.

LONGITUDINAL RESEARCH DESIGNS

Still another problem with research on the technology-structure relationship is that most researchers (with the exception of Aldrich, 1972) seem to imply some sort of causal connection between technology and structure without ever making this explicit. Since all the studies we have reviewed so far were cross-sectional, any sort of causal inference is problematic (Pugh and Hickson, 1972; Donaldson, 1976; Dewar and Hage, 1978). A great many outside variables may intervene in the technology-structure relationship, and many of these may not be in equilibrium. This second possibility is particularly worrisome in comparing variables such as size, technology, and structure, all of which vary over time. As Freeman and Hannan (1975) have demonstrated, the relationship between organization size and certain aspects of structure (i.e., "administrative intensity") can be quite different at different stages in an organization's growth.

In spite of these problems, very few longitudinal studies of organizations have been attempted. We know of only two major, published longitudinal studies of the technology-structure relationship. The first study is that by Van de Ven (1977) of 125 subunits of a large state employment security agency. Two waves of data collected in 1972 and 1973 permitted a cross-lagged partial correlation analysis to determine likely causal priority of variables. Van de Ven found that increasing task uncertainty (in 1972) was most strongly associated with increasing employee and group decisionmaking and decreasing supervisory decisionmaking (in 1973). In addition, increasing workflow interdependence led to increases in employee and group decisionmaking a year later (without any decrease in supervisory decisionmaking). In general, increasing task uncertainty and workflow interdependence led to increasing participation, while increasing unit size tended to have the opposite effect.

A rather interesting but unexpected finding was that "group decisionmaking in 1972 has a greater positive effect on workflow interdependence in 1973 than the latter in 1972 had on the former in 1973" (Van de Ven, 1977:247). That is, the observed direction of the causal relationship was opposite to that hypothesized. Apparently, the more employees were engaged in group (as opposed to individual) decisionmaking in 1972, the greater they perceived their workflow interdependence to be in 1973. As Van de Ven concludes, "one of the real costs of work coordination through group or team decisionmaking may be increasing interdependence and associated problems among unit personnel" (p. 247).

Van de Ven's finding of a strong, positive, time-lagged correlation between task uncertainty and subsequent employee participation in decisionmaking is strong evidence in favor of the hypothesis that changes in technology can bring about changes in the structure of the work unit. Thus, Van de Ven's results confirm the technological imperative hypothesis at the primary work group level.

Fortunately there is also a longitudinal study that focuses at the system level — namely, the one by Dewar and Hage (1978) mentioned previously. These researchers examined three waves of data obtained by Aiken and Hage in sixteen social welfare agencies in 1964, 1967, and 1970 (Dewar and Hage, 1978:118). However, rather than focusing only on relationships between levels of their variables over time as Van de Ven had done, Dewar and Hage also examined relationships between rates of change of their key variables. They argue that

The former [relations between levels] appear to be more indirect causal processes mediated by a number of variables, whereas the latter [rates of change] appear to be more direct. What is crucial, however, is that an examination of both together is necessary to provide a much more complete and complex understanding of organizational change since the level variable may constrain the rate of change or even accelerate it. (1978:118)

Dewar and Hage go on to point out that the main advantage of using rates of change is that this allows one to "approximate an experimental treatment." (On the other hand, the use of change rates alone would be hazardous, due to the fact that they can of course be highly unstable.)

In defining their system level technology variable, Dewar and Hage depart considerably from previous researchers. They point out that measures of "routineness" or of "machine technology" such as automaticity are likely to be significant only to the structure of lower level work units and are unlikely to have an "organizationwide impact" (1978:114). The critical dimension of technology at the system level of the organization is that of the "scope of an organization's task," which would reflect the variety or mix of technologies used by the organization. (Thus, these researchers focused on what we have called the organization's second order technology.)

For cross-sectional comparisons of the levels of their variables, Dewar and Hage found that size was more strongly and consistently related than technology to both vertical and horizontal differentiation, while these relationships were about equally strong with complexity (number of different occupational specialties). However, when both levels and rates of change were used to predict complexity, size was no longer important at all. The strongest determinant of subsequent complexity was the level of complexity in the previous period, and the only other fairly strong determinant was the rate of change in task scope. A similar analysis revealed that size was still the strongest determinant for both vertical and horizontal differentiation, with rate of change in task scope a fairly close second.

Thus, Dewar and Hage found that both organizational growth and increase in task scope or variety were associated with increasing specialization of labor. However, they argue that these two causal variables "make their impact in different areas of the organization" (1978:129). As organizations grow larger, they tend to hire more administrative specialists. On the other hand, increasing technological diversity calls for increasing specialization "on the line." They speculate that the strong association between size and specialization by the Aston researchers (Hickson, Pugh, and Pheysey, 1969) may reflect "the fact that they measured only administrative and support specialization, not that of the line" (Dewar and Hage, 1978:130).

It should be pointed out, however, that Dewar and Hage's measure of change in task scope was different from their other change scores. They did not find much variation between time periods in the level of their task scope variable, so they used the rate of new program introduction in the three year change period instead. This is equivalent to Hage and Dewar's (1973) measure of program innovation and therefore fits our definition of "environmental" (output) technology.

A major contribution of Dewar and Hage's important study is that organizational technology is a key determinant of system level structural variables, provided that the appropriate system level dimension(s) of technology is (are) tapped. Their study is, of course, limited in terms of sample size and the type of organizations examined (health and welfare service agencies), but it does provide some important guides for future system level research. Before we can hope to make progress out of the jungle of conflicting results and models in this area, we must develop an adequate, theory-grounded conception of system level technology. Dewar and Hage have provided a helpful start in that direction.

SUMMARY AND IMPLICATIONS

This review has shown, as have so many others, that empirical evidence on the technology-structure relationship is in a state of considerable confusion and that the notion of a technological imperative has received mixed support at best. However, upon closer examination of the various studies, it becomes readily apparent that the lack of consistent findings is not so much an indictment against technological determinism per se as against the profusion of theoretical models and methodologies employed by researchers in this field. As Fry (1978) has recently demonstrated, a substantial majority of studies have found technology to be significantly related to at least some aspects of structure. Unfortunately, it is difficult to distill any meaningful, consistent relationship(s) from these studies, due to basic conceptual and methodological differences, such as in (1) definitions of both technology and structure, (2) measurement techniques, (3) inclusion of "other" relevant variables, and (4) level and type of organizational unit.

It appears that the level of analysis may be the most critical variation, since those studies focusing on the lower, or work group, level organizational units actually have been quite consistent in their finding that technology and structure are closely related. It is at the systems level of larger, more complex organizations where much of the debate and controversy about technological determinism has taken place.

A major reason for inconsistency at the system level appears to be the fact that the larger and more complex organizations are likely to employ a "mix" of different technologies. As a result, the structure of the organizational system is not likely to be dependent on one homogeneous or even one "dominant" transformation technology, but will, rather, be a function of the "second order" technology of coordination, servicing, and control of the various first order transformation technologies.

When the various studies of technology and structure are examined in this light (as well as in terms of some of the other methodological differences), it becomes apparent that the basic concept of technological determinism is very much "alive and well." Most studies focusing on low level units or task groups (e.g., Mohr, 1971; Van de Ven, Delbecq, and Koenig, 1976) have tended to confirm Woodward's (1965) thesis of a technological imperative. While many system level studies have not (e.g., Hickson, Pugh, and Pheysey, 1969; Child and Mansfield, 1972; Blau and Schoenherr, 1971; Blau et al., 1976), they have added some interesting extensions to Woodward's conclusions, in that all found some aspects of technology to be strongly related to selected aspects of structure.

For example, Hickson, Pugh, and Pheysey (1969) demonstrated that the technology-structure relationship was very much dependent on organization size. They found that operations technology was related to most aspects of structure in very small firms. In large organizations, however, process technology was related only to aspects of structure closely centered on the workflow, such as certain job counts and administrative ratios, and not to system level structural variables like centralization and division of labor. Other researchers, such as Blau and Schoenherr (1971) and Freeman (1973), found strong correlations between technology and certain administrative or clerical ratios centered on the workflow.

Hickson, Pugh, and Pheysey concluded that system level structural variables were far more strongly related to contextual variables such as size and dependence than to technology. Blau and Schoenherr (1971) reached a similar conclusion, but did report fairly high correlations between technology and system level structural variables, such as vertical and horizontal differentiation and centralization within the headquarters of their employment agencies. However, their definition of technology was fundamentally different from that of Hickson, Pugh, and Pheysey in that it was a function of the automation (by computer) of various clerical functions throughout the organization. This measure of computerization probably captured a basic, homogeneous characteristic of the transformation process (clerical function) in these employment agencies.

In a subsequent study of manufacturing plants, Blau et al. (1976) found, again, that the degree of computer use was strongly related to the degree of decentralization from plant headquarters. The functions computerized typically were not manufacturing, but clerical service and control functions such as purchasing, sales, accounting, and production control. Therefore, Blau et al. were measuring the degree of automation of these support functions — that is, what we have labeled the "second order" technology.

A recent longitudinal study by Dewar and Hage (1978) provides still further evidence of the importance of second order or system level technology to organization structure. They propose that the most important determinant of differentiation in the division of labor is not organization size per se, but the increasing scope of an organization's task that increasing size may bring. That is, the complexity of the "mix" of different technologies (processes) and products that the organization must coordinate and control is far more important to structure than sheer size. Moreover, Dewar and Hage base their findings on a longitudinal analysis, focusing both on the current levels of their variables and the changes over time of these levels, permitting them to make some inferences about causal relationships between technology and structure.

Therefore, the findings of various system level studies do not really refute Woodward's thesis, as so many reviewers have concluded; rather, they demonstrate that technological determinism is very much dependent on the level and unit of analysis. When we focus on the structure of the total organizational system, we must be sure to measure technology at the system level.

Furthermore, both the technology and structure variables are clearly multidimensional, heterogeneous categories. Much of the controversy between different researchers can be traced to the simple fact that they have treated their variables as if they were homogeneous and have almost arbitrarily chosen one or a few of many possible dimensions to represent their variables (Stanfield, 1976). This sad state of affairs can be attributed largely to the popular "grounded theory" approach to empirical research in this area (Glaser and Strauss, 1967). That is, rather than being based on a common, underlying theory, research results have been "grounded" in the data gathered in the various studies.

It is not surprising, then, that the extensive debate about the technology-structure relationship that has been taking place in the literature for the past decade or so has not resulted in any kind of meaningful resolution. Before we can hope to make any progress toward such a resolution, we will need a drastic change in future research strategies away from the popular "grounded" theory to "common"-theory-based approaches. That is, before carrying out more empirical studies, we need to develop a useful, common theory of system level relationship between technology and structure. Then, if the variables were derived from this common theory, it would be possible to debate the meaning of each variable in terms of its relationship with the theory (Kaplan, 1964).

In this fashion, we could make some progress toward developing agreed upon definitions of variables that would allow us to clearly distinguish them from each other, as Stanfield (1976) has advocated. Once these conceptual definitions and distinctions had been clarified, it would be possible to develop operational measures for each variable, and the debate could be carried on at this level. Once settled, this debate would lead us to a set of agreed upon measures for a set of agreed upon conceptual constructs. At this point we would be ready to start collecting data to build a solid, empirically tested theory of system level technology and structure.

In developing a basic theoretical model of the technology-structure relationship, we must apply some basic lessons learned from the studies reviewed here. First of all, it seems wise to confine our definition of technology to the transformation process itself, rather than including input or output characteristics as many researchers have done. This will help us in distinguishing the technology variable from other, related organizational aspects, such as various environmental influences, organizational goals, and structure. Second, we must take into consideration the possibility of fundamental differences in transformation technologies between organizations with different purposes (e.g., people processing versus material processing), as well as between different levels in a given organizational system. Third, we still need to include in our model a consideration of the influence of "other" variables, such as various environmental and contextual factors on the relationship between transformation technology and organization structure. That is, our model must include some specific "contingency" considerations. Finally, we must include the organizational effectiveness variable in our model. Very few researchers have followed Woodward's example of relating the technology-structure relationship to organizational performance. However, neither our theory nor its empirical tests will be complete until we can assess the impact of various technology-structure combinations on organizational performance.

Obviously, the development of such a broad-based and universally acceptable theory of technology, structure, and performance will be an extremely difficult task — otherwise we would certainly have done it by now. However, this and many other reviews of the technology-structure literature have made it abundantly clear that the "easy way" has not worked, and it is time to "bite the bullet."

NOTES

1. Mohr chose to average this "subjective" measure with his two "objective" ones in spite of its low correlations with the latter ($r = .19$ and $.28$).
2. It should be noted, however, that Aldrich (1972) came up with a different interpretation of the Aston results by applying path analysis to the data reported by Pugh et al. (1969). He concluded that technology might be a very important variable, "causing" organization size, which in turn would "cause" structure. On the other hand, Aldrich's use of path analysis with cross-sectional data is questionable (see Pugh and Hickson, 1972; Donaldson, 1976).
3. Strictly speaking, this would hold true only to the extent that computer use at the plant level — which is what Blau et al. (1976) focused on primarily — directly reflected the degree of computerization for the larger, or parent, organization.
4. Another study that is typically included by reviewers of the technology-structure literature is Rushing (1968). This research is not really comparable to the above studies, since Rushing used secondary data on forty-four manufacturing industries. He found that the division of labor in these industries was positively related to the hardness of the materials (inputs) being processed. This study has no relevance for the present analysis and therefore will not be considered further.

REFERENCES

Aldrich, H. 1972. "Technology and Organization Structure: A Reexamination of the Findings of the Aston Group." *Administrative Science Quarterly* 17: 26-43.

Amber, G. H., and P. S. Amber. 1962. *Anatomy of Automation.* Englewood Cliffs, N.J.: Prentice-Hall.

Ashby, W. Ross. 1956. *An Introduction to Cybernetics.* New York: Science Editions.

Ayoubt, Z. M. 1975. "Technology, Size, and Organization Structure in a Developing Country: Jordan." Paper presented at National Academy of Management Meeting, August 10-13, New Orleans, La.

Bell, G. D. 1967. "Determinants of Span of Control." *American Journal of Sociology* 73: 100-09.

Benson, J. Kenneth. 1977. "Organizations: A Dialectical View." *Administrative Science Quarterly* 22: 1-21.

Billings, R. S.; R. J. Klimoski; and J. A. Breaugh. 1977. "The Impact of a Change in Technology on Job Characteristics: A Quasi-Experiment." *Administrative Science Quarterly* 22: 318-39.

Blau, P., and R. Schoenherr. 1971. *The Structure of Organizations.* New York: Basic Books.

Blau, P. M.; C. M. Falbe; W. McKinley; and P. K. Tracy. 1976. "Technology and Organization in Manufacturing." *Administrative Science Quarterly* 21: 20-40.

Blauner, R. 1964. *Alienation and Freedom.* Chicago: University of Chicago Press.

Bright, J. R. 1958. *Automation and Management.* Boston: Division of Research, Harvard Business School.

Burack, E. H. 1967. "Industrial Management in Advanced Production Systems: Some Theoretical Concepts and Preliminary Findings." *Administrative Science Quarterly* 12: 479-500.

Burns, T., and G. M. Stalker. 1961. *The Management of Innovation.* London: Tavistock.

Child, J. 1973. "Strategies of Control and Organizational Behavior." *Administrative Science Quarterly* 18: 1-17.

———. 1975. "Managerial and Organizational Factors Associated with Company Performance, Part II — A Contingency Analysis." *Journal of Management Studies* 12: 12-28.

Child, J., and R. Mansfield. 1972. "Technology, Size, and Organization Structure." *Sociology* 6: 369-93.

Child, John. 1972. "Organization Structure and Strategies of Control. A Replication of the Aston Studies." *Administrative Science Quarterly* 17: 163-77.

Comstock, D. E., and W. R. Scott. 1977. "Technology and the Structure of Subunits: Distinguishing Individual and Workgroups Effects." *Administrative Science Quarterly* 22: 177-202.

Dewar R., and J. Hage. 1978. "Size, Technology, Complexity, and Structural Differentiation: Toward a Theoretical Synthesis." *Administrative Science Quarterly* 23: 111-36.

Donaldson, L. 1976. "Woodward, Technology, Organizational Structure and Performance — A Critique of the Universal Generalization." *Journal of Management Studies* 13: 255-73.

Ford, J., and J. Slocum. 1977. "Size, Technology, Environment and the Structure of Organizations." *Academy of Management Review* 2: 561-75.

Freeman, J. H. 1973. "Environment, Technology, and Administrative Intensity of Manufacturing Organizations." *American Sociological Review* 38: 750-63.

Freeman, J. H., and M. J. Hannan. 1975. "Growth and Decline Processes in Organizations." *American Sociological Review* 40: 215-28.

Fry, L. W. 1978. "A Review and Analysis of Studies Examining Technology-Structure Relationships." Paper presented at the National Academy of Management Meeting, August 9-13, San Francisco, California.

Fuchs, V. R. 1968. *The Service Economy.* New York: The National Bureau of Economic Research.

Fullan, M. 1970. "Industrial Technology and Worker Integration in the Organization." *American Sociological Review* 25: 1028-39.

Galbraith, J. 1977. *Organization Design.* Reading, Mass.: Addison-Wesley.

Gerwin, D., and W. Christoffel. 1974. "Organizational Structure and Technology: A Computer Model Approach." *Management Science* 20: 1531-42.

Gillespie, D. F., and D. S. Mileti. 1977. "Technology and the Study of Organizations: An Overview and an Appraisal." *Academy of Management Review* 2: 7-16.

Glaser, Barney G., and Anselm L. Straus. 1967. *The Discovery of Grounded Theory: Strategies for Qualitative Research*. London: Weidenfeld & Nicholson.

Grimes, A. J., and S. M. Klein. 1973. "The Technological Imperative: The Relative Impact of Task Unit, Modal Technology and Hierarchy on Structure." *Academy of Management Journal* 16: 583-97.

Hage, J., and M. Aiken. 1969. "Routine Technology, Social Structure and Organization Goals." *Administrative Science Quarterly* 14: 366-75.

Hage, Jerald, and Robert Dewar. 1973. "Elite Values Versus Organizational Structure in Predicting Innovation." *Administrative Science Quarterly* 18: 279-90.

Harvey, E. 1968. "Technology and the Structure of Organizations." *American Sociological Review* 33: 247-59.

Hickson, D. J.; D. S. Pugh; and D. C. Pheysey. 1969. "Operations Technology and Organization Structure: An Empirical Reappraisal." *Administrative Science Quarterly* 14: 378-97.

Hickson, D. C.; R. Hinings; C. J. McMillan; and J. P. Schwitter. 1974. "The Culture-Free Context of Organization Structure: A Tri-National Comparison." *Sociology* 8: 59-80.

Hrebiniak, L. 1974. "Job Technology, Supervision, and Work Group Structure." *Administrative Science Quarterly* 19: 395-410.

Hunt, R. 1970. "Technology and Organization." *Academy of Management Journal* 12: 235-52.

Inkson, J.; D. Pugh; and D. Hickson. 1970. "Organizational Context and Structure: An Abbreviated Replication." *Administrative Science Quarterly* 15: 318-29.

Jelinek, M. 1977. "Technology, Organization, and Contingency." *Academy of Management Review* 2: 17-26.

Katz, D., and R. Kahn. 1978. *The Social Psychology of Organizations*. 2nd ed. New York: Wiley.

Kaplan, A. 1964. *The Conduct of Inquiry*. San Francisco: Chandler.

Khandwalla, P. 1974. "Mass Output Orientation of Operations Technology and Organizational Structure." *Administrative Science Quarterly* 19: 74-97.

Lawrence, P. R., and J. W. Lorsch. 1969. *Organization and Environment*. Homewood, Ill.: Richard D. Irwin.

Lynch, B. P. 1974. "An Empirical Assessment of Perrow's Technology Construct." *Administrative Science Quarterly* 19: 338-56.

Mansfield, R. 1973. "Bureaucracy and Centralization: An Examination of Organizational Structure." *Administrative Science Quarterly* 18: 477-88.

Miles, R. E., and C. C. Snow. 1978. *Organizational Strategy, Structure, and Process*. New York: McGraw-Hill.

Mohr, L. B. 1971. "Organizational Technology and Organizational Structure." *Administrative Science Quarterly* 16: 444-59.

Mumford, E., and O. Banks. 1967. *The Computer and the Clerk.* London: Routledge and Kegan Paul.

Negandhi, A. R., and B. C. Reimann. 1973. "Correlates of Decentralization: Closed and Open Systems Perspectives." *Academy of Management Journal* 16: 470-582.

Nemiroff, P. M., and D. L. Ford, Jr. 1978. "The 'Fit' between Work Group Structure and Tasks: Its Influence on Task Effectiveness and Human Fulfillment." *Organization and Administrative Science* 8: 15-34.

Ouchi, W. 1977. "The Relationship between Organizational Structure and Organizational Control." *Administrative Science Quarterly* 22: 95-113.

Overton, P.; R. Schneck; and C. Hazlett. 1977. "An Empirical Study of the Technology of Nursing Subunits." *Administrative Science Quarterly* 22: 203-19.

Parsons, T. 1962. *Toward A General Theory of Action.* New York: Free Press.

Pennigs, J. 1973. "Measures of Organizational Structure: A Methodological Note." *American Journal of Sociology* 79: 686-704.

Perrow, C. A. 1967. "A Framework for the Comparative Analysis of Organization." *American Sociological Review* 32: 195-208.

———. 1970. *Organizational Analysis: A Sociological View.* Belmont, Calif.: Wadsworth.

Peterson, R. B. 1975. "The Interaction of Technological Process and Perceived Organizational Climate in Norwegian Firms." *Academy of Management Journal* 18: 288-99.

Pugh, D. S., and D. J. Hickson. 1972. "Causal Inference and the Aston Studies." *Administrative Science Quarterly* 17: 273-76.

Pugh, D.; D. Hickson; and C. Turner. 1968. "Dimensions of Organization Structure." *Administrative Science Quarterly* 8: 289-315.

Pugh, D. S.; D. J. Hickson; C. R. Hinings; and C. Turner. 1969. "The Context of Organization Structures." *Administrative Science Quarterly* 14: 91-114.

Reeves, T. K., and B. A. Turner. 1972. "A Theory of Organization and Behavior in Batch Production Factories." *Administrative Science Quarterly* 17: 81-98.

Reeves, T. K., and J. Woodward. 1970. "The Study of Managerial Control." In Joan Woodward, ed., *Industrial Organization: Behavior and Control.* London: Oxford University Press.

Reif, W. E. 1968. *Computer Technology and Management Organization.* Iowa City: Bureau of Business and Economic Research, University of Iowa.

Reimann, B. C. 1973. "On the Dimensions of Bureaucratic Structure: An Empirical Reappraisal." *Administrative Science Quarterly* 18: 462-76.

———. 1977. "Dimensions of Organizational Technology and Structure: An Exploratory Study." *Human Relations* 30: 545-66.

———. 1978. "The Size of Support Staff in Organizations." Paper presented at National Academy of Management Meeting, San Francisco, California, August 9-13.

Rice, A. K. 1958. *Productivity and Social Organization.* London: Tavistock.

Rousseau, D. M. 1977. "Technological Differences in Job Characteristics, Employee Satisfaction and Motivation: A Synthesis of Job Design Research and Sociotechnical Systems Theory." *Organization Behavior and Human Performance* 19: 18-42.

Rushing, W. 1968. "Hardness of Material as Related to Division of Labor in Manufacturing Industries." *Administration Science Quarterly* 13: 229-45.

Sathe, V. 1978. "Institutional versus Questionnaire Measures of Organizational Structure." *Academy of Management Journal* 21: 227-38.

Scott, W. R. 1975. "Organizational Structure." *Annual Review of Sociology* (October): 1-20.

Stanfield, G. G. 1976. "Technology and Organization Structure as Theoretical Categories." *Administrative Science Quarterly* 21: 489-93.

Starbuck, W. 1965. "Organizational Growth and Development." In J. G. March, ed., *Handbook of Organizations*, 451-533. Chicago: Rand McNally.

Stewart, R. 1971. *How Computers Affect Management*. London: Macmillan.

Thompson, J. D. 1967. *Organizations in Action*. New York: McGraw-Hill.

Thompson, J. D., and F. L. Bates. 1957. "Technology, Organization, and Administration." *Administrative Science Quarterly* 2: 325-43.

Van de Ven, A. H. 1977. "A Panel Study on the Effects of Task Uncertainty, Interdependence, and Size on Unit Decision Making." *Organization and Administrative Sciences* 8: 237-53.

Van de Ven, A. H., and L. L. Delbecq. 1974. "A Task Contingent Model of Work Unit Structure." *Administrative Science Quarterly* 19: 183-97.

Van de Ven, A. H.; A. L. Delbecq; and R. Koenig, Jr. 1976. "Determinants of Coordination Modes Within Organizations." *American Sociological Review* 41: 322-38.

Whisler, T. 1970. *The Impact of Computers on Organizations*. New York: Praeger.

Withington, F. G. 1969. *The Real Computer: Its Influences, Uses and Effects*. Reading, Mass.: Addison-Wesley.

Woodward, J. 1965. *Industrial Organization: Theory and Practice*. London: Oxford University Press.

Zwerman, W. L. 1970. *New Perspectives on Organization Theory*. Westport, Conn.: Greenwood.

Chapter 10

The Interorganizational Network as a System: Toward a Conceptual Framework

Richard Koenig, Jr.*

INTRODUCTION

Interorganizational relations (IOR) focus on transactions among a network of three or more organizations. This unit of analysis has been referred to by Warren (1967) as the interorganizational "field" and defined as "the properties of an aggregate of interacting organizations as distinguished from the properties of the individual organizations themselves" (Warren 1971:54). In a similar vein, Turk (1977) refers to the constellation of interdependent and nonautonomous organizations as a "macrosocial unit."

Common to these and other definitions of IOR is a goal that is unique in that it cannot be achieved by organizations independently pursuing their own self-interests. Examples might include the delivery of health care services among agencies in a community, the distribution of scarce resources by headquarters among their subsidiaries, sharing of information among member organizations of a professional or trade association, and the like.

Granting the large number of practical examples that might be

* Temple University
I would like to thank Mary Jane Huneycutt and Bernard Reimann for their helpful comments on an earlier draft of this chapter.

cited, the bulk of theoretical and empirical work to date has been far more restricted. Two examples of this more limited focus have been open systems analysis and pairwise descriptions of coordination.

1. Open systems analysis seeks to explain the internal structure and properties of organizations in terms of aggregate characteristics of the task environment — variability, complexity, and threat (Child, 1972). Among the early examples of these "contingency" theories was Burns and Stalker's (1961) conclusion that organic and adaptive structures were better suited than mechanistic structures to uncertain environments. Alternatively, Dill (1958) found that greater managerial autonomy was needed in unstable environments. A number of subsequent studies have extended this line of thought (e.g., Lawrence and Lorsch, 1967; Khandwalla, 1972; Duncan, 1972; Negandhi and Reimann, 1973).

2. Pairwise descriptions of coordination sought to determine what processes and activities led to cooperative and harmonious interactions. Awareness, communications, and domain consensus were considered to be among the most salient factors (Tuite, 1972; Van de Ven, 1975; Hall et al., 1977).

Critics of this literature note that although some preliminary insights are provided, these two perspectives alone are too limited for a thorough understanding of IOR. Turk (1970) has bluntly stated that explanations mainly in terms of organization characteristics are inadequate, while Aldrich (1974b) adds that studies must extend beyond simple pairwise relationships. However, in a summary of selected papers presented at prior CARI conferences, Negandhi (1975) concludes that although some researchers have begun using the rhetoric of systems theory, these efforts have been in name only.

This literature review defines IOR as a system. The purpose of the review is not so much critical but rather a constructive attempt to identify salient dimensions of an IOR system and their relationships. The chapter begins by defining a framework, which is then used to discuss some contingency relationships. A concluding section considers issues of dynamics and change.

IOR AS A SOCIAL SYSTEM

Generically, social systems can be defined in terms of the interactions and interdependencies among members — in this case organizations. As goal-oriented, or controlled, systems, these IOR interdependencies are oriented toward one or more objectives that serve as a basis for integrating and governing activities among the organizations. Within these parameters, variations in the degree and type of system can be found. Kuhn (1974) provides an illustration of three degrees of system development — formal, informal, and semi-formal — that can be applied to IOR.

At the formal level, an IOR system can be characterized as having a legitimate hierarchy of authority and an officially mandated, overarching goal. This type of system is reflective of bureaucratic ideologies. At the opposite extreme, an informal system has different means of regulation and control. Subsystem organizations are guided by individual self-interest goals and become interdependent through needs for exchanges and to exploit opportunities in their environments, as has been described by ecological theories (Hawley, 1950; Hannan and Freeman, 1978). However, regularity and stability may result from the development of a market based upon shared prices and commodities of exchange. Economic theories, especially those of competition, are most descriptive of this type of system activity.

In between these two extremes are a broad range of semiformal systems. Dominant characteristics include a low, modest level of formal authority coupled with a rather high level of self-interest orientation by the member organizations. Litwak and Hylton (1962) suggest that organizations exist in a basic condition of conflict with one another, while Guetzkow (1966) suggests that a primary striving is for autonomy. Regulation of interdependencies under these conditions occurs informally via cooperative norms of conduct that are manifest informally through political and altruistic leadership activities on behalf of the system. Descriptions of IOR in this vein have been referred to elsewhere as political economy (Wamsley and Zald, 1973; Benson, 1975).

Four major characteristics common to these varieties of IOR system will serve as the basis for discussion in the remainder of this chapter. These are drawn from the Van de Ven, Emmett, and Koenig (1974) description of IOR as a social action collectivity. The four characteristics are first introduced below and then described in more detail.

1. Transaction Network — Exchange transactions among organizations define the existence and operation of an IOR. These linkages are for the transmission of information and other resources and also serve as the tangible manifestations of IOR. They constitute the marketplace for resource exchanges and the arena for political and regulatory activity as described below.

2. Resources — Procurement of resources necessary for organizational task attainment is one major determinant of transactions. Since organizations are specialized and operate under conditions of scarcity, they are dependent on the network for resources. The type, level and distribution of resources available to the network are determinants of transactions.

3. IOR System Regulation and Governance — This is a second major determinant of IOR transactions. Given the self-interest orientation of organizations in managing their transactions, activities are needed to coordinate and integrate IOR.

4. Environmental Context for IOR — The outside setting provides opportunities for IOR, but also establishes some constraints on exchanges.

Transaction Network

Linkages between organizations have been referred to under a variety of labels, including coupling, connection, interdependence, interaction, linkage, exchange, and the like. As used here, these terms will denote all forms of transmission of information and matter-energy that have relevance for resource transactions and governance of the IOR system. Systems theorists suggest that these transactions can be viewed as actions in the sense that they are designed to have impact and influence on others (Miller, 1972; Kuhn, 1974), while exchange theorists indicate that these transactions are based upon expectations of mutual benefit and reciprocal reinforcement (Blau, 1964; Emerson, 1975).

Linkages can be represented as existing in a network that includes the total set of organizations in the system under analysis. Emerson (1972) specifies that this set consists of three or more organizations, each of which has opportunities for transactions with at least one other member. The hallmark of this perspective, according to Mitchell (1969), is that it permits the analysis of the entire system, including the activities of individual organizations. Rieker, Morrissey, and Horan (1974) suggest further that the network permits a more inclusive study of IOR than the more focused perspectives, such as the pairwise dyad or set.

Clearly, the potential for understanding IOR from a network viewpoint is rich. However, even though references to this perspective are frequent in everyday parlance, it is only in recent years that mathematical formulations have developed. Among the most promising methods are digraph theory (Harary, Norman, and Cartwright, 1965), matrix algebra (Davis, 1965), and block modeling (White,

Boorman, and Breiger, 1976). These approaches, even though in an early state of development, have been useful in delineating several characteristics of transactional networks as described below.

1. Density is the most basic characteristic of a network, describing the extent to which linkages exist. It can be defined as the ratio of the actual number of linkages to the potential number of linkages across the network. More focused measures can be made of the existence of clusters of organizations or subsystems within the network. A select number of organizations might have a high density within their niche, but be generally unrelated to other organizations within their network. This, in fact, was observed by Aldrich (1974b) and by Van de Ven, Walker, and Liston (1976) and supports Turk's (1977) more general observation that organizations interact around very specific and focused objectives.

2. Centrality denotes the extent to which an organization is the source or origin of linkages with others and is defined as a function of two constructs — reachability and distance. Reachability refers to the number of other organizations that one is linked to and distance specifies the extent to which there are intermediaries. The shortest distance is direct, and distance increases positively with the number of intermediaries. In this light, a very central organization would be able to reach all others directly, as characterized by the hub of a wheel configuration. An illustration of this linkage pattern might be a resource distribution system with only one supplier — such as the only bank in a town.

3. Directionality of linkages between organizations may be unilateral and unidirectional or reciprocal and symmetric. When more than two organizations are involved, the relation with a third may be viewed as inverse or negative (e.g., competition) or positive (e.g., collaboration). In general, it is hypothesized that reciprocal and positive relations are evidence of a balance of power and influence and thus are most stable (Blau, 1964; Emerson, 1975).

4. Intensity refers to the degree of involvement by organizations and the overall value of resources included in a particular transaction (Marrett, 1971). This can be defined more specifically in terms of the number of people, the frequency and duration of their interaction, and the size of the resource investment. It is generally suggested that the more important the resource transactions, the more intense and reciprocal will be resource network linkages.

Resources

Resources can be defined as any means or facilities that are potentially usable by organizations in their relationships with other organizations (Yuchtman and Seashore, 1967). A variety of different kinds of resources may be cited, including information, money, physical commodities, clients, customers, and markets to name just a few (Levine, White, and Paul, 1963; Clark, 1968). These resources form the basis for exchange transactions among organizations. The particular type of resource chosen depends upon the need of each organization in terms of its goals and functions (Levine and White, 1961) as well as other factors in the network configuration of resources as described below. It should be noted further that organizations are not necessarily viewed as passive victims of their environments but also may be active participants and strategists in their own self interest (Child, 1972; Aldrich, 1975). Five factors are reported below, and their similarities to Van de Ven et al. (1975), Aldrich (1975), and Benson (1975) are acknowledged.

1. Resource Supply — The level of resources available within the network, which may range from abundant and rich to scarce and lean. To the extent that resources are scarce, it can be expected that there would be an increase in IOR exchange activity (Benson, 1975; Cook, 1977). Under this condition it is not uncommon for organizations to engage in hoarding and possibly to develop competitive strategies (Aldrich, 1974b). At the opposite extreme, an abundance of resources would mean less need for IOR (Katz and Kahn, 1966), and the transaction network would be characterized by a low density of linkages.

2. Resource Distribution — The extent to which resources are dispersed among network organizations. At one extreme, resources may be controlled by one or a few organizations. This condition has been likened to monopoly and is typified by very large organizations, perhaps conglomerates (Turk, 1977). It can be expected that this network would be centralized. At the other extreme, there may be a balanced dispersion of resources across members (Thompson and McEwen, 1958). If the size of the network is large, conditions approaching pure competition become possible. It can be expected, however, that organizations would limit the scope and focus of their interactions to a specific niche or subsystem (Galbraith, 1977; Pfeffer, 197?). Hence, the transaction network would be characterized as dense within subsystems but with holes or gaps between them.

3. Resource Demand — The importance of input resources needed by network members (Aiken and Hage, 1968; Evan, 1966). Hickson et al. (1971) suggest that immediacy and pervasiveness might be measures of the degree of importance. At one extreme, resources in need may be peripheral adjuncts to the operation of the organization, while on the opposite side they may be crucial to survival and operation of the technical core. In this later case, it can be expected that the organization would expend more effort and employ higher level, more professional staff in resource procurement activities (Marrett, 1971). Moreover, to reduce dependencies on other organizations, it is likely that organizations will try to develop transactional linkages that are multiple — redundant as well as reciprocal (Jacobs, 1974; Cook, 1977).

4. Homogeneity — Structural and functional similarity among organizations (Levine and White, 1961; Evan, 1966; Zald, 1966). To the extent that organizations are similar, it is likely that they will be competitors and have little reason to interact on an ongoing basis. However, during an emergency, there may be needs for short-term, direct linkages to borrow supplies or other resources (Perrow, 1970). At the other extreme of more extensive differentiation, an more elaborate linkage network would be needed to deal with pluralistic and potentially conflicting resource needs (Turk, 1977). However, the likelihood of linkages based on symbiotic or vertical interdependencies is greater in competitive situations.

5. Size — The number of organizations in the network. As the number of organizations increases, it becomes more probable that the density of transactions will increase. Moreover, there will be a greater variety of interests and demands, making management a more complex task of formal and informal governance (Turk, 1977; Litwak and Hylton, 1962; Emery and Trist, 1965) and constraining the autonomy of member organizations (Evan, 1966).

Regulation and Governance

Regulation and governance activities are designed to increase complementarity and consistency among transactional linkages. This occurs through both formal and informal means. According to Marrett (1971), formalization can be described in terms of a variety of structural mechanisms, including specification of an intermediary and the development of binding contractual agreements. Informal control refers to the shared norms and values that emerge as a result of transactions and provides a basis for cooperation (Porter, Lawler, and Hackman, 1975).

Formal structures for IOR might vary along a number of dimensions. Warren (1967), in his classic description of the interorganization field, provides an illustration. Utilizing six dimensions abstracted from bureaucratic theory (e.g., inclusiveness of goal, prescribed collectivity orientation, locus of hierarchy and authority, division of labor, etc.), he describes a continuum of systemness. At the least formal level, organizations coalesce around a specific and simple issue, such as to attract new industry to their town or to resist undesired activities by others. In this coalitional system there is no formal authority, relationships tend to be impromptu and for a limited period of time, and organizations retain their autonomy.

Federations are IOR systems at a more formalized level in that they permanently employ a staff that acts together on a range of prescribed tasks or problems of mutual interest to the system members. However, participation of the organizations is generally voluntary, and they retain their autonomy. Federative systems might include chambers of commerce, fiduciary boards, professional associations, coordinating councils, and the like.

At the highest level of formalization is the unitary system, which is characterized by attributes familiar in descriptions of bureaucracy. Included are a legitimate hierarchy of authority, legally binding contractual goals, and a prescribed division of labor. Illustrations of this structure are headquarters-subsidiary relations, conglomerates and mergers in the private sector, and national-regional-local organizations in the public arena.

Shifting to the informal category, Warren, Rose, and Bergunder (1974) suggest that norms may be conceptualized as ranging along a continuum from cooperation to competition. This variable is defined in terms of the overarching purposes and membership of the IOR system. At one extreme members are in agreement about the general state of affairs and rules of operation. At the competitive pole there exists a fundamental disagreement and an accompanying interest in destroying part or all of the total system. For example, the role or legitimacy of a particular agency may be challenged, or the codes of operation and ethics may be violated. In between these two extremes is a more moderate and specific area of norms that is known as contest. According to Warren, Rose, and Bergunder (1974), behavior in this vein is based on overarching norms of cooperation but allows for bargaining and negotiation over one issue in particular — domain.

Domain has been defined variously in terms of goals, functions, operating philosophies, and reference orientations (Levine and White, 1961; Rein and Morris, 1962; Evan, 1966; Thompson, 1967). In more detail, Warren, Rose, and Bergunder illustrate how the domain of community decision organizations might be delineated, including geographic sector of community interest covered, specific activities performed, type of clients served, degree of autonomy exercised, and so forth (1974:27).

The importance of domain, regardless of the level at which it is specified, is twofold. First, domain definition occurs at the level of the system and indicates what activities are appropriate and legitimate for member organizations to perform. Included in domain are the rights, privileges, and access to resources that are crucial to operation. Without legitimacy, an organization's resource dependencies will be frustrated, and ultimately its survival will be threatened (Katz and Kahn, 1966; Pfeffer, 1978). A second reason is internal to the organization and has three parts: (1) Domain agreement increases the degree of predictability among the IOR about their interdependencies, thereby enabling them to operate with less extensive surveillance and greater economies of scale (Emery and Trist, 1965; Terreberry, 1968). (2) Due to limitations on technology, expertise, and the like, organizations are better suited to some environments than others (Shortell, 1977). Galbraith (1977) illustrates this for the coal industry, wherein some firms were designed for small batch, custom operation and others for large volume, continuous processes. (3) Preferences may be based on knowledge that some domains are simpler and more lucrative to operate in than others. Thus, Aldrich (1975) notes that some public employment agencies contest for readily placeable clients, an illustration of the general process known as "creaming."

A number of strategies have been suggested for influencing the outcome of domain contests within a generally cooperative IOR system. These operate mainly informally but have some formal aspects as well. The first of these is co-optation, which involves the solicitation of prestigious and influential individuals, whose support is perceived as beneficial (Perrucci and Pilisuk, 1970; Blankeship and Elling, 1962). Although the involvement of elites may be informal, frequently it is more formalized through membership on committees or boards. Specific purposes may be sought in terms of the persons selected, such as fund raising, policy development, technical administration, or public relations (Zald, 1967, 1969; Perrow, 1965; Pfeffer, 1978). The involvement of elites is promoted when they have similar backgrounds and experiences (Kiesler, 1978) and when there are overlapping, joint memberships on several such committees or boards (Pfeffer and Leblebici, 1973; Pfeffer and Nowak, 1976).

At the opposite extreme, the involvement of some organizations may be regarded undesirable, such as when these organizations are dissonant or uncooperative. In such cases, it may be well to deliberately ignore or exclude these parties (Banfield and Wilson, 1963). Moreover, when such organizations constitute a fundamental threat to IOR itself, coalitions may be formed by other organizations against them (Warren, Rose, and Bergunder, 1974).

Another major strategy used in contests is based on claims to the appropriateness of one's domain. Clark and Wilson (1961) suggest that when organizations have clear goals, measurable standards of action, and determinate rationales, it is possible to justify their domains in terms of efficiency and effectiveness criteria. In these cases, as well as in others where domain is legally prescribed and mandated, it is expected that few transactions would be directed toward dispute.

At the opposite extreme, in many organizations the rationales are less determinate, and knowledge of cause-effect relations is more limited. This latter situation has been said to generally characterize nonprofit organizations (White, 1974; Rushing, 1974). In lieu of a determinate rationale, organizations may employ a number of strategies in domain contests. Many of these are designed to create the appearance of determinateness and objectivity. For example, schools use a number of accreditation and certification procedures and place heavy emphasis on textbooks and other materials in lieu of direct measures of the learning process (Meyer and Rowan, 1978). Alternatively, financial departments in municipal governments were observed to change the charter of their professional association in response to declining goals, while administrative departments claimed expanded domains based on the addition of new, innovative computer facilities (Meyer, 1975). In a more general vein, prestige might be emphasized in terms of various attributes of organization, such as age, size, wealth, and current rate of growth (Caplow, 1964). Perrow (1965) suggests further that public relations activities, mainly information dissemination, would be helpful in making these claims to domain.

Environment

The environment that is relevant to operation of the IOR system forms a setting or context in which transactions occur. Present in the environment are both resource and regulatory influences that may have an impact on the network. Problematic with this conceptualization is the difficulty of precisely separating the network from its externalities because the boundaries sometimes are obscure. This problem is alleviated somewhat when the IOR system is defined a priori (e.g., organizations within a city or with a specific purpose). As Starbuck (1976) observes, the environment is a somewhat arbitrary invention, so that network members may have divergent opinions about what resides outside the IOR system. Acknowledging these difficulties, even though they cannot be resolved, the discussion turns now to the environment as an important source of resources.

The environment is a major source of resources for the IOR system — raw materials, clients, and markets in particular. For example, Pfeffer (1978) notes that governmental agencies may provide cash and other subsidies to particular organizations as well as more general facilities to a community, such as hospitals, roads, or airports, to name a few. Further, the role of the government in funding public welfare and social reform programs is well known. Other avenues for resources might be cited in addition, such as when a local organization receives assistance from headquarters or when prestige or a cosmopolitan orientation necessitate external linkages.

The configuration of these resources may be described in terms similar to those used within the IOR network, as Aldrich (1975) suggests. Thus, for example, distinctions can be made in terms of the level of supply, degree of concentration, differences in type, and importance or need by the network. The analogy, roughly, is of two interacting systems — the environment and the IOR network. Continuing further, the impact of environmental resources on transactional linkages can be suggested as well. For example, when an abundant supply of resources is made available to the network, it can be expected that reciprocity would develop with the external sources. Moreover, if a single organization has its own access to a substantial amount of resources, its need for linkages within the network would be reduced (Levine and White, 1961; Litwak and Hylton, 1962). Alternatively, if resources were made available for local bidding, the outcome might be a general reduction in the density of linkages within the network except for the organization that "won" the contest (Aiken et al., 1975).

A second influence of the environment is in the area of regulation and governance. Formally, laws and procedures may have a strong impact on IOR. Pfeffer (1978) describes the role of government in managing competition. On the one hand, laws may restrict a number of competitors from directly entering a network or offer more limited assistance through protective tariffs. On the other extreme, antitrust laws reduce the chances of monopoly and dominance.

Societal values and beliefs are an informal sanction on networks. Warren, Rose, and Bergunder (1974) describe the institutionalized thought structure in terms of beliefs about legitimacy, authority, social services, pluralism, democracy, and so forth. This fundamental set of beliefs, grounded in the American culture, served as a model and source of legitimacy in the nine cities of their study. Specific interest groups, according to Benson (1975), constitute a second source of influence. Political parties, minority groups, professional societies, and the like may exert influence on network organizations to act in their behalf. The source of power varies with the size of the group, its prestige, and its ability to mobilize itself for action. As a converse, a variant of these external groups, accrediting organizations, are considered to have influence to the degree that they are independent of their members for resources (Pfeffer, 1978).

The above illustrations may be taken to suggest consistency across formalized and informal means of governance. However, this is not always the case, especially when more than one regulatory agency or pluralistic sets of standards affect a network. Witness, for example, differences in eligibility criteria and reporting procedures among interest groups, such as the disabled, the elderly, women, and so forth.

In summary, to this point, four basic components of an IOR system have been described. The transaction network was viewed as an essential condition for the existence of a system, while resources, governance, and environment were determinants. A discussion of relationships or contingencies among these four components is now in order.

CONTINGENCY DESIGN RELATIONSHIPS

Contingency design theories are concerned with the "fit" or congruence between the three major determinants of transactions described in the preceding section. Theories at this level are cross-sectional and make no predictions about change. Moreover, there are no presumptions of effectiveness (as is the case with intraorganizational contingency theories), but these contingencies are related to equilibrium, as will be shown in the next section. In brief, when the components of the IOR system are congruent, it is presumed that they are in a condition of balance, perhaps equilibrium.

The basic argument in contingency designs is stated in terms of complexity, which generally refers to the level of diversity and potential for conflict that affect the transactional network. More specifically, complexity can be related to all of the component variables, but discussions of this topic tend to start with the resource component — and with size in particular (Galbraith, 1977; Turk, 1977). As the number of organizations increases, it is likely that the diversity of goals, purposes, and the like that must be integrated by the governance component will increase. Accordingly, if the type and nature of transactions is to be enlarged, corresponding increases in the scope and level of governance will be required. A number of justifications for this argument can be made, and three of them involve pluralism, power, and ecology.

From a pluralistic view, organizations exist in a basic condition of conflict with one another (Litwak and Hylton, 1962). There are differences in value, goal, and so forth that are irreconcilable, such as between research, church, and state. As the number of organizations increases, diversity becomes more prevalent, requiring additional attention to governance.

The influence and power perspectives are also relevant. According to Cook (1977), power can be defined as the ratio of the need or demand for a resource to the number of alternative sources of availability. When there are only a few sources, it is likely that organizations will enter into exchanges and that these relationships will become reciprocal, balanced, and stable (Emerson, 1972). Alternatively, as the number of organizations increases, resources become more readily available and reciprocal exchange less likely (Blau, 1964). Transactions approach conditions of pure competition.

From an ecological viewpoint, organizations cluster near to others due to exchange dependencies. In addition, there tend to be interests in shared facilities, such as roads, hospitals, common pools of clients, and the like. Many of the dependencies emerge from the intended and goal-directed interests of the organizations. However, others emerge unexpectedly from the field itself, such as changes in zoning laws, tax rates, labor supply, or the number of other organizations.

These three examples serve to illustrate ways in which changes in size trigger rises in diversity, which in turn should be contingent with the level of governance. It can be noted, however, that the size-diversity relation is considered simply a correlation, and no causal implications are made. In essence, size is viewed as an enabling factor, in much the same way that it operates within organizations (Kimberly, 1976).

Within the regulatory factor, the contingency framework includes both informal and formal dimensions. As complexity in the resource sector increases, Turk (1977) suggests that networks specialize in terms of regulation into two types of organization — those that promote consensual, normative solidarity and those that concentrate on the more formal aspects of control and governance. Furthermore, the level of diversity increases the difficulty of reaching normative consensus so that norms tend to become broader and more diffuse. In addition, diversity decreases the likelihood that large but centralized regulatory organizations will be able to represent the total network membership. In consequence, even though the level of governance increases with diversity, it does so by decentralizing into a number of smaller organizations — changes in both amount and type.

Thus far a linear relationship has been suggested between the contingency factors. However, Litwak and Hylton (1962) suggest that IOR is only feasible within an intermediate range of complexity. For example, when there are very few organizations, the level of transactions and potential for interdependencies are small while domains are stable. In this network of low density, cooperation may be attained implicitly through knowledge of another organization's activities, although informal communication may be required on occasion (Galbraith, 1977). Benson (1975) suggests that IOR tends to be unnecessary at this level.

At the opposite extreme, Emery and Trist (1965) refer to a high level of complexity as "turbulence." This may be described as a large size, diverse network so filled internally and externally with unpredictability and contest that chances of cooperation seem remote. The level of contest makes transactions very costly in terms of the need for surveillance, highly skilled staff, and loose structure (Terreberry, 1968; Lawrence and Lorsch, 1967). In this situation, it is not unlikely for organizations to leave the network entirely or to absorb some of the uncertainty by formally bonding together into a single organization by merger. Alternatively, if the network is to be maintained over time, Emery and Trist (1965) and Trist (1976) suggest that shared norms for cooperation must be enhanced.

Thus far, no distinction has been made in the discussion between the IOR network and its environment. However, the analogy applies quite well for both systems. For example, just as there may be a large number and diversity of resources within the network, the same may apply externally as well. Alternatively, in the same way that the network may be governed by a small number of consistent organizations, the environment may exert uniform and compatible pressures. In effect, a parallel is suggested between network and environmental complexities (Turk, 1977).

Contingencies have also been developed at the more specific level of transactions between pairs of organizations, particularly in the work of Thompson (1967) and Galbraith (1977). Three formal mechanisms for regulating transactions have been described — contracting, co-opting, and coalescing. These are said to vary along a continuum in terms of both complexity, as described above, and the intensity of transactions.

Contracts are the simplest formal method for controlling network transactions. By definition, contracts are explicit agreements between two parties that may vary in formality from an understanding based on trust to a legally binding document. The most prominent type of contract is between organizations at the same level of power (Marrett, 1971), although hierarchical mandates are also prevalent. Since they are limited in capacity, contracts are most useful at the lower levels of the complexity continuum. Further clarification of contractual contingencies can be found in the empirical literature.

Hall et al. (1977) studied three kinds of transactions between pairs of organizations dealing with problem youth — mandated by law, voluntary formal contract, and voluntary informal. The results revealed that by far the most transactions were voluntary and that they were a mix of cooperation and conflict. However, there was an overriding positive evaluation of these interactions. When transactions were mandated or contracted, as opposed to voluntary but formalized, there was a significant inverse relation to the presence of conflict. The authors speculate that conflict would be disruptive to an imposed transaction, but quite likely had been resolved previously in one that was voluntary first and formalized later.

In a study of dyadic relationships within the employment service, Aldrich (1975) related the formalization of relationships with intensity, reciprocity, and standardization of units of transactions. Multiple regression analyses revealed that formalization was most predictive of the intensity of transactions. In turn, intense transactions tended to be associated with reciprocity and standardization. Schmidt and Kochan (1977), in other research on the employment service, compared the degrees of perceived symmetry and degree of benefit to the frequency of formalized transactions. As expected, mutually beneficial and symmetrical transactions were the most prevalent, while symmetrical but nonbeneficial exchanges were the least frequent. The asymmetrical condition was moderately frequent and also characterized by the presence of bargaining and conflict. That conflict was not more prevalent in this unbalanced situation, the authors speculate, was because the employment service was more powerful than other members of its set and could suppress that which was not in its best interests.

These three studies, in sum, suggest that a variety of transactions may occur at lower levels of network complexity. These exchanges tend to be informal and voluntary in the absence of dispute. However, in the presence of contest, formalized contracts serve as an enabling mechanism through their operation as a suppressor. In not all cases, it should be noted, are contracts completely successful. Chadwin et al. (1977), in their massive study of the employment service, found many instances of little cooperation in spite of the presence of a legal mandate.

Cooptation is a second mechanism that seeks to influence transactions with other organizations. Potentially more encompassing than contracts, the coopting process occurs most typically through membership on boards. The size, composition, and function of boards can be related to the type and extent of influence that an organization seeks to have on others. Zald (1969), in a theoretical paper, suggests that boards may perform externally oriented activities on behalf of an organization, such as procuring needed resources or maintaining legitimacy. Alternatively, they may represent the environment as monitors of internal administrative activities. Further elaboration can be found in a few empirical studies.

In a study of hospitals, Pfeffer (1973) found that board composition was related to major types of external dependencies. Hospitals whose funds came mainly from the local community were dominated by wealthy and prestigious members of that community and used their boards mainly for fund raising. Alternatively, when funding was from the federal government, boards tended to be less representative of the community, smaller in size, mostly concerned with the appropriate management of funds — and generally less interested in cooptation. In another study of business organizations, similar results were obtained. Firms in greater need of financial resources tended to have a larger number of directors useful for this purpose, while firms in regulated industries favor members with legal backgrounds. Moreover, the size of the board was found to correlate with both the number of functions to be performed and organizational performance. In effect, the results suggest that board composition should be correlated with the degree of external dependencies. There is an optimum range in which boards can function and beyond which too few or too many transactional dependencies will be detrimental.

External legitimation functions may be performed by boards as well. Price (1963), in a study of the Oregon Fish and Game Commission, noted that it was legally designed to perform a selected number of administrative tasks. However, in operation, it served more important buffering and legitimating functions of responding to citizen complaints and promoting new legislation. In a similar vein, Pfeffer (1974) examined the legitimating role of public utilities. He found that in comparison to a random sample of corporations, boards of utilities had a significantly higher number of members with expertise in media and public relations. Furthermore, Zald's (1967) study of local YMCAs showed that boards varied across neighborhoods and that differences could be explained in terms of the socioeconomic characteristics of constituencies.

Coalition, or joint venture, is the highest level of formalized IOR agreement. More encompassing than coopting, coalition involves an arrangement between organizations to engage not only in resource exchanges but also in joint decisions. However, both organizations maintain their own identities, indicating that power and influence are reciprocal and balanced. Unique to the coalition agreement is that it involves a level of transactional intensity beyond the capacity of contracts. Examples may range from sharing patents or licenses to joint research to sharing of production and other facilities.

In summary, the contingency design literature prescribes a congruence between the four IOR system components. Descriptions of IOR from this view frequently begin with an analysis of the complexity of transactions, particularly as reflected in the number and diversity of IOR members. Implicit in this contingency framework is a tendency toward congruence and compatability among the four components of the IOR system, although the methods and processes by which this is accomplished are not discussed. It is to these dynamics that attention now turns.

IOR SYSTEM CHANGE

Change in IOR networks has been referred to under a variety of labels including growth, innovation, development, coordination, and the like. Common to these terms is ambiguity about the meaning of change in the sense that few things are the same as they were ten minutes ago and that the magnitude or severity of difference is a matter of individual perspective. A useful starting point for consideration of change in an IOR system is the assumption of balance or equilibrium. Equilibrium is considered to be a dynamic or steady state, as changes in one factor will be compensated for by changes in others so that the system maintains its overall goal orientation and purpose. As applied to IOR, Benson (1975) suggests that balance includes consensus about domain, ideology, the role of other agencies, and the merits of cooperation. In effect, this would represent a generally stable system of transactions.

Change from an equilibrium or balance condition can occur in different ways. Mayhew (1971), for example, draws a distinction between hierarchical and emergence models. The hierarchical model emphasizes control at the top and resolution of problems via referral up the levels of the hierarchy. When change occurs, solutions are consistent with the preexisting structures at higher levels in the hierarchy and reaffirm the institutional pattern of values. The emergence model, by contrast, is not interested in how higher level stability shapes lower level change, but rather with the initial formation of structure. The development of agreements between organizations is seen as the source of structure, not hierarchically developed norms and values. In fact, cultural norms are seen as contradictory and inconsistent with local interests. Hence, change results from mutual interests among organizations in reducing conflict and increasing stability. The post hoc justification of these activities and agreements gives rise to norms. Further clarification is provided by Turk (1977), who suggests that IOR system change occurs in the presence of two conditions — an external stimulus and an internal linkage mechanism capable of integrating the environmental externality.

External stimuli can be described as of two types. First there are mandates, procedures, rules, needs, and the like that suggest directions or purposes for IOR transactions. In addition, the environment may provide scarce resources or supplies that act as the wherewithal for IOR. Common to these two externalities is that they increase the variety or diversity to which the network must adapt. Quite frequently segments of the environment are disjointed from others, the effect of which is the presentation of contradictory stimuli to the network. However, even if the external forces are positive or complementary, some internal adjustments might be indicated.

Internal linkage capacity refers to the ability of network organizations to forge cooperative agreements and resolve conflicts emanating from external forces. This capability is related to the scale and diversity of governance functions and the extent of norms favoring consensual solidarity. Turk (1977) suggests, based on his survey data of American cities, that the greater the scale of regulation and the more widely shared cooperative values, the higher the capability of the IOR network to deal with influences from its environment.

The change process may be influenced by one or a combination of these two approaches at different times. However, for shifting to a new level of equilibrium in the IOR system, Turk (1977) argues that both the external, or hierarchical, and the internal, or emergent, models must be employed together. Although widespread empirical evidence is lacking, selected case studies support this assertion while illustrating the difficulties of more limited approaches.

Hierarchical, externally induced change is most evident in the public sector, where high levels of government mandate that specific organizations or programs be implemented at the local level. Illustrative of this approach are case studies based on experiences in the War on Poverty during the 1960s. There existed widespread public agreement that the welfare bureaucracy was generally slow and, perhaps, unresponsive in meeting the needs of its clients. In consequence, governments developed and funded new agencies whose purposes were to respond more quickly to their clients and to facilitate more extensive local level cooperation among agencies. The failure of these social change experiments are now history, but the reasons remain somewhat obscure. Some suggestions, however, are provided in the following two case studies.

Pressman and Wildavsky (1973) describe the inception, initial operation and ultimate demise of a local agency designed to stimulate the economic development of welfare level clients through "grassroots" planning and subsequent collaboration among local agencies. Even though there was widespread endorsement throughout the community of welfare reform, little agreement was evident about how agencies might work together. In fact, the existing IOR system was in a primitive state of development and unable to adjust to the new agency. Furthermore, even though local planning was espoused, insufficient time was allotted before all funds had to be obligated. As a result, the new agency was in a dilemma — either spending the money rapidly and alienating the local community or alienating the government in the community's behalf. This double bind doomed the agency to failure in a few short years.

Another case study describes the formation of an advocacy agency designed to stimulate the existing IOR network to be more responsive to clients' needs. In contrast to the previous case, where both coordinated planning and service delivery were mandated goals, the governor's branch offices (GBO) were to have solely an advocacy orientation. Vosburgh and Hyman (1973), in their description of the case, suggest that the close surveillance and active support of the governor's office was crucial to the initial success of the local GBOs. The hierarchical influence suppressed potential controversies related to the GBO's violation of sacred bureaucratic norms. However, when the press of events shifted the governor's attention to other activities, GBOs were forced by the local IOR system to adopt rules and procedures for accountability and to provide more direct than advocacy services. Shortly after the end of the governor's term in office, and without additional sources of support or legitimacy, the GBO program expired.

Thus, hierarchical mandate may serve as a stimulus for change in existing local networks. The availabilities of funds, staff, and external support have been suggested as important ingredients of the changes. However, unless these external stimuli can be integrated at the local level, the promise of sustained change — or even of change at all — was shown to be remote.

Processes initiated at the local level are regarded as a means for developing an IOR network where none existed previously. In its simplest form, cooperative relations can be described between pairs of organizations. Based upon an extensive literature review, Van de Ven (1975) describes three important steps:

1. First, it is assumed that organizations are aware of one another. This is important for locating candidates likely to possess the resources needed in exchanges.
2. Communication and discussion regarding matters of domain and the specific items of exchange constitute the second step. It is proposed that the more frequent the communication, the greater the likelihood of reaching agreements about exchange. Moreover, personal awareness by boundary spanners of one another, based on similarity of background and professional training, is also said to be facilitative.
3. Once exchanges begin, they are considered to increase in intensity over time as the perceived mutual benefit grows. The greater the initial satisfaction, the more likely it is that organizations will increase their involvement.
4. The development of formal structure parallels the growth in intensity of transactions. As the volume and frequency of exchanges increases over time, more formalized agreements and, perhaps, specification of an intermediary role or group are likely to occur.

Trist (1976) extends this description to the network level by a case illustration of the formation of a labor-management committee in a small northeastern community. The committee's general purpose was to promote the industrial development of the city as a whole through such efforts as job training, job redesign, attracting new industries, and applying for governmental assistance. Several factors were cited as instrumental in the formation and operation of this committee.

1. The city had a pervasive and serious problem that served as the basis for cooperation. With a history of poor industrial relations, some major industries had departed recently, and unemployment was rising rapidly.
2. Leadership of this voluntary committee was provided by a newly elected mayor who had bipartisan support and was viewed as charismatic. The mayor was instrumental in convening frequent meetings of the committee to discuss mutual interests.
3. The planning and decisionmaking process of the committee was developmental and incremental. Important considerations included assembling an appropriate cast of organizations, setting relevant boundaries for the committee, and developing internal and external capacities for sustained growth.

The major thrust of this process, according to Trist, is an ecological view of network development based on democratic organizational values. An overriding and urgent purpose, coupled with leadership, prompted transactions toward network formation. At the less complex pairwise level, awareness and self-interest motivations were sufficient to engage in cooperative dialogue processes that over time, could become formalized.

The two change models, when considered separately, can be seen to implicitly include one another. This was particularly true when problems with the hierarchical model were discussed and when longitudinal aspects of the emergent-processual model were noted.

The change process for an IOR network, then, depends on the presence of an external stimulus and the internal potential for cooperative transactions. Moreover, spanning across external and internal factors are both structural and process considerations.

SUMMARY AND IMPLICATIONS

Relationships between organizations are based on exchanges of resources between two or more organizations — our exchange network. Important attributes of these transactions in a network include density, centrality, directionality, and intensity. Variations in exchanges are determined in part by aspects of the resources available for exchange, including level of abundance, dispersion, demand or importance, homogeneity or similarity, and number of resource sources.

A second defining feature of the network concerns its systemic properties. The IOR system is viewed as controlled and oriented toward a condition of equilibrium or balance around mutually shared goals of cooperation. Regulation and governance of the system occur through formal mechanisms, such as hierarchical relations or coordinating agencies, as well as through informal means, including norms and commonly shared values. Moreover, the system is open and subject to influences from its environment.

As described, the IOR system extends the analysis of organizations beyond the more specific pairwise and organization-environment perspectives. Highlighted in this more comprehensive focus are the importance of multiple kinds of transactions between several organizations and/or regulation and governance. In spite of these potential merits of the IOR system unit of analysis, there exist currently unresolved conceptual and empirical problems, two of which concern boundaries and change.

Viewing the IOR network as open and interacting with its environment increases the importance of distinguishing clearly between the two. Three approaches have been employed in the literature, none of which by itself is adequate. First, a distinction often is made in terms of hierarchical levels such as between headquarters and subsidiaries or state and local governments. The headquarters or higher level government is regarded as the environment for local operations. The validity of this distinction, however, is based on more specific information about the relationship. For example, common ancestry and centralized authority may provide the local level minimal discretion, thereby blurring the boundary definition. Alternatively, the local network may exert counterresistance or mobilize resources that help delineate it from the hierarchical environment.

Another approach to identifying IOR networks is based on evidence of transactions. It is suggested that the greater the intensity of transaction, the more liklihood of an IOR network. This view is also promising, but it has limitations. First, it does not account for transactions that are important but occur infrequently, such as those regarding strategic or policy matters. More significant is the observation that the frequency and intensity of transactions is positively related to the degree of similarity. Hence, the higher the level of network-environment interaction (i.e., the more "openness"), the more nebulous boundaries are apt to be.

A third method of defining IOR networks is in terms of geographical boundaries, such as the area encompassing a city voting district and the like. Presupposed is that the member organizations find this distinction meaningful. It may be, however, that an organization has a national or international constituency and just happens to reside in a particular area. In effect, this illustration, along with the other two, serves to emphasize the importance of employing a combination of these three approaches in defining network boundaries. Each of the methods is a simplification of the IOR system and is of limited adequacy.

Turning next to the analysis of change, an important task is establishing a baseline from which to measure change and difference. Typically, change is defined in terms of equilibrium and deviations from it. Problematic, however, is that equilibrium is to some extent a matter of perspective. Thus, for example, Kuhn (1974) suggests that structural change is over a shorter time span and at a lower level than process change. For instance, over a brief time period, relations between organizations may be characterized as dramatic changes in structure, while a longer term view may reveal a repeated cyclical process. Moreover, while processes occur between organizations at a more basic level, these involve structures within the member organizations. In spite of these differences, cross-sectional research implicitly assumes some sort of equilibrium. To the extent that IOR systems are stable, this strategy has some utility. However, if Emery and Trist (1965) are correct that turbulence is on the increase, then a static methodology will be of limited use. Moreover, from a pragmatic standpoint, managers tend to be most interested in research when confronted with serious and current operational problems — or disequilibrium.

The direction of change is another consideration. Assuming that change involves the interface between environmental and IOR system factors, then the tremendous diversity of goals and perspectives is evident. Although most research has traced the impact of a single rule or resource, it seems likely that multiple and possible contradictory environmental forces might operate simultaneously. More important, the integration and resolution of differences in priority is not simply a matter of arithmetic aggregation or averaging, as has been the practice in much of the organizational research. Instead, priorities tend to emerge over time, as the result of behavioral processes of influence and compromise. However, given slack, limited communication, and variations in interdependence (which tend to be prevalent in IOR), it is likely that agreements will develop around the most crucial priorities.

In conclusion, the framework presented in the body of this chapter represents but a first step toward developing a comprehensive understanding of IOR. The conceptualization itself of an IOR system remains difficult, let alone delineation of boundaries and dynamics. The factors included in the framework, however, are among those most frequently cited in the literature. That other dimensions might be added is likely. Laumann and Pappi (1976) approach IOR from an elitist, or leadership, perspective, while White (1974) subscribes to a decisionmaking framework: both of these might be useful additions. However, as Starbuck (1976) notes, the ease with which topics for research can be generated serves as a painful reminder of the barrenness of our knowledge about the organization and its environment.

REFERENCES

Aiken, M., and J. Hage. 1968. "Organizational Inter-dependence and Intra-Organizational Structure." *American Sociological Review* 33: 912-30.

Aiken, M.; R. Dewar; N. DiTomaso; J. Hage; and G. Zeitz. 1975. *Coordinating Human Services*. San Francisco: Jossey-Bass.

Aldrich, H. 1975. "An Organization-Environment Perspective on Cooperation and Conflict between Organizations in the Manpower Training System." In A. Negandhi, ed., *Interorganization Theory*. Kent, Ohio: Kent State University Press.

———. 1974a. "An Interorganizational Dependency Perspective on Relations between the Employment Service and Its Organization Set." Paper presented at the Management of Organization Design Conference, University of Pittsburgh, October 24-26.

———. 1974b. "The Environment as a Network of Organizations: Theoretical and Methodological Implications." Paper presented at International Sociological Association, Toronto, Canada, August.

Banfield, E., and J. Q. Wilson. 1963. *City Politics*. Cambridge, Mass.: Harvard University Press.

Benson, J. K. 1975. "The Interorganizational Network as a Political Economy." *Administrative Science Quarterly* 20: 229-49.

Blankeship, L. V., and R. H. Elling. 1962. "Organizational Support and Community Power Structure of the Hospital." *Journal of Health and Human Behavior* 3: 257-69.

Blau, P. 1964. *Exchange and Power in Social Life*. New York: Wiley.

Burns, T.; and G. Stalker. 1961. *The Management of Innovation*. London: Tavistock.

Caplow, T. 1964. *Principles of Organization*. New York: Harcourt Brace.

Chadwin, M.; J. Mitchell; E. Hargrove; and L. Mead. 1977. *The Employment Service: An Institutional Analysis*. Washington, D.C.: U.S. Department of Labor, R & D Monograph 51.

Child, J. 1972. "Organizational Structure, Environment, and Performance: The Role of Strategic Choice." *Sociology* 6: 1-22.

Clark, B. 1965. "Interorganizational Patterns in Education." *Administrative Science Quarterly* 21: 327-36.

Clark, P., and J. Wilson. 1961. "Incentive Systems: A Theory of Organizations." *Administrative Science Quarterly* 6: 129-66.

Clark, T. 1968. *Community Structure and Decision-Making: A Comparative Analysis.* San Francisco: Chandler.

Cook, K. S. 1977. "Exchange and Power in Networks of Interorganizational Relations." *The Sociological Quarterly* 18: 62-82.

Davis, P. 1965. *The Mathematics of Matrices.* Waltham, Mass.: Blaisdell.

Dill, W. R. 1958. "Environment as an Influence on Managerial Autonomy." *Administrative Science Quarterly* 2: 409-43.

Duncan, R. B. 1972. "Characteristics of Organizational Environments." *Administrative Science Quarterly* 17: 313-27.

Emerson, R. M. 1975. "Special Exchange Theory." *The Annual Review of Sociology* 2: 335-62.

———. 1972. "Exchange Theory, Part II: Exchange Relations, Exchange Networks and Groups as Exchange Systems." In Joseph Berger et al., eds., *Sociological Theories in Progress.* Boston: Houghton Mifflin.

Emery, F., and E. Trist. 1965. "The Causal Texture of Organizational Environments." *Human Relations* 18: 21-32.

Evan, W. 1966. "The Organization Set: Toward a Theory of Interorganizational Relations." In James Thompson, ed., *Approaches to Organizational Design.* Pittsburgh: University of Pittsburgh Press.

Freeman, J. H. 1978. "The Unit of Analysis in Organizational Research." In Marshall Meyer and Associates, eds., *Environments and Organizations.* San Francisco: Jossey-Bass.

Galbraith, J. R. 1977. *Organization Design.* Reading, Mass.: Addison-Wesley.

Guetzkow, H. 1966. "Relations Among Organizations." In Robert Bowers, ed., *Studies in Behavior in Organizations.* Athens: University of Georgia Press.

Hall, R.; J. Clark; P. Giordano; P. Johnson; and M. V. Rockell. 1977. "Patterns of Interorganizational Relationships." *Administrative Science Quarterly* 22: 457-74.

Hannan, M., and J. Freeman. 1978. "The Population Ecology of Organizations." In Marshall Meyer and Associates, eds., *Environments and Organizations.* San Francisco: Jossey-Bass.

Harary, F.; R. Norman; and D. Cartwright. 1965. *Structural Models: An Introduction to the Theory of Directed Graphs.* New York: Wiley.

Hawley, A. 1950. *Human Ecology: A Theory of Community Structure.* New York: Roland.

Hickson, D.; C. R. Hinings; C. A. Lee; R. E. Schneck; and J. M. Pennings. 1971. "A Strategic Contingencies Theory of Intraorganizational Power." *Administrative Science Quarterly* 16: 216-29.

Jacobs, D. 1974. "Dependence and Vulnerability: An Exchange Approach to the Control of Organizations." *Administrative Science Quarterly* 19: 45-59.

Katz, D., and R. Kahn. 1966. *The Social Psychology of Organizations.* New York: Wiley.

Khandwalla, P. 1972. "Environment and Its Impact on the Organization." *International Studies of Management and Organization* 2: 297-313.

Kiesler, S. 1978. *Interpersonal Processes in Groups and Organizations*. Arlington Heights, Ill.: AHM Publishing.

Kimberly, J. 1976. "Organizational Size and the Structuralist Perspective: A Review, Critique and Proposal." *Administrative Science Quarterly* 21: 571-97.

Kuhn, A. 1974. *The Logic of Social Systems*. San Francisco: Jossey-Bass.

Laumann, E., and F. Pappi. 1976. *Networks of Collective Action*. New York: Academic Press.

Lawrence, P., and J. Lorsch. 1967. *Organization and Environment: Managing Differentiation and Integration*. Boston: Harvard University Press.

Levine, S.; and P. White. 1961. "Exchange as a Conceptual Framework for the Study of Interorganizational Relationships." *Administrative Science Quarterly* 5: 583-610.

Levine, S.; P. White; and B. D. Paul. 1963. "Community Interorganizational Problems in Providing Medical Care and Social Services." *American Journal of Public Health* 5: 1183-95.

Litwak, E., and L. Hylton. 1962. "Interorganizational Analysis: A Hypothesis on Coordinating Agencies." *Administrative Science Quarterly* 6: 395-420.

Marrett, C. B. 1971. "On the Specification of Interorganizational Dimensions." *Sociology and Social Research* 56: 83-99.

Mayhew, L. 1971. *Society: Institutions and Activity*. Glenview, Illinois: Scott, Foresman.

Meyer, J. 1978. "Strategies for Further Research: Varieties of Environmental Variation." In Marshall Meyer and Associates, eds., *Environments and Organizations*. San Francisco: Jossey-Bass.

Meyer, J., and B. Rowan. 1978. "The Structure of Educational Organizations." In Marshall Meyer and Associates, eds., *Environments and Organizations*. San Francisco: Jossey-Bass.

Meyer, M. 1975. "Organizational Domains." *American Sociological Review* 40: 599-615.

Miller, J. 1972. "Living Systems: The Organization." *Behavioral Science* 10: 193-237.

Mitchell, J. C. 1969. "The Concept and Use of Social Networks." In James C. Mitchell, ed., *Social Networks in Urban Situations: Analyses of Personal Relationships in Central African Towns*. Manchester, England: Manchester University Press.

Negandhi, A. R. 1975. *Interorganization Theory*. Kent, Ohio: Kent State University Press.

Negandhi, A., and B. Reimann. 1973. "Task Environment, Decentralization and Organizational Effectiveness." *Human Relations* 26: 203-14.

Perrow, C. 1970. *Organizational Analysis: A Sociological View*. Belmont, Calif.: Wadsworth.

———. 1965. "Organizational Prestige: Some Functions and Dysfunctions." *American Journal of Sociology* 66: 335-41.

Perrucci, R., and M. Pilisuk. 1970. "Leaders and Ruling Elites: The Interorganizational Bases of Community Power." *American Sociological Review* 35: 1040-56.

Pfeffer, J. 1978. *Organizational Design.* Arlington Heights, Ill.: AHM Publishing.

———. 1974. "Cooptation and the Composition of Electrical Utility Boards of Directors." *Pacific Sociological Reviews* 17: 333-63.

———. 1973. "Size, Composition and Function of Hospital Boards of Directors: A Study of Organization-Environment Linkage." *Administrative Science Quarterly* 18: 349-64.

———. 1972. "Size and Composition of Corporate Boards of Directors: The Organization and Its Environment." *Administrative Science Quarterly* 17: 218-28.

Pfeffer, J., and H. Leblebici. 1973. "The Effect of Competition on Some Dimensions of Organization Structure." *Social Forces* 52: 268-79.

Pfeffer, J., and P. Nowak. 1976. "Joint Ventures and Interorganizational Interdependence." *Administrative Science Quarterly* 21: 398-418.

Porter, L.; E. Lawler; and J. R. Hackman. 1975. *Behavior in Organizations.* New York: McGraw-Hill.

Pressman, J., and A. Wildavsky. 1973. *Implementation.* Berkeley: University of California Press.

Price, J. 1963. "The Impact of Governing Boards on Organizational Effectiveness and Morale." *Administrative Science Quarterly* 8: 361-68.

Rein, M., and R. Morris. 1962. *Social Work Practice.* New York: Columbia University Press.

Riecker, P.; J. Morrisey; and P. Horan. 1974. "Interorganizational Relations: A Critique of Theory and Method." Paper presented at American Sociological Association Meeting, Montreal, Canada, August.

Rushing, W. 1974. "Differences in Profit and Non-profit Organizations: A Study of Effectiveness and Efficiency in General Short-Stay Hospitals." *Administrative Science Quarterly* 19: 474-84.

Sarason, S.; C. Carroll; K. Maton; S. Cohen; and E. Corentz. 1977. *Human Services and Resource Networks.* San Francisco: Jossey-Bass.

Schmidt, S., and T. Kochan. 1977. "Interorganizational Relationships: Patterns and Motivations." *Administrative Science Quarterly* 22: 220-34.

———. 1976. "An Application of a 'Political Economy' Approach to Effectiveness: Employment Service-Employer Exchanges." *Administration and Society* 1: 455-73.

Shortell, S. M. 1977. "The Role of Environment in a Configurational Theory of Organizations." *Human Relations* 30: 275-301.

Starbuck, W. 1976. "Organizations and their Environments." In Marvin Dunnette, ed., *Handbook of Industrial and Organizational Psychology.* Chicago: Rand McNally.

Terreberry, S. 1968. "The Evolution of Organizational Environments." *Administrative Science Quarterly* 12: 590-613.

Thompson, J. 1967. *Organizations in Action.* Chicago: McGraw-Hill.

Thompson, J., and W. McEwen. 1958. "Organizational Goals and Environment: Goal-Setting as an Interaction Process." *American Sociological Review* 23: 23-31.

Trist, E. 1976. "A Concept of Organizational Ecology." Paper presented at the Australia Universities Conference, Melbourne, July 29.

Tuite, M. 1972. "Toward a Theory of Joint Decision Making." In Matthew Tuite, Roger Chisholm, and Michael Radnor, eds., *Interorganizational Decision Making*. Chicago: Aldine.

Turk, H. 1977. *Organizations in Modern Life*. San Francisco: Jossey-Bass.

———. 1970. "Interorganizational Networks in Urban Society: Initial Perspectives and Comparative Research." *American Sociological Review* 35: 1-19.

Van de Ven, A. H. 1975. "A General Theory of Interorganizational Relationships." Unpublished paper, Kent State University.

Van de Ven, A. H.; G. Walker; and J. Liston. 1976. "Coordination Patterns within an Interorganizational Network." *Human Relations* 29: 19-36.

Van de Ven, A. H.; D. Emmett; and R. Koenig. 1974. "Frameworks for Interorganizational Analysis." *Organization and Administrative Sciences* 5: 113-29.

Van de Ven, A. H.; J. Liston; R. Koenig; and B. Esterline. 1975. "Pair-Wise Inter-Agency Relationships Among Local Texas Early Childhood Service Organizations." Austin, Texas: Texas Department of Community Affairs.

Vosburgh, W., and D. Hyman. 1973. "Advocacy and Bureaucracy: The Life and Times of a Decentralized Citizen's Advocacy Program." *Administrative Science Quarterly* 18: 433-48.

Wamsley, G., and M. Zald. 1973. "The Political Economy of Public Organizations." *Public Administration Review* 33: 62-72.

Warren, R. 1971. "The Interactions of Community Decision Organizations: Some Conceptual Considerations and Empirical Findings." In Anant Negandhi, ed., *Modern Organization Theory*. Kent, Ohio: Kent State University Press.

———. 1967. "The Interorganizational Field as a Focus for Investigation." *Administrative Science Quarterly* 12: 396-419.

Warren, R.; S. Rose; and A. Bergunder. 1974. *The Structure of Urban Reform*. Lexington, Mass.: D. C. Heath.

White, H.; S. Boorman; and R. Breiger. 1976. "Social Structure from Multiple Networks. I. Blockmodels of Roles and Positions." *American Journal of Sociology* 81: 730-80.

White, P. 1974. "Intra- and Inter-Organizational Studies — Do They Require Separate Conceptualizations?" *Administration and Society* 5: 107-51.

Yuchtman, E., and S. Seashore. 1967. "A System Resources Approach to Organizational Effectiveness." *American Sociological Review* 32: 891-903.

Zald, M. 1969. "The Power and Functions of Boards of Directors: A Theoretical Synthesis." *American Journal of Sociology* 75: 97-111.

———. 1967. "Urban Differentiation, Characteristics of Boards of Directors, and Organizational Effectiveness." *American Journal of Sociology* 73: 261-72.

———. 1966. "Organizations as Policies: An Analysis of Community Organization Agencies." *Social Work* 2: 56-65.

Zaltman, G., and R. Duncan. 1977. *Strategies for Planned Change*. New York: Wiley.

Chapter 11

Sociocultural Influences on Organizations: An Analysis of Recent Research

Mary Elizabeth Beres and James D. Portwood*

As thought and research have progressed in the areas of management and organizational theory, it has become increasingly clear that the structure and functioning of organizations may be significantly influenced by the proximate environmental context. One major environmental aspect that has been identified as a possible influencing factor is the sociocultural milieu surrounding the organization. Reviewers of applicable cross-national/cross-cultural research in the early 1970s (Ajiferuke and Boddewyn, 1970a,b; Barrett and Bass, 1970; Boddewyn and Nath, 1970; Goodman and Moore, 1972; Hesseling, 1973, Nath, 1968; Roberts, 1970; Schöllhammer, 1969), however, noted that progress toward establishing the exact nature and dynamics of this influence process has been limited. It was generally concluded that research prior to 1970 was primarily anecdotal and exploratory empirical work with little conceptual development. The current study proposes to review work published since 1970, with emphasis on its possible contribution to sociocultural theory building.

* Temple University

The authors wish to thank Mohamed Latib and John Dugan for their valuable assistance in preparing this review, and the sponsors of Conference on Complex Organizations for their suggestions and their interest in the project.

The present effort is intended not only to review specific studies, but also to identify avenues for future research that are suggested by the collective body of findings. This objective has led to a distinctive review strategy in which the problem of understanding sociocultural influences on organizations served as the sole guide in selecting and analyzing research. As a result, the review includes studies from a diversity of disciplines, including anthropology, sociology, and psychology, in addition to comparative management research. Each of these studies has been considered in terms of its contribution to sociocultural theory building, rather than in terms of its methodological characteristics or its place in the development of a particular discipline. This approach has resulted in the identification of several findings implicit in the cumulative body of research, but unrecognized due to the isolation in which interrelated studies have often been pursued.

In order to reduce the review task to manageable proportions, several restrictions have been imposed on its scope. First, in view of the extensive reviewing done around 1970, this review concentrates on work published between January 1970 and June 1978. Second, the review is limited to English language publications, with the recognition that this introduces a bias due to the omission of information from untranslated, non-English sources. Third, studies are included only if they have a cross-national or cross-cultural perspective and focus on organizational issues. Finally, because of its largely anecdotal nature and its pragmatic, rather than theoretical, orientation, international business literature (Schöllhammer, 1973) has been omitted. Application of these criteria has resulted in the identification of 105 reports of models or empirical research, which form the basis for the review. Because of space limitations, only the more significant studies and general conclusions from the review are presented here. (A more complete analysis of the research is available from the authors.)

FINDINGS IN RECENT CROSS-NATIONAL RESEARCH

Existing cross-national research can be grouped along two dimensions — research objective and organizational focus. The first of these dimensions distinguishes research in terms of the types of contributions it makes to theory development. In this regard, cross-national studies tend to fall into three distinct categories — (1)

studies that propose and/or test models explicitly addressing relationships between sociocultural variables and the functioning of organizations; (2) empirical studies that test in cross-national settings the universality of propositions developed in specific sociocultural contexts; and (3) exploratory or descriptive studies that make no a priori assumptions about the nature of cultural influence.

The first group of studies is concerned with sociocultural processes and indicates how scientists currently think about sociocultural influence. The second set serves as tests of the hypothesis that sociocultural variables are irrelevant and thereby helps to identify the limits of cultural influence and points to potential dependent variables. The third group of studies supplies data for inductive theory building and generates instruments for empirical research. Because of the intent of this review, studies are analyzed in terms of these contributions, regardless of their original purposes.

From the perspective of organizational focus, studies also group into three categories — (1) structurally oriented macrostudies of organizational properties, such as size, goals, and authority structure; (2) process-oriented macrostudies of organizational activities, such as decisionmaking, planning, and socialization; and (3) behaviorally oriented microstudies of the attitudinal and behavioral bases of organization functioning. Of these three groups, the two macrolevel approaches are more directly concerned with organizational functioning. Several recently proposed models, however, explain societal influences by means of microlevel processes (e.g., Beres and Portwood, 1979; Gillespie and Mileti, 1976; Negandhi, 1973a). Because they contribute to development of this dimension of the models, a sample of recent cross-national behavioral studies has been included in the review.

The distribution of recent research efforts along the dimensions of research objectives and organizational focus is indicated in Table 11-1. As can be seen from the differences between column totals and the number of unique studies, some researchers have begun to address multiple levels of organizational functioning. On the other hand, only a few researchers, notably Negandhi, have conducted research across the spectrum of research objectives. The major contributions that each of the various groups of studies make to understanding sociocultural influences on organizations are briefly identified below. The final section of the review is devoted to a discussion of the research directions suggested by the collective pattern of findings.

Table 11-1. Types of Cross-National Studies of Organizations, 1970-1978

Organizational Focus	Research Objectives		
	Sociocultural Theory Development	Tests of Universality	Exploratory Studies
Structural	8	15	21
Process	7	4	14
Behavioral	11	9	28[a]
Total unique studies	18	28	59

[a]Selected sample of relevant research.

SOCIOCULTURAL THEORY DEVELOPMENT

An overview of recent theoretical studies indicates that they are for the most part a variety of independent research efforts that represent diverse phases of the theory-building process. In terms of levels of abstraction, they range from general models concerned with multiple levels of organizational functioning to limited domain models that offer more concrete conceptualizations, linking sociocultural processes to (1) characteristics of an organization's authority structure; (2) processes of decisionmaking, organizational change, recruitment, socialization, and communication; and (3) the attitudes and behavior of organization members. In terms of the object of explanation, some of the conceptualizations identify causal relationships between environmental and organizational variables, while others focus on the mechanisms of cultural influence, particularly socialization processes.

A third group of models, concerned with the definition of culture, has begun to develop a descriptive theory of the culture construct. The few empirical studies of sociocultural processes have been in this area (e.g., Beres and Portwood, 1979; Child and Kieser, 1977; Kelley and Reeser, 1973; Triandis and Vassiliou, 1972). Table 11-2 indicates which models relate to each of these theoretical functions.

Because they were developed largely in isolation from one another, recent models present a relatively fragmented view of sociocultural influence and leave several theoretical gaps. Across the models, however, two common themes emerge — first, the view that culture is an environmental factor influencing organizations; and,

Table 11-2.   Theoretical Functions of Sociocultural Models

	Object of Explanation		
Level of Abstraction	Causal Relationships	Causal Process	Culture Construct
General	Long and Seo, 1977 Negandhi, 1973a Negandhi, 1975	Beres and Portwood, 1979	
Limited domain structure	Poblador, 1975	Brossard and Maurice, 1976	Child and Kieser, 1977
Process	Heller, 1973 Gillespie and Mileti, 1976		Evan, 1974–1975
Behavior	Granick, 1972 Robey, 1974	Moore, 1974	Kumar and Singh, 1976

second, the assumption that organizations are behavioral phenomena. These themes give the models a sufficiently common foundation so that they could be integrated into a more comprehensive explanation of sociocultural processes.

Early sociocultural research was criticized for failing to define culture and failing to provide a theory of cultural influence. While these problems continue to exist, some attempts have been made to address them. Theorists concerned with the culture construct have begun to define culture in terms of basic value dimensions. Recent models offer three variations of this approach. In one case, theorists view culture as a personal set of constructs, measurable at the individual level (Kumar and Singh, 1976; Triandis and Vassiliou, 1972). Others see culture as a set of values, norms, and behavior dispositions shared with contemporaries and measured by means of contemporary, group level indicators (Evan, 1974–1975; Gillespie and Mileti, 1976). The third approach defines culture as a set of cognitive and behavioral patterns socially inherited from previous generations, a definition that requires measurement in terms of ancestral group values (Beres and Portwood, 1979; Child and Kieser, 1977). While none of these approaches has strong empirical support, Triandis' work demonstrates that a systematic study of cultural orientations can lead to accurate predictions of individual behaviors (Triandis and Vassiliou, 1972; Triandis et al., 1972, 1973).

The second problem in sociocultural models has been a lack of clear distinctions between cultural systems and other environmental variables. This ambiguity arises in part because the environmental variables are never clearly defined. It also results from the custom of treating culture as a national characteristic. This custom makes it easy to identify cultural boundaries, but impossible to separate culture operationally from the legal, political, and social characteristics of national systems. Recently, several models have defined culture independently of national boundaries (Beres and Portwood, 1979; Child and Kieser, 1977; Evan, 1974–1975; Gillespie and Mileti, 1976; Moore, 1974), and a few empirical studies have provided evidence of intranational cultural variation (Beres and Portwood, 1979; Kelley and Reeser, 1973). These studies are a significant step forward, but they fail to specify where cultural boundaries are, if not on national lines; and hence, the ambiguity of the distinction betwen cultural systems and other environmental systems remains.

Recent models have offered a variety of explanations of cultural influence. Negandhi's (1974a) comprehensive conceptualization of the environment identifies social and cultural variables as two of many environmental forces in a complex system of influence. Within this environmental complex, some theorists view culture as an independent influence acting in parallel with other forces (Heller, 1973; Negandhi, 1974a). Another group of theorists considers culture a primary force, influencing other environmental and organizational processes (Evan, 1974/75; Gillespie and Mileti, 1976). Finally, the cultural change (Gillespie and Mileti, 1976) and feedback models (Beres and Portwood, 1979; Brossard and Maurice, 1976; Child and Kieser, 1977; Crozier, 1973; Long and Seo, 1977; Boddewyn, 1973) suggest that environmental and organizational processes can influence culture.

With regard to the way culture influences organizations, four types of models have been proposed, which vary in terms of relationships hypothesized between culture and organization and individual behavior. Culture is either seen as (1) interacting with organizational properties to influence behavior (Granick, 1972; Heller, 1973; Moore, 1974; Negandhi, 1973a; Tobey, 1974); (2) directly shaping organizational characteristics, that in turn influence behavior (Long and Seo, 1977); or (3) interacting with environmental constraints to influence behavior, which in turn shapes organizations (Beres and Portwood, 1979). In view of the rather vague and general formulations of each of these models, it is unclear whether they are in actual conflict or have described cultural influence in superficially simple terms. By taking such diverse perspectives, they have at least identified the alternative explanations with which a comprehensive theory of sociocultural influence must deal.

In summary, the last eight years have produced several sociocultural models, but little hypothesis-testing research. Some of the promising developments include (1) a greater effort to define culture; (2) some attempts to explain cultural influence; and (3) general agreement about basic assumptions. Before these models can be useful guides for rigorous, deductive research, however, there is need for a more precise concept of culture, clearer differentiation between cultural systems and national systems, and clearer specification of influence relationships.

Tests of Universality

Universalistic organization theories focus on variables frequently neglected in sociocultural studies. As a result, this research helps to identify alternative environmental forces and to clarify the nature of sociocultural influence processes. In recent years, the most systematic generalizability research has been concerned with various influences on organizational structure. A few unrelated cross-national studies have examined the universality of organization process relationships and nonsociocultural influences on attitudes and behavior. Table 11–3 lists these studies in terms of the independent-dependent variable relationships studied.

From the findings in these studies, two patterns emerge that suggest areas where cultural influence is more likely to occur. In the first pattern, the consistency of results varies by independent variable. Clearest support is shown for the universality of technology and size relationships. Qualified support is shown for contingency theories, and mixed results are reported in studies concerned with the influences of management policy. This pattern of findings suggests that organizational functioning may be more systematically influenced by physical variables, such as size and technology, and less consistently affected by social psychological variables, such as environmental uncertainty and management policy. In more concrete terms, machinery may have a more universal impact on organizations than management policy.

Although there may be a variety of explanations for the inconsistent findings in these studies, the pattern of results suggests the following hypothesis:

> The greater the physical constraints on organizational functioning, the less variance there will be across cultures in the organization's mode of functioning.

Table 11-3. Recent Cross-National Studies of Universal Theories

	DEPENDENT VARIABLE		
Independent Variable	Organization Structure	Organization Processes	Factors/Behavior
Technology	Zwerman, 1970	Cascio, 1974	Peterson, 1975 Orpen, 1976 Form, 1972 Reimann, 1973
Size	Child, 1973 Hickson et al., 1974 Inkson et al., 1970 Tracy and Azumi, 1976		
Environmental/ Situational Contin- gencies	Tracy and Azumi, 1976 Negandhi and Reimann, 1972 Ruedi and Lawrence, 1970	Heller and Wilpert, 1977, 1979	
Management Policy/Strategy	Negandhi, 1974b Negandhi and Reimann, 1971, 1973 Simonetti and Simonetti, 1974	Pavan, 1976	
Economic Development			Gruenfeld and Mac- Eachron, 1975
Decisionmaking Style		Rosner et al., 1973	
Universal Attitude Configurations			Burger and Doctor, 1976 Krus and Rysberg, 1976

Such a hypothesis implies that automobile assembly lines would be more similar across cultural boundaries than administrative systems and that manufacturing firms would be more similar than service organizations. In suggesting these comparisons, cross-national tests of universality identify a new direction for sociocultural research.

The second consistent finding across generalizability research is that relationships between environmental, organizational, and individual characteristics are far more universal than the distributions of these characteristics. This pattern suggests, on the one hand, that organizational characteristics occur in highly interdependent clusters and, on the other hand, that the likelihood of developing or adopting particular clusters (i.e., types of organizations) varies across nations.

In practical terms, these findings imply that types of organizations predominant in one society may be less prevalent, or nonexistent, in other societies with divergent sociocultural milieus (Ruedi and Lawrence, 1970). It further implies that relatively unique mixes of organizational types would appear in different societal settings. Interpreting these research results from a sociocultural perspective leads to the hypothesis that:

Within a society, culture (1) encourages the emergence of certain types of organizations; (2) determines the types of organization that will be most common; and (3) influences the distributional mix of organizational types.

The research efforts of Udy (1965, 1970) are based on a similar hypothesis, but unfortunately, his approach to the study of cultural influence has been largely ignored.

When viewed from a methodological perspective, there are several characteristics of recent research on universal theories that raise questions about the reported findings and serve to emphasize the need for an operational definition of culture. The major limitations lie in three areas — representativeness of the data bases, quality of measurements, and objectivity of data analysis. With regard to sampling, nearly all the studies are on manufacturing organizations located either in industrialized nations in North America and Western Europe or in developing nations in Asia, Africa, and Latin America. The studies frequently include only a small number of countries, a small number of organizations, and a small number of people. Given these sampling processes, the cross-national representativeness of the findings is highly questionable.

The problems involving measurement and data analysis are closely related. First, the unsystematic use of varying instruments and the failure to use multiple measures of a construct leave open the possibility that results are due to method effects. Only in the area of technological influence do consistent results obtained using diverse measures give confidence that the findings represent the relationship studied.

Second, because of the ambiguous way in which variables are operationalized, findings attributed to universal influences may sometimes be the result of cultural processes. In one case, management policy, an organizational variable, is measured by aggregating individual perceptions. Some theorists have argued that such perceptions are indicators of cultural influences on an individual's cognitive frame of reference and, hence, are measures of culture. In other cases, nation has been used as a measure of industrialization, socialization as an indicator of economic development, and basic value dimensions as a measure of worker attitudes. All these measures have also been referred to as indicators of culture. This confusion reflects the tendency of researchers to focus on arbitrarily restricted sets of variables and to find what they are looking for.

Resolution of each of these methodological difficulties depends on the development of a clearly operationalizable definition of culture that can be used to identify the population boundaries for sampling; as a standard for evaluating the cross-national equivalence of measures; as a basis for distinguishing indicators of culture from measures of other environmental or organizational variables; and to enable researchers to design studies that more adequately represent the complexity of the environment. In turn, testing of the two hypotheses suggested by past findings, and verification of the original findings, depend on resolution of those methodological difficulties.

Exploratory Research

A large portion of cross-national/cross-cultural research continues to be primarily exploratory or descriptive in nature. These studies, which gather data bases richly descriptive of their research populations, can make three types of contribution to sociocultural theory building. First, they can contribute conceptually to model formulation by identifying individual or organizational characteristics and activities that may be influenced by the existing cultural context and by identifying environmental conditions that provide alternative explanations for differences observed across groups. Second, inductive data-gathering research can develop or validate instruments and research designs for use in studies of cultural influence. These studies may be especially helpful in developing functionally equivalent measures and measures for the multiple method designs that are strongly advocated for future cross-cultural research (Nath, 1968; Reimann, 1974). Third, these studies can help provide the empirical data needed to develop "cultural maps" that identify similarities and differences across potential study populations and describe the effects of different cultural systems. Reliable mapping is critical to the understanding of cultural influence and development of powerful models. As noted previously (Beres and Portwood, 1979; Evan, 1974-1975; Roberts, 1970), researchers cannot legitimately attribute observed differences across populations to cultural influences without prior knowledge of the structure, dynamics, and boundaries of cultures within given study populations.

The quality of the various contributions made by recent exploratory studies tends to vary according to the level of the phenomena they address. Most of the macrolevel research is limited in scope, discussion oriented, utilizes no culturally based theoretical framework, and lacks rigorous methodology. Researchers have done little to build on previous work in the field. As a result, the contributions from this research come from a limited set of studies and are primarily in the area of suggestions for future study. Many microstudies, on the other hand, exhibit considerable rigor, a feature that reflects the influence of methodologies and instrumentation borrowed from the broader fields of industrial psychology and organizational behavior. One of the most interesting and promising contributions of these studies is the emergence of several coherent streams of research that have generated comparable sets of data involving several variables across a wide range of countries.

In terms of conceptual contributions, several studies suggest some potential links between culture and certain organizational properties. The strongest evidence of a relationship comes from several studies that used strikingly different methodologies, data sources, and settings, but obtained comparable results linking culture to the degree of formality in macrolevel control structures (Azumi and McMillan, 1975; Dore, 1973; McMillan et al., 1973; Sim, 1977). Another body of research on participative management structures (Farris and Butterfield, 1972; Rosner et al., 1973; Tannenbaum et al., 1974) has led to the suggestion that past cultural traditions may affect the ease with which participative structures are established in given settings (Tannenbaum et al., 1974). There has also been some evidence of cross-national variation in industrial relations processes (Peterson, 1976; Shapira and Bass, 1974; Zupanov, 1973) and in the relationship between managerial attitudes and success (England, 1975; Bass and Eldridge, 1973; Ryterband and Barrett, 1970).

With regard to alternative explanations of observed differences, there is some evidence that organizational structuring may be affected by political and economic factors (Beyer and Lodahl, 1976; Dore, 1973; Franko, 1974; Tannenbaum et al., 1974); product lines, industry, technology, organizational age, and size (Azumi and McMillan, 1975; Negandhi and Prasad, 1971; Sim, 1977); and employee demographics (Nightingale and Toulouse, 1977). A sequence of studies assessing the impact of management philosophy on organizational structuring and planning activities reports that these variables are related across a variety of countries, but also gives evidence that the distribution of types of structures varies with country (Negandhi, 1973b; Negandhi and Prasad, 1971; Simonetti and Boseman, 1975; Simonetti and Simonetti, 1977; Wright, 1971). Finally, studies of organizational decisionmaking have discovered cross-national differences in the extent of shared responsibilities (Obradovic, 1975; Tannenbaum et al., 1974; Zimbalist, 1975), but one study links differences in participatory behavior to perceptions of subordinate skill (Heller and Wilpert, 1977, 1979). Collectively, these exploratory findings show the same pattern of results as the universal, hypothesis-testing research. Technology shows the most consistent influence across countries, and distributions of various types of organization differ cross-nationally.

Two of the most important conceptual contributions of recent research come from Nightingale and Toulouse's (1977) study of cultural differences in Canada. First, their findings clearly demonstrate that cultural boundaries do not always correspond to national boundaries. Second, the study's research design allows the researchers to compare culture's relative influence on structure, process, and attitude levels of organization behavior. Results indicate that the two cultures involved are most distinguishable on the basis of individual values and least so in terms of organizational structural charcteristics. The magnitude of differences in organizational processes fell between these two extremes. These findings suggest that cultural processes may be most influential at the individual level and less influential, due to other factors, at the organizational level.

Methodologically, recent exploratory research makes only a few contributions. Some studies have developed strategies for controlling potential confounding environmental variables. These include the use of matched samples, holding constant the location or type of organization studied, and representative sampling of organizations in a culture. Studies have also introduced the use of simulation as an alternative to questionnaires or field observation (Shapira and Bass, 1974; Graves, 1972) and the use of paired subordinate perceptions as a control measure for managers' perceptions (Heller and Wilpert, 1977, 1979).

In the area of design, Cole's work (1971) illustrates the value of an anthropological case approach to data collection, while Tannenbaum et al. (1974) and Rosner et al. (1973) demonstrate how cross-national research teams can reduce ethnocentric influences on research design and data interpretation. Microlevel studies have provided well-validated instruments for the cross-cultural study of attitudes and values. Finally, Schuh (1974) has developed a method for independently operationalizing "culture" and "nation." His results indicate a significant independent effect for both constructs, a finding that is particularly important in view of questions being raised about the relationship between nation and culture.

In the area of cultural mapping, macrolevel studies are too diverse and too limited in their sampling of populations to make any significant contribution to the identification of cultural systems. Recent efforts at the microlevel (Bass and Eldridge, 1973; England, 1975; Ronen and Kraut, 1977; Simonetti and Weitz, 1972), however, have made significant advances in the mapping of individual values and needs. These studies utilize results from research streams initiated by the work of Haire, Ghiselli and Porter (1966; see also Ajiferuke and Boddewyn, 1970a; Clark and McCabe, 1970; Cummings and Schmidt, 1972; Redding and Casey, 1976; Smith and Thomas, 1972); England (1975; see also England and Koike, 1970; England and Lee, 1971, 1973, 1974, England, Dhingra, and Agarwal, 1974; Whitely and England, 1977); and Barrett and Bass (1970, 1972; see also Bass and Eldridge, 1973; Burger and Doktor, 1976; Ryterband and Barrett, 1970).

Patterns of responses in each of these sets of studies show that certain countries may be clustered in terms of similarities in managerial values. While the national groupings generated do not always coincide, the general consistency of results across a wide range of countries and numerous studies gives reasonably strong evidence that some cultural boundaries may well extend across two or even more national boundaries. In addition to studying managerial values, microresearchers have also begun to examine need structures and the dynamics of employee motivation in different countries (Harrell, 1971; Simonetti and Weitz, 1972; Slocum, 1971; Slocum and Topichak, 1972; Slocum et al., 1971). As yet, these efforts are not as organized or focused as those on managerial values, but they do provide a beginning for the mapping of individual need patterns.

In summary, recent exploratory cross-national research makes some incremental contributions to the understanding of sociocultural influence. The types of conceptual, methodological,, and empirical insights offered are summarized in Table 11-4. Problems remain, however, because there is too much of what Berrien (1970) calls "safari research" — namely, opportunistic study in which little thought is given to rationale or research design.

Table 11-4. Contributions of Recent Exploratory Research

Conceptual

1. Certain organization level phenomena (control structures, participative management strategies, selection, collective bargaining, and dispute settlement activities) and individual level phenomena (managerial values and need structures) appear to vary as a result of cultural influence, while others (organizational planning strategies, decisionmaking structures) are less clearly influenced.
2. Independent environmental characteristics (political and economic history, management philosophy, technology) may provide alternative explanations to the cultural influence proposition.
3. Cultural boundaries cannot necessarily be equated with national boundaries.
4. Empirical data provide some support for hypotheses derived from generalizability research and the suggestion that cultural influence is more pronounced at the micro-versus macrolevel in organizations.

Methodological

1. Multiple strategies have been introduced that control for potentially influential environmental differences.
2. Several promising methodological innovations (simulation, manager-subordinate pairing, anthropological case study, multinational research teams) have been introduced.
3. A valid system of measurement for individual values has been developed and used across a wide range of national environments.

Empirical Mapping

1. A mapping process, using cross-national data on managerial values and need structures, has begun. As yet, the process is fairly limited.

Summary

From the perspective of understanding sociocultural processes, one general conclusion reached by these reviewers is that considerably more work is needed to provide a clear understanding of the nature and extent of sociocultural influences on organizational functioning. Research continues to have many of the limitations described by earlier reviewers. More particularly, studies have frequently focused on a limited number of countries and organizations; little attention has been given to operatives versus managers; studies have tended to measure organization structures and processes by means of managerial perceptions; and the quality of data manipulations sometimes has exceeded the quality of data (Lenski, 1976). The differences between cultural boundaries and national boundaries, discussed by earlier reviewers (Ajiferuke and Boddewyn, 1970a; Goodman and

Moore, 1972; Hesseling, 1973; Schöllhammer, 1969) and evidenced in a few recent empirical studies (Beres and Portwood, 1979; Heginbotham, 1975, Nightingale and Toulouse, 1977), have not been recognized in most conceptual models.

Instead, ambiguities in the definition of environmental variables have led to conflicting interpretations of data, a problem that also reflects the random nature of much research effort in the area (Berrien, 1970). Because the interests and methods of researchers have varied greatly, cross-national research has addressed a broad range of countries and variables in a variety of different ways, making it difficult to generalize or even discern trends in the findings.

The grouping of studies according to research objectives and organizational focus, however, has brought attention to several points. First, grouping by objectives has made clear the strong influence that researcher orientation has on data interpretation. Cultural theorists see cultural differences, and universalists see universal relationships. Second, a sociocultural analysis of universalistic research findings has led to hypotheses relating (1) cultural variation to biophysical constraints on behavior and (2) cultural influence to the types of organizations in a society. Third, grouping by organizational focus has called attention to the scattered nature of empirical research at the macrolevel and the atheoretical state of research at the microlevel. Finally, the pattern of findings regarding cultural influences on macro- and microlevel variables has led to a suggestion that cultural influences may be greater at the microlevel.

In the area of theory, the review has identified some general and limited domain models that describe the cultural influence process and some attempts to conceptualize the culture construct. These models and conceptualizations begin to address the relevant theoretical questions. However, considerable work is needed before these models can be fully developed. One area especially in need of some clarification and elaboration is the description of the organizational environment. In too many models, the relationship between cultural and environmental effects is unclear, making it virtually impossible to assess the independent effects of variables. Models are also vague or contradictory in their representation of the causal relationships among sociocultural processes, other environmental processes, organizational characteristics, and individual attitudes and behavior.

Contributions from recent exploratory research include the identification of several specific organizational characteristics that may be influenced by culture. Microlevel studies are beginning to provide the type of broad mapping of managerial values that can be helpful in identifying cultural boundaries. Some of the more stubborn problems that remain are in the area of methodology where researchers are struggling to develop culturally equivalent measures, identify appropriate sampling procedures, and operationalize the culture construct.

DIRECTIONS FOR THE FUTURE

Having examined the recent past in cross-national organization research, this concluding section of the analysis looks into the immediate future. Beginning with an identification of some of the more pressing research issues, the discussion turns to the practical, conceptual, and methodological problems that make progress difficult and concludes by suggesting some steps that can be taken, given current constraints.

Research Issues

There are two major theoretical obstacles to the development and understanding of sociocultural influences on organizations. First, comparative theorists do not have an operationalizable definition of culture, and second, the causal role of culture has been only superficially addressed. While these are old problems, recent studies suggest some specific directions for future model building.

In the past, culture has either been operationalized as national or as the shared values of a group of respondents. The first of these methods makes it impossible to distinguish culture from the political, legal, social, and economic variables associated with nation. The second approach makes it impossible to measure culture and its attitudinal effects independently. Recognizing these difficulties, several researchers have recently adopted an anthropological approach, defining culture in terms of patterns of basic value orientations (Child and Kieser, 1977; Evan, 1974-1975; Kumar and Singh, 1976; Triandis, 1975). This approach shows considerable promise, and its development should be a priority effort.

To make a values definition of culture operationally useful, several problems must be solved. First, basic value dimensions must be identified. Second, the types of patterns in which these dimensions combine must be determined. In addition, a theory linking these patterns to observable indicators must be developed and tested (see Nath, 1970). Once the culture construct is clearly operationalized, the attitude-mapping activities already begun can be used to identify the boundaries of cultural systems. The same techniques can also be used to determine the cultural composition of a country's "national character" (Inkeles and Levinson, 1969). Measurement of culture must reach this stage before models of cultural influence can actually be tested.

A conceptually clear definition of culture would help to solve several methodological problems that are obstacles to inductive theory development. First, an operationally unambiguous definition of culture would provide a standard against which to judge the functional equivalence of different instruments, making it possible to compare findings from different studies. Second, a clear definition would help to identify the appropriate unit of analysis for studying cultural systems. This problem has plagued anthropologists (Huff, 1974; Whiting, 1968), but has been largely ignored by management theorists who have equated culture with nation. Finally, a measurable definition of culture would lead to resolution of the representative sampling problem by helping scientists identify the population boundaries of cultural systems.

The second theoretical area that requires attention concerns culture's causal role. Currently, most comparative theorists view culture as one of a set of environmental influences, but propose several different theories about culture's role in the environment. One set of theorists argues that cultural differences are disappearing because industrialization is leading to convergence in social structures (e.g., Bertrand, 1976; Kaplan, 1976). Universalistic theories treat culture as a nonexistent or nonsignificant factor in organizational processes. At the opposite extreme are theorists who view culture as a primary causal factor that influences the selection of forms of industrialization and/or technology (Frost and Hayes, 1979; Zwerman, 1970); types of organization (Ruedi and Lawrence, 1970); and types of social structures (Triandis, 1975; Triandis et al., 1973). From this perspective, organizations themselves are measures of culture (Crozier, 1973; Form, 1969; Hickson et al., 1974; Ruedi and Lawrence, 1970). Finally, some theorists suggest that culture influences social processes within the constraints imposed by ecological conditions (Beres and Portwood, 1979; Endruweit, 1979; McMillan, 1973; Whitely and England, 1977). Thus, there are four different types of explanations advanced regarding the nature of cultural influence in the environment.

The models that include culture as a variable treat it either as a dependent variable constrained by the process of industrialization, as an independent variable determining the technological and administrative development of organizations, or as a variable intervening between environmental constraints and the development of organizations. Since there are reasonable arguments and evidence supporting each of these types of models, the possibility exists that all of them represent aspects of cultural processes. Endruweit (1979), in fact, has suggested that the rigid classification of variables as independent and dependent imposes artificial constraints that make it difficult to analyze the influence of culture.

A more appropriate approach may be to view culture in terms of a hierarchy of influences, in which the environment first constrains variance. Culture then determines, within the constraints, which of the possible behaviors will be selected. The behaviors in turn shape the environment, so that the next choice would take place within the new constraints set by a culturally altered environment, and so on. In addition to this sequential hierarchy of influence, such a model would include a cross-sectional hierarchy in which the choice of any one individual would be limited to the set of options resulting from the contemporaneous choices of others. At each point where choice exists, this model suggests that culture would influence the selection of an option. Thus, cultural influence would successively channel behavior within the environmental and concomitant choice constraints it had previously influenced.

Two patterns of findings in recent generalizability studies tend to support a complex model of culture's causality. In the first pattern, technological variables appeared more consistently correlated with organizational properties than social psychological variables. These results are consistent with the view that environmental conditions limit cultural influence. In the second pattern, the distribution of types of organizational characteristics varied more by country than the correlations between organizational characteristics. These findings are consistent with the view that culture influences the choices made from among options composed of interrelated characteristics. Together these patterns support the suggestion that culture intervenes between the environment and possible outcomes to determine which outcome will actually occur. They also leave open the possibility that culture can function as an exogenous variable "causing" an observed relationship between variables, as long as the variables are both social in character.

In view of the support these findings give to a complex model of cultural causality, future theorizing ought seriously to consider a hierarchical model of influence. The two hypotheses generated from recent findings offer a starting point for such an approach.

The greater the physical constraints on organizational functioning, the less variance there will be across cultures in the organization's mode of functioning.

Within a society, culture (1) leads to the emergence of certain types of organization; (2) determines the types of organization that will be most common; and (3) influences the distributional mix of organizational types.

The issue of causality is further complicated by feedback models of culture (Beres and Portwood, 1979; Crozier, 1973; Long and Seo, 1977; Thomis, 1976). In addressing the dynamics of influence, these models suggest that culture can lead to choices that in turn create situations that give rise to new cultural value patterns. This view reintroduces the possibility that culture may be a dependent variable. It also suggests that there may be significant shifts, or even discontinuities, within a developmental sequence of cultural influence. In this vein, Hesseling (1973) and Suryadinata (1976) have proposed that the establishment of nations may lead to the development of national cultures. By providing a conceptual link between culture and nation, this suggestion makes it clear that feedback models not only add complexity to causal modeling, but they also raise questions about the approrite unit of analysis for cultural systems. Each of the issues raised by the cultural feedback models must be addressed if models of sociocultural processes are to reflect the complexity of their dynamic dimensions.

In addition to addressing culture's relationship to other environmental influences, theorists have also considered the specifics of how culture influences an organization. One suggestion is that culture shapes an organization through the aggregate of its influence on individual behavior (Beres and Portwood, 1979). Support for this view appears in the findings of studies that address micro- and macrolevels of behavior. In each case, culture's influence was clearest at the microlevel, less clear at the process level, and least clear at the structure level. If this is the case, then the process level of organizations becomes an especially important focus for research, since it is the meeting point between structural constraints and individual differences. From this perspective, the study of culture would become the study of *how* what *must* be done *is* done.

One problem with the studies that show culture relating more strongly to micro- than macrolevel variables is that they all use attitudinal measures of culture. It is possible that the findings are simply the cumulative evidence of a method effect in which micromeasures correlate more highly with other micromeasures than with macromeasures. To distinguish potentially real relationships from method effects, future studies should include macromeasures of culture, such as use of time and space (Hall, 1959; Riemer, 1975), as well as micromeasures.

Recapitulating, then, several recent studies suggest that culture be operationally defined in terms of basic value dimensions. Future research needs to identify the dimensions, the patterns in which they group, their observable indicators, and the unit of analysis that is appropriate for representing a cultural system.

In regard to causality, the studies collectively present a relatively complex view of culture's role. Future models should address the relationship between cultural influence and other environmental processes, such as industrialization; the apparent dependent, independent, and intervening roles of cultural influence; and the relationship between cultural influence and cultural development. Models also need to identify the processes by which culture influences organizations. In the latter area, findings that link culture more closely to microlevel variables should be tested using macromeasures of culture.

Current Problems in Cross-national Research

The practical problems in cross-national research are many, ranging from obtaining functionally equivalent measures to funding (Berrien, 1970; Goldberg, 1977). Political sensitivities are a particularly critical factor, often affecting what can be studied in different countries (Boddewyn, 1976; Tannenbaum et al., 1974) and how results may be interpreted (Hesseling, 1971). Because these problems are not new to the field, there is a shortage of data from which to develop theories or by which to test them.

Not only is data scarce, but what exists reflects the diverse interests of researchers who become involved in cross-national studies for a variety of theoretical and/or pragmatic reasons (Grochla, 1977). The theoretical studies focus on the explanation of social processes, as has been seen in this review. Pragmatically oriented research (e.g., Graves, 1970; Schöllhammer, 1973) is concerned with prognosis and design and has been pursued by researchers interested in the development of multinationals, the international transfer of management technology, and the adaptation of organizations to new settings or changing conditions. These differences in purpose, together with the wide range of potential variables, make cross-national research relevant to scholars and practitioners in many areas. This, in turn, has resulted in an extensive amount of work being reported through widely dispersed channels. The absence of linkages between these outlets leads to duplication of effort and noncomparability across studies. In general, the scattered nature of current research limits the ability of researchers to capitalize on cumulative findings.

Ideological bias is one of the major conceptual limitations in current cross-national research. Hesseling (1971) has suggested that current organization theories are largely Anglo-American. Several other researchers (Ferrari, 1974; Glaser, 1971; Goldman and Van Houten, 1977; Grochla, 1977; Gvishiani, 1972; Hofstede and Kassem, 1976; Kassem, 1977) have identified distinctive features of various European traditions. Maruyama (1974) argues that these differences in approach are rooted in different structures of reasoning, and Huff (1974) relates them to differences in ecology. Apparently, the orientations of researchers may be influenced by the same cultural processes they attempt to study. Not only do ideological biases affect models, but since methodologies are strongly influenced by theory, the biases make it difficult to design a truly cross-national study. Instead, most research indicates how other nations compare with a researcher's own society in terms of variables and/or processes relevant in the researcher's society. Thus, the studies themselves are culturally biased.

Because the attempt to understand cross-national differences in organizations is a research topic that draws models and methodologies from a variety of disciplines, cross-national research is shaped not only by ideological influences, but also by the levels of development in contributing fields. As has been seen, for example, psychology offers much more rigorous measurement methodologies, while sociology offers theoretical frameworks. Currently, the unevenness of development across different fields makes it difficult, if not impossible, to design research that is equally rigorous at macro- and microlevels. Hence, it is likely to be some time before macro- and micromodels can be adequately tested.

The quality of models and empirical studies depends also on whether cross-national researchers utilize the contributions of relevant disciplines. In this regard, much recent research has ignored anthropological concepts and methods, an unfortunate omission, since culture is a central concern of anthropologists. In view of the wide range of processes potentially involved in sociocultural influences on organizations, cross-national research is likely to be dependent on the state of the art in an increasing number of related disciplines. Constructing integrated models and research designs from theories and methods that have developed around the specialized views of reality of different disciplines will be a continuing problem in this area.

Possibly because of the problems described above, cross-national research is often inadequately designed. Ambiguous operationalizations of variables and arbitrarily restricted conceptualizations of the environment leave findings open to numerous alternative explanations. In addition, studies rarely build on one another. Until researchers begin working systematically to construct a consistent body of knowledge, it will be difficult to make any progress in understanding sociocultural influences on organizations. What appears to be needed at this point are methodological and conceptual frameworks to guide data-gathering efforts across studies.

Given the practical, conceptual, and methodological problems cited, it is obvious that any comparative research effort is a major undertaking. Conducting a well-designed study depends, on the one hand, on adequate funding and, on the other hand, on a clear and comprehensive conceptual scheme. In view of the high cost of cross-national research and the problematic support of funding sources, it is important that future studies be "efficient" as well — that is utilize the best available measures, gather data that can be compared with related earlier studies, and cumulatively advance knowledge of sociocultural variations and/or understanding of sociocultural processes. These norms apply to any good research project: however, they have been particularly difficult to follow in cross-national studies. The concluding section of this review offers some suggestions on how to improve the efficiency of future efforts given the current state of the art.

Recommendations for Future Research

Progress in understanding something as complex as sociocultural processes is likely to be slow and painstaking. There are several ways, however, in which cross-national research efforts could be made more systematic and cumulative. Some possibilities are suggested here in relation to (1) the organization of past findings; (2) coordination of different types of research; and (3) the use of conceptual and methodological guidelines for design. In many cases, the individual recommendations are not new, but they have greater significance when seen in terms of a total program aimed toward the integration of various cross-national efforts.

To begin with, there already exists a widely dispersed data base describing organizational and behavioral characteristics in a large number of national settings. A first step in the organization of findings would be to review and catalog these studies in terms of countries, measures, and results. By including single country case studies in such a data matrix, the comparative potential in these intensive efforts could be developed. Hesseling (1971) has also suggested that the in-house research units of multinationals could be a good source of data, providing of course that anonymity is preserved. Cataloging all these results would help to identify consistent and discrepant findings across past studies; indicate research areas that have been neglected; and from the patterns of findings across variables, suggest hypotheses for further research.

Recently, several scholars have begun to organize existing studies that relate to the organizational characteristics of particular groupings of nations (Boddewyn, 1976; Davis and Goodman, 1972; Graves, 1970). While these collections indicate clearly the broad scope of relevant materials, they tend to focus on discussions rather than data. Given the evidence of biases in data shown in this review, it is recommended here that a systematic compilation of data should be organized and available for analysis from the diverse perspectives of different researchers. Murdock's (1957, 1965) human relations area files, created for anthropologists, present a model for such a cumulatively compiled data base.

Development of a central data file is directly related to a second organizational recommendation — namely, creation of a clearing house for cross-national research (Graves and Hesseling, 1970). The centers begun by scholars such as Negandhi, England, and Bass and Barrett, as well as the Science Center Berlin and the quarterly abstract, *The International Executive,* are steps in this direction, but the establishment of a centralized repository for cross-national data would offer the opportunity for a more complete integration of the field.

Not only is there a need for a central clearing house, there is also one for a setting in which theorists from different countries could interact and further the formation of cross cultural research teams (Nath, 1977). During the recent past, the Science Center Berlin has been performing such a role (e.g., Goldberg, 1977; International Research Group, 1977). Schöllhammer (1975) suggests that the professional associations could also perform such a function. In addition to having scholars from different countries, research teams studying sociocultural processes would also benefit from having members representing ·different disciplines. By having such a diverse group of planners, research designs could incorporate the contributions of varying ideologies and disciplines while avoiding some of their biases.

With regard to future research, the diversity of purposes characteristic of cross-national research can be used to advantage. By recognizing the functions of various types of research and maintaining appropriate linkages between them, researchers can benefit from a division of labor, while pursuing the common goal of understanding sociocultural influences on organizations. In addition, because so little is known about sociocultural processes, even as organizations increasingly operate across national and cultural boundaries, it is important that both theoretical and pragmatic research efforts be promoted.

On the one hand, cross-cultural theoretical studies are needed to identify basic human processes and to determine how these processes are affected by environmental conditions. At this level, comparative organization research has much in common with cultural anthropology (Evan, 1974-1975; Gillespie and Mileti, 1976; Udy, 1970) and cultural psychology (Berry and Dasen, 1974; DeVos and Hippler, 1969), among other disciplines and would gain by drawing upon these fields. Nonetheless, acquiring an understanding of basic processes is a difficult and long-term activity that at times may appear irrelevant and nonproductive. Systematic theoretical research must be supported, however, because it provides the knowledge that enables practitioners to anticipate and shape the directions in which organizations develop.

At the other end of the research continuum, pragmatic studies help managers understand and deal with their immediate situations (Hesseling, 1973). Such studies have a short-term focus. In the comparative management area, they have concentrated on the development of multinationals or the development of administrative and management capacities in industrializing nations. The weakness in much of this research is its tendency to accept some existing system as a norm. On the other hand, these studies supply important information to practitioners who cannot suspend decisions until the results of theoretical research are available. They also supply data on current practice. Thus, both pragmatic and theoretical research activities have critical roles in developing an understanding of sociocultural processes.

Theoretical and pragmatic studies could make important contributions to one another (Schöllhammer, 1973). Unfortunately, however, cooperative interactions between these efforts have not been characteristic in the past, except where the same researcher pursued both purposes (e.g., England, 1975; Negandhi and Prasad, 1971). The central data file recommended earlier is one way in which the data from applied research could be made readily available to theorists. In return, current conceptual schemes ought to be translated into guidelines identifying the types of information that should be sought in future descriptive and exploratory research. By following such guidelines, pragmatically oriented studies would be less biased by researchers' subjective views of reality. In addition, studies conducted in different settings by independent researchers would still provide comparable results and thereby contribute to a cumulative description of organizations throughout the world. Several such schemes have already been offered (Frew, 1977; Hesseling, 1973; Schöllhammer, 1969), but these need to be updated in the light of more recent knowledge, and their use should be more actively promoted.

The role of conceptual frameworks in the design of empirical research, including exploratory studies, is described in two recent methodological models (Grochla, 1977; Wind and Douglas, 1971). Wind and Douglas' explanation of how research objectives can be translated into valid designs is particularly helpful. The methodological problems in cross-cultural research have also been addressed from a variety of perspectives by other theorists (Bennett, 1977; Brislin et al., 1973; Cummings, Harnett, and Schmidt, 1972; Graves, 1970; Miller, 1972; Nath, 1968). In order to avoid the design problems prevalent in so many past studies, future research efforts should pay special heed to the advice available from such sources.

Because they have focused on the study of culture longer than any other group of scientists, anthropologists' insights deserve special attention (Etzioni and Dubow, 1970). Their clinical case study approach seems a particularly promising way of meeting the need for data that captures the complex interrelations in sociocultural processes. By combining this approach with a common conceptual and methodological framework for data gathering, single country studies could generate comparable cross-cultural data and thereby avoid some of the practical problems that arise in comparative studies. At the measurement level, several resarchers have also suggested some nonattitudinal indicators of culture, such as content of religious and ethical teachings (Beres and Portwood, 1979; Long and Seo, 1977; Robey, 1974); content of newspapers and magazines (Marquez, 1975); responses to socially ambiguous stimuli (Nelson and Jorgensen, 1975); and the uses made of physical space (Riemer, 1975). Development of these measures could lead to the macrolevel operationalizations of culture that are needed to determine culture's relative influence on macro- and micro-organizational properties. Thus, methodological resources have much to offer at both the design and measurement levels of empirical research. Wherever these contributions are relevant, they should be utilized to increase the rigor of future cross-cultural organizational research.

In conclusion, the primary recommendations emerging from this review are that (1) a central data file should be developed; (2) a clearing house for cross-national research should be established; (3) cross-cultural research should be designed by cross-national, cross-disciplinary research teams; (4) both theoretical and pragmatic research should be rigorously pursued, but with future efforts linked to one another; (5) conceptual frameworks should be developed and used to guide data-gathering activities; and (6) existing methodological resources should be used to improve the rigor of research designs. These suggestions seem reasonable in light of current practical, conceptual, and methodological problems in cross-national research. In promoting a more integrated approach to cross-cultural study, particular attention should be given to the research issues identified earlier — namely, development of an operationalizable definition of culture and clearer specification of culture's causal role.

The goal toward which this review attempts to contribute is a clearer understanding of sociocultural influences on organizations. Taken together, recent research suggests that nearly all currently studied social and ecological processes are involved in this influence in some way. This further implies that if cultural studies are broadly and rigorously pursued, they could provide a catalyst for a new synthesis in organization theory. At such a point, the conflict between convergence and pluralism theories becomes resolved into a universal theory of ethnocentrism (Wind and Douglas, 1971), and the research activity completes yet another cycle.

REFERENCES

Ajiferuke, M., and J. Boddewyn. 1970a. "Socioeconomic Indicators in Comparative Management." *Administrative Science Quarterly* 15, no. 4 (December): 453–58.

———. 1970b. "Culture and Other Explanatory Variables in Comparative Management Studies." *Academy of Management Journal* 13, no. 2 (June): 153–63.

Azumi, K., and C. J. McMillan. 1975. "Culture and Organization Structure: A Comparison of Japanese and British Organizations." *International Studies of Management and Organization* 5, no. 1 (Spring): 35–47.

Barrett, G. V., and B. M. Bass. 1970. "Comparative Surveys of Managerial Attitudes and Behavior." In J. Boddewyn, ed., *Comparative Management: Teaching Training and Research*, pp. 179–217. New York: Graduate School of Business Administration, New York University.

———. 1972. "Cross Cultural Issues in Industrial and Organizational Psychology." Rochester, N.Y.: Technical Report 45, Management Research Center, University of Rochester.

Bass, B. M., and L. D. Eldridge. 1973. "Accelerated Managers' Objectives in Twelve Countries." *Industrial Relations* 12, no. 2 (May): 158–71.

Bennett, M. 1977. "Response Characteristics of Bilingual Managers to Organizational Questionnaires." *Personnel Psychology* 31: 29–36.

Beres, M. E., and J. D. Portwood. 1979. "Explaining Cultural Differences in the Perceived Role of Work: An Intranational Cross Cultural Study." In G. England, A. Negandhi, and B. Wilpert, eds., *Organizational Functioning in a Cross Cultural Perspective*, pp. 139-74. Kent, Ohio: Kent State University Press.

Berrien, F. K. 1970. "A Super-Ego for Cross Cultural Research." *International Journal of Psychology* 5, no. 1: 33-39.

Berry, J. W., and P. R. Dasen. 1974. *Culture and Cognition: Readings in Cultural Psychology*. London: Methuen.

Bertrand, W. E. 1976. "Attitudinal Components of Changing Social Institutions: A Methodology for the Comparative Analysis of Social System Modernity." *Cornell Journal of Social Relations* 7, no. 1 (Spring): 79-86.

Beyer, J. M., and T. M. Lodahl. 1976. "A Comparative Study of Patterns of Influence in United States and English Universities." *Administrative Science Quarterly* 21, no. 1 (March): 104-29.

Boddewyn, J. 1973. "Ambiguous Relationship Between Culture and Organization: One-Way Relationship or Interdependency?" In A. Negandhi, ed., *Modern Organizational Theory*, pp. 319-22. Kent, Ohio: Kent State University Press.

———. ed. 1976. *European Industrial Managers: West and East*. White Plains, N.Y.: International Arts and Sciences Press.

Boddewyn, J., and R. Nath. 1970. "Comparative Management Studies: An Assessment." *Management International Review* 10, no. 1: 3-11.

Brislin, R. W. et al. 1973. *Cross Cultural Research Methods*. New York: John Wiley and Sons.

Brossard, M., and M. Maurice. 1976. "Is There a Universal Model of Organizational Structure?" *International Journal of Sociology* 6, no. 1 (Spring): 41-75.

Burger, P. C., and R. Doktor. 1976. "Cross Cultural Analysis of the Structure of Self Perception Attitudes Among Managers from India, Italy, West Germany and the Netherlands." *Management International Review* 16, no. 3: 71-78.

Cascio, W. F. 1974. "Functional Specialization, Culture and Preference for Participative Management." *Personnel Psychology* 27: 593-603.

Child, J. 1973. "Predicting and Understanding Organization Structure." *Administrative Science Quarterly* 18, no. 2 (June): 168-85.

Child, J., and A. Kieser. 1977. "Contrasts in British and West German Management Practice: Are Recipes for Success Culture Bound?" Paper presented at the Conference on Cross National Studies of Organizational Structure and Functioning, Honolulu, Hawaii, September.

Clark, A. W., and S. McCabe. 1970. "Leadership Beliefs of Australian Managers." *Journal of Applied Psychology* 54, no. 1 (February): 1-6.

Cole, R. E. 1971. *Japanese Blue Collar: The Changing Tradition*. Berkeley: University of California Press.

Crozier, M. 1973. "Cultural Determinants of Organizational Behavior." In A. Negandhi, ed., *Modern Organizational Theory*, pp. 219-28. Kent, Ohio: Kent State University Press.

Cummings, L. L., and S. M. Schmidt. 1972. "Managerial Attitudes of Greeks: The Roles of Culture and Industrialization." *Administrative Science Quarterly* 17, no. 2 (June): 265-72.

Cummings, L. L.; D. L. Harnett; and S. M. Schmidt. "International Cross Language Factor Stability of Personality: An Analysis of the Shure Meeker Personality/Attitude Schedule." *The Journal of Psychology* 82: 67-84.

Davis, S. M., and L. W. Goodman, eds. 1972. *Workers and Managers in Latin America*. Lexington, Mass.: D. C. Heath.

DeVos, G. A., and A. A. Hippler. 1969. "Cultural Psychology: Comparative Studies in Human Behavior." In Lindsey and Aronson, eds., *The Handbook of Social Psychology*, 2nd ed., vol. 4, pp. 323-417. Reading, Mass.: Addison-Wesley.

Dore, R. 1973. *British Factory — Japanese Factory: The Origins of National Diversity in Industrial Relations*. London: George Allen & Unwin.

Endruweit, G. 1979. "Relations Between Organizational Goals and Structure: A Comparison of German and U.S. Police Organizations." In G. England, A. Negandhi, and B. Wilpert, eds., *Organizational Functioning in a Cross Cultural Perspective*, pp. 225-50. Kent, Ohio: Kent State University Press.

England, G. W. 1975. *The Manager and His Values: An International Perspective from the United States, Japan, Korea, India and Australia*. Cambridge, Mass.: Ballinger.

England, G. W., and R. Koike. 1970. "Personal Value Systems of Japanese Managers." *Journal of Cross Cultural Psychology* 1, no. 1 (Spring): 21-40.

England, G. W., and R. Lee. 1971. "Organizational Goals and Expected Behavior Among American, Japanese and Korean Managers: A Comparative Study." *Academy of Management Journal* 14, no. 4: 425-38.

———. 1973. "Organizational Size as an Influence on Perceived Organizational Goals: A Comparative Study Among American, Japanese and Korean Managers." *Organizational Behavior and Human Performance* 9, no. 1: 48-58.

———. 1974. "The Relationship Between Managerial Values and Managerial Success in the United States, Japan, India and Australia." *Journal of Applied Psychology* 59, no. 4: 411-19.

England, G. W.; O. P. Dhingra; and N. C. Agarwal. 1974. "The Manager and the Man: A Cross Cultural Study of Personal Values." *Organization and Administrative Sciences* 5, no. 2 (Summer): 1-97.

Etzioni, A., and F. L. Dubow. 1970. *Comparative Perspectives: Theories and Methods*. Boston, Mass.: Little, Brown & Co.

Evan, W. M. 1974-1975. "Culture and Organizational Systems." *Organization and Administrative Sciences* 5, no. 4 (Winter): 1-16.

Farris, G. F., and D. A. Butterfield. 1972. "Control Theory in Brazilian Organizations." *Administrative Science Quarterly* 17, no. 4 (December): 574-85.

Ferrari, S. 1974. "Cross Cultural Management Literature in France, Italy and Spain." *Management International Review* 14, nos. 4 and 5: 17-26.

Form, W. H. 1969. "Occupation and Social Integration of Automobile Workers in Four Countries: A Comparative Study." *International Journal of Comparative Sociology* 10, nos. 1 and 2: 95-116.

———. 1972. "Technology and Social Behavior of Workers in Four Countries: A Sociotechnical Perspective." *American Sociological Review* 37: 727-38.

Frew, D. R. 1977. "Organization Theory Development in England: The Conceptual Framework of Pugh." *Management International Review* 17, no. 3: 37-43.

Franko, L. A. 1974. "The Move Toward a Multidivisional Structure in European Organizations." *Administrative Science Quarterly* 19: 493-506.

Frost, P. J., and D. C. Hayes. 1979. "An Exploration in Two Cultures of Political Behavior in Organizations." In G. England, A. Negandhi, B. Wilpert, eds., *Organizational Functioning in a Cross Cultural Perspective.* Kent, Ohio: Kent State University Press.

Gillespie, D. F., and D. S. Mileti. 1976. "Organizational Adaptations to Changing Cultural Contingencies." *Sociological Inquiry* 46, no. 2: 135-41.

Glaser, W. A. 1971. "Cross National Comparisons of the Factory." *Journal of Comparative Administration* 3, no. 1: 83-117.

Goldberg, W. H. 1977. "Tripartite Study into 'Organizations in Crises' — Some Observations." Paper presented at the Conference on Cross National Studies of Organizational Structure and Functioning, Honolulu, Hawaii, September.

Goldman, P., and D. R. Van Houten. 1977. "Managerial Strategies and the Worker: A Marxist Analysis of Bureaucracy." *The Sociological Quarterly* 18, no. 1 (Winter): 108-25.

Goodman, P. S., and B. E. Moore. 1972. "Critical Issues of Cross Cultural Management Research." *Human Organization* 31, no. 1 (Spring): 39-45.

Granick, D. 1972. *Managerial Comparisons of Four Developed Countries: France, Britain, U. S. and Russia.* Cambridge, Mass.: MIT Press.

Graves, D. 1972. "The Impact of Culture Upon Managerial Attitudes, Beliefs, and Behavior in England and France." *Journal of Management Studies* 9: 40-56.

———, ed. 1970. *Management Research: A Cross Cultural Perspective.* San Francisco: Jossey-Bass.

Graves, D., and P. Hesseling. "Towards a Centre of Cross Cultural Studies." In D. Graves, ed., *Management Research: A Cross Cultural Perspective,* pp. 323-36. San Francisco: Jossey-Bass.

Grochla, E. 1977. "Organization Theory: Present State of the Science and Actual Challenges — An Analysis with Special Regard to the Development in the German-speaking Countries." *Management International Review* 17, no. 3: 19-36.

Gruenfeld, L. W., and A. E. MacEachron. 1975. "A Cross National Study of Cognitive Style Among Managers and Technicians." *International Journal of Psychology* 10, no. 1: 27-55.

Gvishiani, D. M. 1972. *Organization and Management: A Sociological Analysis of Western Theories.* Moscow: Progress.

Haire, M.; E. E. Ghiselli; and L. W. Porter. 1966. *Managerial Thinking: An International Study.* New York: John Wiley.

Hall, E. T. 1959. *The Silent Language.* New York: Doubleday.

Harrell, T. W. 1971. "Some Needs of Iran Managers." *Personnel Psychology* 24: 477-79.

Heginbotham, S. J. 1975. *Cultures in Conflict: The Four Faces of Indian Bureaucracy.* New York: Columbia University Press.

Heller, F. A. 1973. "Leadership, Decision-Making and Contingency Theory." *Industrial Relations* 12, no. 2 (May): 183-99.

Heller, F. A., and B. Wilpert. 1977. "Limits to Participative Leadership: Task, Structure and Skill as Contingencies — A German-British Comparison." *European Journal of Social Psychology* 7, no. 1: 61-84.

——. 1979. "Managerial Decision-Making: An International Comparison." In G. England, A. Negandhi, and B. Wilpert, eds., *Organizational Functioning in a Cross Cultural Perspective*, pp. 49-71. Kent, Ohio: Kent State University Press.

Hesseling, P. 1971. "Organizational Behavior and Culture: The Case of the Multinational Enterprise." *Quarterly Journal of Management Development* 2, no. 3 (March): 1-23.

——. 1973. "Studies in Cross Cultural Organization." *Columbia Journal of World Business* 8, no. 4 (Winter): 120-34.

Hickson, D. J. et al. 1979. "The Culture-Free Context of Organization Structure: A Tri-National Comparison." *Sociology* 8, no. 1 (January): 59-80.

Hofstede, G., and S. Kassem, eds. 1976. *European Contributions to Organization Theory.* Amsterdam: Van Gorcum.

Huff, T. E. 1974. "Is a Theory of Sociocultural Process Possible without Reference to Civilization Complexes?" *Social Analysis* 35, no. 2 (Summer): 85-94.

Inkeles, A., and D. J. Levinson. 1969. "National Character: The Study of Modal Personality and Sociocultural Systems." In Lindsey and Aronson, eds., *The Handbook of Social Psychology*, 2nd ed., vol. 4, pp. 418-506. Reading, Mass.: Addison-Wesley.

Inkson, J. H. K. et al. 1970. "Organization Context and Structure: An Abbreviated Replication." *Administrative Science Quarterly* 15, no. 3 (September): 318-26.

International Research Group. 1977. "Industrial Democracy in Europe (IDE): An International Comparative Study." *Social Science Information* 15, no. 1: 177-203.

Kaplan, P. F., and C. H. Huang. 1976. "The Individual Modernity of Filipino Small-Scale Industrial Workers." *Economic Development and Cultural Change* 24, no. 4 (July): 499-514.

Kassem, S. 1977. "Organization Theory: American and European Styles." *Management International Review* 17, no. 3: 11-18.

Kelley, L., and C. Reeser. 1973. "The Persistence of Culture as a Determinant of Differential Attitudes on the Part of American Managers of Japanese Ancestry." *Academy of Management Journal* 16, no. 1 (March): 67-76.

Krus, D. J., and J. A. Rysberg. 1976. "Industrial Managers and n Ach: Comparable and Compatible?" *Journal of Cross Cultural Psychology* 7, no. 4 (December): 491-96.

Kumar, U., and K. K. Singh. 1976. "The Interpersonal Construct System of the

Indian Manager: A Determinant of Organizational Behavior." *Indian Journal of Psychology* 51, no. 4: 275-90.

Lenski, G. 1976. "The Need for Reader Access to the Measures of Variables Used in Quantitative Cross National Studies (Comment on Jackman)." *American Sociological Review* 41, no. 4 (August): 751.

Long, W. A., and K. K. Seo. 1977. *Management in Japan and India — With Reference to the United States.* New York: Praeger.

Marquez, F. T. 1975. "The Relationship of Advertising and Culture in the Philippines." *Journalism Quarterly* 52, no. 3 (August): 436-42.

Maruyama, M. 1974. "Paradigmotology and its Application to Cross Disciplinary, Cross-Professional and Cross Cultural Communication." *Dialectica* 28, nos. 3 and 4: 135-96.

McMillan, C. J. et al. 1973. "The Structure of Work Organizations Across Societies." *Academy of Management Journal* 16, no. 4 (December): 555-69.

Miller, D. C. 1972. "Measuring Cross National Norms." *International Journal of Comparative Sociology* 13, nos. 3 and 4: 201-16.

Moore, R. 1974. "The Cross Cultural Study of Organizational Behavior." *Human Organization* 33, no. 1 (Spring): 37-45.

Murdock, G. P. 1957. "World Ethnographic Sample." *American Anthropologist* 59: new series no. 14: 664-87.

———. 1965. *Culture and Society.* Pittsburgh: University of Pittsburgh Press.

Nath, R. 1968. "A Methodological Review of Cross Cultural Management Research." *International Social Science Journal* 20: 35-62.

———. 1970. "Proposition-Building and Other Methodological Issues in Comparative Management." In J. Boddewyn, ed., *Comparative Management: Teaching, Training and Research*, pp. 137-59. New York: Graduate School of Business Administration, New York University.

———. 1977. "Comparative Management and Organizational Theory: Linking the Two." *Columbia Journal of World Business* 12, no. 2 (Summer): 115-24.

Negandhi, A. 1973a. "A Model for Analyzing Organization in Cross Cultural Settings: A Conceptual Scheme and Some Research Findings." In A. Negandhi, ed., *Modern Organizational Theory*, pp. 285-312. Kent, Ohio: Kent State University Press.

———. 1973b. *Management and Economic Development: The Case of Taiwan.* The Hague: Martinus Nijhoff.

———. 1974a. "Cross Cultural Management Studies: Too Many Conclusions, Not Enough Conceptualization." *Management International Review* 14, no. 6: 59-67.

———. 1974b. "A Cross Cultural Comparative Study of Management." *Omega: The International Journal of Management Science* 2, no. 6: 785-91.

———. 1975. "Comparative Management and Organization Theory: A Marriage Needed." *Academy of Management Journal* 18, no. 2 (June): 334-44.

Negandhi, A., and S. B. Prasad. *Comparative Management.* New York: Appleton-Century-Crofts.

Negandhi, A., and B. C. Reimann. 1971. "Task Environment and Some Structural Characteristics: A Cross Cultural Study." *Quarterly Journal of Management Journal* 2, no. 3 (March): 39-52.

———. 1972. "A Contingency Theory of Organization Re-examined in the Context of a Developing Country." *Academy of Management Journal* 15, no 2 (June): 137-46.

———. 1973. "Correlates of Decentralization: Closed and Open System Perspectives." *Academy of Management Journal* 16, no. 4: 570-82.

Nelson, J. L., and C. L. Jorgensen. 1975. "The Green Bag: The Uses of Ambiguity in Eliciting Covert Cultural Assumptions." *Human Organization* 34, no. 1 (Spring): 59-61.

Nightingale, D. V., and J. M. Toulouse. 1977. "Values, Structure, Process, and Reactions/Adjustment: A Comparison of French and English-Canadian Industrial Organizations." *Canadian Journal of Behavioral Science* 9, no. 1: 37-48.

Obradovic, J. 1975. "Workers' Participation: Who Participates?" *Industrial Relations* 14, no. 1 (February): 32-44.

Orpen, C. 1976. "Job Enlargement, Individual Differences, and Worker Responses." *Journal of Cross Cultural Psychology* 7, no. 4 (December): 473-80.

Pavan, R. J. 1976. "Strategy and Structure: the Italian Experience." *Journal of Economics and Business* 28, no. 3 (Spring-Summer): 254-60.

Peterson, R. B. 1975. "The Interaction of Technological Process and Perceived Organizational Climate in Ten Norwegian Firms." *Academy of Management Journal* 18, no. 2: 288-99.

———. 1976. "A Cross Cultural Study of Secondary School Teachers' Attitudes Regarding Job Satisfaction, Professionalism and Collective Negotiations (Sweden and State of Washington)." *Journal of Collective Negotiations* 5, no. 2: 113-24.

Poblador, N. S. 1975. "The Structure of Authority and the Distribution of Rewards in Philippine and American Banks." *International Studies in Management and Organization* 5, no. 1 (Spring): 48-67.

Redding, G., and T. Casey. 1976. "Managerial Beliefs Among Asian Managers." In *Academy of Management Proceedings, 36th Annual Meeting.* August.

Reimann, B. C. 1973. "On the Dimensions of Bureaucratic Structure: An Empirical Reappraisal." *Administrative Science Quarterly* 18, no. 4 (December).

———. 1974. "Task Environment and Decentralization: A Cross National Replication." *Human Relations* 27, no. 7: 677-95.

Riemer, J. W. 1975. "A Typology of Work Settings: A Model for Comparative Analysis." *Human Mosaic* 9, no. 1 (Fall): 33-41.

Roberts, K. H. 1970. "On Looking at an Elephant: An Evaluation of Cross Cultural Research Related to Organizations." *Psychological Bulletin* 74: 327-50.

Robey, D. 1974. "Cultural and Environmental Determinants of Worker Response: A Research Model." *Management International Review* 14, nos. 2 and 3: 75-83.

Ronen, S., and A. I. Kraut. 1977. "Similarities Among Countries Based on Employee Work Values and Attitudes." *Columbia Journal of World Business* 12, no. 2 (Summer): 89-96.

Rosner, M. et al. 1973. "Worker Participation and Influence in Five Countries." *Industrial Relations* 12, no. 2 (May): 200-12.

Ruedi, A., and P. R. Lawrence. 1970. "Organizations in Two Cultures." In J. W. Lorsch and P. R. Lawrence, eds., *Studies in Organizational Design*, pp. 54-83. Homewood, Ill.: Irwin and Dorsey Press.

Ryterband, E. C., and G. V. Barrett. 1970. "Managers' Values and Their Relationship to the Management of Tasks: A Cross Cultural Comparison." In B. M. Bass et al., eds., *Managing for Accomplishment*, pp. 226-61. Lexington, Mass.: Lexington Books.

Schöllhammer, H. 1969. "The Comparative Management Theory Jungle." *Academy of Management Journal* 12, no. 1 (March): 81-97.

———. 1973. "Strategies and Methodologies in International Business and Comparative Management Research." *Management International Review* 13, no. 6: 17-32.

———. 1975. "Current Research in International and Comparative Management Issues." *Management International Review* 15, nos. 2 and 3: 29-45.

Schuh, A. J. 1974. "An Alternative Questionnaire Strategy for Conducting Cross Cultural Research on Managerial Attitudes." *Personnel Psychology* 27: 95-102.

Shapira, Z., and B. M. Bass. 1974. "Settling Strikes in Real Life and Simulations in North America and Different Regions of Europe." *Journal of Applied Psychology* 27: 95-102.

Sim, A. B. 1977. "Decentralized Management of Subsidiaries and Their Performance: A Comparative Study of American, British and Japanese Subsidiaries in Malaysia." *Management International Review* 17, no. 2: 45-51.

Simonetti, J. L., and F. G. Boseman. 1975. "The Impact of Market Competition on Organization Structure and Effectiveness: A Cross-Cultural Study." *Academy of Management Journal* 18, no. 3 (September): 631-37.

Simonetti, J. L., and F. L. Simonetti. 1974. "The Impact of Management Policy and Organization Structure on the Management Effectiveness of Firms Operating in Italy." *Journal of Economics and Business* 27, no. 28 (Fall): 249-53.

———. 1977. "American and Italian Management Policy Toward Task Environment Agents: Is There a Difference?" *Management International Review* 17, no. 1: 77-87.

Simonetti, J. L., and J. Weitz. 1972. "Job Satisfaction: Some Cross Cultural Effects." *Personnel Psychology* 25: 107-18.

Slocum, J. W., Jr. 1971. "A Comparative Study of the Satisfaction of American and Mexican Operatives." *Academy of Management Journal* 14, no. 1 (March): 89-91.

Slocum, J. W., and P. M. Topichak. 1972. "Do Cultural Differences Affect Job Satisfaction?" *Journal of Applied Psychology* 56, no. 2: 177-87.

Slocum, J. W. et al. 1971. "A Cross Cultural Study of Need Satisfaction and Need Importance for Operative Employees." *Personnel Psychology* 24: 435-45.

Smith, B. E., and J. M. Thomas. 1972. "Managers: A Case Study." *Sloan Management Review* 13, no. 3: 35-51.

Suryadinata, L. 1976. "Ethnicity and National Integration in Indonesia: An Analysis." *Asia Quarterly* 3: 209-34.

Tannenbaum, A. S. et al. 1974. *Hierarchy in Organizations*. San Francisco: Jossey-Bass.

Thomis, M. J. 1976. *Responses to Industrialization: The British Experience*. Hamden, Conn.: Archer Books.

Tracy, P., and K. Azumi. 1976. "Determinants of Administrative Control: A Test of a Theory with Japanese Factories." *American Sociological Review* 4 (February): 80-94.

Triandis, H. C. 1975. "Social Psychology and Cultural Analysis." *Journal for the Theory of Social Behavior* 5, no. 1: 81-106.

Triandis, H. C., and V. Vassilou. 1972. "Interpersonal Influence and Employee Selection in Two Cultures." *Journal of Applied Psychology* 6, no. 2: 140-45.

Triandis, H. C. et al. 1972. *The Analysis of Subjective Culture*. New York: John Wiley.

———. 1973. "Psychology and Culture." In P. H. Mussen and M. R. Rosenzweig, eds., *Annual Review of Psychology*, vol. 24, pp. 355-78.

Udy, S. 1965. "The Comparative Analysis of Organizations." In J. G. March, ed., *Handbook of Organizations*, pp. 678-709. Chicago: Rand-McNally.

———. 1970. "The Development of Differentiation in Organized Work." In J. W. Lorsch and P. R. Lawrence, eds., *Studies in Organizational Design*, pp. 101-12. Homewood, Ill.: Irwin and Dorsey Press.

Whitely, W.; and G. W. England. 1977. "Managerial Values as a Reflection of Culture and the Process of Industrialization." *Academy of Management Journal* 20, no. 3 (September): 439-53.

Whiting, J. W. M. 1968. "Methods and Problems in Cross Cultural Research." In Lindsey and Aronson, eds., *The Handbook of Social Psychology*, 2nd ed., vol. 2, pp. 693-728. Reading, Mass.: Addison-Wesley.

Wind, Y., and S. Douglas. 1971. "On the Meaning of Comparison: A Methodology for Cross Cultural Studies." *Quarterly Journal of Management Development* 2, no. 4 (June): 105-21.

Wright, R. W. 1971. "Organizational Ambiente: Management and Environment in Chile." *Academy of Management Journal* 14, no. 1 (March): 65-74.

Zimbalist, A. 1975. "The Dynamic of Worker Participation: An Interpretative Essay on the Chilean and Other Experiences." *Administration and Society* 7, no. 1 (May): 43-55.

Zupanov, J. 1973. "Two Patterns of Conflict Management in Industry." *Industrial Relations* 12, no. 2 (May): 213-23.

Zwerman, W. L. 1970. *New Perspectives on Organization Theory*. Westport, Conn.: Greenwood.

Chapter 12

Organizational Research: Needed Steps for Future Studies

George W. England,* Anant R. Negandhi,** and Bernhard Wilpert‡

In the preceding chapters, we presented eleven papers, summarizing and analyzing major conceptual orientations and empirical findings concerning the functioning of organizations at four different levels — individual, group, organizational, and societal. In so doing, our aim was to integrate the impact of these four level variables on the overall functioning of complex organizations. More specifically, the levels and subtopics considered were:

1. Individual Level
   a. Competence Potential: The area included the individual's aptitude, ability, skill, education, training, and experience as they relate to the organizational functioning. (Chapter 1)
   b. Motivational Potential: This area covered motivation theories and empirical research studies concerning motivation aspects, including values, needs, and expectations. (Chapters 2, 3, and 4)
2. Group Level
   a. Intergroup Bargaining Processes and Decisionmaking: This area covered the impact of organizational roles, information

* University of Oklahoma
** University of Illinois
‡ Science Center Berlin

and resource control means, and the dynamics of subunit interactions and their impact on organizational decision making processes. (Chapter 5)

b. Governance of Organization and Leader-Led Roles: The area covered the governance systems and changes occurring in such systems. (Chapters 6 and 7)

3. Organizational Level

a. Task and Technological Aspects: The area covered the impact of task structure and technology on organizational functioning. (Chapter 9)

b. Interorganizational Dependence and Influences: The area explored the theoretical and conceptual developments in the interorganizational field and sought the impact of interorganizational dependency on organizational functioning. (Chapter 10)

4. Societal Level

a. Political Factors: The area covered the impact of political factors on organizational governance (leadership) and on overall organizational functioning. (Chapter 8)

b. Sociocultural Factors: The area covered the theoretical and conceptual developments in cross-cultural organizational studies. (Chapter 11)

In an attempt to integrate the above diverse levels in the overall functioning of complex organizations, we provided an overall concept of organizational functioning as dependent variable(s). We conceived organizational functioning in terms of structuring, organization design processes and mechanisms, and organizational performance variables. The authors of the various chapters were asked to relate their specific independent concepts and variables to the above concept of organizational functioning. As stated, our intent was not only to seek an understanding of how each level of independent variables affects the overall functioning of organizations, but also to examine the interlocking of various parts of subsystems and how this interconnectedness affects the working of a system as a whole.

PURPOSE OF THIS CHAPTER

The main purpose of this chapter is to highlight some of the problems we face at the present juncture in organizational studies in achieving the cross-level integration outlined above. These comments and suggestions are not contrived as criticism on any specific points presented in the preceding chapters. They are simply an attempt to chart a map of activities that await our attention as we move into new and challenging horizons in studying complex organizations.

THE SYSTEMS JARGONS, BUT CONCERN FOR SIMPLE CAUSATION

It is obvious that in spite of serious attempts made by the various authors in integrating their specific area variables with other area variables within an organizational system in the overall functioning of complex organizations, such attempts merely pinpoint the excessive levels of specialization of organizational researchers. In other words, although the jargons and concepts of systems and the systems' frameworks are often articulated by scholars working at different levels of organizational phenomena — individual, group, organization, society — the actual focus utilized in various organizational studies reported in this volume and elsewhere is either at a subsystem level or a small component of a given subsystem. Moreover, in actual conduct of the specific studies, the overwhelming concern exhibited is the discovery of causal relationships between two or more sets of variables. And yet, we all know very well that the most differentiating characteristic of a system is the pattern of relationships and not the simple bivariate causal relationships.

Although Scott, some twenty-three years later, seemed convinced time in the field of organization theory, the applications of systems concepts in studying the organizational life is long in coming. For example, Barnard, in 1938, used a basic concept of systems in explaining the functions of the executive. He stated: "A cooperative system is a complex of physical, biological, personal and social components which are in a systematic relationship by reason of the cooperation of two or more persons for at least one definite end. Such a system is evidently a subordinate unit of larger systems . . . ." (p. 65).

Although Scott, some twenty-three years later, seemed convinced that the modern organization theorist had succeeded in comprehending and utilizing systems framework, the progress evidenced in various organizational studies reported in this volume and elsewhere casts serious doubts on both our desire and ability to do so. Writing in 1961, Scott stated:

The distinctive qualities of modern organization theory are its conceptual-analytical base, its reliance on empirical research data, and above all, its integrating nature. These qualities are framed in a philosophy which accepts the premise that the only meaningful way to study organization is to study it as a system . . . . (P. 15)

He further states: "Modern organization theory and general system theory are similar in that they look at organizations as an integrated whole" (p. 21).

Has the prophecy or wishful thinking of Scott and other systems thinkers proven right? Are we now pursuing in our studies a range of interrelated questions as Scott then thought we were asking, such as:

(a) What are the strategic parts of the system?
(b) What is the nature of their mutual dependency?
(c) What are the main processes in the system which link the parts together, and facilitate their adjustment to each other?
(d) What are the goals sought by the systems? (P. 15)

As the reader can judge from the review of studies at various levels of the organizational phenomenon presented in this volume, we have definitely become more conceptual and analytical, and our studies are more empirically based, but our inquiry still remains at subsystem levels. To put it differently, as Kast and Rosenzweig echoed in 1972:

Even though we preach a general systems approach, we often practice subsystems thinking. Each of the academic disciplines and each of us personally has a limited perspective of the system we are studying. While proclaiming a broad systems viewpoint, we often dismiss variables outside our interest or competence as being irrelevant, and we only open our system to those inputs which we can handle with our disciplinary bag of tools. (P. 454)

Put simply, to comprehend the overall functioning of complex organizations in systems of networks, researchers have to pay attention to cross-level influences and the impact of variables existing within a given layer as well as those outside of one's chosen layer of the organizational phenomenon. This may itself require a shift from a bivariate causation orientation to a multiple causation investigation. Our conceptual and theoretical models, in his regard, have to be of a multivariate type. Given the discipline and overspecialized orientations of many of us in the organization theory area, it may thus require teamwork of an interdisciplinary type, if we have to change our present focus to a systems framework.

In recent years, some researchers have indeed addressed the above problems and made a useful beginning in constructing multivariate models. A case in point is the recent framework provided by Melcher. As shown in Table 12-1, Melcher's (1973) conceptual scheme has identified both structural and process variables affecting organiza-

Table 12-1.   Structural-Behavioral Model

A.   Primary Structural Variables

1. Size	Small	to	Large
2. Workflow	Nonintegrated	to	Integrated
3. Work demands	Stable	to	Unstable
4. Spatial-physical-temporal factors	Concentrated	to	Dispersed
5. Heuristics	Programmed	to	Unprogrammed

B.   Mediating Structural Variables

1. Formal authority relationships	Diffuse	to	Specific
a. Departmentation	Autonomous	to	Interdependent
b. Delegation	Decentralized	to	Centralized
c. Levels	Few	to	Many
2. Control systems	Institutional	to	Individual
a. Standards	Undefined	to	Defined
b. Measurement	Ad hoc	to	Formal
c. Rewards-sanctions	Institutional	to	Individual
3. Information system	Spontaneous	to	Rationalized
a. Networks (linkage)	Complete	to	Single
b. Channel density (means)	Single	to	Multiple
c. Speed (time)	Real	to	Delayed
d. Storage-retrieval	Limited	to	Extensive

C.   Leadership Dimensions

1. Representation	Downward	to	Upward
2. Interactions	Vertical	to	Lateral
3. Standards	Low	to	High
4. Participation	Low	to	High
5. Goals	Group	to	Individual
6. Direction	Loose	to	Tight
7. Rule adherence	Low	to	High
8. Motivation	Rewards	to	Sanctions
9. Technical	Limited	to	Extensive
10. Action	Passive	to	Active
11. Problem skills	Limited	to	Extensive
12. Personal abilities	Emotional	to	Nonemotional

D.   Personality

1. Independence	Dependent	to	Independent
2. Authoritarianism	Autocratic	to	Nonautocratic

Source: Melcher (1973).

tional functioning. These include size, workflow (technology), work demands (environmental variables), spatial-physical-temporal factors, and heuristics as primary organizational context variables. His mediating structural variables include factors concerning formal authority relationships (departmentation, delegation, levels of hierarchy) and control and information subsystems variables. At the individual level, the model includes personality variables and the individual's skills and abilities. At the intra- and intergroup levels, he has included many of the variables generally considered in the leadership studies (e.g., kinds of representation, interaction, participation, direction, etc.).

Melcher's conceptual scheme and his initial operationalization of variables are exhibited in Tables 12-1 and 12-2. Although Melcher and his colleagues have made some attempts to test this model, greater efforts are needed both to refine such a model and to conduct empirical studies. Particularly, his model still ignores many of the environmental and sociocultural factors affecting organizational functioning.

Table 12-2. Behavioral Profile

	1	2	3	4	5	6	7	8	9
Individual Behavior									
1. Job Involvement	Low							High	
2. Commitment to standards	Rarely							Almost always	
3. Job initiative	Little							High	
4. Self-improvement	Little							High	
5. Work goal commitment	Rarely							Almost always	
6. Sense of frustration	Almost always							Rarely	
7. Sense of achievement	Rarely							Almost always	
8. Absenteeism	Almost always							Rarely	
9. Turnover	Almost always							Rarely	
Group Relations Lateral									
10. Confidence and trust	Rarely							Almost always	
11. Job-related communication	Rarely							Almost always	
12. Non-job-related communication	Rarely							Almost always	

Table 12-2. (continued)

	1	2	3	4	5	6	7	8	9
13. Cooperation patterns	Rarely								Almost always
14. Group unity	Rarely								Almost always
15. Interaction off the job	Rarely								Almost always

Group Relations: Vertical

	1	2	3	4	5	6	7	8	9
16. Trust downward	Rarely								Almost always
17. Trust upward	Rarely								Almost always
18. Flow of requested information upward	Almost always								Rarely
19. Communication screening	Almost always								Rarely
20. Job information	Rarely								Almost always
21. Human relations information	Rarely								Almost always
22. Cooperation and teamwork	Rarely								Almost always
23. Acceptance of immediate superior's decisions	Rarely								Very often
24. Acceptance of higher level decisions	Rarely								Very often
25. Acceptance of staff decisions	Rarely								Very often

Intergroup Relations: Lateral

	1	2	3	4	5	6	7	8	9
26. Confidence and trust	Rarely								Almost always
27. Communications accuracy	Rarely								Almost always
28. Communications screening	Almost always								Rarely
29. Social communications	Almost always								Rarely
30. Cooperation	Rarely								Almost always
31. Team spirit	Rarely								Almost always
32. Acceptance of decisions	Rarely								Almost always
33. Interaction patterns	Rarely								Almost always

Source: Melcher (1973).

In this volume itself, some of the authors, especially Hall (Chapter 5) and Koenig, (Chapter 10), have made useful attempts toward utilizing a systems framework. More recent European studies take important steps in the direction of systematically including national environment and sociocultural factors in studies of organizations. One example is the study by Maurice, Sorge, and Warner (1980), where the analytic framework comprises national traditions and educational systems of three European countries and their specific relationships to organizational structures of manufacturing units. Another example is the IDE (1980a, b) study of industrial democracy in Europe, which scrutinizes the impact of national industrial democracy schemes of twelve countries on the distribution of power and influence within industrial establishments.

IT IS EASIER SAID THAN DONE

We recognize that the plea for utilizing a systems framework is easier to make than to practice. Time, money, and personal resources in terms of our specialized discipline-oriented training are indeed real factors that play an important role in what we do at the present time — that is, our continued reliance on variables within a given level (individual, group, organizational, or societal) and our concentration on establishing bivariate causation between variables lying within a given level. However, if we are to comprehend the total functioning of complex organizations, a change in our present focus is an absolute necessity. In the preceding pages, our intention was to highlight some of the limitations of our current approach in conducting organizational studies. In the following pages, we will briefly outline some of the steps necessary to change our current focus.

As Melcher (1973:4) has indicated, a number of factors have inhibited the development and use of systems framework. These are:

1. The limited critical dialogue among systems adherents and those utilizing traditional perspectives.
2. The diffuseness of definitions of many systems and general systems concepts, such as holism, open systems, system boundaries, negative entropy, steady state, dynamic equilibrium, and so forth.
3. The lack of operationalization for the above systems' concepts.
4. The overreaching of goals before basic foundations have been established.
5. The difficulty of developing a methodology to describe and analyze complex interrelationships in dynamic models.

Beyond removing the above limitations to successfully utilizing a systems framework, we also need to pay attention to our existing preoccupation with respect to (1) present overemphasis on structural versus functional or process approach, (2) present bias concerning our modus operandi in studying organizations, and (3) reliance on traditional variables as dependent variables.

STRUCTURAL VERSUS FUNCTIONAL APPROACH

The examination of empirical and conceptual studies of organizations reveals a preponderance of concern for the structural approach. Many sociological studies emphasizing this aspect can be traced to the original insights provided by Weber (1947). Since the time that Weber formulated his concept of bureaucracy, many refinements have been made in the original bureaucracy concept. Yet to date, not much has been done to utilize this concept as a variable in the empirical study of organizations. As Pugh and his colleagues have noted:

> All the studies appear to regard bureaucracy as a unitary concept . . . . Surprisingly little work has been devoted to an examination of [bureaucratic] characteristics with a view to reifying and developing the concept . . . . The literature has also lacked empirical studies of bureaucracy as a *structural* variable applied to organizations, in spite of the many studies that stress the continuous growth of bureaucratic forms. (1963:295-96)

All social organizations are basically purposive and goal-directed systems. It is therefore necessary to specifically identify both the intrinsic and extrinsic functions of a given organization and then to examine the consequences of a particular structural arrangement on the achievement of these functions. As Pugh and his colleagues have noted, "The empirical study of the structure of an organization cannot be carried out except in relation to its functioning. Its structure is indeed a construct derived from its activities" (p. 300).

Of course, a number of scholars have provided typologies that can be extremely useful in linking structural variables with the functions of organizations. To cite a few examples, Gouldner (1954) has classified the bureaucracy into three ideal types — mock, punishment centered, and representative. Similarly, Etzioni (1964) has classified social organizations on the basis of their predominant pattern of compliance, which includes coercive, utilitarian, and normative.

With respect to the function of organizations, Bakke (1966) has provided the generalized description of the process of work organization that is shown in Table 12-3. Similarly, Wofford (1967) has attempted to classify personal qualities of individuals and to link those qualities to given tasks and goals of organizations. Although his functional classification scheme closely resembles those of the so-called classical management theorists (i.e., planning and setting objectives, organizing, leading, controlling, etc.), his attempts to link those functions with the personal qualities of individuals and the types of goals organizations strive to achieve is indeed novel and thoughtful.

In summary, despite a useful beginning toward functionalism (or the functional approach), organization theorists have generally shown little concern for linking structural variables with the functions, activities, and goals of organizations. This has made our discipline very restrictive in explaining and predicting the total workings of social organizations. Our knowledge about organizational functioning at the present time is perhaps too narrow to identify nonfunctional organizations in the social system that have ceased to contribute to social needs but still operate. Another serious limitation in current studies is the lack of concern for establishing relevant linkages

Table 12-3. Processes of Work Organizations

Process	Definition	Organizational Activity
Identification	Developing, legitimatizing, and symbolizing the organization charter	
Perpetuation	Acquiring, maintaining, transforming, and developing basic resources	Thoughtways (ideas), personnel (people), services (material), finance (money), conservation (nature), cultivation (operational field)
Workflow	Producing and distributing output	Production, distribution
Control	Directing, coordinating, stimulating, regulating, appraising, and clarifying all operations	Direction, motivation, evaluation, communication
Homeostatic	Preserving the integrity of the organization in an evolving state of dynamic equilibrium	Fusion, leadership, problem solving, legitimization

Source: Bakke, 1966.

between organizational variables. In other words, the question of "structure for what" has not been adequately raised. Researchers have stopped short by considering structural variables as the ultimate dependent variables. Hence, structural properties have not been systematically linked to such important variables as human resource utilization, behavior patterns, and measures of organizational effectiveness. Indeed, very few studies attempt such linkage.

MODUS OPERANDI

One basic premise underlying the development of various organization theories is that conflict is harmful and dysfunctional in achieving organizational objectives and therefore should be avoided. Conversely, cooperation and harmony among different subsystems and/or individuals and groups are useful for the effective functioning of an organization. The origin of this basic assumption can be traced to the thoughts of Marx (1906) at the societal level, and to Follet (1918) and Mayo (1946) at the organizational level.

Perhaps because of this premise, much effort has been devoted to the issue of managing and controlling conflict and fostering cooperation and harmony between different units and/or individuals and groups in an organization. At the same time, we have made little effort to understand the dynamics of conflict and its creative role in achieving organizational goals and objectives.

Of course, many organization theorists might agree with Caplow that the destructive and dysfunctional aspects of interunit and intergroup conflict should be minimized. As he has stated:

> Since organizations are sub-divisible, self-maintenance always involves protections against those forms of internal divisions which threaten the existence of the whole . . . . many organizations encourage conflict under the name of competition . . . . spontaneous and unregulated conflict, however, is a direct threat to the organization's existence. (1957:113)

Notwithstanding the validity of such arguments, a number of other studies, such as those by Baker, Dembo, and Lewin (1941), Goldstein (1951), Allport (1953), Rogers (1959), and Abell (1975) do indicate that a certain degree of conflict, tension, and frustration within and between individuals and groups may actually increase creativity, innovation, satisfaction, performance, and effectiveness.

Without taking a specific viewpoint on either side of the fence, it is necessary to note that conflict per se is a reality for many social organizations. It is therefore necessary to treat this aspect in a more realistic manner when building our theories about organizational functioning.

NEW AND RELEVANT DEPENDENT VARIABLES IN ORGANIZATIONAL STUDIES

Our preoccupation with establishing harmony and cooperation in an organization has led us to utilizing harmony-related dependent variables as measures of organizational effectiveness. Such dependent variables as absenteeism, turnover, employee morale, alienation from work, and interdepartmental relationships have been accepted as "universal" variables without much questioning or scrutiny. Hence, they have been applied to studies of different social organizations pursuing different goals and objectives and operating in different time and space horizons. This tendency to "universalize" dependent variables indeed puts us back, both in time and perspective, and acts as an inhibiting force in the search for more relevant dependent variables more appropriate for a specific context.

For example, given the contingencies created by labor contracts and other social forces, many industrial as well as nonindustrial organizations may not have much option in reducing manpower as they see fit. Yet the market for their products and services may have reached a saturation point. In such a situation, high absenteeism and turnover may be an advantage. However, the organization theorist, hoping to reduce absenteeism and turnover with his traditional value of maintaining harmonious relationships, may indeed be suggesting the exact opposite of what the organization needs.

This is precisely the point where the organization theorist is drastically confronted with an intrinsic dilemma of his own role. The dilemma is posed by the very fact that he, too, finds himself in an open systems field of possibly conflicting value demands. Should he take the view of the individual employee; of the organization; of wider societal concerns? Already by the choice of his subject of study — but more strongly by any action recommendation he might make — he demonstrates the difficulty of remaining a "pure scientist"; he rather is already — knowingly or unknowingly — of the "heroic-applied" variety (Churchman, 1968). We are not able to resolve such dilemmas once and for all. However, what counts is to become aware of them and to decide consciously.

As stated at the beginning of this chapter, the above comments and observations are not directed toward criticism of specific chapters presented in this volume. Our attempt was to direct attention to some of the present-day limitations in our studies and hopefully to improve our collaborative efforts as we move into the 1980s with a new worldwide challenge of coping with fast-changing environments. It is hoped that our initial attempt to bring together scholars working at different levels of the organizational life may prove as a worthwhile beginning toward a challenging end.

REFERENCES

Abell, P., ed. 1975. *Organizations as Bargaining and Influence Systems.* London: Heinemann.

Alport, G. W. 1953. "The Trend in Motivational Theory." *American Journal of Orthopsychiatry* 23: 107-09.

Baker, R.; T. Dembo; and K. Lewin. 1941. "Frustration and Regression." *University of Iowa Studies in Child Welfare* 78, no. 7.

Bakke, Edward W. 1966. *Bonds of Organizations: An Appraisal of Corporate Human Relations.* Hamden, Conn.: Shoe String Press.

Barnard, Chester. 1938. *The Functions of the Executive.* Cambridge, Mass.: Harvard University Press.

Caplow, Theodore. 1957. "Organizational Size." *Administrative Science Quarterly* 7: 485-505.

Churchman, L. W. 1968. *Challenge to Reason.* New York: McGraw-Hill.

Etzioni, Amitai. 1964. *Modern Organizations.* Englewood Cliffs, N.J.: Prentice-Hall.

Follet, Mary Parker. 1918. *The New State: The Group Organization. The Solution of Popular Government.* London: Longmans, Green, and Co.

Goldstein, K. 1951. *Human Nature.* Cambridge, Mass.: Harvard University Press.

Gouldner, A. W. 1954. *Patterns of Industrial Bureaucracy: A Case Study of Modern Factory Administration.* Glencoe, Ill.: Free Press.

Industrial Democracy in Europe (IDE), International Research Group. 1980a. *Industrial Democracy in Europe.* London: Oxford University Press.

———. 1980b. *Industrial Relations in Europe.* London: Oxford University Press.

Kast, Fremont E., and James E. Rosenzweig. 1972. "General Systems Theory: Applications for Organization and Management." *Academy of Management Journal* 4: 447-65.

Maurice, M.; A. Sorge; and M. Warner. 1980. "Societal Differences in Organizing Manufacturing Units: A Comparison of France, West Germany, and Great Britain." *Organization Studies* 1, no. 1: 59-86.

Marx, Karl, and Fredrick Engels. 1906. *Manifesto of the Communist Party.* Chicago: Kerr.

Mayo, Elton. 1946. *The Human Problems of an Industrial Civilization.* Cambridge, Mass.: Harvard University Press.

Melcher, Arlyn J. 1973. "A Systems Model." In Anant R. Negandhi, ed., *Modern Organizational Theory*, pp. 9-34. Kent, Ohio: Kent State University Press.

Pugh, D. S. et al. 1963. "A Conceptual Scheme for Organizational Analysis." *Administrative Science Quarterly* 8: 289-315.

Rogers, Carl. 1959. "A Theory of Therapy, Personality, and Interpersonal Relations as Developed in the Client-Centered Framework." In S. Koch, ed., *Psychology: A Study of Science.* New York: McGraw-Hill.

Scott, William G. 1961. "Organizational Theory: An Overview and an Appraisal." *Academy of Management Journal* 2: 15-21.

Weber, Max. 1947. *The Theory of Social and Economic Organizations.* Glencoe, Ill.: The Free Press.

Wofford, J. C. 1967. "Behavior Styles and Performance Effectiveness." *Personnel Psychology* 20: 461-95.

Name Index

Subject Index

Ability(ies): in competence potential, 14-15; taxonomy of, 16-18

Absenteeism, and job satisfaction, 64, 65, 66

Absolutism: in autonomous, creative functioning, 38; in conventional thinking and behavior, 33; in empathic people orientation, 37; in negativism and self-assertion, 35

Abstractness: and functioning of complex organizations, 43-48; measuring, 3; and theory of bureaucracy, 48. *See also* Concreteness-abstractness

Acceptance: in conventional thinking and behavior, 34; in empathic people orientation, 37

Achievement, and job satisfaction, 61

Achievement motivation theory, 106; construct validity of, 81-82; and external influences, 82; measuring procedures in, 80; prediction of performance in, 80-81; prediction of work satisfactions in, 81; theoretical domain of, 81

Administration, and job satisfaction, 61. *See also* Management

Advancement, and job satisfaction, 61

Age, and conceptual system, 34, 36, 38

Anthropological approaches, 229

Aspirations, and job satisfaction, 56-61. *See also* Expectations

Assessment procedures, 18

Attitude research, 29-30

Attribution theory, 153, 175-176

Authoritarianism: in autonomous, creative functioning, 38; in conventional thinking and behavior, 33; in empathic people orientation, 37; in negativism and self-assertion, 35

Authority, changes in attitudes toward, 183

Automation, and delegation of authority, 260. *See also* Computerization

"Baby boom," 45

Behavior, performance as, 64. *See also* Performance

About the Editors

George W. England is Professor of Management and Director of the Center for Economic and Management Research in the College of Business Administration at the University of Oklahoma, Norman, Oklahoma. Previously, he was Professor of Psychology and Industrial Relations at the University of Minnesota. Professor England has served as visiting professor, lecturer, or researcher at institutions in North Carolina, California, Colorado, Australia, Canada, Japan, India, Korea, and Germany, including the International Institute of Management of the Science Center Berlin, where he was Senior Research Fellow. A well-published writer of both books and articles, he is the author or coauthor of several books in the field of industrial relations and management, including *The Manager and the Man* and *Organizational Functioning in a Cross-cultural Perspective.* Professor England received his Ph.D. in Industrial/Organizational Psychology from the University of Minnesota, where he also received his undergraduate education.

Anant R. Negandhi is Professor of International Business at the University of Illinois at Urbana-Champaign. He earned his B.A. and B. Com. degrees from the University of Bombay; his M.B.A. from Texas Christian University; and his Ph.D. from Michigan State University. Prior to joining the faculty at the University of Illinois, he taught at the University of California at Los Angeles and at Kent State University. During the years 1976-1978, he served as Senior Research Fellow at the International Institute of Management of the Science Center Berlin. Professor Negandhi has published over sixty articles in various scholarly journals; in addition, he is the author of *Quest for Survival and Growth: A Comparative Study of American, European, and Japanese Multinationals.* He was founder-editor of the quarterly journal *Organization and Administrative Sciences.*

Bernhard Wilpert, who was educated at the Universities of Tubingen, Oregon, and Bonn, is Professor of Psychology at the Technical University of Berlin, Visiting Professor at the Institut d'Etudes Politiques de Paris, and Associate Research Fellow at the International Institute of Management, Science Center Berlin. Previously, he served as Professor of Psychology at the Padagogische Hochschule Berlin and as a Research Fellow and Lecturer at the German Development Institute. Professor Wilpert has also been affiliated with the German Volunteer Service (in Bonn) and the International Secretariat for Volunteer Service (in Washington, D.C.). The author or coeditor of several books about organizational psychology and the psychology of work, from 1973-1980 he served as international coordinator of a study of the functioning of industrial democracy in eleven European countries and Israel.

About the Science Center Berlin

The Wissenschaftszentrum Berlin (Science Center Berlin), a nonprofit corporation, serves as a parent institution for institutes conducting social science research in areas of significant social concern.

The following institutes are currently operating within the Science Center Berlin:

1. The International Institute of Management
2. The International Institute for Environment and Society
3. The International Institute for Comparative Social Research

They share the following structural elements: a multinational professional and supporting staff, multidisciplinary project teams, a focus on international comparative studies, a policy orientation in the selection of research topics and the diffusion of results.